THE CREDIBILITY OF DIVINE EXISTENCE

Other works of Norman Kemp Smith

Studies in the Cartesian Philosophy
A Commentary to Kant's Critique of Pure Reason
Prolegomena to an Idealist Theory of Knowledge
Translation of Immanuel Kant's Critique of Pure Reason
Hume's Dialogue concerning Natural Religion
The Philosophy of David Hume
New Studies in the Philosophy of Descartes
Descartes' Philosophical Writings

NORMAN KEMP SMITH
1872—1958

The Credibility of Divine Existence

THE COLLECTED PAPERS OF
NORMAN KEMP SMITH

EDITED BY

A. J. D. PORTEOUS, R. D. MACLENNAN

& G. E. DAVIE

MACMILLAN

LONDON · MELBOURNE · TORONTO

ST. MARTIN'S PRESS

NEW YORK

1967

MACMILLAN AND COMPANY LIMITED
Little Essex Street London WC 2
also Bombay Calcutta Madras Melbourne

THE MACMILLAN COMPANY OF CANADA LIMITED
70 Bond Street Toronto 2

ST MARTIN'S PRESS INC
175 Fifth Avenue New York NY 10010

Library of Congress catalog card no. **67–11284**

PRINTED IN GREAT BRITAIN
BY W. & J. MACKAY & CO LTD, CHATHAM, KENT

Contents

Preface

Some time before his last illness Professor Kemp Smith had brought together a number of his more important papers and addresses, which had already appeared elsewhere, with a view to publication after his death. As Professor Maclennan has explained in Section II of the Introduction, Kemp Smith left instructions in his will as to their editing, designating as possible editors the three of us, his friends and former students, whichever was available and willing to undertake the work. When at last, after many delays, we were able to meet, we decided on a joint editorship and on our respective contributions to the Introduction which, we thought, should be prefixed to the volume.

Apart from the nature and composition of the Memorial Introduction, our editorial task seemed to be mainly one of finding a publisher; and we were fortunate in securing the interest and co-operation of Messrs. Macmillan & Co., who had published most of Kemp Smith's major works in the past. Kemp Smith had already arranged the papers in the order and context in which he wished them to appear, and had submitted them to a thorough revision; and in this matter we felt bound by his wishes.

The papers now collected in this volume contain some of Kemp Smith's most original work in philosophy, and one or two of them are almost the only source of our knowledge of his views on ultimate issues in religion. The articles on universals deal with logical and epistemological problems that still have relevance to modern debate, and show how radical was his divergence from the Idealism of Bradley and Bosanquet prevalent in his early manhood.

In providing a biographical sketch of Kemp Smith we were faced by the difficulty that he had left behind no autobiographical material; and for the facts of his youth and early career there were few among his contemporaries and acquaintances who could supply authentic reminiscences. We are greatly indebted to his daughter, Janet (now Mrs. Martin Ludlam), who most willingly supplied us with such family details as she knew or was able to recall from her father's conversations in later life; and for an account of his Glasgow days we gratefully acknowledge the help of Miss Marion Buchanan and Emeritus Professor J. W. Scott of Cardiff. We would also like to thank Dr. A. C. Ewing of Cambridge, who wrote the Memoir of Kemp Smith for the *Proceedings of the British Academy* in 1959 and passed on to us the information he obtained from Emeritus Professor A. D. Ritchie, Kemp Smith's successor in the Edinburgh Chair, and Professor W. F. M. Stewart, Professor of Philosophy in the University of Alberta, Calgary, who was Lecturer in Logic at Edinburgh from 1955 to 1959.

The present writers were Kemp Smith's pupils in Edinburgh, two of them members of his first class (1919–20), and the third a pupil and then Assistant in the thirties; and we all knew him intimately during his middle and later life. But accurate dating of the events of his London and Edinburgh periods would have been difficult but for the fortunate existence of a fairly continuous series of letters, extending from 1916 to 1938, written to his intimate friend and former pupil at Princeton, Emeritus Professor Charles W. Hendel, Jr., of Yale University, who had been a colleague of two of us at McGill University, Montreal. With the help of this correspondence it was possible to give a fairly accurate account of his later life and to illustrate his views on current affairs and on the teaching of philosophy. To Professor Hendel we would like to express our gratitude for his kindness and interest in our task, and for valuable suggestions as regards the narrative. Among Kemp Smith's literary remains there were also found a number of letters of considerable interest from correspondents, some of them distinguished philosophers, which helped to fill out the picture of the man as we remembered him.

It remains only to record our thanks to the Editor of the *Proceedings of the Aristotelian Society*, and to the Editors of the various philosophical journals and other periodicals where the papers first appeared, for their kind permission to reprint them in a more permanent form.

G. E. DAVIE
R. D. MACLENNAN
A. J. D. PORTEOUS

Memorial Introduction

I. Biographical Sketch:

Norman Kemp Smith (1872-1958)

A. J. D. PORTEOUS

NORMAN KEMP SMITH occupied the Chair of Logic and Metaphysics in the University of Edinburgh from 1919 to 1945. He was great not only as a philosopher, a scholar and a teacher—he is one of the few eminent philosophical scholars whom this country has produced—but also as a man. To those, like the present editors, who were fortunate enough to have been his pupils and intimate friends, he has seemed in retrospect to have been one of the most potent single influences in their lives; and his stature seems to grow with the years, making it difficult to write dispassionately about him. Readers of the papers collected in the present volume, including former pupils and scholars familiar with his published writings,[1] may wish to know something of the life and character of the author; and for this reason the following biographical sketch has been attempted, with the help of available letters and of information gleaned from the memories of friends and colleagues. It is a record of unremitting thought and splendid academic achievement.

Norman Duncan Smith—to give him his full baptismal name, Duncan being his mother's surname—was born in Dundee on 5 May 1872, in the same year as Bertrand Russell and a year before G. E. Moore, who outlived him by less than two months. He was called

---

[1] In particular *Studies in the Cartesian Philosophy* (1902), *A Commentary to Kant's Critique of Pure Reason* (1918), *Prolegomena to an Idealist Theory of Knowledge* (1924), *Hume's Dialogues concerning Natural Religion* (1935), *The Philosophy of David Hume* (1941), and *New Studies in the Philosophy of Descartes* (1952).

Norman after Dr. Norman Macleod, the famous Church of Scotland preacher of the Barony, Glasgow, who died on 16 June 1872, about the time of his christening; and in this choice of a name we can perhaps discern a mother's hope that her son might be destined for the ministry. He seems to have made little use of his middle name in early life, preferring the simple 'Norman Smith'. However, in 1910, after his marriage to Miss Amy Kemp, he substituted her name by deed poll for his middle name, and desired henceforth to be known as 'Kemp Smith'. We shall, accordingly, by anticipation, use this designation throughout.

His father was Andrew Watson Smith, a cabinet-maker in Dundee, and Norman was the youngest child by five years in a family of six, three boys and three girls, none of whom other than himself had a university education. One of his brothers became a highly respected solicitor in Dundee, and the other a tea-planter in India. Two of his sisters were married, and one of them visited him shortly before he died when she was ninety-six years of age. Kemp Smith often used to joke about how young he felt after he had been to visit her. Attached though he was throughout his life to his family, and especially to his mother, who died in the autumn of 1916 after his return from America to this country, none of them could fully share his intellectual interests. This fact, coupled with his position as the youngest of the family, appears to have engendered a feeling of loneliness and isolation which remained with him, according to his daughter, to a greater or lesser extent all his life. She has sometimes wondered whether without it he could have become so great as a philosopher or as a person. He used to say to her—the phrase recurs in his letters—'Life is a battle'; and again, 'Human relationships are the most difficult in the world'. This may seem incredible to those who knew him; for though he was sometimes shy and awkward in general company and had little social 'small talk', to his many intimate friends he seemed to possess a remarkable genius for friendship; and he had a natural fondness for children. In his old age he greatly enjoyed the company of his grandchildren, with one of whom, Ailsa, a kindred spirit, he developed, despite the disparity in age, a delightful *camaraderie*.

When Kemp Smith was only five years old his father went bankrupt and the family had to move to a smaller house in Coupar Angus. This misfortune involved removing the child from his small private school and sending him to the local primary one, and this separation from his friends remained for him a sad memory. Another early recollection was of the Tay Bridge disaster in the winter of 1879: it was impressed on his mind by the fact that on the previous day he had been trying to build castles out of corks during a strong gale. He became a pupil at Dundee High School, where he was a prize-winner; and some time subsequent to 1885 he transferred to Harris Academy, from which, in 1888, at the age of sixteen-and-a-half, he entered the University of St. Andrews. In the Bursary Competition he was placed third out of twenty-six candidates, and on this basis was awarded a Foundation Bursary of £20 for four years. The previous year he had sat the entrance examination but had wisely decided to remain an extra year at school in order to improve upon his results. Not much is known of his school days, of which he seldom spoke. But one gathers from remarks in later life that he did not find them very enjoyable or the teaching particularly inspiring: he used to complain of the routine grind and the narrowness of the curriculum, a feature common to many secondary schools in Scotland of the period.

When, therefore, in October 1888, Kemp Smith matriculated at St. Andrews and entered upon a five-year course for an Honours Arts degree, he found in its freer atmosphere the exhilarating intellectual stimulus which his school had failed to give; and after life in Dundee the cultural and aesthetic attractions of St. Andrews made a strong appeal. Here he soon made the acquaintance of David Irons and William Menzies, two of the ablest students of the time, both at least two years his senior, and with both of whom he formed a lifelong friendship. With Irons he was invited to 'read philosophy', a signal privilege for a junior undergraduate, and one which must have influenced his early development. Irons graduated with Honours in Philosophy in 1891, gaining the Ferguson Scholarship in Philosophy the following year. After a period of study in Berlin he eventually became a professor of philosophy at Bryn Mawr College, Pennsylvania, U.S.A. He probably influenced Kemp Smith's decision in 1906 to apply for a Chair at Princeton, and it seems likely that he was present at the interview which Kemp Smith had with Woodrow Wilson in

Edinburgh. He died prematurely in 1907. William Menzies won the Ferguson Scholarship in Classics in 1891 and graduated with first-class Honours in Classics and Philosophy in 1892. To him we are indebted for a vivid sketch of university life at St. Andrews at this time and of its leading academic personalities.[1]

Conspicuous among these were Lewis Campbell, the revered Professor of Greek and distinguished Platonic scholar, then reaching the end of his long tenure of the Chair, and Andrew Seth (after 1898, Pringle-Pattison) who had come from Cardiff in 1887 to the Chair of Logic, Rhetoric and Metaphysics, and was responsible for the teaching of English as well as of Logic in the University. Menzies went from St. Andrews to Balliol for two years, and, after assisting Professor John Burnet in Greek at St. Andrews from 1896 to 1898, elected to become a teacher of Classics and eventually H.M. Inspector of Schools in Scotland, first in the far north and subsequently in the Borders. In later years in Edinburgh he and Kemp Smith maintained their early friendship and, until Menzies' death in November 1951, they saw a good deal of one another.

In the Greek classes Kemp Smith sat under Lewis Campbell during Campbell's final years; and in 1890–1 he was second prizeman in the Third Greek class. In the Honours Greek class he was taught by John Burnet, who returned to St. Andrews in 1891 to fill Campbell's place when the latter went abroad for his health, and succeeded to the Greek Chair in 1892 after Campbell's death. From these distinguished scholars Kemp Smith no doubt acquired his lasting interest in Early Greek Philosophy and in Plato.

It was, however, in the philosophy classes that Kemp Smith revealed his real bent. He received his first introduction to the subject from Andrew Seth in the Ordinary Logic class, little thinking that he was destined to succeed him in the Edinburgh Chair twenty-nine years later, on which occasion he paid a graceful tribute to Seth as a teacher of Philosophy.[2] Unfortunately he did not have the benefit of Seth's

[1] In his contribution to G. F. Barbour's Memoir of Andrew Seth Pringle-Pattison in the volume entitled *Balfour Lectures on Realism*, pp. 59–67 (Blackwood & Sons, 1933).

[2] In his Inaugural Lecture, 'The Present Situation in Philosophy', published in *The Philosophical Review*, xxix (January 1920).

Advanced class which was, as Menzies wrote, 'the really important one, for it was in it that the professor gave of his best and that the significance of Philosophy was first revealed to us'. For Seth was called to Edinburgh to succeed his old teacher, Alexander Campbell Fraser, in the autumn of 1891. Thus Kemp Smith's Honours work in logic and metaphysics was done under Henry (later Sir Henry) Jones, the eloquent Welsh Idealist philosopher who succeeded Seth.[1]

At this time the Chair of Moral Philosophy at St. Andrews was occupied by William Knight, of whom Kemp Smith gives an interesting account in the opening number of *The Philosophical Quarterly*,[2] characterizing him as 'a very colourful figure, enterprisingly self-reliant'. Knight was a man of diverse interests and an ardent supporter of the higher education of women. He was general editor of the Blackwood series of philosophical monographs, and himself contributed the volume on Hume. He was also the prime mover in the foundation of the Scots Philosophical Club in 1900. But, according to Menzies, he was not a very effective teacher of philosophy and he did not have an Advanced class in Moral Philosophy. His chief interest was in literature, and he is now chiefly remembered as the editor of Wordsworth's writings, together with a life, in eleven volumes; and with the editing of a selection from Dorothy Wordsworth's Journals.

In all the philosophical classes at St. Andrews, Kemp Smith was first prizeman, gaining in addition the Gray Essay Prize and the Tyndall Bruce Logic Prize. He won Henry Jones's admiration and affection and was, as Sir Henry wrote in 1919, 'the ablest student I had in St. Andrews, whether in English Literature or in Philosophy'. In March 1893 he concluded his brilliant career by taking his degree with first-class Honours in Mental Philosophy under the Old Regulations, and winning the Ramsay Scholarship. In the following year, in competition with unusually able candidates from the four Scottish universities, he won the Ferguson Scholarship in Philosophy, the examiner being Professor Adamson. In those days the academic year consisted of only two terms, from October to March, leaving the summer free for work

[1] For a vivid account of his election see *Old Memories*, by Sir Henry Jones, pp. 201–21 (Hodder & Stoughton, 1923).

[2] Vol. i, no. 1 (October 1950), pp. 1–2.

or travel; and, presumably on Henry Jones's advice, he spent the whole summer of 1894 in Germany, as was a usual practice with Scottish graduates in philosophy, as a student at the University of Jena. Little is known of these months; but it is said that he took to rowing and that he was condemned by the alphabetical arrangement of the class to sit next to a contentious American fundamentalist! He does not appear to have mentioned Rudolf Eucken, who occupied the Chair there: perhaps he was not lecturing at the time. This opportunity for foreign study was made possible by a special grant awarded to him by the Senatus, and his University course was partly financed by means of scholarships and prizes, for it is unlikely that his family was in a position to give him much assistance.

When Henry Jones succeeded Edward Caird in the Chair of Moral Philosophy in Glasgow in 1894, on the latter's election as Master of Balliol, he invited Kemp Smith to be his Assistant for the session 1894–5, and later bore tribute to the help he received in his first difficult year in the new Chair: 'I cannot speak too highly, or with too much gratitude, of the care, the accuracy, the judgment and the faithfulness with which Mr. Smith performed his work.' Thus began Kemp Smith's long career as a teacher of philosophy, extending over more than half a century.

It is probably to this time that the story belongs, which he was fond of relating to his friends, though it is just possible that it happened later when he was Assistant to Adamson. Being 'overwhelmed', as he expressed it, by a feeling of his inadequacy for the teaching of philosophy, he decided to resign his appointment and called one evening at his chief's home to announce his intention. As luck would have it, Henry Jones was out and his wife persuaded him to come in and await her husband's return. When the Professor finally arrived he invited Kemp Smith to stay to dinner, and would not hear of any discussion of the purpose of his visit until the meal was over. At its conclusion, such was the effect of the food and wine, that his outlook on life had completely altered and there was now no more thought of resignation. Nevertheless, he resolved to return to the Continent and equip himself more adequately for his future vocation. Thus he spent the following eighteen months of the years 1895 and 1896 in study abroad at the

Universities of Zürich, Berlin and Paris, laying a firm foundation for his later work by a thorough knowledge of the French and German languages and philosophies.

In the autumn of 1896 Kemp Smith returned to Glasgow, this time as Assistant to Robert Adamson, who had come to Glasgow the previous year to occupy the Chair of Logic and Rhetoric. Before this, Adamson had been for seventeen years (1876–93) in Manchester as Professor of Philosophy and Political Economy and two years (1893–5) in the Aberdeen Chair of Logic, and was regarded as the foremost Kantian scholar in the country. As Adamson's Assistant, Kemp Smith gave special courses of lectures both to the Ordinary and to the Honours classes. To this Assistantship in Logic there was added in 1897 an independent Lectureship in Logic and Metaphysics at Queen Margaret College, where women could attend all their degree courses if they did not choose to join the men's classes on Gilmorehill. Some of the professors came and gave lectures there, but this was not the practice of the professors of philosophy; thus Kemp Smith had full responsibility for the degree courses there in Logic and Metaphysics.

One cannot doubt that the close association with Adamson during the remaining six years of Adamson's life was the major determining influence on Kemp Smith's philosophical development. Not only did he find Adamson's critical approach to philosophy thoroughly congenial, but he owed a deep debt to the Professor's friendship and many acts of kindness. Adamson's premature death from enteric fever, at the age of fifty, in February 1902, after only a brief illness, was a terrible shock to him; when he arrived at a friend's house with the news he is said to have been speechless with grief and to have left almost immediately. At the funeral he gave the second of the two addresses, following that of Henry Jones, and after speaking of the force, originality and modesty of Adamson's teaching he went on:

'Of Professor Adamson as so much more than the teacher, as a personal influence that once felt can never be forgotten, I shall not trust myself to speak. Those of us who have been privileged to know him in any intimate way feel that he has laid upon us by the influence, moral as well as intellectual, which he exercised, a fresh obligation to a higher way of life; an obligation which we can only discharge by a more sincere devotion to the pursuit of truth and the service of our fellow-men.'[1]

After Adamson's death Kemp Smith was entrusted by the University Court with the entire work of the Logic Chair, and he conducted both the Ordinary and the Honours classes single-handed throughout the rest of the session, the Ordinary class having then one hundred and fifty-six students. Robert Latta, whose lectures he had attended at St. Andrews when Latta was Assistant there, was appointed to succeed Adamson, and with him Kemp Smith worked harmoniously for the next four years.

Adamson's influence and guidance is strongly seen in Kemp Smith's first and for many years his only book, *Studies in the Cartesian Philosophy*, which was published in 1902 and won for him in 1903 the Doctorate in Philosophy of St. Andrews. Adamson's help and criticism, as also that of Henry Jones and A. S. Pringle-Pattison, are freely acknowledged in the Preface. This very able and mature work was a remarkable achievement for a young man and received deservedly high praise from leading philosophers for its learning and the freshness and originality of its approach, not to speak of the lucidity and trenchancy of its style. To Adamson Kemp Smith probably owed his initial interest in Descartes' philosophy and its development by his successors, both in Britain and on the Continent, which culminated in Kant; and he shared Adamson's conviction that a thorough study of the Kantian philosophy was a necessary preliminary to any attempt to solve modern problems of epistemology. This is evident both from his *Commentary to Kant's Critique of Pure Reason* and from his *Prolegomena to an Idealist Theory of Knowledge*: he did not take the view of Caird that Kant was merely a half-way house to the system of Hegel. Likewise he held firmly to Adamson's belief that the best approach to philosophy was through a study of the historical evolution of ideas in the works of its greatest practitioners.

On the strength of his first book, *Studies in the Cartesian Philosophy*, he applied, in March 1903, for the Logic Chair at St. Andrews, then rendered vacant by the death of D. G. Ritchie, receiving powerful support from his teachers and other leading philosophers in Scotland

[1] *Glasgow University Magazine*, 12 February 1902, pp. 183–4.

and elsewhere; but G. F. Stout was the successful candidate. He applied again in May, unsuccessfully, for the Chair of Philosophy in the South African College, Cape Town; but at the age of thirty-one, with an already established reputation, he could afford to wait for promotion.

Few now survive who can supply details of Kemp Smith's life during his Glasgow days. One is Miss Marion Buchanan, whose mother was a writer of poetry, and whose brother, the late Rev. R. M. Buchanan, had been a fellow-student of his in Paris[1] and later was a United Presbyterian minister at Kirriemuir and librarian at Trinity College, Glasgow. Kemp Smith was a welcome visitor at their Glasgow home and used to discuss philosophy with Miss Buchanan, for she had been a student in Edward Caird's class. One winter they went together to an evening bookbinding class at the Glasgow School of Art, but the days were not long enough for the very slow and elaborate work involved.

At this time Kemp Smith had lodgings near the University off Woodlands Road, and not far from the Royal Botanic Gardens and Kelvingrove Park; and, being a splendid walker, he rejoiced in the beautiful surroundings of the Campsie Hills and Strathblane. On Saturday evenings he and his friends used to attend the orchestral concerts in St. Andrews Halls. Dr. Buchanan was then an assistant United Presbyterian minister in Troon, Ayrshire, and his lodgings at Dundonald were a favourite meeting-place for those, like Kemp Smith, who enjoyed walks and discussions. The group included among others the Rev. Dr. James Moffatt, later of New Testament fame, and Dr. Ernest F. Scott, a distinguished graduate of Glasgow and Oxford, then a United Presbyterian minister at Prestwick, who later went to a Chair at Queen's University, Kingston, Ontario, and subsequently to Union Theological Seminary, New York. He is chiefly noted for his work on St. John's Gospel. Kemp Smith's continuing interest in problems of New Testament theology probably stemmed from these early associations.

According to the testimony of surviving pupils, Kemp Smith lectured in those days from carefully prepared notes, which were largely dictated

---

[1] Another was the late Dr. Stevenson, Professor of Hebrew and Semitic Languages in Glasgow University.

and proved invaluable to his students when they came to prepare for examinations. At the Berkeley bicentenary celebrations in Dublin in 1953, when the wife of a well-known Professor of Philosophy confessed to Kemp Smith that she still had his notes, dating from Queen Margaret College days, he exclaimed in a tone of assumed horror, 'Oh, burn them, burn them!' Perhaps the ten years he spent in America, from 1906 on, caused a considerable change in his lecturing technique, for in Edinburgh he adopted a much freer style.

Among his Glasgow pupils at this time were two future professors of philosophy, John W. Scott and Archibald A. Bowman, Ferguson Scholars in Philosophy in 1905 and 1906 respectively. J. W. Scott became Sir Henry Jones's Lecturer in Moral Philosophy from 1905 to 1920, and was for a year a colleague of Kemp Smith's at Queen Margaret College. From 1920 to 1944 he held the Chair of Logic and Philosophy at Cardiff and from 1925 to 1943 was Hon. Secretary of the Homecroft Association. In retirement he has devoted his energies to the compilation of a valuable index to the Proceedings of the Aristotelian Society. Bowman, as we shall see, was to become not only one of Kemp Smith's distinguished students but one of his most intimate personal friends. He succeeded Kemp Smith as Lecturer in Logic and Metaphysics in 1906, and went to Princeton in 1912 to fill the Stuart Chair of Logic, which he occupied (apart from the War Years, 1915–19, when he was on active service in Europe and latterly a prisoner of war) until 1926. He then returned by invitation to the Glasgow Chair of Logic and Rhetoric, transferring after a year to the Chair of Moral Philosophy, when it was vacated by H. J. W. (later Sir Hector) Hetherington on becoming Vice-Chancellor of Liverpool University.

In the spring term of 1906, towards the end of his Glasgow period, Kemp Smith went to Manchester as Assistant to his friend, Professor Samuel Alexander, at the latter's special request. The two men had come together in the late nineties, drawn by a bond of common interest in Malebranche's philosophy and the Realist features which it exhibited; and Alexander had introduced him to the works of Avenarius, which led to the writing of the two articles in *Mind* here reprinted. Thus began a lasting friendship, though Kemp Smith found himself unable to accept many of Alexander's views. Apropos of these articles on

Avenarius he received a postcard from William James, dated 2 February 1908:

'I have only just "got round" to your singularly solid and compact study of Avenarius in *Mind*. I find it clear and very clarifying after the innumerable hours I have spent trying to dishevel him. I have read the *Weltbegriff* three times and have half expected to have to read both books over again to assimilate his immortal message to man, of which I have hitherto been able to make nothing. You set me free! I shall not re-read him but leave him to his spiritual dryness and preposterous pedantry. His only real original idea seems to be that of the vital *Reihe*, and that, so far as I can see, is quite false, certainly no improvement on the notion of adaptive reflex actions.'

Prompted to some extent, no doubt, by his old friend of student days, David Irons, then at Bryn Mawr College, Kemp Smith, in 1906, applied for the Stuart Chair of Psychology at Princeton University, New Jersey, a Chair, the holder of which had to give courses not only in psychology but in general philosophy as well. At some date in the early summer of that year he was interviewed in the North British Hotel, Edinburgh, by Woodrow Wilson, the future war-time President of the United States, and at that time President of Princeton, who duly had him appointed. Thirteen years later, in June 1919, when Kemp Smith had applied for the Edinburgh Chair, Wilson, then engaged at the Peace Conference in Paris, was to support him with a very cordial testimonial. In describing the interview many years later Kemp Smith was wont, with humorous self-depreciation, to attribute his success to Wilson's being so enraged by the views of his chief rival applicant on the subject of William Ewart Gladstone, that 'he was glad'—to use Kemp Smith's own words—'to embrace even me!'

Thus, in the autumn of 1906, he went to Princeton; and so there began a fruitful decade of teaching in this famous American university with its long-standing Scottish connexions. Here Kemp Smith broadened his experience as a teacher and was afforded the leisure to embark on his great work of Kantian scholarship. The life of the College and its surroundings appealed greatly to him and, as he wrote later,[1] 'Only

---

[1] In his Memoir of A. A. Bowman, prefixed to the latter's *Studies in the Philosophy of Religion* (Macmillan, 1938), vol. i, p. xxxi.

those who have enjoyed the privilege of life in Princeton and have shared in the academic and social life of that delectable little town, can know the strength of the spell which it casts upon the dwellers within its bounds.' In a letter to Professor C. W. Hendel some years later he spoke of America as his 'second fatherland'.

He still, however, kept in close touch with the Old Country; and during a visit in the summer of 1910 he married Miss Amy Kemp, whom he had known for some years, having met her through cousins of hers who lived in Dundee. She was roughly his contemporary in age, the only one who married of the six daughters of Francis Kemp, a Scotsman, Manager of the District Bank in Manchester. She had been trained as a teacher and had had a successful career, latterly as head-mistress of a private school at Haslemere, Surrey. Without sharing much, or at all, in his technical philosophical interests, she was a woman of great charm and social gifts, a warm and generous personality, who gave her husband not only her name but—what he had hitherto lacked —a happy and congenial home life, and a place where pupils and friends could always count on a friendly welcome, as many generations of students and younger staff in both Princeton and Edinburgh can testify. Their only child, Janet, was born in July 1912, and she became her father's continual joy and pride both as a young child and as she grew to womanhood.

For Kemp Smith the last few years at Princeton, prior to 1914, seem to have been very happy ones. They were the years of his marriage, of the birth of his daughter, and of the arrival (in 1912) of the Bowmans to join the small Scottish circle in the University. Those years served specially to renew and deepen the old friendship with A. A. Bowman and created lasting ties between the two families. By this time Kemp Smith was becoming well known at the University by his conspicuous success as a stimulating teacher, both of large classes of over two hundred and of advanced students; and by his effectiveness in committees and in administration. In the philosophical world outside, through his articles and contributions to the meetings of the American Philosophical Association, he was already regarded by his colleagues as one of the leaders of the younger generation of philosophers in America. In 1913 he became Chairman of the Department of Philosophy and Psychology, which comprised seven professors and three assistant professors; and in 1914, on the death of the then incumbent of the McCosh Chair of Philosophy, Professor A. T. Ormond, he was made, by the unanimous vote of the Board of Trustees, the McCosh Professor of Philosophy. This change enabled him to devote his whole teaching effort to the history of philosophy and to the central problems of logic and metaphysics. In 1912 he received an invitation to the Mills Professorship of Philosophy in the University of California in succession to Dr. Howison; and a year later he was invited to give courses there in the winter term; but he felt obliged to decline both these invitations. At this time he was working steadily on his *Commentary to Kant's Critique of Pure Reason*; and by 1914 the first draft had been practically completed, though it was to undergo constant revision during the subsequent two years. But he did accept an invitation, in the spring term of 1914, to deliver a course of lectures on 'British Philosophy in the Seventeenth and Eighteenth Centuries' at Columbia University, New York City. With the *Commentary* well under way he began a new translation of the *Critique of Pure Reason*, and had completed about a third of it before the outbreak of the First World War and its attendant distractions forced him to lay it aside; and it was not resumed until 1927. Kemp Smith used to say that he regarded the translating, whether of Kant or of Descartes, as more like recreation than work, having in it something of the attraction of crossword puzzles.

The Kemp Smiths made many friends among their colleagues in Princeton, with whom contact was maintained long after they had returned to Scotland. Chief among them were Paul Elmer More, Lecturer in Philosophy, an eminent Platonic scholar and author of a sequence of books on Platonism; Warner Fite, the Stuart Professor of Ethics; and George McLean Harper, Professor of English; together with their respective families. Three of his outstanding pupils at this time, who became lifelong friends and correspondents, were Edmund Wilson, Carl F. Taeusch and Charles W. Hendel, Jr. Edmund Wilson became a distinguished literary critic and novelist and regularly visited his old teacher when he was in Europe. He has left a vivid picture of a visit to Kemp Smith, paid shortly after the end of the war in 1945, when the latter had just entered upon retirement and before his family returned from India.[1] Taeusch taught philosophy for a time, later becoming a professor of Business Ethics at Harvard Business School. Subsequently he transferred to educational work in the Extension Department of the United States Department of Agriculture, where he did good work convening meetings of farmers all over the country. But it was Charles W. Hendel, who first made the acquaintance of Kemp Smith in his third college year in 1910–11 and graduated in 1913 with Honours in Philosophy, whom he inspired to devote his life to the subject and who is well known for his writings on Hume and Rousseau. After the war and a year at Williams College, Hendel returned to Princeton as an Assistant Professor; and then, for eleven years (1929–40), he occupied with distinction the Chair of Moral Philosophy at McGill University, Montreal, where for two years the present writer was his colleague. Hendel returned to the States in 1940 to become Sheldon C. Clark Professor of Moral Philosophy and Metaphysics and Chairman of the Department of Philosophy at Yale University for the next nineteen years (1940–59), retiring in 1959. Recently he had the honour of being Gifford Lecturer at Glasgow University for the years 1962 and 1963.

Owing to Hendel's kindness in making available to the present editors his fairly continuous correspondence with Kemp Smith from 1916 to 1938, it has been possible to reconstruct the events of his life in war-time London and in Edinburgh more accurately than if one had to depend on memory. And the characteristic comments which Kemp Smith makes in these letters on men, books and current affairs help to revive the image of the man as his friends knew him. Two comments of Hendel referring to Kemp Smith's later Princeton days are perhaps worth quoting, reminiscent as they are of the walks and informal hospitality subsequently enjoyed by his Edinburgh pupils.

> It had been our custom in days past at Princeton to take long walks together in the country, often silent for as much as an hour, then discussing philosophy, and of course I profited immensely by the discourse. Nor was our association limited to that, for he opened his home to me and to other graduate students, and we felt free to

[1] *Europe without Baedeker* (Secker & Warburg, 1948), pp. 238–40.

repair there, night or day. His ever-ready welcome, always with a little quizzical smile, but warm and inviting, wherein his wife always joined, made his home a place where we younger men were tided over our many days of discouragement or bewilderment with philosophy, and as we walked back to our quarters after a session with him at tea we would be clearer in purpose and heartened. Those occasions of personal and informal association taught us what it meant to be a philosopher.

Again in another passage:

> I am inclined to think that his practice as professor was based on this lesson that the home, in the teaching of philosophy, is a valuable adjunct of the classroom. Before breaking off this train of memories I wish to say something about these 'conversations' alluded to. They were never a continuous discussion. They were often not even overt, strange as this language may seem. Long silences would occur as we walked far out on the roads and fields. The only sound would be that of his stout walking stick with the silver head that pounded vigorously along at a rapid pace, neither of us saying anything. One learns indeed from quiet understandings and unexpressed sympathies as well as from explicit discussion. When it is really a man's example and wisdom that educates us it is tradition working in silence rather than by the explicit word.

These idyllic days were destined soon to end. The European war was already casting its shadow across the Atlantic; and in the summer of 1915 Bowman and his family departed for Scotland on the *Tuscania*, where he was to seek and soon obtain a commission in the Army. The Kemp Smiths had been in Europe in 1913 and 1914; but this summer they spent quietly in the country, first on an island off the coast and then in New York State, where Kemp Smith was revising the *Commentary* and preparing it for the press. By the beginning of 1916, with the war still dragging on, Kemp Smith's desire to return to Britain and offer his services became more and more insistent. He finally obtained leave of absence from his academic duties for the duration of the war, and on 20 March 1916 sailed with his family from New York. Meanwhile Hendel had returned from a year of study and travel in Europe, and, as a graduate student, was working on a dissertation on Hume's

Dialogues; and from then until the middle of 1917, even when he was in camp in the Army, he was continuing to help Kemp Smith with the revision, proof-reading and verifying of references.

After a brief and unsuccessful attempt to join the Army, which was ruled out by his age, Kemp Smith was given a civilian post in the Intelligence Section of the Ministry of Munitions in London and for the ensuing three years was busily engaged on Government work. In May he was transferred to a more interesting post in the Department of Information of the War Office and Admiralty, then located in the Royal Geographical Society's rooms in Kensington. These first months of war-work were a time of unremitting labour, involving long hours, which left him in the evening physically and mentally exhausted, with little energy for the work of revision and proof-reading of the *Commentary*, on which he was steadily engaged. In this work he was receiving the assistance of his philosophical friends, Mr. H. H. Joachim of Merton College, Oxford, Professor G. Dawes Hicks of University College, London, and his old teacher, Sir Henry Jones, whose help and criticisms he gratefully acknowledged. Hendel, still in Princeton, was in almost weekly correspondence with him over the proofs, and in one letter Kemp Smith speaks of his war-work as 'interesting and pleasant enough, though, of course, it does not come up to Philosophy'. In October 1916 he took a small flat at 3 Heath Mansions, The Grove, Hampstead, where his family could be with him for the winter months. It was next door to a house where the painter Romney had lived in the eighteenth century. The following year, in March 1917, before America had formally entered the war on 6 April, Kemp Smith was transferred to an organization for promoting the Allied Cause in neutral countries; and he later served in the American Section of the Ministry of Information. Throughout these dark days he never doubted the rightness of the Allied stand and the war guilt of Germany or the necessity to prosecute the struggle to a victorious conclusion. A peace, he thought, which left Germany free to pursue her ambitions in Eastern Europe unchecked would in the long run be fatal. Nor had he any doubts of our ultimate ability, with American aid, to win the war.

For two of these years in London Kemp Smith was working in close association with Professor Macneile Dixon of the Chair of English

Literature in Glasgow, who later, in 1935–7, delivered a notable series of Gifford Lectures there, entitled 'The Human Situation'. Between the two men there grew up an intimate friendship, which was continued and deepened in the years following the war. When Macneile Dixon was released to return to academic work in the early autumn of 1918, he wrote a graceful letter of appreciation to his colleague, part of which is worth quoting for the light it sheds on Kemp Smith at this period and the impression he made on his friends:

> . . . As to what you say on our personal relations during the two eventful years I need not tell you how I appreciate the affectionate and friendly character of it, and that none the less that, of course, the truth is all the other way. I am your debtor and profoundly. The job itself apart, which would have been devilish badly run by me without you; in which you did most of the work and I got all the advertisement—though as regards that I don't fancy you grudge it and I can honestly say I regard it as a barren and empty thing—the two years with you were a joy and an education. I'll say this that I've got more philosophy, honest stuff, from your conversation than from that of any living man, and I would rather have your judgment in any matter concerned with it, as indeed with most other things, than that of any person of my acquaintance. Of course I am no judge of technical values, but I've wandered around in a desultory way among the thinkers and venture to think you have a breadth and an honesty, a depth and an acuteness not ladled out in profusion in any given generation. Of course you know where you're weak or think you are weak, and naturally the opinion of experts would with you outweigh that of a mere outsider, such as I obviously am. But philosophers should, I think, take notice of poor 'ignorants' like myself, and I hold to it that you have done me more good than anyone else. Then there's the personal and still more precious side. I might have liked your philosophy and not you! But except that I've sometimes felt a worm, you have given me a lot of happiness, and I'm not going to try to do justice to the innumerable courtesies and considerations I've had from you. The two years' sojourn in our little island, surrounded by the vexed waters of personal animosities, intrigues and charlatanism, none of which disturbed for a moment our harmonious co-operation, will remain with me to

the end as a delightful memory, unspoilt, undarkened, a rounded and charming thing. That is secure, nothing can touch it further. I won't say any more, though I could say a good deal, save to hope that the conditions may be such as to make your remaining time at the Ministry at least tolerable and, if possible, enjoyable. I'm not very sure that the Germans are yet in mind to throw up the sponge. They may rally on a shorter line and try to bargain. But it's clear that the pressure is pretty nearly unbearable. . . .[1]

In March 1918 Kemp Smith sought an opportunity to meet Baron F. von Hügel, and the mutual liking of the two men for each other ripened into a warm and intimate friendship, which lasted until von Hügel's death in 1925. Among Kemp Smith's literary remains were found a number of personal letters from the Baron dealing with religious matters.

After the Armistice, and shortly before his release from Government work, Kemp Smith wrote to Hendel, on 30 December 1918:

> It is an immense relief to have the slaughter over and past. But life is likely to be very uncomfortable and uneasy for some time to come, before established peace conditions can be restored.
>
> Wilson has received a magnificent welcome in France and in this country. I trust all will go well and that the Allies will amicably agree on a common policy in all essential matters.
>
> The Coalition Unionists have swept into power again with an immense majority. Indeed Lloyd George seems to me to have overreached himself; and by lack of generosity to his former Liberal colleagues, and especially to Asquith, has landed himself in a difficult position, with the Unionists in an absolute majority in the Commons, and almost 2 to 1 over the Coalition Liberals.

His *Commentary* on Kant had, after many printing delays, been published in July 1918; and Kemp Smith decided to spend the intervening months, before returning to Princeton in August, in getting back to philosophy and doing a little writing. After a week or two in Surrey the family moved north to Edinburgh, with a short interval at Windermere. Kemp Smith was able to pay a brief visit to Alexander in

[1] Letter dated 18 October 1918.

Manchester, who was then engaged in seeing his Gifford Lectures 'Space, Time and Deity' through the press. His address for the next few months was 16 Corrennie Gardens, Edinburgh; while there, he saw both Pringle-Pattison and his brother James Seth and paid a short visit to G. F. Stout in St. Andrews.

The Kemp Smiths had already booked passages for a return to Princeton when, on 14 May, Pringle-Pattison announced his resignation from his Chair, for which applications were invited forthwith; and without much hesitation Kemp Smith decided that he ought to become a candidate, even though a return to the life in America still held strong attractions for him. Having taken this difficult decision he at once communicated it to Hendel, in a letter dated 16 May, and indicated how uncertain were his chances of election. Not only would there be a very strong field of possible applicants—he mentioned J. B. Baillie of Aberdeen, A. E. Taylor of St. Andrews, A. D. Lindsay of Balliol, John Laird of Belfast and G. Dawes Hicks of London as likely candidates among others—but the composition of the electing body, the Curators of Patronage, made their action incalculable. He went on:

> I know that the news will be very disturbing to you, my dear Hendel, for I know the affectionate friendship you bear me; and the loss of your companionship will be one of the many evils, and a great one I count it, incident to this uprooting, if that comes about. But it is well not to cross bridges till we come to them, and meantime I am trying to avert such thoughts.
>
> The reasons determining my action are many and varied, and into them I cannot now enter. At the worst we should be able to keep contact, one way and another. . . .
>
> This earthly life is a pilgrimage, remember; so let us shoulder our packs and face the next bit of the road as befits philosophers. All sorts of jolly things may happen—*must* happen, let us say, to us both.

The next few weeks were very unsettling ones for Kemp Smith and his friends, as we know from his correspondence with Macneile Dixon in Glasgow. He was able to muster very powerful support from both sides of the Atlantic; and his volume of testimonials, numbering twenty from Britain and twelve from America, makes most impressive reading.

Included is support, not only from internationally known names like Woodrow Wilson and John Grier Hibben, the President of Princeton, and Henri Bergson and Émile Boutroux in France, but from the occupants of the Chairs of Philosophy in Glasgow, St. Andrews, London, Birmingham, Manchester, Liverpool and Cardiff, and from leading philosophers in Oxford and Cambridge, not to speak of his friends and colleagues in Princeton and prominent American philosophers and theologians elsewhere. Many of them had been impressed by the massive scholarship and clarity of his *Commentary* on Kant. His chief rival appears to have been J. B. (later Sir James) Baillie, who shortly afterwards was appointed Vice-Chancellor of Leeds University.

Kemp Smith's election was announced in *The Times* of 26 June, and he decided to remain on in Edinburgh to prepare for his duties in the autumn. The day before the announcement, A. S. Pringle-Pattison wrote:

> My dear Kemp Smith,
> Now that the great issue is decided I wish to say how completely satisfied I am that the future of my old Chair is in good hands. May you have a long and happy tenure, bringing to it, as I know you will, fresh distinction in the years to come.

And so, in October 1919, at the age of forty-seven, Kemp Smith succeeded his old teacher in the Edinburgh Chair of Logic and Metaphysics, conscious of its historic traditions and resolved to be worthy of the succession. Looking back in later life on his long occupancy of it, extending over twenty-six years, he must have felt that his ambitions had been realized. On the rostrum, as an exponent of philosophy, few could equal him, and his ascendancy over the large Ordinary class, numbering between two and three hundred, was complete. The force of his personality and his stern gaze could on occasion quell any potential trouble-maker; and he made all but the dullest feel that philosophy was an exciting and serious business. As was said by one of the present editors, Professor R. D. Maclennan, in an appreciation in the *Scotsman* on the day of his funeral (6 September 1958):

> One's mind goes back at this time to his first Philosophy lecture at this University. One recalls the crowded classroom of nearly

300 students, most of them ex-servicemen, restless and expectant, ready to show their impatience of teaching which seemed to be merely a carry-over from pre-war days, then the realization, when Kemp Smith began to speak, that they were in the presence of a supremely great teacher and a personality of commanding force.

Kemp Smith's Inaugural Lecture, delivered in the late afternoon of 16 October 1919 and entitled 'The Present Situation in Philosophy',[1] was an impressive survey of the mutual relations of Idealism, Naturalism and Scepticism and the issues that divided them in various fields. It formed the subject of discussion at the winter meeting of the Scots Philosophical Club, at which Lord Haldane of Cloan and the Earl of Balfour, both Honorary members, were present and took part in the discussion.

From 1919 to 1924 Kemp Smith's colleague in the Chair of Moral Philosophy was James Seth, the younger brother of Pringle-Pattison, and in his own way a great and beloved teacher. He died in his sixty-fifth year in the summer of 1924, before his resignation could take effect, and was succeeded by Professor A. E. Taylor from St. Andrews. From then on, until Taylor's resignation in 1941, Philosophy in Edinburgh was represented by two of the most distinguished names in philosophical scholarship. But the two men, though both Idealists in philosophy, were of very different outlook, training and temperament.

During Kemp Smith's first year in his Chair various changes were made in the syllabus and in the structure of the Department. The name of the Ordinary degree class was changed from 'Logic and Philosophical Introduction' to 'Philosophy'; and a new three-term Intermediate Honours course was instituted, each term dealing with a separate topic, taken by a different teacher. In the autumn term the Professor himself lectured on Fundamental Problems of Philosophy; then in the spring term Mr. R. P. Hardie, the Lecturer in Logic, now promoted to an independent Readership in Ancient Philosophy, discussed Fundamental Problems in Logic, dealing mainly with Bradley, Bosanquet and Russell; and in the summer term, Mr. Henry Barker, the Lecturer in Social Ethics, considered Philosophical Problems in the field of Psychology.

---

[1] Published in *The Philosophical Review*, vol. xxix (January 1920).

'Advanced Metaphysics' was renamed 'Philosophy Honours'. John Anderson was appointed Lecturer in Logic and held the post until he left, in 1927, to fill the Challis Chair of Philosophy in the University of Sydney. He was succeeded by R. D. Maclennan, one of the present editors, who went out to McGill University, Montreal, in 1933, and held successively the Frothingham Chair of Logic and Metaphysics and the Chair of Moral Philosophy. His successor at Edinburgh was W. A. Sinclair, who had returned from a Commonwealth Fellowship at Harvard in 1932 to be one of the two Assistants (there had been only one previously); and he was still a Reader in the Department at the time of his tragic death in December 1954.

For Kemp Smith these early years were fully occupied with heavy teaching duties, broken only by a visit to America in the spring and early summer of 1923, on the occasion of his appointment as Mills Lecturer in Philosophy in the University of California at Berkeley. In his absence his work was taken by Professor J. H. Muirhead, an old friend, then recently retired from his Chair in Birmingham. This appointment gave Kemp Smith the opportunity to revisit his many friends in Princeton and elsewhere, and he made a great impression in Berkeley. Writing to him of this visit on 1 January 1925 Bowman says:

> You have left a *tremendous* reputation behind you in California. At Berkeley, whenever I was introduced to anyone, the first question was, Did I know *you*? And that was followed by an account of yourself that was always the same, always delightful to hear. I felt that even to be able to claim intimate acquaintance with you added a cubit to my stature.

The fruit of his Mills Lectures was his *Prolegomena to an Idealist Theory of Knowledge*, published in 1924, which propounded a Realist solution to the epistemological problems of sense-perception on Kantian lines within the framework of a spiritual interpretation of reality. This volume was a most original contribution to contemporary debate and shows Kemp Smith's constructive powers; but it had a mixed reception from the critics, and the ingenious solution it offered was not free from difficulties, though Whitehead is said to have accepted it gratefully.

During these early years in Edinburgh, Kemp Smith took his full share of the burden of administration which falls to the lot of the Head of a large Department. Apart from the usual committees of Faculty and Senatus, he was for two four-year periods a Senatus representative on the University Court (1924–32), and for four years (1929–33) Dean of the Faculty of Arts, discharging the duties of that onerous office with characteristic efficiency and conscientiousness. He possessed undoubted gifts in this direction, and, had he so wished, could easily have had his energies diverted into administrative channels. He is known to have declined the tentative offer of a Principalship in 1929. For his heart was in teaching and writing and he was never happy unless he had some task of authorship in hand.

Kemp Smith's quick wit and resource as a speaker is amusingly illustrated by a small incident that occurred at this time during a 'Religion and Life' week in February 1925, to which Dr. Julian Huxley had been invited as the principal outside-speaker. Kemp Smith himself was giving an address, and in it he had been discussing the many unfounded assumptions upon which our so-called established knowledge rests. As he reached the end of his peroration he stepped backwards to resume his seat on the platform. Unfortunately he misjudged the position of his chair and literally 'fell between two stools'. A rueful expression was quickly followed by a twinkle as he picked himself up and calmly announced to the audience, 'Just another unfounded assumption!'

A number of important papers in this collection belong to his first decade in Edinburgh. The three articles on 'The Nature of Universals' were published in *Mind* in 1927, followed by the Aristotelian Society paper on 'The Fruitfulness of the Abstract' in 1928, which, as we see from a letter, had been germinating in his mind as early as 1920. They represent an important attempt, through criticism of the Hegelian type of Idealism represented by Bradley and Bosanquet, and of the modified position of Cook Wilson and Stout, to find a more tenable basis for his own version of Idealism. The penetrating essay on Fear, which only appeared in print in the year before his death,[1] was already in existence in 1925 and had been given to the Faculty of Divinity Theological Society. In a letter to Hendel (dated 29 March 1925), who had expressed a wish to see it, he writes:

[1] *Philosophy* (January 1957).

You see, being only a lecture as it stands, it needs more added supplement than it gives by itself, and unless I'm there to adapt to my hearers, the poor thing might mislead more than edify. See? Meantime you can be reflecting upon the fact that it was *not* among the nobler animals who know not fear, but among the timorous inhabitants of the tree-tops, that Nature found its opportunity to create man.[1]

To this period there also belongs the publication of his translation of *Kant's Critique of Pure Reason*, begun in 1913 and resumed in 1927. It appeared in 1929 and at once superseded all other English translations, being followed in 1934 by an abridged edition for the use of students.

By the early thirties the idea of a book on Hume, which would develop further the ideas adumbrated in two early articles in *Mind* in 1905, here reprinted, began to form in his mind. He was attracted by temperament to the great Scottish philosopher and felt that the aim and nature of his philosophy had been misunderstood by previous writers. He prepared the way for his new interpretation with an edition of Hume's *Dialogues concerning Natural Religion*, which was published in 1935. Here, in the course of a long and illuminating Introduction, he discusses Hume's views on religion and the difficult problems presented by this famous work. Kemp Smith's own views on these ultimate issues are represented in print only by his British Academy paper of 1931, 'Is Divine Existence Credible?', which provides the title for this volume, and by a short broadcast talk, also here reprinted, entitled 'Immortality'. In a letter to Hendel, dated 27 September 1933, he defends this talk against Hendel's questioning of the appropriateness of the medium:

I note what you say about my talk on 'Immortality'. I'm not sure, however, that I agree about its not being worth-while. To do it at all, even badly, I find much more difficult than the more technical stuff. It forces one to write more simply, and therefore, if at all, more clearly and to be more definite on ultimate issues. Writing about 'values' can be so vague and hazy.

It is one of the chief regrets of his friends that he declined, so it is said, more than one invitation to be a Gifford Lecturer and preferred to

[1] Cf. p. 437.

devote his last years to philosophical scholarship. This leaves a sad gap in our knowledge of his religious views which memories of casual conversations only partially fill.

Kemp Smith's method of working, in his study of a great philosopher like Kant or Hume or Descartes, was to concentrate on the text, supplemented by surviving letters, thus getting to know the author's idiom and the historical context of his thought, and so tracing out the conflicting tendencies in the development of his views. '*Festina lente*', he once wrote in a letter to Hendel (25 January 1916), 'is an excellent motto in things philosophical, though it never had any application in matters of love.' In the same letter of September 1933, mentioned above, he records his progress with the Hume studies:

> Iona grows on us all, the better we know it. I should gladly spend a whole year, or more, amidst its quiet: nothing could be better for work. Even these two months I have got quite a lot, leisurely too, done on Hume, whom I feel I'm beginning to know. It is queer, isn't it? how one goes on getting to know a dead author— just as if he were alive and in the flesh, to show [*sic*] new sides of himself to us. And writing, I always find, helps that process better than any other: simple reading of him doesn't do it. I wish you were here to talk him over. I'll not attempt to write of it: it is in incubation; and to enter upon it at all would be profitless, unless at length. But I seem to find things shaping out, and things fitting in, which I take to be a sign that my back is not wholly to the light.

Kemp Smith's letters to Hendel in 1932 and 1933 give some account of his philosophical reading. In addition to Price's *Perception* and Hallett's *Aeternitas*, of which he strongly approved, Troeltsch's *Sociallehre* and Nicolai Hartmann's *Ethics*, which had recently appeared in English translations, were occupying his attention and, above all, Whitehead's and Bergson's recent books. A letter dated July 1932 is worth quoting, as it sheds light on his attitude to philosophy and his views on the teaching of it:

> Have myself been reading and re-reading [Whitehead's] *Process and Reality*—with great enjoyment and profit; but there is still

much which baffles me. But I feel very sure that it is a great work and will be a ferment in Philosophy for some decades, till it is assimilated in some degree. Philosophy, it seems to me, is over-exciting these days; certainly it is alive: I wish I were your age instead of my own, if only for this reason, to have time to digest it all quietly before decrepitude or the grave closes upon me. Bergson, too, has been joining in. Seen his book? It is very readable; but hardly, I think, important as Whitehead's are.

And in the same letter he dealt with questions raised by Hendel, then writing from McGill University, giving his views on the teaching of philosophy:

I agree with you as to *Honours* classes, that it is best to fit them in with what one is working at oneself, if happily that be not too much off the main line. But I do think that every teacher, at starting, should spend some years in very carefully working out courses on the line of his own views, that will serve as adequate introductions to the main fundamental problems of the subject. And, of course, it is they that are the recruiting ground for the Honours classes. I have almost stopped reading lectures in the Honours classes; reading books with them instead. But quite a different method is required for classes of beginners, I think. Doubtless you agree in the main.

Kemp Smith's method in the Ordinary class was, for the most part, to talk freely from notes, illustrating from his wide knowledge of psychology and anthropology, and pausing at intervals to dictate a few carefully phrased sentences so as to provide an accurate record of an argument or point. The blackboard would often be covered with writing before the lecture commenced and he would sometimes lean perilously on a long slender pointer as he talked.

Both in his teaching and in his writing he set for himself the most exacting standards of excellence. He revised and rewrote continually. One got the impression that writing did not come easily to him and that the succinct and elegant beauty of his style was the result of strenuous and unremitting effort. He demanded the same effort of his advanced pupils, with whom he was sparing of praise: when it came, it was felt to be high indeed. In contrast, he was kind and lenient with the 'weaker brethren', as he termed them. Some quotations from his correspondence with Hendel will illustrate his attitude.

As he was leaving for Europe in June 1913, on the eve of Hendel's graduation from Princeton, he wrote:

> I am greatly rejoiced that you are deciding for Philosophy and the teaching of it. When you come to do it, you will find it, in spite of its delights, a very heart-breaking task (I mean especially the teaching of it),

and later in the same letter:

> [You] need only to be strict enough with yourself, discontented enough with what you can yet do, and hard-working enough to become—let us lower our ideal for a moment—one of the leaders in Philosophy (and Philosophy itself means light and leading) in your own day and generation. Only don't forget to aim higher than that.

And in similar terms, in a letter dated 3 February 1919:

> You are rather severe, I think unduly so, on teachers of Philosophy. Remember teaching that may not suit one may suit others. I agree that in this field there are many incompetents and not over-deserving of charity in that they show no sign of being weighed down by their short-comings. But, as Matthew Arnold replied to the poetess from Ohio, who praised her own verses and then excused herself on the ground that she liked to think that excellence is 'common and abundant', 'No, madam, excellence is not common and abundant—but (what were his words?) dwells among rocks, almost inaccessible, and man must well-nigh wear his heart out e'er he can reach her.'

Such rigorous standards alone would have made him work slowly on his cherished book on Hume. He had planned that *The Philosophy of David Hume* should be published in 1939, the bicentenary of the publication of Hume's *Treatise*; but other circumstances and close personal concerns intervened to preoccupy him and, as we shall see, it did not finally appear until 1941.

Some details of the domestic life of the Kemp Smiths in Edinburgh should perhaps be recorded here, familiar though they are to a wide circle of their Scottish friends. After a brief stay at 14 Lennox Street, on the north side of the city beyond the Dean Bridge, they removed to 'Ellerton', a large house in Grange Loan, the back of which faces on to Blackford Hill. This was their home until 1937, and here they offered hospitality to their friends and colleagues, and to many generations of students and overseas graduates. Iona was a favourite retreat in the summer months, as was Windermere, both of which offered opportunities for quiet work. Occasional Continental holidays made a welcome break with routine. They spent an enjoyable three weeks' holiday in Ajaccio, Corsica, in 1925 and another on the Adriatic coast of Jugoslavia in the early summer of 1929. At Easter 1933 they went for a trip to Holland, and in August 1935 they were in Switzerland, Austria and Germany. In August and September 1936 they paid a five weeks' visit to South Germany and Austria at a time when the Nazi movement was gaining control and beginning to menace the peace of Europe. Giving his impressions of this holiday to Hendel, in a letter dated 15 November 1936, Kemp Smith wrote:

> The material prosperity of that part of Germany—and I fancy of Germany as a whole—is amazing. The more intelligent sections in the Universities are having a difficult time, and have to lie very low, but the rest of Germany seems in the highest of spirits. The country, I take it, is governed by a Mrs. Grundy, supposed to be an embodiment of the *Volksgeist*, and with Hitler as her mouthpiece and conscience. She is a vulgar woman, but in tremendous spirits; and like all Mrs. Grundys is very intolerant of opposition. The young people of Germany seem very happy, and of remarkably fine physique. Would ours were of such physique! It is sad to think that while France is standing for some of the higher elements in our civilization she is so divided and so unhappy these days, while Germany with all her vulgarities and tyrannies is so unified and so in spirits! How will it all be ten years hence?

The same summer, on 12 June 1936, his great friend Bowman died unexpectedly after a brief illness at the early age of fifty-three, having occupied the Chair of Moral Philosophy in Glasgow for only nine years, and left behind a mass of unpublished material. Kemp Smith wrote an obituary notice for *Mind*,[1] and, with the help of Professor J. W. Scott, undertook the laborious task of editing the two sets of manuscripts, with a view to the publication of two books which would be a fitting memorial of a remarkable teacher and thinker. Kemp Smith made himself chiefly responsible for the bulky papers which he edited and published in 1938 in two volumes, with a memorial introduction, entitled *Studies in the Philosophy of Religion*. Scott devoted himself to the unfinished manuscript of the Vanuxem Lectures which Bowman had delivered in Princeton in 1934, and published them under the title *A Sacramental Universe, being a Study in the Metaphysics of Experience*.

Soon further bereavements followed for Kemp Smith. On 16 December 1936 his wife died suddenly from an attack of pneumonia, and his elder sister's death followed on 8 July 1937. He and his daughter decided to sell 'Ellerton' and to build a small modern house at the foot of the large garden; this—14 Kilgraston Road—was to be his home for the rest of his life. As architect he chose a young man at the outset of his career and himself took great interest in the design of the new house. The architect is now Sir Robert Matthew, who occupies the Chair of Architecture in the University of Edinburgh, and who, among other achievements, was responsible for the design of the Festival Hall in London on the South Bank. His daughter Janet, who had graduated in Arts at St. Andrews in 1934 and was finishing a course for the Social Science Diploma at Edinburgh, accompanied her father this summer on a long holiday in Austria and Italy, in the course of which they went from Innsbruck through the Brenner Pass as far as Venice, and thence by Padua, Verona and Lago di Garda back to Innsbruck and home via Munich. In the autumn Janet announced her engagement to Martin Ludlam, a young doctor who had just completed his medical course. He came of a Quaker family, his father, Dr. E. B. Ludlam, being a near neighbour and a Lecturer in Chemistry in the University. The match delighted Kemp Smith, who felt that his daughter's happiness was now assured. He obtained leave of absence from his teaching duties in the University for the spring term of 1938, to allow him leisure to complete his book on Hume, and on this account declined, in January 1938, the offer of a visiting appointment at McGill University. His daughter had

[1] No. 181 (January 1937), pp. 123–7.

a post at Newbattle Abbey, the Adult Education College in Midlothian, and their temporary home was at the Braid Hills Hotel, where they remained until their new house was ready for occupation in the late spring. Janet's marriage took place on 14 September 1938, in the beautiful little church at Dalmeny near South Queensferry; but the couple remained in this country until early in August 1940, when their first child was about eight months old. They then sailed for India, where Dr. Ludlam was engaged on medical work for the duration of the war; and they did not return to this country until 1946, the rest of their family, except the last two children, being born in India.

The Philosophy of David Hume, as I have noted, was originally intended to appear in 1939. Though Kemp Smith had still not finished it, he presented the substance of chapter xxiv as his Inaugural Address at the memorable Joint Session of the Aristotelian Society, the Scots Philosophical Club and the Mind Association at Edinburgh from 7 to 10 July 1939. The outbreak of the Second World War in September, with the inevitable delays in printing that ensued, further hindered the production of the book; and it was not published until 1941.[1]

During the years since he came to Edinburgh many honours had come to Kemp Smith in recognition of his eminence as a scholar and a philosopher. St. Andrews honoured him in 1920 with its LL.D. and Glasgow was to give him a similar degree in 1951. Durham bestowed on him an honorary D.Litt. in 1930. He became a Fellow of the Royal Society of Edinburgh in 1921, and in 1924 he was elected a Fellow of the British Academy.

Throughout the war Kemp Smith remained at his home in Edinburgh, obeying the Government's injunction to avoid unnecessary travel, and, with a dog as his companion, was looked after by his devoted housekeeper. He had learnt to drive a car when he was sixty-six years of age, and from 1940, for a few years, was able to use it to take him into the country for short walks. The war brought additional burdens. He served for a period on the South-East of Scotland Tribunal dealing with conscientious objectors, and found it 'weird work' and 'on the whole

---

[1] *Aristotelian Society Suppl.*, vol. xviii; C. W. Hendel, *Studies in the Philosophy of David Hume*, Introduction, p. xxxiv (Library of Liberal Arts. Bobbs-Merrill Co. Inc., 1963).

depressing, even if frequently with comic relief'. His two Assistants, one of them George E. Davie, one of the present editors, were soon called up to the Forces; and after the first year W. A. Sinclair, who, during the first months of the war, had rendered valuable service to the Ministry of Information, by his broadcasts entitled 'The Voice of the Nazi', felt obliged to join his artillery regiment. In the autumn of 1940 Professor A. E. Taylor suffered a slight stroke, and for a good part of the session Kemp Smith had to take his Honours class, while Reginald Jackson, the Reader in Ancient Philosophy, lectured to the Ordinary one. Taylor partially recovered, but retired in 1941 from his Chair. He was still able to do some teaching until 1944, when John Macmurray, Grote Professor of the Philosophy of Mind and Logic in the University of London, was invited to succeed him. During all this period Kemp Smith was left almost single-handed to administer both Departments. He tendered his own resignation in 1944, but was persuaded to continue in office for a further year, in order to enable the Selection Committee to find a suitable successor. In 1945 the resignation took effect and Professor A. D. Ritchie of the University of Manchester was elected to the Chair.

In the tribute paid to Kemp Smith at the time of his retirement it was said that 'he had been a powerful, stimulating and humane influence, and the friend, counsellor and host of students and colleagues'.[1] And at the meeting of the Senatus on 14 November 1945 a special minute dealing with the careers and achievements of the professors who had retired contains the following personal appreciation of Kemp Smith:

> As a teacher Professor Kemp Smith was in the front rank. The subtlety of his thought was happily combined with a power of lucid exposition and a direct simplicity of manner. He could allow himself to be carried away by his theme; and when he did, he carried his hearers with him. But what his students will recall with the warmest gratitude is the unfailing sympathy with which he helped them through their difficulties and the personal interest which he took in their activities. To his colleagues his generous sympathy, his ready friendliness, and his soundness in counsel were a tower of strength; while his balanced humanity symbolized, even as it expressed, what is most valuable in our academic tradition.

[1] *University of Edinburgh Journal* (Autumn 1945).

It is impossible to do justice in a few words to Professor Kemp Smith's work in Philosophy. He did for the greatest of modern philosophers what Professor Burnet did for the greatest of the ancients. Both Plato and Kant had been seen too much through the eyes of a later tradition and interpreted as forerunners.

In December 1945 an Appeal was made by his friends for a fund to enable two portraits of him to be painted by the same artist, one of which was to be hung in the University 'where it would always be seen by students in the Department of Logic and Metaphysics'. Some months later he was presented with his portrait.

Freed from his onerous duties Kemp Smith now entered, at the age of seventy-three, upon a period of retirement which was to last for thirteen years, during all but the last year and a half of which he was to remain amazingly active, physically and intellectually. His daughter and her husband with their family returned from India in two stages during the course of 1946 and settled in Carlisle, where Dr. Ludlam opened a practice. With their return a new and absorbing interest came into Kemp Smith's life and he rejoiced greatly in the role of grandfather.

He now proceeded with an attempt to revise his first book, *Studies in the Cartesian Philosophy*, which had long been out of print, in the light of all the work that had been done by Gilson and other scholars since its publication in 1902. He soon found that a mere revision was impossible and courageously set himself to produce an entirely new work on Descartes; this engrossed him for six years, taking up a large part of his energies. The book, *New Studies in the Philosophy of Descartes*, together with a companion volume of selected translations, *Descartes' Philosophical Writings*, was at last published in his eightieth year, exactly half a century after the earlier book. It was a remarkable achievement for a man of his age and showed no flagging of his intellectual powers. It has already become a classic in the interpretation of Descartes.

In the summer of 1953 Kemp Smith travelled by air for the first time when he flew from Liverpool to Dublin to attend the bicentenary of Bishop Berkeley's death, held in Trinity College. These celebrations were followed by the annual meeting of the Mind Association and the Aristotelian Society, where he acted as Chairman at one of the symposia. For the next four years he remained active and apparently in good health, visiting his family in Carlisle from time to time and having some of his grandchildren to stay with him; and for his friends, when they called, there was always a warm welcome.

He was deeply affected at this time by the tragic and unexpected death of his former pupil and colleague, W. A. Sinclair, only four months after his marriage. Sinclair collapsed and died of exposure and heart failure on 21 December 1954 during a blizzard in the Cairngorms, where, as Colonel and Commanding Officer of the University Training Corps, he had gone to visit the contingent in their winter camp. Kemp Smith had been a very close friend and he did what he could to help and comfort his young widow and his invalid mother. In January 1957 he himself suffered a slight 'black-out', which necessitated a short period in the Royal Infirmary and several weeks of convalescence. By May he seemed to have recovered, though his handwriting was very shaky, and the autumn saw a recurrence of his illness. The next eleven months were spent in an Edinburgh nursing-home in increasing weakness. He was visited regularly by members of his family from Carlisle and by his many friends. Among his most faithful visitors were Miss Marion Buchanan, his friend of Glasgow days, who was with him almost to the last, the late Miss Florence Philip, and Mrs. Suzanne Sinclair. To the distress of his family Kemp Smith seemed to consider that his life-work was done and longed wistfully for the end. This came mercifully on 3 September 1958, when he slept peacefully away in his eighty-seventh year. The cremation service, held at Warrington Crematorium on 6 September, was conducted by two of his Edinburgh pupils.

One may ask what were the qualities of mind and character that made Kemp Smith so great as a teacher and inspired the devotion of so many of his friends and pupils. As an exponent of philosophy he was able to present it, despite its abstract nature, as something supremely important for life and worthy of the utmost endeavour. The tributes of two of his American pupils well express what we who were his Scottish disciples likewise felt. Hendel wrote in 1959:

> Kemp Smith was the first teacher to interest me deeply in Philosophy. He observed that interest and he cultivated and disciplined it. When I had once committed myself to the life of learning he made sure that I should always keep aspiring to merit

the title of philosopher and he never tolerated any complacency about apparent attainments.

And the late Professor Arthur E. Murphy, who heard his Mills Lectures in California in 1923, and two years later followed him to Edinburgh, wrote:

> I was then an undergraduate at Berkeley, a 'pre-legal' major in philosophy and political science, with no serious intention in my College work but to become a lawyer and, if possible, a good one. Philosophy I found an amusing game of ideas and a good means of developing a skill in argument that could later, I hoped, be put to more practical use. It was from Kemp Smith that I learned that Philosophy could be more than this,—that it could be an enterprise in which a man found and gave the best of himself in a just understanding of the greatest issues of human life. I decided that semester that I wanted to become Kemp Smith's kind of philosopher. To this continuing task my life has since that time been devoted. . . . Since then I have seen him only once, in 1938. We talked again about philosophy and about the sense of life in a world then obviously on the way to a second and more destructive global war. And again I found in him the strength, integrity and steadiness of mind I needed to go on with the job to be done.[1]

It was a common experience of many of his pupils to feel a certain awe of Kemp Smith, even after years of intimacy. Hendel has expressed this feeling, which he had retained at the age of sixty, and Bowman felt it in the earlier years of their acquaintance, as indeed did many of us in Scotland. Perhaps this was partly due to his natural reserve and partly to the sheer force and depth of his personality. But what more than anything else endeared him to his friends was his intense humanity. Along with his acute analytical powers he possessed a remarkable interest in people and in human concerns, combined with a fund of common sense and an eminently practical judgment, which led his friends to seek his advice in times of perplexity or distress. They sensed that he really cared what happened to them and that they could count on his sympathy in their successes and comfort in their sorrows. He was faithful

---

[1] In a letter to Hendel, dated May 1959.

and assiduous as a correspondent, and his letters, often brief and dashed off in his inimitable handwriting, frequently very difficult to decipher, contained wise advice and shrewd comments on events and ended invariably with warm and affectionate greetings.

Lastly, he was in himself a fully balanced and integrated person who, one felt, had come to terms with himself and with life, and could face the future with cheerful optimism. 'How, I have long felt', he wrote in December 1954, 'can we consort with our young people and still doubt the future of our civilization?' In consequence he was honest and direct in his dealings, with no trace of affectation or insincerity, and he was humble regarding his own achievements. As Hendel wrote: 'There were never merely verbal gestures in anything Kemp Smith said. All was honesty. It was that in his own life and demeanour that drew his pupils to him with confidence in his wisdom and friendship.'

Perhaps the most eloquent tribute was paid to him by Arthur E. Murphy, in the letter quoted above, in words reminiscent of the closing lines of the *Phaedo*:

> I was never a disciple of Kemp Smith's doctrines, where he had doctrines to offer as, for example, in *Prolegomena to an Idealist Theory of Knowledge*. But in the way in which Socrates had disciples I am proud to count myself in that category and to say, in gratitude and deep affection, that 'of all the men of his time whom I have known he was the wisest and justest and best'.

A. J. D. P.

II. *Divine Existence*

A PERSONAL RECOLLECTION

R. D. MACLENNAN

THE choice of the title for this collection of the late Professor Kemp Smith's articles and addresses calls for some explanation if not justification. In the first place I should say that although the selection and arrangement of papers was his own, he left no instructions about a title, the choice of which is therefore the responsibility of the Editors. Secondly the task of editing was entrusted 'according to their availability' to one or other of the three colleagues and former pupils whom he named in his will. When at last, after long and unavoidable delays, we met together to discuss the problems of editing and which of us should accept the responsibility, we found that while all of us retained the most vivid memory of Kemp Smith as a teacher and friend, we each of us would have given somewhat different versions of his philosophical influence, according to whether our own philosophical interests were predominantly historical, or logical or religious and, I had better add, metaphysical; certainly metaphysical, as he understood that word to mean the legitimate extension beyond the frontiers of sense perception of every inquiry into reality and truth. It seemed best therefore that an introduction, besides providing a biography as its principal aim, should reflect something of the manner in which his thought and personal beliefs had influenced his pupils, and this might emerge if we each contributed what we could from our understanding and personal recollection of his teaching and of conversations with him. This we thought might be of interest to those that knew him only through his authoritative works on Descartes, Hume and Kant, and a help to the reader who has a philosophical interest but has had no special philosophical training. Further we decided that we should in no way attempt

38

an interpretation of his philosophy as a whole and burden this volume with a lengthy introduction.

Professor Kemp Smith's eminent position in the philosophical world has rested almost wholly upon his studies, translations and expositions of the three classical philosophers mentioned above, but those that were fortunate enough to have been his pupils, and later his friends, were aware of a range and originality of thought which could not find full scope in historical interpretation and that he was moving towards positions which would ultimately commit him to an orientation of his entire philosophical outlook. He had so far written only one comparatively short systematic work on our perceptual knowledge of the external world, entitled *Prolegomena to an Idealist Theory of Knowledge*. The word *Prolegomena* is instructive of the intention of this work, but the term *Idealist*, except in the sense in which he himself understood the word (which will be mentioned later), has acquired a meaning which would be entirely misleading if applied to Kemp Smith. Looking back upon this work now with the thought of his paper on Divine Existence in mind we can see how in this Prolegomena he was concerned not with one but with two problems; or perhaps we should say that the problem of perception (what the data of the senses disclosed of a real exterior world), led directly to the larger and more inclusive question whether the senses, in serving our practical needs which are none the less needs for true knowledge of that world, also relate us to a transcendent reality. This collection of his papers is the nearest we shall ever come to a general philosophy of nature, history and Divine Existence such as he could, and probably would, have developed, had not failing health and the strain of writing his last major work on the philosophy of Descartes rendered a task of such magnitude impossible. The fact that he made the selection himself, that it contains by no means all his articles and addresses, does also encourage us to believe that he intended it to be in some not inadequate degree representative of his personal philosophy.

Only one paper bears a title corresponding to the one chosen to head this volume, but the choice of this title seemed to the editors an inevitable one. Professor Kemp Smith not only regarded Divine Existence as the most fundamental of all questions, philosophical or practical, but he also maintained that no philosophical problem can ever be isolated.

This is not because philosophical problems belong to a single system, as the Idealists held, or indeed to any system; Kemp Smith had attained through his studies of Descartes, Hume and Kant a mastery of the historical approach to philosophy. When he turned to a critical and analytic discussion of problems, he did not abandon his historical perspective which enabled him to see each problem as the historian sees his facts—not as isolated phenomena but as acquiring meaning and significance as they are seen to involve other facts. In the philosophical field, then, the more fundamental the problem, the more it would disclose the complexities of the issues and its interrelation with other philosophical questions involved. Kemp Smith acquired his mastery of this historical method through his own studies of Descartes, Hume and Kant, but in the paper on 'How far is Agreement Possible in Philosophy?'—one of his early papers—he had already formulated the principles of the historical approach to philosophy. Speaking of the problems of philosophy as non-isolable he says,

> They differ from the problems of the positive sciences, not only in the complexity of their data, but also in the impossibility of adequately treating them by any method exclusively analytic. They likewise demand an orientation towards history, and the application of the insight thereby acquired.

Perhaps I should also add that this discussion of Divine Existence does represent the emergence of his mature views and that it was written while he was at the height of his intellectual powers. The reader who is concerned and perplexed over recent discussions of this question and disquieted over the negativity of the outcome, will find that Kemp Smith's critique of the anthropomorphic concepts of the Divine contains all that has been urged in this negative but necessary attack upon an uncritical and widely held strain in traditional theism (eighteenth-century, certainly, rather than Biblical); but he will also discover that, in the negative and critical parts of the argument, he is at once clearing the ground and preparing the foundations of a far more constructive theism. In what follows I will confine my remarks mainly to some comments on this lecture, drawing upon personal recollections here and there and just barely indicating where it reaches out to views expressed in earlier or later papers or where the argument rests upon logical positions which are fully considered in the three articles on 'Universals' and in the paper on 'The Fruitfulness of the Abstract'.

Though in making these comments I have tried to bear in mind the reader whose interest in the problem of God in contemporary thinking could be called philosophical rather than theological, but who as already mentioned has had no special training in philosophy, I am well aware that comments which aim to avoid the inherent complexities have little value, even if at the time they might seem to be illuminating. At the risk of intelligibility, I have accordingly made rather brief references from time to time to his treatment of other closely related problems which will be found among these papers. There is some advantage even in gaining an appreciation of the complexities of the problem, for the mind of the reader is thereby protected against the pretensions of the philosophical journalist. Faith and difficulties, as Newman has said, are compatible; faith and doubt are not, but 'ten thousand difficulties do not make one doubt'. Kemp Smith remarks in his paper on 'How far is Agreement Possible in Philosophy?' that one function of philosophy is 'to enforce breadth of outlook and catholicity of judgement. It stands for the general human values as against excessive pretensions, whether in science, in religion, or in practical life, for the past and the future as against the present, for comprehensiveness and leisure as against narrowness and haste.' He was a Humanist, not in the narrow, exclusive and negative usage by which that word has been debased in our time. He stood for the general human values, but he would have deplored the attempt to establish them upon human nature and human society alone as in the end destructive of these values themselves.

It is worth while recording two expressions of his attitude to philosophy both of which Kemp Smith firmly held and which at first sight seem difficult to reconcile, though in fact they are complementary. One of these is his already mentioned view of the nature of philosophical problems. This he was fond of impressing upon his students on their first advance beyond an historical introduction towards the discussion of 'problems' when that sense of endless complexity (and indeed perplexity) begins to grow upon the mind. No philosophical problem, he maintained, can ever be solved in isolation. Any philosopher who has reached his philosophical position through critical and competent thinking will have realized that the position he has adopted on any one problem commits him to congruent views on all the others. It is possible of course to state this doctrine in such a way as to attribute to reason a primacy over fact as well as the possession of ultimate criteria of truth in its own right. Kemp Smith's complete divergence from this lies in his own approach to philosophical questions, which I have already referred to as a carry over of the historical perspective into the philosophical field. In consequence, while he accepted a coherence of fact and theory as a test of truth, it was a coherence not imposed by reason, but disclosed to reason through patient dealing with facts and the insight which is its reward. While each problem must be examined and analysed so far as possible in and by itself, such analysis will yield no solution in and by itself. The kind of solution which philosophy offers is the point of view to which the philosopher attains when he can view his problems for the first time both in distinctness and yet together. Why then, he asks, do philosophers differ?

> The really fundamental reason why equally competent philosophical thinkers may arrive at diametrically opposite results is not I believe to be looked for in temperament, but rather in the complexity of the problems, and in the limitations which personal experience, necessarily incomplete, and differing from one individual to another, imposes upon us.

The other expression of his attitude, so entirely characteristic of Kemp Smith's thinking, concerns the role of reason, both in science and in philosophy. On first encounter, the teaching that philosophical problems are non–isolable does suggest, and had formerly implied, the conception of a philosophical system in terms of which problems are said to be soluble. Philosophical reason concerned with theory, and speculative hypotheses, and scientific reason dealing with fact, can be contrasted, as they have commonly been in the recent past, very much to the detriment of philosophical reason and the general disparagement of metaphysical inquiry. The originality of Kemp Smith's attitude is that, in rejecting the idea of a system, it unites the two functions of reason, the philosophical and the scientific, the historical and the analytical. Both deal with facts and neither ever completely excludes the other, for the role of reason is seen to have a fundamental similarity in both. When this historical orientation of reason is thus maintained, there must be a legitimate and indeed necessary scope for metaphysics. I quote this passage from his article on 'Whitehead's Philosophy of Nature'. Speaking of the fundamental facts and conditions of human existence he says:

> We cannot by means of reason establish their necessity. The most that we can do is to determine their actual nature and the consequences that follow therefrom. And in so doing, we generally succeed in finding that, under the conditions prescribed, a rationality or order appropriate to them, determined by them, gradually discloses itself—an order which is richer and more wonderful than any that unassisted . . . reasoning could ever have anticipated . . . It is not indeed the task of the human mind to prove the rationality of the Universe or any part of it. It is for the Universe, on detailed study, to reveal the kind of rationality which does, as a matter of fact, belong to it.

In the brief references I have made here and elsewhere to his logic, I have tried to avoid the 'whole and part' language of Idealist logic which would give a quite false impression if applied to Kemp Smith's procedure. He did not believe that the nature of the part is determined by that of the whole. He rejected the Idealist doctrine of Coherence completely as a definition of truth, though he retained it as a test of truth. The nature of man, his freedom and destiny, is not determined by his being merely part of this universe. One of the important lessons of Kemp Smith's logic is that through the rejection of the Idealist doctrine of the Concrete Universal, which interprets the qualities of numerically distinct things as qualities of a single whole, we are led to affirm the only real and true alternative, namely that Universals are abstract and that it is by way of comparison and contrast with the abstract that we are brought to an appreciation of the fact of individuals. To assert that universals are abstract is certainly not to say that they are abstractions: universals are the recurring rhythms and patterns of nature; they are what we call *types* by means of which our natural reason can discern order and regularity in what would otherwise be a flood of unpredictable events. Individuals of course are also parts of this universe, but so long as they are in existence they are irreducibly individuals. We as individuals respond to other individual persons and things and to the Universe itself as individuals, and every response, though it may conform to a pattern or type, is in itself a unique occurrence in space and time. Thus the space-time world we live in is characterized by continuous creativeness. It is in Whitehead's phrase 'creatively advancing into novelty'. It is a world in which we must recognize contingency as well as the emergence of order, and to assert the non-isolability of philosophical problems is also to assert that it is only as we discern order and connexion among events that we can take account of the contingent happenings as well.

★   ★   ★

The paper on Divine Existence was originally written for delivery to the Faculty and students of New College, Edinburgh, and, as I recall the occasion, the title was then 'The Credibility of Divine Existence'. I should say in passing, that it made a profound impression on the students. In part this was due to the force and clarity of his delivery and to the almost unique emphasis which he was able to impart to the spoken word. It was not so well received by some members of the Faculty, who were uneasily aware that his uncompromising rejection of anthropomorphism might not accord with the Christian doctrine of Incarnation. Thereafter it was revised many times, Kemp Smith as was his custom submitting it to various friends and colleagues for criticism. Finally it was redrafted for the British Academy 1931 without any substantial modification of the original argument.

The title, however, was changed into the form of a question 'Is Divine Existence Credible?' Kemp Smith felt that a far more detailed development of the positive side of the argument would be required for a philosophical justification of belief in God. On the other hand, the question: 'Is Divine Existence Credible?' could be intelligibly asked in a single paper and answered to the extent of indicating the kind of evidence that a positive answer would require. In the end, as the reader will see, the author goes further:

> The answer to my question is therefore this: Divine Existence is more than merely credible: it is immediately experienced; . . .

It is perhaps needless to say that all this is very far removed from any thought of 'proof' of Divine Existence. He was completely out of sympathy with all attempts to revive the traditional arguments, including, of course, the argument based on analogy of human and divine purpose. I remember him remarking to me that by choosing the words 'credible' and 'credibility' he hoped to emphasize the fact that he was not advancing one more argument for the existence of God, but inquiring into the source and status of a belief, which, if we knew its generating conditions and could relate them to the historical faith with which our specific beliefs are bound up, would be seen to evoke the most profound responses and emotions at their deepest level in human nature. One feature of religious experience which fascinated Kemp Smith was precisely its capacity of self-renewal: this he believed was due to the fact that its roots lie both in an historical faith and in the immediate experiences embedded in our encounter with those situations in the natural world which arouse the deep-seated emotions of reverence, awe, hope, fear, grief. Although this position is made abundantly clear in the discussion, it cannot do any harm to restate it with reference to some currently expressed opinions. It would not, I think, be misrepresenting Kemp Smith to say that if a distinction is to be made between historical faith and religion, and certainly the demand for a 'religionless Christianity', whatever that may mean, seems to indicate the possibility at least of such a distinction, it must never be carried through to a denial of one of the terms. Religion, which has its source in those immediate experiences within the natural world which involve the sense of mystery, would degenerate into a mere nature worship or pantheistic mysticism unless it found expression in an historical faith. On the other hand, to deny the relevance, the validity, the necessity of religion for an historical faith is to deprive the latter of one of its continued and abundant sources of life: the day inevitably comes when our words, our forms, and the doctrines in which an historical faith is clothed seem to lose their power to create the way of life which every great historical creed and faith inculcate. When supplementing an historical faith and being modified by it these immediate experiences immeasurably deepen the quality of worship by inducing in the mind of the worshipper the sense of a 'presence'. Above all they engender the sense of our creaturely dependence upon God which is fundamental to belief in Divine Existence. So essential in Kemp Smith's teaching is this notion of the creaturely consciousness and its relation to the creative that I will direct most of my remaining comments towards it. A brief return to the logic is necessary at this stage.

★   ★   ★

Now the fact of a logical connexion between the technical logical issues examined in certain of these papers and the vivid and concrete treatment of the belief in Divine Existence might not be questioned and yet the question be raised whether this pursuit of logical connexion holds any real value for one whose interest is intelligent and critical but not specialized. The difficulty is increased by the fact that the philosophical background against which Kemp Smith developed his own logic is unfamiliar even to the philosophically trained of this generation and has therefore ceased to make any direct impact on literature or theological thinking, though its influence is by no means exhausted and we meet it in unexpected places. English Idealism, represented by such figures as Bradley and Bosanquet, was then the dominating philosophical influence and it was against this draft of Idealism that the critics of the time, G. E. Moore and Bertrand Russell, directed their attack. These are regarded today as the deadliest enemies of this Idealism, and the reader may wonder why so few references to Moore and Russell are to be found among all the papers. The reason is that Kemp Smith's own critique of Idealism which will be found in such articles as 'The Nature of Universals' and 'The Fruitfulness of the Abstract' is quite different in intention. His criticisms of Idealism are certainly not less radical than those of Moore and Russell, but these were destructive anti-metaphysical thinkers, whereas Kemp Smith's method was to find his way through criticism of opposing views to a constructive philosophy. Should it turn out that metaphysical presuppositions were after all involved, they could be justified only if shown to be inescapable. It is for us a misfortune that a logic at once so original, critical and yet constructive, should have been expounded against the background of a philosophical system in its essentials alien to his own temper of mind. Furthermore, he published his articles on logic at a time when the influence of this English version of Absolute Idealism was already on the wane. The consequence was that Kemp Smith's contributions to logic and epistemology never did receive the critical attention they merited.

I think, then, that the answer to this question is that the inquiries in this collection dealing with the facts of human life and religious beliefs do lend themselves to intelligent non-specialized discussion. Professor Kemp Smith intended them so and took the greatest pains to attain lucidity and simplicity without sacrifice of truth. But the clarity and emphasis he did attain was due to the mastery he had himself acquired over logical issues, and it was this, perhaps more than anything, that enabled him to give full weight both to the elements of rationality calling for precise formulation and to the non-rational or intuitive, and yet show how the two may unite to form an intelligible if incomplete account of the status of our fundamental beliefs. It is surely then a worthwhile, and, with the help Dr. Davie has given, not too difficult a task, to take a little time and trouble to try and see for oneself the interdependence of the concrete and the abstract. I have spoken above about the non-rational elements which inevitably enter into this discussion of Divine Existence. The non-rational does not mean the irrational; it can mean what we apprehend through a mode of knowledge into which the inferential processes of reason do not enter, or it can mean that which we name as infinite, omnipotent, omnipresent, and yet are unable to talk about except in a language adapted to finite things.

When one looks back upon this period of the late twenties, it now seems clear that constructive philosophical thinking in Britain suffered a disastrous set-back just through the absence of such a philosophical foundation as Kemp Smith's work in logic might have laid, and if the reader thinks this is far too large a claim, I can only refer him to Kemp Smith's three articles on Universals and to the brilliant paper on 'The Fruitfulness of the Abstract'. But the younger critical minds were then turning away from the traditional ideal of philosophy as the search for 'a coherent view of existence', nor could any new constructive outlook develop out of the atomism of Moore.

* * *

But the logical questions must not be dealt with in this summary fashion.

Perhaps it is better to say, simply, that in his logical studies Kemp Smith was working his way towards a concept of the natural world which did not at all conform to the Idealist pattern. Though he was prepared to call himself an Idealist, he was a Realist (if one may use for once these time-worn labels) in all except this one conviction that ideal values, the highest of which was personality, play a commanding role in human destiny. This concept of nature, which had reached its fullest development in his philosophical thinking at the time of writing on Divine Existence, shows the contemporary influence of Bergson and Whitehead, of Whitehead much more than Bergson; but to me it is clear that it was through his own peculiar insight into the natural world that he could come to speak of it as characterized by continuous creativeness wherein, despite the limitations of our temporal and creaturely consciousness, we may yet, in a mode which he calls mysterious, be made aware of non-creaturely reality.

No doubt if it could be established that we are creaturely beings it could only be through prior knowledge of the existence of God. 'By no idealization of the creaturely can we transcend the creaturely.' Apart from our repetitive actions, where plan and foresight enter in and which cover so large an area of our conscious lives—actions which can only in the least degree be called creative at all—there is creativeness in the Universe at three levels. There is the natural order wherein events, unique and one-time, are continuously brought into being in its creative advance. There are types of human action which we speak of as creative in distinction from the repetitive. These Kemp Smith calls purposive and creative to the extent that they bring something genuinely new into existence. Yet the sculptor, painter, musician, scientist or man of letters who exemplify these types are creative only within a pre-existent environment which includes their own past experience. Then there is the highest level where neither plan nor pre-existence can have any meaning, the level of Divine Existence where God alone is fully creative. Kemp Smith used to speak of creativeness in the human and natural orders as a delegated creativeness which yields no clue to the nature of creativeness itself. The inability to understand creativeness might well lead the reader to think in like manner of the existence of God as wholly incomprehensible and inconceivable, and I well remember certain of

Kemp Smith's colleagues who, while fully agreeing with his negative criticisms, thought that a wholly negative conclusion was their only logical outcome. Kemp Smith's answer was to point out that it is not the fact of God's existence but the mode that is inconceivable, and that to argue in the manner of his critics was still to argue on the basis of human analogy, and human analogy, based even on what we call the creative activities, such as the arts and sciences, is agreed to be totally inadequate; but to attribute creativeness to God, or rather to say that this is what the Divine is, is precisely to depart from human analogy. 'Creativity is a theomorphic, not an anthropomorphic concept.' Also while it is true to say that we do not have the least idea of the mode of creative action, we do have actual awareness of the fact of creativeness extending throughout the natural order 'occurring at every moment and in all places'. Creativity is an ultimate 'and like all ultimates, it has to be used in explanation while remaining itself unexplained'. It is also a striking fact that the severest critics of the old argument towards design (Hume and Kant) could not escape an experience which was borne in upon the mind, in despite of reason, with the force of a direct impression or sensation. This they wrongly interpreted as an impression of design in nature; rightly understood it is a sense of the mysteriousness of the natural order.

*   *   *

I have often wished over the years since he died that I had asked him if he could be more specific about his use of the word 'mysterious'. We are so accustomed in our day to hear the word used in the shallowest of contexts that to appeal to our sense of the mysterious in personal existence and in nature as the ultimate source of belief in Divine Existence is to invite a smile of scorn from the sceptic. But Kemp Smith never used a fundamental term which was not deeply weighed, all the more so a word so liable to encourage loose thinking and false emotional attitudes. Creativity is mysterious and there is no other word for it. Furthermore in his theory of knowledge he was an apostle of objectivity; he maintained that the colours and sounds whose combinations in the natural world delight us and sometimes appal us are really there, just as much as the abiding objects, though we need not suppose they are occurring all the time; they have the status of events and some events require more complex generating conditions than others, such as, in the case of colours and sounds, the presence of perceiving organisms.

Those features of the natural order which arouse in us emotions like fear, terror, awe and reverence, are as truly objective as the events of which we have been speaking above. Above all, and only to be significantly experienced in connexion with the cosmic setting of our human life, is the 'mysterious' in response to which the appropriate emotion is awe, which he describes in the final article on Fear as

> an emotion into which there would appear to be almost no human factor that does not enter. Peculiar to this type of experience is a sense of being drawn—*in spite of fear*—to the object which is arousing it, leaving us with the desire for future experience of it.

These features would seem to belong to religious experience in its advanced forms as well as to it as it emerges from its initial sources, and the reader may find it of interest to trace their many and various manifestations in historical forms of worship. Man is both drawn towards the mysterious and alarmed by it. He is attracted because he senses in it, in spite of fear, a deep kinship with himself; he is repulsed and alarmed because it is too much for him, its sheer otherness invites him to self-abasement. I think that in part, certainly only in part, his concern with religious belief lay in the sheer intellectual fascination and bafflement which these ideas—the creative and the mysterious—exercise upon the mind. The mysterious is not the unanalysable but the unfathomable. The first term describes only what is simple, the second what is of unending depth and complexity.[1]

---

[1] Kemp Smith commends, but does not adopt, Otto's concept of the numinous, as that which gives rise to awe. Further, he is in agreement with Otto that belief in Divine Existence is of the direct, intuitive order and not inferential. He mentions that had he been engaged in an epistemological discussion of the nature of our apprehension of the Divine, far more would have to be said about the *a priori* elements involved. Otto treats the numinous as an *a priori* category, the proof of which is in part reached through introspection, in part through a critical examination of reason, following Kant—a very curious combination indeed! Otto's approach is through analysis of situations which yield the experience of awe, then gradually building up to an attempt to determine the numinous element itself. The background of Kemp Smith's approach is a philosophy of nature as creative, where creativity is itself the ultimate, and it is with

In these last comments I am drawing upon my remembrance of talks with him. What seems extraordinary, looking back, is the lack of any very specific conclusions we could have drawn from them. This seems all the more strange when one remembers how enriching and enlightening these conversations were. In his presence we all felt some of the 'awe' of which Professor Hendel writes, and even when admitted to his most intimate friendship we could not always overcome a sense of his 'aloneness', as though his vision was reaching out to horizons far beyond our own. Perhaps it was just this experience that precluded us from carrying away much that could be put into the form of conclusions in words. From these long quiet conversations interspersed with silences we came away feeling that a change had taken place in ourselves, something far more fundamental than a merely intellectual illumination.

I do however remember a talk I had with him, perhaps two years before he died. He was talking about our knowledge of God and he said that he personally could not now go beyond an 'Ordering Principle'. Some months later when he was recuperating in the Royal Infirmary of Edinburgh from the onset of an illness which was later to recur and to be his last, he asked me to visit him one evening when he expected to be alone. Almost at once he brought up the subject of our talk of months earlier and said that he feared he had left me with a far more negative impression than he had intended. God is creative power with all that is involved in such attributes as omnipresence and omniscience, of which we have no understanding. This he had not intended to deny. But, of course, when we assert such attributes we are only affirming that God's being is not subject to the limiting conditions of space and time. But to evolve a concept of Divine activity, or of the Divine Nature, or of God's relation to man, he could not go beyond an 'Ordering Principle'. If it is possible to do so it can only be through the medium of the historical religions with their special revelations. But for him an ordering principle was not nearly so negative and formal a concept as might appear to us,

---

creativity that the mysterious is bound up. Although we do and must experience the element of the mysterious in specific situations, it is in the *cosmic* setting of our human life, as he very significantly says, in the effort to discover meaning and abiding value, that we are made most poignantly aware of this unfathomable, mysterious character of Divine Existence. (See Rudolf Otto, *The Idea of the Holy*, pp. 117 ff.)

for he held firmly to the objectivity of the ultimate values, above all those that condition personal life.

The reader will find that the implications of this become clearer in the broadcast address on Immortality where he rests the case upon our belief that personality is the highest value we know; and if this then is the end towards which the Principle of Order shapes the creative process, we live in a Universe where the good must be yet more durable, more prevalent than the ill. If this be optimism, Kemp Smith did not come by it lightly, nor did he underestimate the ills, though he would not have gone as far as Cardinal Newman: 'I look out of myself into the world of men', says the latter, 'and there I see a sight which fills me with unspeakable distress. The world seems simply to give the lie to that great truth, of which my whole being is so full, and the effect upon me is, in consequence, as if it denied that I am in existence myself. If I looked into a mirror and did not see my face, I should have the sort of feeling, which actually comes upon me, when I look into the living busy world, and see no reflection of its creator.' At any rate, Kemp Smith had found a far more objective basis for belief than Newman's 'voice of conscience' and would have regarded the fact of conflict between the appearances and the belief in Providence, which Newman himself regarded as a mystery, and our inability to accept or explain this conflict, as equally owing to the conditions of our creaturely consciousness.

I could not help noticing, and others besides myself noticed, that during his latter years he seemed almost to have more assurance of an 'after-life' than of the existence of God. Yet in his broadcast discussion he quite decisively rejected any approach to an after-life other than through Divine Existence. I do not doubt in the least that he never departed from the philosophical views expressed in that address. Once during these latter years while we were walking together he remarked with a little bitterness—the only bitterness I have ever seen in him—that he was sure of other regions in the Universe where life would be more satisfactory than here. Personality he held to be the highest achievement of our world as we know it; yet, as Professor Porteous has noted, he used to say that nothing was more difficult than personal relations. There is about personality something incomplete, something crying out to be completed.

He greatly admired W. P. Montague's remarkable Ingersoll Lecture of 1932, 'The Chances of Surviving Death'. Montague's problem was not the same as Kemp Smith's. As the title indicates he was discussing survival rather than immortality, but in the last section of the lecture he turns to the question of eternal life. What are the prospects for eternity, he asks. The highest we can conceive of is personality and the possibility of its continued growth. The words which so deeply impressed Kemp Smith in this context are from Montague's final paragraph: 'precious and indispensable for value as personality appears, there is about it something tragically wanting; and as in every finite thing, but more acutely, a sort of wound that cries for healing'. Is it possible that in personalities like Kemp Smith's, where life seemed to be lived most fully, this wound is felt most acutely?

If personality is our highest measure of value must it not exist in God in the fullest possible measure? So reasoned Kemp Smith's friend, the most learned, distinguished and beloved Catholic lay philosopher, Baron von Hügel. Kemp Smith agreed with much else of von Hügel's teaching about God, namely that God is truly other, that He is incomprehensible to finite minds and that Divine transcendence is essential to the religious consciousness. But personality cannot be other than a concept of our finite, creaturely consciousness, and between the creaturely and the creative the difference is absolute: God is the wholly other. The kinship we feel towards the mysterious, creative source of our being we experience as a personal response on our own part; but does this imply that God's activity towards ourselves is likewise personal or personal even in a far higher degree? His activity, His initiative towards us is indeed always prevenient. We feel kinship with the Divine because we sense in it the creative conditions whereby our own beings are sustained in space and time and this sense is reinforced by the belief that there also are the conditions for the continued growth and fulfilment or perfecting of our personal natures. The former is an immediate sense of our dependence upon God, the latter an act of faith inseparable from historical religion.

It is then hardly possible to say, on Kemp Smith's premises, that God is personal, and it is best to avoid phrases which do nothing to clarify the problem, such as 'personality is in God' or 'God is supra-personal', in order to circumvent the difficulty. Surely the difficulty is of our own making. There is, as Kemp Smith has argued, an abidingly mysterious character about the self: the self can be apprehended in relation to the body and other physical conditions, in fellowship with others, never in and by itself and never fully comprehended. There is therefore that about personality which eludes definition and description, and it is that, and its being also the highest we know, that seems to allow of it being extended to the being of God. But if we are to take the doctrine of creation seriously then we are committed to the rejection of anthropomorphic thinking all the way. What is really important to understand is that the alternative to *personal* is not *impersonal*. If the word personal as applied to God is wholly inadequate, impersonal is wholly misleading. What is essential to belief is that God as creator must transcend the world, that as Creator His Nature must contain all the conditions for the perfectibility of our natures, the chief of which is grace or love. 'By the Divine,' he says, 'we must, at the least, mean that upon which all things rest.' He is here referring to the attribute of power, upon which the higher attributes such as love and wisdom depend, and he does not mean that all things rest upon the Divine in a static or qualitative manner, for the Divine is above all the creative, the supernatural. The use of this last word may appear shocking in certain quarters, where it is associated with superstition and not with enlightened discourse about God. Kemp Smith, writing to Montague, remarks: 'I am glad to see that you do not shirk using the term "supernatural". It is surely a good, and even indispensable term, absurdly misrepresented when it is equated, as it generally is, with the miraculous.' It is important to insist, as he does elsewhere, that if the term 'supernatural' is to be correctly used, then the word 'natural' must be allowed to have full positive meaning and reality. As he points out in criticism of Bergson's use of the former term, an extreme supernaturalism deprives the natural of positive meaning, and makes it merely resistant to instead of receptive of the supernatural.

Again, personality, as known to us within the limits of our human experience, is bound up with what we call the empirical self, the self that rises in the morning, feeds itself when hungry, needs rest and sleep at night. We have no reason to suppose that this empirical self has any potency to survive bodily death, otherwise we should have to suppose that an after-life simply continues the conditions which have sustained the self during its present existence. Kemp Smith's view, as set forth in the address on Immortality, is that immortal life begins not after death but in the here and now and is, for the self, an entry into a new way of life. This must mean that, within our human personality, there is a potentiality which our knowledge of the empirical self has not been able to take account of. In other words, from our knowledge of the human personality gained through normal experience, we would never be able to assert or predict an immortal destiny. The whole problem of immortality has been transformed by the abandonment of the doctrine of an immaterial soul-substance not subject to disintegrating processes, and the recognition that all objective claims for a meaningful after-life must be based upon the kinship of the personality with the Divine, and that, although the initiative comes from the Divine, there is in the human personality this potentiality for kinship. Kemp Smith's insistence that there is a mysterious character to the life of the self will be remembered at this point, also Montague's 'something tragically wanting . . . a sort of wound that cries out for healing'.

If human personality is no measure at all of Divine Existence, human consciousness sheds no more than the faintest glimmer of light upon the nature of Divine knowledge, which is taking account of the least, the most minor happenings in the Universe, just as much as of those which to our sense of time and space are its major events. This taking account of the least is incomprehensible to our finite minds, but is precisely what we must postulate of the mind of God in attributing to it omniscience and omnipresence.

★   ★   ★

Edmund Wilson, America's distinguished critic and man of letters, who has sat under him at Princeton, records in his *Europe Without Baedeker* a visit to Kemp Smith's house in Edinburgh in 1945. He describes it as one of the most fortifying experiences of his trip, and gives a charming and, as we would say, homely account of his former teacher now in retirement and aged over seventy, but evidently in unimpaired activity of mind and body. When they sat down to breakfast Kemp Smith 'insisted on my eating porridge in the traditional Scottish way: you had to take with each spoonful of porridge a spoonful of cold milk' thus to bring out the real nutty flavour of the porridge. Before they parted their conversation came round to more serious topics; the outlook for the future, the outworn beliefs which stood in the way of constructive thought. Edmund Wilson said he thought it was time to get rid of the word *God*, since we had 'no need of that hypothesis' to account for the life that was in us and the coherence of the Universe. Kemp Smith replied 'I don't know any better word'. Wilson goes on to reflect that Kemp Smith being of an older generation than himself and being brought up in Scotland had no doubt had a more rigorous religious training. 'For myself,' he goes on to add, 'I am extremely reluctant to call anything whatever "God", for the word had too many connotations of obsolete and miraculous mythologies; and what Kemp Smith called God was, I think, something mainly identifiable with a vigorous physical persistence, a rectitude in relation to others and to one's own work in the world, and a faith in the endurance of the human mind.'

It would be difficult to imagine a less adequate notion of what Kemp Smith meant by God than the above propositions convey, and it is evident that the genuine bonds of affection and respect, which continued to unite teacher and pupil over all those years, since Princeton days, were not due to a shared philosophical outlook. Kemp Smith was enthusiastic about Edmund Wilson's pioneer work in making known to the American public the discovery and promise of the Dead Sea Scrolls; and when the series of articles, which he wrote for *The New Yorker*, subsequently appeared in book form, I remember Kemp Smith joyfully presenting copies to his friends. Of more concern is Edmund Wilson's implication that Kemp Smith's very use of the word 'God' was a carry over from his Scottish upbringing and 'more rigorous religious training'. Once this kind of question is raised, it is always difficult and unsatisfactory to answer, and I do not think it would ever have occurred to any one to raise it who had been in direct contact with Kemp Smith's critical habit of mind. In this case one has to bear in mind Edmund Wilson's own confessed reluctance 'to call anything whatever God', likewise his unwillingness to attribute to Kemp Smith, whom he admired, a word so suggestive to his mind of the obsolete and the miraculous. Kemp Smith's early religious training would have exposed him, like almost every other young person in Scotland at that time, to a popularized type of Calvinism, and there is no reason to doubt that the influence of this teaching was a lasting one. But what did it amount to in his case? Discussing David Hume's early religious education, when Hume was exposed to a Calvinism of a far more extreme type, he makes this comment:

> No teaching—it is probably correct to say—is so ill suited for popularization, and loses so much in the process as the teaching of Calvin. (*Dialogues concerning Natural Religion,* ed. Kemp Smith, p. 11.)

If this comment reveals anything of Kemp Smith's attitude to his own early training, it surely reveals that it was largely an intellectual one, neither reactionary nor uncritical in acceptance or rejection. What it did do was to lead him to a thorough-going reappraisal of aspects which his early training had obscured or ignored, notably Calvin's relation to the medieval tradition and his doctrine of man. There was also another and later influence which may well have been a strong encouragement. His years at Princeton introduced him to the writings of Jonathan Edwards whose endeavour to find a philosophical foundation for Calvin's doctrines, if unsuccessful, was none the less deeply impressive. Kemp Smith once said to me that Edwards' treatise on the Will was the most powerful argument for determinism he had ever encountered.

The article on 'The Middle Ages, the Renaissance and the Modern Mind' is a remarkable piece of work, and certainly one of the most important in this collection, in respect of its profound analysis of the Medieval and Protestant traditions, and its relevance to the problems of Christianity and culture in our own society, and to the present concern of the Christian Churches to review their own traditions and to find a common basis of co-operation. I should apologize for taking up only one point and that briefly. Kemp Smith has emphasized the fact that religious belief must be sustained by both immediate experience and historical faith which inculcates a way of life. Being concerned with the fundamental belief in God, the article on Divine Existence has said little about historical faith, beyond pointing out its necessity for the higher forms of religious practice which come only later. It is here that religion comes into contact and frequently into conflict with morality. Speaking of religion in its relation to morality Kemp Smith says 'just as it starts by being other than morals, so it continues to the end to be more than morals'. He allows for a moral autonomy, indispensable to religion, if religious practice is to benefit from informed ethical criticism; and ethics, in turn, if it is to deepen its concept of man through this contact, must recognize that religion has independent roots. Thus there grows out of this uneasy but immensely fruitful partnership an ethico-religious concept of man.

According to one such concept man's essential need is for self-knowledge, yet he cannot attain to it for the reason that his nature, infected by evil, is prone to self-deception and only by rising to the contemplation of God can he contemplate himself. And then the picture is anything but an attractive one. This is Calvin's understanding of human nature; it is the realistic view and, Kemp Smith believed, far closer to the truth than all theories of progress and of the natural goodness of man. His doctrine of creativeness would preclude him from accepting Calvin's predestinarian concepts, but the doctrine of man in its essentials is psychologically and ethically sound. It is the ultimate justification of the use of force in civilized society and the ultimate source of the will to wage war and resort to violence. It is also that which makes fear an indispensable motive of human conduct: 'Not a craven fear that swamps the mind, but a fear that searches the spirit, steadying it to clearer vision and awakening it to consciousness of the serious issues of life.' From this quotation the reader will see that in this, one of the earliest of his articles, Kemp Smith had already formulated the chief principle of his thesis in the final article on Fear.

★   ★   ★

While he was in London towards the end of the First World War, he met Baron von Hügel and the two men, so apparently different in temperament and background, formed a deep friendship unbroken till von Hügel's death in 1925. During these years there was a continued exchange of letters, Kemp Smith writing for the most part once a week and the Baron as often as his precarious health and gradually failing strength would allow. The Baron's letters—those that were found among Kemp Smith's private papers—are nearly all intimately personal, an outpouring of affection and gratitude for the blessings of this friend-ship and the help these weekly letters had given him. The great interest of the letters is personal rather than philosophical and, so far as we could discover, Professor Kemp Smith had had no thought of their publica-tion. One letter, however, in particular attempts to answer a question to which he gave much thought in later years. The question was that of the Christian Church and Culture today. It was the question he had asked in his article on the Middle Ages. Could the Baron (who, though re-garded as a modernist, was a convinced and devoted Catholic) conceive of the Christian Body as capable of assimilating the best in the modern world, interpenetrating its Culture, as it did in the Golden Middle Age? Von Hügel's answer could not have been fully satisfying, for I remember Kemp Smith many years later expressing his own doubts on this, in his view, crucial question. All the same the Baron's answer is impressive. He first stated his own conviction that a few of the ablest thinkers in the Catholic Church, both lay and priests, had already achieved this assimi-lation, but the fact that single individuals had accomplished this was one thing, a huge entire institution was quite another thing; that it could and would eventually do so was for him a matter of undoubting faith. The answer could not, however, rest there. 'The essential, the most indispensable of the dimensions of religion is *not breadth but depth*, and above all *the insight into sanctity and the power to produce saints*. Rome con-tinues—of this I am very sure—to possess this supernatural depth—possesses it in far greater degree than Protestantism, and still more than the unattached modern.'

Kemp Smith's sympathy with the Christian Faith and Church in its encounter with the vast and yet unformed forces of modern secular culture should be evident from these papers. Did he himself belong to any Christian denomination? The answer is no. Kemp Smith would have found the dogma or doctrine of any of the traditional Christian denominations too confining. 'Impossibly orthodox' is an expression I have heard him use of Brunner and Barth, though he had great respect for the latter. So called 'Liberal Christianity' I never heard him discuss at all. The fact is that he shared a considerable part—one would say the best—of the Catholic and Protestant traditions with, however, an acceptance of the fact that he belonged to the latter; but how far he was prepared to go along with that tradition, I never precisely understood. On one matter he was emphatic: the Professor of Philosophy at Edinburgh University had special responsibilities towards his students. He was himself the humblest of men, but he must have known that his influence was exceptional, and that one in his position would be expected to have thought out his own views carefully. To partake of Communion would, he felt, create the impression that he fully accepted an orthodox Christian position. On the other hand he was meticulous in his attendance at the monthly University Services, and while on holiday in the Highlands, or at Iona, he regularly attended the local church. He once remarked to me that if he lived in a rural community he would probably become a member of the Church and participate in the Sacraments. His sympathy with the Christian tradition, his concern over the Church's conflict with secularist culture and his own inability to accept any one tradition opens up a question which I cannot pursue here, though it seems to be one of momentous consequences if the Christian Churches are to be able to draw upon the most talented minds. I will just add that some of the ideas Kemp Smith contributed in answer to this question find at least partial expression in the article on 'The Middle Ages, the Renaissance and the Modern Mind', and that von Hügel's answer that the Church's 'indispensable dimension is not breadth but depth' may well be true for its survival, but for its task in the world more is required.

To try to write about Kemp Smith as a teacher and thinker is to become increasingly aware of one's inadequacy. I was a member of his first Philosophy Class at Edinburgh University and shared with three hundred others, most of them ex-servicemen of the First World War, the privilege of being introduced to philosophy by one whom we immediately recognized to be a great teacher. We also shared the feeling that we were in the presence of a great man who, in our estimation, would have been equal to any office in public life. As some of us came to know him more intimately in later years we found that the sense of his greatness remained, but we altered our views about public life. He would have been wasted doing anything other than being the great teacher he was.

R. D. M.

III. The Significance of the Philosophical Papers

G. E. DAVIE

AS a philosopher, Kemp Smith was at once refreshingly different and remarkably solid. Reacting early against the rival extremes of English-speaking philosophy (monism *v.* pluralism, subjectivism *v.* behaviourism), he took his stand on a principle of intellectual moderation, which, owing something to the Scottish philosophical inheritance, at the same time drew its chief inspiration from the modern as well as the classical philosophers of France and Germany. The result is a philosophy which is of the greatest interest both in technical and in human terms. On the one hand, Kemp Smith successfully wrestles with central themes which, of crucial importance in modern Continental philosophy, are only now coming into prominence in the English-speaking world—notably, the reflective distinction between 'act-character' and 'content' in mental states (*anglice*, 'speech-acts'), as well as the interrelationship of colour and extension ('can the same spot be red and green all over?'). On the other hand, sustained by the kindred tradition of the Princeton and the Edinburgh Chairs, Kemp Smith magnificently managed to bring out the direct relevance to the human situation of these apparently recondite topics by making them the basis of a critique of modern optimism involving a certain reappraisal of the doctrine of original sin. The outcome is a series of essays in philosophy of a calibre whose interest is likely to increase rather than diminish with the passage of time.

I. THE INESCAPABILITY OF HISTORY

To appreciate Kemp Smith's starting-point, it is necessary to pay attention to his distinctive doctrine about the nature of philosophy. 'Bertrand Russell', he notes, 'has advocated the limiting of philosophy to the strictly *a priori*.[1] But for Kemp Smith, such a sharp separation of the *a priori* and the empirical denatures philosophy, which, he argues, 'is more closely bound up with the historical and humanistic disciplines than with those of the deductive and demonstrative type'. Philosophy is, no doubt, up to a point analytic in the sense of seeking to discover the *pervasive features* of the human situation, but its problems emerge only in and through preliminary anthropological survey of the past in relation to the present, and of one way of life by comparison with others.

To make this view more precise, let us glance at the paper on the possibility of agreement in philosophy. The kind of thoroughgoing specialization which obtains in the laboratory-based and technical disciplines is not in the nature of the case a practical possibility in library-based disciplines such as the humanities are. In a subject like chemistry, 'the results of former research sum themselves up in definite principles and prescribed methods. To that extent, a chemist can dispense with the study of history', just as he can dispense with the study of philosophy or literature. On the other hand, this sort of isolationist policy won't work with regard to the humanities. In particular, philosophy cannot be cut off sharply from history. In philosophy, there are no laboratories, no scientific instruments to serve as means of teaching the tyro the methods of formulating questions; there are only books. But where so much depends on the presentation of selected texts, the business of understanding involves a perpetual battle against inherited stereotypes. In philosophizing we do not start with a *tabula rasa*; we start with prejudices in regard to the visible and unread books which surround us. Inevitably,

---

[1] *The Present Situation in Philosophy* (Edinburgh, Thin, 1919), p. 27.

the would-be philosopher finds himself involved with the problem of the intellectual inheritance of his subject, and thereby of the culture-history of mankind.[1]

The commitment of philosophy to history is as far-reaching as it is inevitable. In vain do philosophers of the Russell–Moore school protest that they are not historians of ideas; their own writings make it clear that it is not possible to do philosophy without pontificating about intellectual history—'the ghost in the machine', etc. The alternative is thus, for Kemp Smith, not between the historical and the systematic treatment of any problem, but between all-round 'intellectual mastery' and 'unconscious preconceptions' about the history of ideas. 'An adequate solution of philosophical problems and a valid interpretation of past systems, must', Kemp Smith points out, 'develop together.'

To illustrate this doctrine of the interpenetration of philosophy and history, look at Kemp Smith's contributions to the history of philosophy represented here by the articles on Hume and on Locke. Kemp Smith's great achievement here has been to challenge the progressive view (what one might call the Whig view) of intellectual history. From first to last, the central theme of his Kant and Hume and Descartes books has been a calling in question of the Romantic-optimistic dialectic alike in the 'Germano-Coleridgean' version according to which one-sided outlooks of a pluralistic and subjective kind prepare the way for a final revelation of monistic mysticism, and equally in the Benthamite-utilitarian version according to which a primitive legacy of mystical monism is in process of being replaced by the ultimate clarity of a behaviouristic-pluralistic logic. Setting aside altogether this progressivism, Kemp Smith brings out in lucid detail how the great philosophers (including David Hume and Descartes) were not tied to the artificially simplified extremes of either monism or pluralism, of either subjectivism or behaviourism, but were, one and all, striving to express, in one form or another, the balanced tensions of complicated position or counter-position. In this way, Kemp Smith sees historical philosophy as a series of recurrent intellectual crises in which a position of moderate centrality is each generation struggling to reassert itself and to reformulate itself

---

[1] Kemp Smith's position rests on his critique of the *cogito* of Descartes, as discussed below, pp. 85 ff.

(not always successfully) in the face of the competition and clamour of one-sided extremisms.

Exceptional for modern Britain and not yet properly appreciated here, Kemp Smith's interpretation of intellectual history has close affinities with the living trends on the Continent. We think in particular of M. Jean Laporte, pupil of Bergson, teacher of Sartre, the starting-point of whose researches[1] was, avowedly, Kemp Smith's 'très remarquable article' on Hume, here reprinted. The significance of Kemp Smith's position emerges clearly in those books and articles where M. Laporte presents 'a Descartes who is not just a rationalist, but also empirical, a Hume who is not only atomistic but also holistic, even vitalistic in tendency'.[2] Equally, the Kemp Smith spirit strongly survives in those disciples of M. Laporte who struggle against the optimistic-progressive view of intellectual history revived by M. Goldmann,[3] with its resurrected stereotype of a one-sided Hume 'empiricist and sensualist', and a one-sided individualistic Descartes.

Bearing in mind Kemp Smith's distinctive view of the history of philosophy, let us come closer to the starting-point of his own philosophy proper by looking at his powerful analysis of the moral crisis of our own time, as given in 'The Middle Ages, the Renaissance and the Modern Mind'. Already before 1914, Kemp Smith repudiated the social optimism which formed the predominant outlook of intellectual Britain, uniting Bradley's school with Russell's. Modern philosophy, Bosanquet said, speaking not only for himself and Bradley, but for the rival party of Russell and Moore, regards the future 'not as a painful preservation of equilibrium, but as a free and natural growth towards perfection'.[4] Tired of this inflated optimism, Kemp Smith took his stand on a renovated version of a position Bosanquet and Russell thought out-

---

[1] *Rev. Philosophique* (1933 and 1936), 'Le scepticism de Hume'. It is hoped that M. Laporte's writings on Hume will be presented in book-form, as promised by his editors.

[2] *Rev. Philosophique* (1941), p. 447.

[3] *Le Dieu Caché*, pp. 37–38, 40, 42 (Paris, Gallimard, 1955). English translation, *The Hidden God*, by Philip Thody.

[4] B. Bosanquet, *The Civilization of Christendom*, p. 85 (London, Swan, Sonnenschein; New York, The Macmillan Co., 2nd ed. 1899).

moded. What the scientific revolution of the twentieth century required as its moral counterpart was not a utopian or even a melioristic perfectibilism, but a return to something like the standpoint of original sin. For Kemp Smith, the triumphant advance of natural science inevitably introduced an era, not of increasing contentment, but of increasing instability and danger to civilization. In short, the kind of moral philosophy required by a science-based 'Age of anxiety' is a revival of Calvinistic values.

In the paper on 'The Moral Sanction of Force', Kemp Smith's 'neo-Calvinist' thesis is applied with great freshness and force to problems of twentieth-century politics. The danger is that 'we fall victim to the Pelagian fallacy, blinding ourselves to the complexity of the situation'. Kemp Smith warns against the intellectual optimism of the times. The ultimate heresy of the modern mind is the eighteenth-century doctrine, revived by such as Russell, that the social tensions which make force and compulsion necessary, are an accidental intrusion into the human situations, capable of being eliminated from society, and destined to 'wither away'. On the contrary, from Kemp Smith's point of view, the mark of advancing civilization is increased social tension and intensified state-compulsion. In this sense, strife is incapable of being eliminated from society. The utmost which can be achieved in the name of the moral and religious ideal is such a reorganization of social conditions as will shift the incidence of the tensions, making them take new forms. Thus the price of the abolition of duelling was the creation of the modern state with novel machinery of compulsions to cope with transformed and intensified unrest. Kemp Smith does not want to deny the validity of the moral ideal—he puts that point beyond question in his discussion of the same subject in the paper on Bergson's political and social views; at the same time his main concern is to point out that we make nonsense of the ideal if we fail to acknowledge the fundamental role of tensions.

Kemp Smith returned to this same theme in the splendid paper on 'Fear', which was the last thing he published. Acknowledging its affinity with 'the magnificent opening chapter of Calvin's *Institutes*', it is directed against the doctrinaire humanitarians who regard fear as a disease to be eradicated from society, and who suppose the intellectual element is separable from the emotive. As against them, Kemp Smith argues that the tenseness of fear is not a sort of St. Vitus's dance which surges up in the body as an alien intruder, clouding one's consciousness of the situation. The mistake of the humanitarian logician is, as usual, the atomistic outlook which treats fear as a single isolated impulse, failing to note its complexity. 'In fear impulsive tendencies are at once excited and obstructed; in one aspect, the emotion presses towards action, in the other, it checks action and throws the individual back upon himself, imposing the delay requisite for reviewing the situation.' In this sense, the apprehensiveness which is inseparable from fear, far from clouding the mind, has a genuinely cognitive role. The vital point for Kemp Smith is that, in and through these intellectual tensions, 'fear holds the painful before consciousness'. Eliminate fear from human nature, and 'how is attention to the disagreeable to be secured?' This view of the educative, intellectual function of fear is not, Kemp Smith points out, a donnish and ineffectual theory; it is what Wordsworth as well as Calvin held. The article ends with a remarkable analysis of those passages in the *Prelude* where Wordsworth, drawing on his own experiences, criticized the Enlightenment ideal of a terror-free world.

Kemp Smith's analysis of our historical situation, so far noteworthy for a realistic moderation, first begins to reveal its metaphysical depths when, leaving behind superficial British thinkers, he sets himself to appraise 'Bergson's Manner of Approach to Moral and Social Questions'. Going over the topics already discussed in 'The Moral Sanction of Force', Kemp Smith notes that, up to a point, Bergson and himself agree as to the indispensable role of moral or aesthetic ideals in the creative process whereby a society criticizes and abolishes an institution like the duel or whereby an architect evolves an original solution of a building problem. According to Bergson and to Kemp Smith, 'the spirit can discover itself only in antagonism to natural conditions'. In the sequel, however, a disagreement soon arises as to the source of the spirit's inspiration. Bergson, for his part, accepts a 'Neo-Platonic' separation, according to which, 'in proportion as our human activities are truly creative' 'the insights which guide them are due to supra-natural influences, breaking in upon the normal course of our usual activities'. Kemp Smith, on the other hand, maintains 'in opposition to such contentions, that, in the mastery of natural necessities, the inspiration comes'

—in part, at least— 'through new possibilities detected in these necessities', i.e. not through inspired prophecy, but through rational analysis of the given.

Expounded more thoroughly in the last five pages of the paper on 'Whitehead',[1] the present point at issue with Bergson is of capital importance for Kemp Smith's philosophy. The embarrassing fact about this Bergsonian irrationalism, so far as Kemp Smith was concerned, was its intimate connexion with the very part of Bergson with which Kemp Smith sympathized most strongly—the doctrine of *durée*. It was essential to Kemp Smith's social critique to accept from Bergson the view that 'time is not an independent variable'—i.e. historical events are internally related, and it is this internal relatedness that Kemp Smith relies on in denouncing the Russellian view that social tensions are accidental intrusions into history. So, too, Kemp Smith enthusiastically accepted the Bergsonian view of nature as 'at every moment creatively advancing into novelty', with the unpredictable 'rhythm' of a melody in process of composition. But if we accept this *durée* view of time are we obliged to 'depreciate reason' as 'too inflexible' to allow for 'the freakishness of life'? Such was Kemp Smith's dilemma.

Kemp Smith begins by pointing out that Bergson's time-stream is unanalysable only because he sets aside the conjunct experience of spatiality. Reintroduce space, and an analytic apprehension of the time flow becomes possible. How, for example, is it possible to distinguish Scottish history from English within the complex web of events constituting the British past? Great Britain's 'being an island', 'grotesquely shaped', Kemp Smith says, 'has largely determined the history of England and of Scotland'. The point apparently is that, owing to the contrast between the relatively impenetrable mountain-mass in the North, and the flatlands in the South, the island of Britain reacted differentialy to invasions like those of the Romans and of the Normans. In this sense, not only is the historical division of Britain incomprehensible without reference to geographical facts, but, in a more general and more profound sense, it would appear as if the distinctive tempo and rhythm of one country's history stands out as comprehensible only if

[1] Confessing indebtedness to Whitehead's teaching about space, Kemp Smith is obviously less satisfied with the 'eternal objects' which serve Whitehead as universals.

viewed against the background of the different rhythms of historical movement elsewhere.

However, this division of time by space still does not properly meet Bergson's objection to rational analysis, since from his point of view these multiple histories would each be so multifarious and creative as to elude any but artificial classifications and periodizations. 'Types and patterns', 'rhythms and recurrences' 'are but artificial schemes devised by our merely anthropomorphic reason', which, 'under the stress of our practical needs', are 'read into the ever-changing freely creative processes'. The Bergsonian scepticism about analysis thus still maintains its ground.

Kemp Smith's reply constitutes perhaps his greatest intellectual achievement. Bergson's view of analysis as merely anthropomorphic and arbitrary is due to a misunderstanding of the abstractive process involved in our experience of universals. The essence of analysis is not that, in a purely subjective way, we 'read' rhythms and patterns into the objects given in experience, but that the objects of experience *reveal to us*, in a non-arbitrary and objective way, new and hitherto latent qualities, according as we look at them in the light of unfamiliar background objects. In this sense, the reply to Bergson already contains the germ of the doctrine which is not fully developed till 'The Fruitfulness of the Abstract'. Bergson's misunderstanding of the role of intellect is due to a failure to appreciate *the abstraction i.e. analysis by comparisons*, in which the object studied, e.g. a historical situation, discloses itself and its distinctive aspects in virtue of its noticeable resemblances to and differences from contrasting objects elsewhere. For instance, the educational inheritance of Scotland appears in a very different light when compared with the French or the American than when compared with the English inheritance.

In the light of these principles, let us reconsider the line Kemp Smith takes in regard to the Bergsonian question of the nature of the intellectual or artistic creation, raised towards the end of 'Bergson's Manner of Approach to Social and Moral Questions': 'It is', he says, 'only under stress of natural necessities that we can ever succeed in obtaining effective contact . . . with the values (aesthetic, etc.) to which we have access by direct awareness.' Applied to Kemp Smith's favourite case of architectural creation, this principle means that the architect's work involves only 'the positive *modification* of natural necessities, not the *elimination* of them'. That is to say, whatever is devised has to harmonize with the constants of the historic heritage involved—townscapes, social and institutional customs, etc. In this sense, the architect must live himself into the history and cannot escape it. But at the same time it is not enough for the architect to remain exclusively within this historical stream and the conditions it prescribes. What he is seeking is 'a solution which, in satisfying all these prescribed conditions, will also satisfy his more general demands for effectiveness and beauty'. What this means is that the architect must analyse the possibilities inherent in the given situation, by looking beyond it and away from it to other comparable situations, involved in different and alien historical circumstances. On this view, architectural creation involves an intellectual balance between divergent demands. If the given situation is not compared with other, external situations, its possibilities will not emerge at all, whereas, on the other hand, the inappropriate possibilities cannot be ruled out except in the light of the historical movement inherent in the situation.

In this way, Kemp Smith sets aside the Bergsonian view of the creative movement as *wholly* irrational and a gift from above. In part at least, he argues, the abstract disciplines, outlined above, and to be discussed in detail later, form an essential precondition of artistic and other invention. The intellectual restraint they impose provides the same sort of stimulus to the spirit as does 'the prescription of a traditional technique in the arts' such as verse-form.

II. THE LIBERATING ROLE OF ABSTRACTION

This problem of how to do justice to the Bergsonian concrete *durée* without rejecting intellectual analysis is the starting-point alike of the three articles on Universals of 1927 and their remarkable sequel of the next year—'The Fruitfulness of the Abstract'. The effect of his struggle with Bergson was to convince Kemp Smith that 'the illusion of the epoch' so far as philosophy was concerned, was the preference for the concrete over the analytical and abstract. In the first two articles on Universals, Kemp Smith confronts the Hegelian version of this heresy, while the third deals with the corresponding attempts of the empiricists to depreciate the abstract in favour of the concrete. Finally in 'The Fruitfulness of the Abstract' Kemp Smith completes this remarkable project by expounding his own balanced views on the subject.

Granted, this long series of articles is pretty hard reading—narrowly ascripted to shape–colour perception, ill-supplied with examples, always involved and often elliptical in its arguments, sometimes infected with the confusion inherent in a terrific effort to get things clear. Yet at the same time, these difficult pages of Kemp Smith have compelling interest and high authority, just because, in the midst of all these detailed technical struggles, he never loses sight of the ultimate moral purpose. For as plainly appears in the articles, what was at stake in this grand debate of the mid-twenties on universals and particulars, was nothing less than the future of intellectual standards in the Britain of our time. The central question was about what kind of logic was to succeed the internal relations scheme of Bradley and Bosanquet, which, because it blurred basic distinctions in a complacent way, was now totally discredited. Was this outmoded Victorian optimism to give place to an equally extravagant theory of external relations which couldn't see the wood for the trees? Or was there at last to prevail some principle of sagacious moderation which neither absorbed the parts into the whole nor reduced the whole to its parts? Debated between Moore and Whitehead and Ramsey and Russell and Joseph, these issues, so fateful for our Britain of forty years later, form the background to Kemp Smith's research into universals and particulars, giving it both point and excitement.

Let us then start from 'The Fruitfulness of the Abstract', as being Kemp Smith's final word on the subject. If we wish to do justice to the facts of cognition, we must always keep in view the fundamental relationship between a thing—e.g. a horse—considered concretely in its individuality, i.e. in the continuingness of its life-history, and the same thing considered abstractly as a type, i.e. as the recurrence of a complex pattern which is elsewhere also embodied simultaneously, with some variations. When we consider the horse as an individual, we consider it as a sort of organic unity of its qualities—as, for example, a shape internally related to its colour, in the sense that it would be impossible in practice to alter the horse's shape (by dieting, etc.) without to some extent affecting its colouring. When, on the other hand, we consider the horse as a type, we are not comparing its continuance at one stage of its life-history with its appearance at a previous stage, we are comparing its appearance at its present stage with that of other horses and other things set alongside it, so as to note how it resembles these other things in certain ways and differs in others; and what we find, as the result of this latter sort of comparison, is that shape in our horse now presents itself no longer as internal to the colour, but externally related to, or independent of it.

Already at the time of writing his *Kant*, Kemp Smith was aware that this latter relationship of the externality or contingency of a thing's qualities in reference to one another goes hand in hand, in a remarkable way, with their being also, in this other sense, internally or necessarily related. 'Colour is a variable quality of the genus horse, but, in the individual horse, is necessarily determined in some particular mode. If a horse is naturally white, it is necessarily white.'[1] The customary sharp separation between contingent and necessary, external and internal, must therefore be, Kemp Smith concludes, a mistake. In 'The Fruitfulness of the Abstract' Kemp Smith chooses a terminology which will at one and the same time exhibit the subtle intimacy and the sharp separateness of knowledge of the individual on the one hand, and knowledge of its type on the other, contrasting them respectively as knowledge of *identity in and through difference* (organic unity of the qualities) and '*identity amidst difference*' (mutual independence of the qualities). 'The individual', he says, 'is not merely, like the type, an identity amidst difference; it is an identity in and through difference. The differences enter into its inmost being.' The art of epistemology thus consists in keeping these two aspects of cognition distinct, while refusing to isolate them.

About identity in and through difference, what Kemp Smith says is clear and to the point, although brief. In order to bring out what is

[1] Norman Kemp Smith, *A Commentary to Kant's Critique of Pure Reason* (London, Macmillan, 2nd ed. 1923), p. 40.

meant by the internal relatedness of qualities, it is not necessary to cite an organic being like a horse, let alone a human self-consciousness—a billiard ball exhibits the same quality. When Bosanquet pointed out that an individual like Julius Caesar reacts as a whole to whatever is done to it, Kemp Smith retorted that 'this is quite as true of anything else—e.g. a spherical body'.[1] Presumably, what he means is that the colour and the shape of the billiard ball are internally related in the sense of its being impossible to alter the colour (e.g. by painting) without affecting its shape and size qualities, and of its being equally impossible to alter the shape (e.g. by squeezing and flattening) without to some extent affecting the surface-texture and so the colour.

Intent on a justification, Kemp Smith concentrates on the really original items in his formula—namely the relations of identity amidst difference. As in the comparable discussion of Jean Laporte,[2] his starting-point is the Humeian doctrine of the distinctions of reason, the importance of which had long before been emphasized by both Meinong[3] and Husserl.[4] Given the experience of a white sphere, how do we manage to distinguish empirically the case of attending to the shape and neglecting the colour from the case of attending to the colour and neglecting the shape. According to Hume, the shifts of attention cannot be made, the colour and the shape remain indifferentiable, until we compare our white ball with two other appropriate objects—e.g. a white cube and a black (or red) sphere, thus noting how it is exactly similar to the former in one way, and to the latter in another. As is clear, not only from 'The Fruitfulness of the Abstract', but also the relevant pages of his book on Hume, Kemp Smith's point is not different. The shifts of attention cannot consciously take place except on the prior basis of the kind of double comparison Hume speaks of. What makes possible the abstract distinction is the experience of 'same shape, differing colour; same colour, differing shape'. Take away the comparisons with these addi-

[1] 'The Nature of Universals: I', p. 259 n. 2.

[2] *Le Problême de l'Abstraction*, passim (Princeton, 1940).

[3] J. N. Findlay, *Meinong's Theory of Objects and Values* (2nd ed.), pp. 118–23, (O.U.P., 1963).

[4] Marvin Farber, *Foundations of Phenomenology*, pp. 271–82 (New York, Paine-Whitman, 2nd ed., 1962).

tional environmental things, and the colour–shape distinction vanishes from the sphere, depriving its individuality of its clear-cut qualities and reducing it to a vague indescribable *durée*.

In the hope of clarifying this fundamental distinction between identity amidst difference and identity in and through difference, let me give an illustration which may bring out Kemp Smith's point. Consider the case of three faces, belonging to three identical triplets—one face normal, the second blushing but ordinarily composed, and the third both blushing and distorted with passion, and compare the case of a single face which in immediate succession loses its normal colour and begins to blush, while retaining its composure, and then still blushing, becomes distorted. The point of the illustration is that for all their analogy— 'same shape, differing colour; same colour, differing shape'—these contrasting cases are still significantly different. The first case permits of a Humeian distinction of reason between colour and shape, because, as Hume says, it can be made the basis of two *separate* experiences: as well as seeing all three faces together, we can look at them two at a time, thus separating the experience of the respect in which the blushing face resembles the distorted face from the experience of the respect in which the blushing face resembles the normal face. On the other hand, the contrasting case lacks this property which permits the abstraction of shape from colour, just because the three states of the one face cannot be set side by side and must be experienced in irreversible succession. But once granted this fact, it becomes at last possible to indicate what this experience of the changing states of the one face would be like, considered in itself and divorced from the first experience, i.e. what identity in and through difference might be in the absence of identity amidst difference. Suppose we experience the face change from normal to blushing, and thence to a flushed distortion, *without being able to distinguish colour from shape*, what terms would remain to describe it? Crescendo of passion, decline and fall of a façade—the only terms available would be those appropriate to a pure Bergsonian *durée*.

To look at Kemp Smith's philosophy in this light is to bring out an affinity with the twentieth-century Continental movement. For example, the balanced antithesis between abstract and concrete presents a certain parallelism with a line of thought which, nascent in Bergson, is still traceable in Sartre[1] and Merleau-Ponty[2]; indeed Kemp Smith is remarkably close to Jean Laporte in combining a respect for the Humeian doctrine of the abstract and the Bergsonian doctrine of the concrete. By contrast he is more distant from German phenomenology as represented by Husserl,[3] who, along with a certain admiration, criticizes Hume's distinction of reason very sharply indeed and whose view of time appears unindebted to Bergson.

At the same time, in spite of these affinities, Kemp Smith was no exotic, and was developing a line familiar in classical Scottish philosophy.[4] From a point of view like his, penetrated by inherited values of 'moderate realism', the Continental follow-up of Bergson concentrated too much on the concrete, too little on the abstract. Jean Wahl put forward a very dangerous slogan with his 'vers le concret'. Concentrate your attention, in an ultra-specialist manner, on one sphere of existence, one department of study, and you will infallibly fail to pick out its basic aspects. What makes analysis possible, alike in natural science and in history, is the comparison in point of resemblance and of difference with what lies beyond one's sphere or in the background. It was this sort of extra-departmental comparison which illuminated the mysteries of the glacier for Clerk Maxwell's master J. D. Forbes, by revealing its behaviour-pattern as that of a viscous fluid; it was this sort of non-specialist, cross-cultural contrast with a settled Europe which led the American historian Turner to his fruitful insight into the crucial importance of the frontier to development in the U.S.A. Taken in this sense, the principle

---

[1] Cf. p. 3 of *Being and Nothingness* (English trans., H. E. Barnes; London, Methuen, 1957) with p. 186 for a contrast, analogous to that of Kemp Smith (though not identical), between a sense in which colour is not, and a sense in which it is, internally related to extension.

[2] *Phenomenology of Perception*, p. 372 (Paris, Gallimard, 1945)—the reference to Cézanne.

[3] Kemp Smith, however, was both impressed and influenced by Husserlian views of Hume, as expounded in C. V. Salmon's distinguished *Central Problem of David Hume's Philosophy* (Max Niemeyer, 1929).

[4] Warned by the example of English empiricism, Scottish philosophy long continued to be aware of the role of intellect and the importance of abstraction. It is this fact C. S. Peirce presumably had in view when he commended Thomas Reid as being both 'well-balanced' and 'subtle'.

'towards the abstract', far from being secondary to 'vers le concret', is rather the key to the latter. As Kemp Smith says, 'the chief mode in which the abstract exhibits its fruitfulness' is that 'it makes possible the apprehension of its counterpart, the uniquely individual'. If, therefore, you do not take your abstractive procedures seriously, if, as so often happens, your guiding comparisons are limited to one privileged model, and do not play off a variety of models against one another, you will certainly misunderstand the peculiar individuality of the object you study, you will remain insensitive to its distinctive historical rhythm, to the principle which holds it together as an organic unity. It was thus that the British administrators created chaos in the Tiv tribe of Nigeria,[1] because their preliminary analysis of its social arrangements depended exclusively on a comparison with English custom and omitted the contrast with other relevant communities. Neglect the abstract in this way, and you will lose touch with the concrete. That is Kemp Smith's message to his generation.

Let us pass abruptly from 'The Fruitfulness of the Abstract', to the third of the articles on the nature of Universals, in which Kemp Smith's object is to reinstate the abstract in the face of the dogma of the concrete-minded nominalists of Britain. The argument which Kemp Smith singles out for criticism is one which, from Berkeley onwards, has been a stronghold of logical atomism—the argument which denies the presence in red, green and yellow of any identical and invariable item called 'colour'. In certain cases, it is admitted, when we are asked to identify an unfamiliar individual thing (pick out a ten-amp plug from the box) comparison in point of likeness and unlikeness enables us to 'abstract' it from the surrounding objects. But by the same token, comparison of this red, that yellow, yonder blue, does not reveal them as resembling one another in respect of possessing a certain invariable quality called 'colour'. Hence there is no sense in speaking of colour as a common quality which we abstract.

Kemp Smith's mode of meeting this argument is a fine specimen of his philosophical acumen. What, he asks, if 'the fundamental fact of visual experience is not colour but colours?' In other words, the thing responsible for this atomizing approach is the inveterate prejudice of empiricism

[1] Margaret Mead *et al.*, *Cultural Patterns and Technical Change* (Unesco, 1953), p. 143.

against the notion of inextricable complexity. On Kemp Smith's view the purely uniform red patch, the bedrock of an atomism like Moore's, is an unnatural conception capable of being taken seriously only by the sort of philosopher for whom a paint-pot is the normal source of colour. As against this, Kemp Smith contends that the basic visual experience is thus, so to speak, necessarily the experience of the parti-coloured, not of the monochrome. Once the complex nature of colour-experience is recognized, the whole problem is transformed. Ask in terms of the atomistic approach to colour if there is any element common to this green and that red, and of course the question will prove unanswerable. Substitute the different question as to whether there is anything in common as between the experience of red-in-contrast-to-green and the experience of yellow-contrasted-with-blue, and you will no longer be at a loss for an answer. What is common to this pair of experiences is that, in each case, the experience of the colour-contrast is inseparable from an experience of boundary or outline in the visual field. But what if the nominalists, to controvert this new case, raise the question whether, over and above the admitted resemblance in the matter of revealing outline, there is any further thing in common between the case of red-green and that of yellow-blue, such as might found the notion of colour in general? Is not the red-green which reveals outline as sheerly different, in the given context, from the blue-yellow which reveals outline as a visual experience of shape would be from the corresponding tactual experience of the shape? In what he calls 'the most difficult part of my inquiry', Kemp Smith gives his reply. 'Visual definition of outline', he says, 'can be achieved through the contrast of red and green, or through the contrast of yellow and blue; and adequately to apprehend the two situations involves identification through each of the four qualitative types.' What Kemp Smith has here in view is, apparently, the contrast of two different cases: (i) that of a visual experience so contrived that red and green were never experienced except together and in contrast, and in a similar way, yellow and blue were inseparable, and (ii) that of a visual experience akin to the normal one in which all the various permutations and combinations were found of red with green, red with blue, red with yellow, green with blue, green with yellow as well as yellow with blue. Given this contrast of cases, the whole difficulty begins to clear up. The main point is that, in case (i) it is not merely impossible to pick out the genus 'colour in general', it is also impossible to pick out the colour species, i.e. to distinguish between, for example, the inseparable red and green, for the simple reason that the requisite comparisons cannot be made. Or, in other words, within the given experience, the colour-genus and the colour-species remain indistinguishable for the same reason as, in Hume's 'globe of white marble', *considered in itself*, colour and shape are indistinguishable. On the other hand, as soon as we turn to case (ii), the wider range of comparisons enables us to effect 'the distinction of reason'. That is to say, by studying the likeness and unlikeness of red-yellow, red-blue, and blue-yellow, we find ourselves in a position to 'entitle colour any and every sensum which, in contrast to another, discharges the function of defining outline' in the visual field.

As we look back over this argument of Kemp Smith against the pluralists, what strikes us most strongly is that its principle consists in exploring the further conditions and implications of the 'distinction of reason' between colour and shape which formed the central theme of 'The Fruitfulness of the Abstract'. So too we are going, in an analogous way, to find in a moment that the critique of Hegelian monism, undertaken in the first and second articles on 'The Nature of Universals', involves as its vital centre, a redeployment of the topics of spatiality, foreground-background and external relations which we encountered before in Kemp Smith's argument against Bergson's depreciation of rational analysis. In this sense, the attack on Hegelianism, like the attack on pluralism, serves largely to illustrate and reinforce, in new matter and a new manner, the items previously discussed.

As usual, Kemp Smith deals very fairly with the concrete dialectic of Bosanquet as expressed in the doctrine that any given individual or organic whole must itself be understood as a part of a wider organic whole. They are not talking nonsense when they talk of a transition from the 'generic' to the 'corporate', from speaking about the rose considered as a class-concept, i.e. an identity amidst difference (the individual roses regarded as independent of one another) to speaking of the rose in the sense of the Rose family, 'a vegetable stock with an evolutionary history', which is in some sort an identity in and through difference. This distinction between the generic and the corporate underlies, for

Kemp Smith too, the familiar contrast between the particular family as a unity with a history of its own, and its individual members, each with his own biography. 'The ideal of a family is other than the ideal for an individual, and this is especially so as regards the kind of unity for which each has to strive.' Kemp Smith gives an impressive analysis of the sense in which a family is a sort of 'organic unity'.

The difficulty with Hegelianism is not this distinction, but rather the way in which it is used to depreciate the individual as compared with the corporate or higher unity of which he is a part. Why does monism maintain the biography of an individual person is superficial and misleading as compared with, say, the family-history? From this point of view, Kemp Smith is able to get a grip of the central principle of Bosanquet's slippery argument. It depends on Hegel's principle of the truth as the whole. 'No finite entity, a family or a race just as little as an individual, is knowable in and by itself. Everything finite functions as a part in a wider whole, and, only through the understanding of its context, can it itself be understood'. In this way, the concept of humanity, like the concept of the Orchidean order or the Rose family, have no meaning apart from the Universe in which they have made their appearance, and in terms of which their past history, or their future destiny can alone be understood.

From Kemp Smith's point of view, the error here has considerable affinities with the error Bergson makes in attempting to see everything as part of a single complex time-flow or history. The counterpart of Bergson's neglect of space is Bosanquet's blindness to the background–foreground relation. Or to be more precise, the trouble with Bosanquet's thesis that 'every finite entity is knowable as a part of a wider whole' is his failure to recognize its ambiguity. Excessively aware that being an inseparable part of a wider whole means in one sense being involved in something like a historical development, the Anglo-Hegelians are ignorant of the counter-sense in which being part of a wider whole involves necessarily development in contrast to stable background, and in relative independence to things which constitute the background. Abolish the relatively stable background, and the foreground movement becomes imperceptible.

The principle which thus brings down both Bosanquet and Bergson is not only true of the perception of movement; it likewise applies to our knowledge of evolutionary development. 'It is', Kemp Smith says, 'characteristic of the organic and the individual at every level, that their development presupposes an environment which is not itself self-variable (at least not in the same degree) and which is, therefore, in its relative fixity, a sufficiently stable field for the acquisition of habits', etc. such as make evolutionary development possible.

Thus, for Kemp Smith, there are two senses, distinguishable yet inseparable, in which human history has to be understood as part of a wider whole. In one sense, it has to be understood as a continuation of, an organic phase in, animal evolution, but in the other sense, it can be understood only against the background of the stable environment of living and geological nature—i.e. as somehow independent of nature and a breakaway. That is how Kemp Smith clears accounts with the Anglo-Hegelians.

In this hurried sketch of Kemp Smith's discussion of the monists, as also in our exposition of his critique of the pluralists in Universals III—I have had to omit many interesting things. Much of the matter thus left aside is, no doubt, concerned with topics already treated—all these articles on universals being, in their different ways, preparations for and previews (sometimes tentative) of the fundamental distinction, finally drawn in 'The Fruitfulness of the Abstract' between *identity amidst difference* and *identity in and through difference*. At the same time, it has also been necessary to leave out of account altogether certain original and interesting points Kemp Smith makes.

However, if we are to understand Kemp Smith's balanced critique of the Monists and the Pluralists, the thing of capital importance is not the details but the general spirit of intellectual moderation. What Kemp Smith was concerned to point out is that internal relations could lead to intellectual and moral extravagances just as outrageous as those of the rival doctrines of external relations. Just as a modern professor of psychiatry may be misled by the model of Russell's external relations into regarding a phenomenon like teenage sex as if it could be contained in a watertight compartment and could be developed freely without spilling over into adjacent and interconnected sectors of social life, so in an analogous way, the monistic principle of Hegel, as implying unity through differentiation of function, furnished Bernard Bosanquet with the means for a doctrinaire defence of that most questionable of twentieth-century British trends—the policy of extreme specialization in education, and of rigid demarcation-lines between employments.[1] In this sense, the Hegelians, equally with the pluralists, were apostles of a social-intellectual immoderation of the sort Kemp Smith abhorred, and in this sense, far more is at stake in these three difficult, technical articles on 'The Nature of Universals' than merely academic dialectic.

III. THE EMBODIED CONSCIOUSNESS

To grasp Kemp Smith's philosophy the following contrast conceived somewhat in the Bergsonian style will perhaps be illuminating. Think of a musical phrase, or melody, considering it on the one hand from the standpoint of the composer actively engaged in its creation, and on the other hand from the standpoint of an impresario with a box-office mentality. For the former, there is a private consciousness of the notes as a phase in the organic unity of a melody which is in process of coming into being. On the other hand, in the case of the latter, nothing exists except the measurable audience reaction, i.e. what is publicly observable; and the music is treated, not as an organic unity, but a series of notes in an externally related succession.

Taking this antithesis as a guide, we can soon see Kemp Smith's significance. The immediate background to his work was the conflict between rival extremist groups, one of which (Bradley and Bosanquet) emphasized the combination of privacy and internal relations, whereas the other (Russell) upheld external relations and publicity. The key to Kemp Smith would seem to be his search for a mediating position between these opposites. The article on universals tries to effect this for the quarrel between external relations and internal relations; those on perception and consciousness (the 'Avernarius', 'Subjectivism and Realism', and a third—unfortunately not included here—on 'The Problem of

[1] Bosanquet, op. cit., pp. 352–6.

Knowledge') aim, on the other hand, at reconciling the standpoint of the public with that of the private.

No doubt, the model for Kemp Smith's discussion of the outer–inner problem was Bergson's attempt in *Matière et Mémoire* to mediate between idealism and realism. However, it is important to note that Bergson made an impact on him only after he had prepared himself for it as the result of profound original researches on Avernarius (in the articles included here), and on Malebranche (both in the *Cartesian Studies* (1902) and in an interesting article not included here). The articles on Avernarius and the work on Malebranche are thus of capital importance for Kemp Smith's views of inner–outer, etc., and of the two, it was Malebranche who is the key-figure.

Two things in Malebranche indelibly impressed Kemp Smith, determining his whole approach to the inner–outer problems. In the first place, there was Malebranche's stimulating critique of the inwardness of the Cartesian *cogito*.[1] Descartes had gone astray in claiming that we know the mind better than the body. On the contrary not only is the experience of the inner incapable of being clearly described except in the light of outer experience, but further, this necessary involvement of introverted knowledge with extraverted carries with it, Malebranche pointed out, consequences fatal to the Cartesian doctrine of a diaphanous self-consciousness. For just as visual experience cannot itself inform us about the natural, bodily condition of our experience of visual blackouts or of pitch darkness, so my experience in general is incapable of illumining the ontological foundations of my unconsciousness. In saying this, Malebranche inspired Kemp Smith's favourite doctrine 'there is no awareness of awareness'. But secondly this criticism of the *cogito* was not the only thing to impress Kemp Smith; he was also equally impressed by what he called 'the realist tendency' in Malebranche. Why, Malebranche asks, are things normally seen as having their 'common sense' size, and why is their perspective size noticed only rarely? Because,

[1] Kemp Smith, *A Commentary to Kant's Critique of Pure Reason*, p. xliii, n. 1; 'The Problem of Knowledge', in *Journal of Philosophy*, ix (1912): '[Malebranche's] delightful and most unfortunately neglected philosophy'. See also British *Journal of Psychology*, vol. i, pt. 3, pp. 191 ff., and the relevant parts of *Studies in the Cartesian Philosophy* (London, Macmillan, 1902), by Norman Smith (i.e. Kemp Smith).

he replies, in a manner which anticipates Gestalt, a sort of organic unity principle operates in seeing. The size we see things as having in the normal way is a function of the things we see beside them; you get the experience of 'perspective size' only by artificially isolating the thing seen from the visual background of other things. Anticipating Bergson, he points out that this holistic view of things seen is adapted 'to the practical purposes of life', whereas the isolated, atomistic vision which shows odd perspective sizes is not so adapted. Kemp Smith never forgot Malebranche's realism or his critique of the *cogito*. Put together and subtly developed, they constitute Kemp Smith's 'first and fundamental ideas' about inner–outer, consciousness, perception, etc.

To appreciate the Avernarius articles, we must forget about their destruction role in supplying Lenin with materials for his *Dialectical Materialism* and *Empirio-criticism*.[1] From Kemp Smith's own point of view, the great merit of Avernarius was the pertinacity with which he kept to the two great problems opened up by Malebranche—that of the ontological conditions of our consciousness, and that of evolving a realist view in reference to the facts of visual size. Ultimately a failure, Avernarius's philosophy is nevertheless very instructive.

For Kemp Smith the really stimulating feature of Avernarius seems above all to have been his treatment of the relationship of consciousness to its objects. By using the 'new' German method of reflective analysis, Avernarius had been able to explore the foundations of the distinction between act and object of experience much more carefully than English-speaking philosophers were doing, such as G. E. Moore in his *Refutation of Idealism*. Following the German fashion, Avernarius used the sophisticated procedure of differentiating act and object ('character' and 'content', he calls them) by the application of a Humeian distinction of reason, analogous to the colour–shape one discussed earlier, which did justice both to the connectedness and the independence of these contrasting elements of experience.

It is in this way, for instance, that Meinong deals with the distinction of the 'ing' and the 'ed', as J. N. Findlay shows.[2] 'The distinction between

---

[1] V. I. Lenin, *Dialectical Materialism* and *Empirio-criticism* in vol. xi of *Selected Works* (London, Lawrence & Wishart, 1958), pp. 137, 138 and 156.

[2] Findlay, op. cit., pp. 122, 123.

the content and the act-element rests on the fact that the mental states exhibit an independent variability in two directions; we can direct our minds in various ways to the same object or to different objects in the same way.' Kemp Smith fixed on precisely the same feature in Avernarius. To distinguish between 'the two inseparable aspects, inner and outer', Avernarius points out that 'each aspect may vary independently of the other. On the one hand, we may perceive, believe, know one and the same content; and, on the other hand, we may take up the same mental attitudes to different things.'

This 'act-character'–'content' distinction was, then, a standard technique in Germany, soon to develop under Husserl into the doctrine: 'all consciousness is consciousness of——'. Apparently, these phenomenological tactics were too subjectivist for Avernarius, who—Kemp Smith tells us—refused to recognize any such thing as 'perception *of*' an object. Instead, by a kind of abstraction peculiar to himself, Avernarius used the contrast between 'act-character' and 'content' as the basis of a distinction between *the absolute standpoint* (i.e. what we would call 'behaviourist' or 'observationalist') in which the material objects, organic and inorganic, forming the content of experience, could be considered out of relation to my experience of or feelings towards them, and, on the other hand, the *relative standpoint* (we might call it 'reflective' or 'introverted') in which the objects are considered in relation to my feeling about them.

According to Avernarius, the insoluble metaphysical problem disappears for ever as soon as we adopt this 'pure experience' approach, based on the distinction of absolute and relative standpoints. Confronted by this claim, Kemp Smith proceeds to criticize it in terms of the principles he was learning from Malebranche. First, what about the mysterious foundations of my consciousness of the world? Avernarius replies that there is no mystery. I experience a change of feelings from delight to disgust in reference to the picture I look at, and simultaneously I can observe a change in the nerve-process of the brain corresponding to the felt change of attitude. But how, Kemp Smith asks, can I observe my brain? Avernarius replies that 'the brain can be brought within the experienced field first by opening the skull and then using a suitable arrangement of mirrors'. Kemp Smith, however, remains unimpressed: Avernarius evidently is ignorant of the facts which Augustine and

Malebranche knew so well about the systematic elusiveness, so far as my experience is concerned, of the ontological and physiological conditions of my consciousness.

The debate now shifts to the traditional problem of our perception of an external world. What does Avernarius make of that? In reply, he attempts to reformulate it, with special reference to the problem of visual size. Look at size-perception from the absolute standpoint, i.e. behaviouristically, physiologically: evidently the things perceived retain their sizes and their shapes quite independent of the embodied human beings who perceive them. But now turn to the relative standpoint and it will be found the shape and size of the things perceived depend on the brain-process, retinal imprints, etc., of the perceiver, in the sense of varying concomitantly with them. Formulate the question in these terms, Avernarius claims, and the difficulties will soon disappear. But once again Kemp Smith is unimpressed. In making the visible sizes vary with the brain-processes and retinal sizes, Avernarius has forgotten about the Gestalt principle, announced by Malebranche and explored by Bergson, according to which visible size does not vary with retinal size, but depends functionally on the objects visible along with it and in its background.

The themes of the 'Avernarius' at once look back to Malebranche and forward to the 'Subjectivism and Realism' and 'The Problem of Knowledge'. The former article (on Avernarius and Bergson) draws attention to Bergson's attempt to defend realism in reference to size-perception, etc., by means of an organic principle like Malebranche's. The latter (on Bergson and Kant) makes Avernarius's 'character'–'content' distinction the basis of a far-reaching restatement of the critique of the diaphanous *cogito*.

To take first the last and highly original theme—Kemp Smith points out that the distinction of reason technique permits me to differentiate between the picture I see and my delight in seeing it, only because experience enables me to feel my delight change to boredom. But, by the same token, it follows that I cannot distinguish between the given picture and my consciousness of it, for the reason that experience could not possibly enable me to feel my attitude to the world change from consciousness to blank unconsciousness. Understood in this way, the distinction between sleeping and waking, as applied to myself, is one which I could not learn through my own experience. Hence of course the difficulty which partisans of the diaphanous *cogito* experience when trying to account for the fact of unconsciousness. So, too, 'sleep is, for this reason, something of which objective idealists have never been able to give a reputable account'.

If we are not to miss the profundity of Kemp Smith's distinctive doctrine that *there is no awareness of awareness*, it is above all necessary to bear in mind that he is not concerned only with the empirical elusiveness to me of my own body—e.g. the incapacity of knowing what I look like when asleep, except by asking others. What he is concerned with rather is the sort of intellectual blind-spots, afflicting the others as well as myself, which arise through the social fact of organized educational routines. When therefore Kemp Smith denies awareness of awareness, what interests him is not just the limitations of one's ordinary knowledge of the physical, etc., conditions of awakening from sleep, but especially the limitations on one's powers of detecting, by self-analysis, the methodological presuppositions one inherits as the result of one's upbringing in that society—habits of organized silence in reference to certain problems, certain books, etc. In the case where a country is gripped by a group-prejudice in intellectual matters, how can the practice of enclosed solitary self-doubt make the philosopher aware of blinkers imposed by the scholastic machine? Hence the indispensable duty for philosophers to study the history of their subject. The 'past history of philosophy'—as handed down in tradition—'predetermines, consciously or unconsciously, our attitude to present-day problems'. To neglect the history of philosophy involves entangling one's philosophizing in 'unconscious preconceptions'. Hence too the dangers for philosophy of the sort of officially organized orthodoxy characteristic of 'France under Cousin's domination of University teaching'. In this sense, the philosophical *prise de conscience* is impossible except through the medium of such intellectual exchanges as enable us 'to see ourselves as others see us'.[1]

Criticizing the pretensions of metaphysicians, Kemp Smith regularly appeals to this fruitful principle of our limited awareness of awareness.

[1] This part of Kemp Smith's thought is impressively developed by Angus Sinclair in his unduly neglected *Conditions of Knowing* (London, Routledge & Kegan Paul, 1951); see pp. 11–18.

The chief weakness of Hegelianism, for example, is its acceptance of the Cartesian position that we know the mind better than the body. 'If consciousness knows itself in its ultimate nature—and such is Hegel's contention', then we are already involved in 'a spiritual monism which does violence to the highest interests'. So, too, phenomenology was suspect to Kemp Smith just because the 'bracketing' procedure seemed to imply the claim to a knowledge from the inside of oneself and my relation to the world, which was not complemented by a knowledge from the outside. 'Is it possible', Kemp Smith asked Professor H. H. Price in a letter (1944), 'to have a purely phenomenological description' of an encounter with an object? 'Must not the description to be adequate be realist, allowing for bodily factors which, even when not directly experienced, have yet to be reckoned with or causally operative?— unless, that is, you fall back on a sheerly visual description, and can show it to be adequate and descriptive [i.e. realist].' What Kemp Smith means, apparently, is that a purely visual description could not be realist, be- cause it would have to omit reference to the invisible fact of one's eye's externality to the objects seen. In other words, the difficulty of pheno- menology is that it aspires to knowledge from the inside in the absence of knowledge from the outside.[1]

In this way, Malebranche—always a stimulating influence in Scottish philosophy[2]—had, by his 'realist' critique of the *cogito*, confirmed Kemp Smith in the kind of realism he had learned from his original teachers and mentors, especially Robert Adamson. 'Experience does not initially contain any clear cut distinction between mind and its objects— the inner and the outer. The distinction between inner and outer pro- ceeds *pari passu*, and one must not say that all our knowledge is of the inner, as the subjectivist maintains'.[3] Adamson's realism anticipates and elucidates that of Kemp Smith; and the criticism cited above on pheno- menology—its neglect of the indispensable tension in conscious experi-

---

[1] Kemp Smith, *A Commentary to Kant's Critique of Pure Reason*, p. xlv.

[2] See Hamilton's *Reid*, p. 265b and p. 266b; Thomas Brown's *Lectures*, vol. xxx (Tait, 1828), p. 193; Sir W. Hamilton, *Lectures on Metaphysics*, vol. i, p. 262—a re- markable set of testimonies.

[3] Adapted from J. A. Passmore's illuminating discussion of Scottish Realism. *A Hundred Years of Philosophy* (London, Duckworth, 1957), pp. 281–3.

ence between the object *as seen* and the object *as eyed*—presupposes precisely this inherited contrast between inner and outer.[1]

By contrast with phenomenology Bergson[2] avoids the subjectivism of Descartes. For Bergson 'our starting-point is the world of bodies in space. The problem is not to account for our consciousness of it, but to explain why we know it in a form relative to our individual position.' That is to say, Bergson, in a certain sense, gives a priority to our perception of the bodies out there, treating as secondary and subsequent our experience of their interrelation to the elusive *corps propre* with the distinction thereby entailed of inner and outer. For Bergson, as for Kant (to whom Kemp Smith assimilates him), 'the problem is not how, starting from the subjective, the individual can come to a knowledge of the independently real, but how, if a common world is alone immediately apprehended, the inner private life of the self-conscious being can be possible'.[3]

Following Kemp Smith's lead, let us go behind the 'perilous popularity' which, after *L'Évolution Créatrice*, overwhelmed Bergson, in order to uncover the solidity and promise of his central teaching about perception. In the first place, his starting-point is free from subjectivism: in perceiving the brown table, I consciously experience it as external to organs of sight which, though tactually explorable by myself, are visually off-stage. Secondly, he does not dodge difficulties. Sense-data phenomenalism, common-sense realism, the microscopic viewpoint of scientism all are true from their own standpoint, and the question is: how to reconcile them?

But let us turn at once to Bergson's actual principle of solution, noting how it manages to combine the two contrasting moves which later were to mean so much to Kemp Smith—the appeal to a concrete

[1] For the classic source we must look, beyond Adamson, to the brilliant but forgotten pages of J. F. Ferrier, *Lectures and Philosophical Remains* (Edinburgh, Blackwood, 1866), vol. ii, pp. 365-404.

[2] It should be noted that in Bergson's case as in Kemp Smith's, the mentors and teachers they respected most were deeply involved in the international argument about the value of classical Scottish philosophy—e.g. Ravaisson in France (*Rev. des Deux Mondes*, November 1840) and A. Seth in Scotland (*Scottish Philosophy*, Edinburgh, Blackwood, 1885).

[3] Kemp Smith, *A Commentary to Kant's Critique of Pure Reason*, p. 280.

principle of organic unity, and the appeal to an abstractive principle of perceptual discrimination. Deprive me of a sense (e.g. sight), and not only does my way of dealing practically with things have to alter (e.g. the way I eat) but my hearing sharpens as if in compensation. What Bergson argues is that this compensation is not accidental. My perceptual discriminativeness is internally related to my practical situation. The qualities I discern in bodies are those I am in a position to use. Inner (thought) implies outer (action).

Take Bergson's discussion of realism *versus* sense-data. The contrast between seeing a house in the far distance and seeing it near is not between seeing it tiny and seeing it normal-sized, but between, on the one hand, seeing it along with its surroundings, but deprived of definite details, and, on the other hand, seeing it in relief, definite in its qualities, without being able to see its setting. Look at the situation in this light, and it becomes clear that we discriminate in the house the sort of qualities which our standpoint equips us to deal with. When seen close-up, it reveals the qualities (relief, etc.) appropriate to our dealing with it by practical manipulation; when very far off, it reveals to us its whereabouts and its environment, enabling us to approach or recede.

What finally clinched Kemp Smith's admiration for Bergson was the way the same principle may be used to reconcile the scientist's experience of things with common sense. Change the mode of dealing with a body from that of ordinary handling to that of experimental analysis under laboratory conditions, and the qualities in the objects relative to our ordinary vision disappear, to be replaced by qualities which are discriminable only by microscopic procedures. The blood-drop seen microscopically can no longer be mopped up with cotton wool, but requires for its manipulation delicate instruments.

In later life, this Bergsonian stimulus continued to reverberate through Kemp Smith's writings on perception. Indeed, the essential contribution of his *Prolegomena*[1] (1924) is perhaps simply this: that it kept before the

---

[1] *Prolegomena to an Idealist Theory of Knowledge* (London, Macmillan, 1924), e.g. pp. 190–4, etc., and also pp. 114–22. Apart from this Bergsonian interest, the whole discussion of Alexander's realism has contemporary relevance in connexion with the topics discussed in D. M. Armstrong's *Perception and the Physical World* (London, Routledge & Kegan Paul, 1961), chs. 14 and 15.

'realist' generation the need for a theory of perception which stressed not only the cognitive but also the biological–practical relation to the object. Whitehead[1] himself has acknowledged his indebtedness to Kemp Smith on this very point. With his usual flair, Kemp Smith had, from the start, fixed upon the very things in *Matière et Mémoire*, whose originality was going, nearly fifty years later, to astonish the phenomenologists.[2]

Looking at Kemp Smith's general significance as a philosopher, we are left in no doubt as to the intellectual appropriateness of his enthusiasm for *Matière et Mémoire*. From Kemp Smith's point of view, a perception-theory on Bergsonian lines was just what was required to carry on to completion the work begun by his revival of the Malebranchian *cogito*. Just as, in the matter of self-knowledge, there cannot be any consciousness of the inner except through consciousness of the outer (my own body, my historical situation, etc.), so knowledge of the material world rests, in a similar way, on a combination of perceptual discrimination (inner) and of action (outer) in regard to the object. In this sense philosophy, as reflection on my intellectual presuppositions, goes hand in hand with the history of ideas in somewhat the same way as theoretical analysis of nature and experimental work become sterile if separated from one another. Kemp Smith's study of the inner–outer problem thus converges with his view about abstract and concrete. As, there, he distinguishes without separating, between experience and comparison, so, here, he insisted on the fruitfulness of the inherent tension between introspection and observation, theory and practice. Inspired by Malebranche and Bergson, Kemp Smith's Scottish realism pioneered a philosophical moderation which not merely avoids the various extremisms of the Bosanquets and the Russells, the Ayers and the Ryles, but which, breaking through conventional academic reticences, probes intellectual blind-spots of British society with a responsibility and depth unmatched in latter-day debates about the two cultures.[3]

---

[1] A. N. Whitehead, *Symbolism* (Cambridge, 1927), p. 57.
[2] Ian Alexander, *Bergson* (London, Bowes & Bowes, 1957), p. 30, and M. Merleau-Ponty, *Signes* (Paris, Gallimard, 1960), p. 233.
[3] See Descartes's *Rules*, Rule I.

Concluding the systematic analysis, let us restore a sense of chronological perspective, by following up the one clear clue to Kemp Smith's inner development which these papers furnish—his changing relationship to Henri Bergson. Let us note at once that Kemp Smith began where we have just ended—with the critique of Cartesian intellectualism, in which, partly under the inspiration of *Matière et Mémoire*, he developed, before the First World War, a distinctive view of perception as involving both inner and outer, thought and action. The middle phase of Kemp Smith's career involved, on the other hand, the beginning of a move beyond Bergson, first announced in 1923 in the paper on Whitehead. The powerful papers on the abstract and the concrete thus arise out of the attempt to preserve what is valuable in *Les Données Immédiates*, while getting rid of the irrationalism. Defining carefully his relationship to Bergson in the 1941 obituary, Kemp Smith singles out for commendation these two early works. Bergson's inspiration later slackened, but nevertheless his works, studied as a whole, have still much to give. Finally, in the 1947 paper on *Les Deux Sources*, Kemp Smith, reaffirming his 'Calvinist' values, closes the account by criticizing Bergson sharply for sundering the experience of history's complexity from the awareness of the moral and religious ideal of unity, and thereby destroying the fruitful tension which unites them.

Leaving Bergson behind in his last years, Kemp Smith began to move forward to Whitehead and back to Descartes. Yet it would be a complete mistake to regard either move as a sharp break with his earlier Bergsonian interests, let alone a concession to the fashionable positivism of post-war Britain. The alliance with Whitehead still had as its centre the question of mediating between the *durée* on the one hand and reason on the other. The intensive preparation for the *New Studies in the Philosophy of Descartes*[1] involved, in a somewhat similar way, participation in the post-Bergsonian quest[2] of contemporary French scholarship —Laporte, Gouhier, Alquié, etc.—for a Descartes who would transcend

---

[1] Published by Macmillan, 1952, along with *Descartes' Philosophical Writings*, selected and translated by Norman Kemp Smith—fifty years after its publication by the same house of his *Cartesian Studies*.

[2] Merleau-Ponty, *Signes*, p. 165.

the time-worn antithesis of 'intellectualisme' and of 'empirisme'. Looking beyond regions where philosophy, he felt, was 'in the doldrums', Kemp Smith saw the chief hope for intellectual progress in the metaphysical dialogue between the new world and the old, which Whitehead had kept going.

G. E. D.

Collected Papers

The Naturalism of Hume[1]

I

Hume's philosophic writings are to be read with great caution.
His pages, especially those of the *Treatise*, are so full of matter,
he says so many different things in so many different ways and
different connexions, and with so much indifference to what he
said before, that it is very hard to say positively that he taught, or
did not teach, this or that particular doctrine. He applies the same
principles to such a great variety of subjects that it is not surprising
that many verbal, and some real inconsistencies can be found in his
statements. . . . This makes it easy to find all philosophies in
Hume, or, by setting up one statement against another, none at
all.[2]

THE latter is, in effect, what Green has done in his *Introduction to
Hume's Treatise*. Green's interpretation of the *Treatise* leads to the
conclusion that Hume has no set of positive beliefs, and merely develops
to a sceptical conclusion the principles which he inherits from Locke
and Berkeley. Nothing exists but subjective states, organized by the
brute force of association. There is no self, no external world. Hume,
Green contends, is more of a subjective idealist than even Berkeley, and
so thorough a sceptic that he denounces all belief in permanence, in
identity, in activity, whether in the self or outside it, as fiction and
illusion. All is change: change governed by no law.

This, however, is now generally recognized as being an unfair statement of Hume's position, and as ignoring all that is most characteristic

---

[1] *Mind*, vol. xiv, N.S., no. 54.
[2] Selby-Bigge, ed., *Hume's Enquiries concerning the Human Understanding and concerning the Principles of Morals*, 1894 edn. (Oxford), Introduction, p. vii.

in his teaching. In answer to Green I may quote the words of another member of the Idealist School:

> It is evident that Hume was not lost in the quagmire of subjective idealism. The objective and the subjective are with him akin: the objective is the subjective, which is universal, permanent, and normal. The causal relation has, in the first instance, only a subjective necessity; it generates an objective world. . . . Kant's Hume is therefore a somewhat imaginary being: the product, partly of imperfect knowledge of Hume's writings, partly of prepossessions derived from a long previous training in German rationalism.[1]

In these articles I shall try to determine how far, and in what sense, these statements, which Wallace merely makes by the way, and without attempting to justify them in a detailed manner, may be regarded as true. My general conclusion will be, that the establishment of a purely naturalistic conception of human nature by the thorough subordination of reason to feeling and instinct is the governing principle of Hume's philosophy; and in order to bring out clearly the significance of this general principle I shall dwell only on the central aspects of his teaching, omitting, for instance, his views on mathematical science, in which he was not really at home and in reference to which his teaching appears in its least fortunate light. I shall keep almost entirely to his theory of ordinary consciousness and to his theory of morals.

I shall begin by considering whether Green is justified in asserting that Hume denies the existence of the external world and of the self. It is still the prevalent view that Hume agrees with Berkeley in the denial of a material world. Hume undoubtedly accepts Berkeley's arguments against the knowability of such a world; and to their number he himself adds another derived from his own philosophy.[2] Also, though he lays little

---

[1] Wallace, W., *Prolegomena to Hegel's Logic*, 2nd edn. (Macmillan, 1874), ch. viii, pp. 96–97.

[2] *Treatise*, bk. I, part IV, § ii; Green and Grose's edition (1874), pp. 499–500; Selby-Bigge's edition (1888), p. 212. Hereafter I shall refer to Green and Grose's edition as 'G', and to Selby-Bigge's edition as 'S–B'. I assume—the evidence (cf. Selby-Bigge's Introduction to the *Enquiries*) seems fairly conclusive—that Hume's philosophy must primarily be judged by the *Treatise*. But I shall make use of the *Enquiries*, and also of

stress on these arguments—they are barely mentioned in the *Treatise*—
the sufficient reason is that he believes himself to have demonstrated, by
his more thoroughgoing analysis of sense-experience and of reason,
that it is impossible by either of these, the only two sources of knowledge, to establish the existence of body. But while thus strengthening
Berkeley's position, he denies its relevancy. What we may perhaps
describe as the chief aim of Hume's philosophy is to prove that, save as
regards those relations upon which the mathematical sciences are based,
belief never rests on reason or insight, and that, on the contrary, what
we may call synthetic reason is itself merely generalized belief. The
assumption of the existence of body is a 'natural belief' due to the ultimate instincts or propensities that constitute our human nature. It cannot
be justified by reason, and this unaccountability it shares in common
with our moral and aesthetic judgements and with all those theoretical
beliefs which concern matters of fact. Green, in ignoring this new doctrine of belief, certainly one of the most essential, and perhaps the most
characteristic doctrine in Hume's philosophy, and in regarding Hume as
attempting to generate experience out of simple impressions by the
mechanism of association,[1] in the manner of Mill and Spencer, misrepresents both the spirit and the letter of the *Treatise*.

Green by his close-knit massive argument has certainly succeeded in
showing that Hume, in developing the line of thought of Locke and

---

the *Dialogues concerning Natural Religion*, when they seem to support or to extend the
conclusions come to in the *Treatise*. Hume's philosophy as expounded in these three
works seems to me to form, on the whole, a consistent system.

[1] 'The vital nerve of his philosophy lies in his treatment of the "association of
ideas" as a sort of process of spontaneous generation, by which impressions of sensation
issue in such impressions of reflection, in the shape of habitual propensities, as will
account, not indeed for there being—since there really are not—but for there seeming
to be those formal conceptions which Locke, to the embarrassment of his philosophy,
had treated as at once real and creations of the mind' (*Introduction to the Treatise*,
pp. 162–3). In opposition to such statements we must insist that Hume does not
regard association as 'explaining' or 'generating' ideas or feelings, but only as stating
the conditions under which, as matters of fact, we find them to occur. The same
misinterpretation of Hume's use of association appears in Green's criticism of Hume's
doctrine of the disinterested passions.

Berkeley, reveals the incapacity of their principles to account for experience. But to that general conclusion Hume would in great part agree. His predecessors were, he believed, bound to fail in the establishment of their philosophy;

> Most of the writings of that very ingenious author [Berkeley] form the best lessons of scepticism, which are to be found either among the ancient or modern philosophers, Bayle not excepted. . . . That all his arguments, though otherwise intended, are, in reality, merely sceptical, appears from this, *that they admit of no answer and produce no conviction.* Their only effect is to cause that momentary amazement and irresolution and confusion, which is the result of scepticism.[1]

This failure he regards as contributing to the proof of his own. Their failure leads him, however, not to reject their view of sense—it was not rejected even by Kant—but to criticize their view of the function of reason. We cannot by means of reason explain any of the ultimate characteristics of our experience—the origin of our sensations, the true 'secret' nature of causal connexion, apprehension of external reality, appreciation of beauty, judgement of an action as good or bad. And the alternative is not scepticism, but the practical test of human validity. Certain beliefs or judgements (Hume makes no distinction between belief and judgement, or indeed between judgement and reasoning[2]) can be shown to be 'natural', 'inevitable', 'indispensable', and are thus removed beyond the reach of our sceptical doubts.

> The sceptic . . . must assent to the principle concerning the existence of body, though he cannot pretend by any arguments of philosophy to maintain its veracity. Nature has not left this to his choice, and has doubtless esteemed it an affair of too great importance to be trusted to our uncertain reasonings and speculations. We may well ask, *What causes induce us to believe in the existence of body?* but 'tis vain to ask, *Whether there be body or not?*

---

[1] Cf. *Enquiry*, part I § xii; G, note to p. 127; S–B, note to p. 155. Italics are Hume's own.

[2] *Treatise*, I, III, vii; G, note to p. 396; S–B, note to p. 96.

That is a point which we must take for granted in all our reasonings.[1]

Belief in causal action is equally natural and indispensable; and Hume freely recognizes the existence of 'secret' causes, acting independently of our experience. This causal action shows itself both in the mental and in the natural world. Association is

> a kind of Attraction, which in the mental world will be found to have as extraordinary effects as in the natural, and to show itself in as many and as various forms. Its effects are everywhere conspicuous; but as to its causes, they are mostly unknown, and must be resolved into *original* qualities of human nature, which I pretend not to explain.[2]

And speaking in the *Enquiry* of causes in the natural world:

> [The really] ultimate springs and principles [of natural operations] are totally shut up from human curiosity and inquiry. Elasticity, gravity, cohesion of parts, communication of motion by impulse; these are probably the ultimate causes and principles which we shall ever discover in nature; and we may esteem ourselves sufficiently happy, if, by accurate inquiry and reasoning, we can trace up the particular phenomena to, or near to, these general principles. The most perfect philosophy of the natural kind only staves off our ignorance a little longer: as perhaps the most perfect philosophy of the moral or metaphysical kind serves only to discover larger portions of it.[3]

To turn now to the self. Hume contends that we have no grounds either in experience or in reason for declaring the self to be a simple

---

[1] Ibid. I, IV, ii; G, p. 478; S–B, p. 187. Italics are Hume's own.

[2] Ibid. I, I, iv; G, p. 321; S–B, pp. 12–13.

[3] *Enquiry*, IV, I; G, p. 27; S–B, pp. 30–31; cf. *Treatise*, I, III, v; G, p. 385; S–B, p. 84: 'As to those *impressions* which arise from the *senses*, their ultimate cause is, in my opinion, perfectly inexplicable by human reason, and 'twill always be impossible to decide with certainty, whether they arise immediately from the object, or are produc'd by the creative power of the mind, or are deriv'd from the author of our being. Nor is such a question any way material to our present purpose. We may draw inferences from the coherence of our perceptions, whether they be true or false; whether they represent nature justly, or be mere illusions of the senses.'

unchanging substance. Complexity and change are the most prominent characteristics of our human nature.

> The identity which we ascribe to the mind of man is only a fictitious one, and of a like kind with that which we ascribe to vegetables and animal bodies.[1]

> In a very few years both vegetables and animals endure a *total* change, yet we still attribute identity to them, while their form, size, and substance are entirely alter'd. An oak that grows from a small plant to a large tree, is still the same oak; tho' there be not one particle of matter, or figure of its parts the same. An infant becomes a man, and is sometimes fat, sometimes lean, without any change in his identity.[2]

By calling such identity 'fictitious', Hume, as his comparison of the self with plants and animals would seem to show, does not mean to assert that strictly there is no such thing as an identical self, but only that an absolute constancy is not part of its essential nature. As he indicates in the *Treatise*, all that seems to correspond to this assumed metaphysical constancy is identity of function. In the self, as in a plant or animal, the parts of each conspire to a common end, and this end persists throughout the most radical transformations.[3]

The complexity of the self is as obvious as its changeableness:

> Nothing seems more delicate with regard to its causes than thought. . . . A difference of age, of the disposition of his body, of weather, of food, of company, of books, of passions; any of these particulars, or others more minute, are sufficient to alter the curious machinery of thought, and communicate to it very different movements and operations. As far as we can judge, vegetables and animal bodies are not more delicate in their motions, nor depend upon a greater variety or more curious adjustment of springs and principles.[4]

---

[1] *Treatise*, I, IV, vi; G, p. 540; S–B, p. 259; cf. ibid., G, p. 535; S–B, p. 253; *Dialogues*, VII; G, pp. 422–3.

[2] *Treatise*, loc. cit.; G, p. 538; S–B, p. 256.

[3] Loc. cit.

[4] *Dialogues*, part IV; G, p. 408.

It may be noted how Hume, in spite of his speaking of the self as a 'bundle or collection' of distinct impressions, constantly compares it with organisms, with the unity of a plant, of an animal, of society.

> I cannot compare the soul more properly to anything than to a republic or commonwealth, in which the several members are united by the reciprocal ties of government and subordination, and give rise to other persons, who propagate the same republic in the incessant changes of its parts. And as the same individual republic may not only change its members, but also its laws and constitutions; in like manner the same person may vary his character and disposition, as well as his impressions and ideas, without losing his identity. Whatever changes he endures, his several parts are still connected by the relation of causation. And in this view our identity with regard to the passions serves to corroborate that with regard to the imagination, by the making our distant perceptions influence each other, and by giving us a present concern for our past or future pains or pleasures.[1]

Hume's analysis of the self is unfairly treated when contrasted only with that of Kant, and not rather, as it also ought to be, with the views of Locke and Berkeley. On the fundamental point that the self is not to be described as a simple substance, Kant is in agreement with Hume. When Hume states that the self is *for us* (the limitation is important and should always be noted) only a 'bundle or collection' of perceptions, he is overstating his position in opposition to the equally one-sided view of his opponents.

Our belief, then, in the identity and unity of the self, like our belief in an external world, though determined for us by nature, cannot be justified by reason. The ultimate nature of the self cannot be known, and on theoretical grounds no abiding personality can be proved. But so far from denying the existence and reality of the self, Hume seeks—like Kant, though in so different a manner—in its ultimate constitution, in its propensities, instincts, feelings, and emotions, the explanation of all experience, whether theoretical or practical.

'Tis evident, that all the sciences have a relation, greater or less, to

---

[1] Cf. *Treatise*, I, IV, vi; G, p. 542; S–B, p. 261.

human nature; and that however wide any of them may seem to run from it, they still return back by one passage or another.[1]

It is the capital or centre of all knowledge, and once masters of it we can extend our conquests over all those sciences which intimately concern us.

> In pretending, therefore, to explain the principles of human nature, we in effect propose a complete system of the sciences, built on a foundation almost entirely new, and the only one upon which they can stand with any security.[2]

Many difficulties in the way of this interpretation of Hume's position will at once suggest themselves, especially as regards his frequent and very confusing use of the words 'fiction' and 'illusion' in reference to causality, and material body, but consideration of these difficulties I shall defer until I have more completely stated what I regard as being Hume's actual position.

As already pointed out, Green seems to hold that Hume's principles are all borrowed from Locke and Berkeley, and that his philosophy may be adequately regarded as simply the consistent and thorough development of their fundamental principles. There is, however, much positive teaching in the *Treatise* which is not to be found anywhere in the writings of his predecessors; and his philosophy is throughout inspired by a new conception of knowledge which is in certain respects analogous to Kant's Copernican idea. This new conception of the nature of experience and of the function of reason, if explicitly formulated, would run as follows. The function of experience is not to supply a metaphysic, but only to afford us guidance in practical life. If we are content to regard our beliefs as the outcome of the ultimate propensities that constitute our human nature, they can be shown, in their fitness to the calls which things make upon us, to be as wonderfully adapted as any of the animal instincts; but when, on the other hand, we wrongly insist on interpreting them as the conclusions of supposed inferences, they will be found to rest on contradictory and theoretically unjustifiable assumptions. Even when philosophers reinterpret the ordinary consciousness, modifying this or that belief, so as to attain a consistent system, they merely

---

[1] *Treatise*, Introduction to bk. I; G, p. 306; S–B, p. xix.
[2] Ibid.; G, p. 307; S–B, p. xx.

propound additional beliefs, which, while they do not stand the test of practical life, still continue to contain 'all the difficulties of the vulgar system, with some others, that are peculiar to themselves'.[1]

Hume is thus no sceptic as to the powers of reason, but quite positive that its sole function is practical. The question that has primarily to be decided is not how the fundamental characteristics of experience are to be rationally explained, but what function rational insight can have in our lives. That can only be discovered by observation of the facts, and as man is essentially an active being, these are above all else those of morals. Hume therefore fitly adds as sub-title to the *Treatise* which contains his whole philosophy, that it is 'an attempt to introduce the experimental method of reasoning into moral subjects'.[2] Reason is not the guide to action, but, quite the reverse, our ultimate and unalterable tendencies to action are the test of practical truth and falsity. Reason, he contends, is nothing distinct from our natural beliefs, and therefore cannot justify them. His attitude in ethics—that

> reason is, and ought only to be the slave of the passions, and can never pretend to any other office than to serve and obey them[3]

—has its exact counterpart in his theory of knowledge. 'Giving a different turn to the speculations of philosophers', Hume seeks to establish

> a system or set of opinions, which if not true (for that, perhaps, is too much to be hop'd for) [may] at least be satisfactory to the human mind, and [may] stand the test of the most critical examination.[4]

That this is really Hume's conception of the function of reason, and that it leads to a genuinely fresh conception of the nature and conditions of experience, will best be shown by a brief account of the main argument of the *Treatise* and *Enquiry*. But before doing so, we may in passing note the two very distinct meanings which he ascribes to the term 'reason'.

---

[1] *Treatise*, I, iv, ii; G, p. 499; S–B, p. 211.
[2] Hume uses the term 'moral' in a very broad sense.
[3] *Treatise*, II, iii, iii; G, p. 195; S–B, p. 2.
[4] Ibid., I, iv, vii; G, pp. 551–2; S–B, p. 272.

> All reasonings may be divided into two kinds, demonstrative reasoning, or that concerning relations of ideas, and moral reasoning, or that concerning matter of fact and existence.[1]

The first kind of reasoning is analytic. Since the relations discovered are involved in the ideas compared, being such as cannot be changed without change in the ideas, their truth is guaranteed by the law of non-contradiction. The relations thus revealed are those of resemblance, contrariety, degrees in quality, and proportions in quantity or number; and as the mathematical sciences of geometry, algebra, and arithmetic, involve only such relations, they are rendered possible by such discursive analytical thinking.

> That three times five is equal to the half of thirty, expresses a relation between these numbers. Propositions of this kind are discoverable by the mere operation of thought, without dependence on what is anywhere existent in the universe. Though there never were a circle or triangle in nature, the truths demonstrated by Euclid would for ever retain their certainty and evidence.[2]

This logical necessity, which consists in the impossibility of conceiving the opposite, is the sole form of rational necessity known to us, and it supplies a standard in the light of which we are enabled to detect its complete absence from all our knowledge of matters of fact. When we seek by means of inference to extend our knowledge of real existence, we make use of certain non-rational synthetic principles which can only be explained as blind instinctive propensities of the human soul. And as this second, synthetic, form of reasoning embraces all knowledge outside mathematics (for even the present testimony of sense and the records of memory involve synthetic principles), it is much the more important, and Hume constantly equates it with reason in general. Reason, he roundly declares, is 'nothing but a wonderful and unintelligible instinct in our souls': though it may justify itself by its practical uses, it can afford no standard to which objective reality must conform. 'There is no

---

[1] *Enquiry*, IV, ii; G, p. 31; S–B, p. 35. This broad use of the word 'moral' is in keeping with Hume's view of our knowledge as determined throughout by practical considerations, and as possessing no absolute metaphysical truth.

[2] *Enquiry*, IV, i; G, pp. 21–22; S–B, p. 25.

room in mind for any synthetic operation. Analysis Hume admits, but not synthesis. . . . What is called Necessity of Reason, if it does not mean the impossibility because contradictoriness of the opposite (and that is only analytical), has no objective significance; it is merely the expression for a tendency in mind; it is only subjective: "necessity is something that exists in the mind, not in objects".'[1]

So long as we move about within experience, determining the nature of our given ideas and their discoverable interrelations, analytical thinking with its absolute standard enables us to gain true and certain knowledge. Experience is, however, conditioned by what lies outside it;[2] and as there is no transition, by way of analytical thinking, to these external conditions, they control the mind from without by a merely brute necessity. Through feeling and instinct they determine the mind both in thought and in action.

> Nature by an absolute and uncontrollable necessity has determined us to judge as well as to breathe and feel.[3]

> All these operations (judgement as to matters of fact, appreciation of beauty, estimation of an action as good or bad) are a species of natural instincts, which no reasoning or process of the thought and understanding is able, either to produce, or to prevent.[4]

Hume has even attempted in the *Treatise* to bring the knowledge of relations into line with this account of empirical reasoning. All ideas are simple and relationless. They do not compare, but are as they are; and hence in them lie no relations.

> The necessity which makes two times two equal to four, or three angles of a triangle equal to two right ones, lies only in the act of the understanding by which we consider and compare these ideas.[5]

This view of mathematical reasoning is, however, inconsistent with

---

[1] Adamson, *Development of Modern Philosophy*, i, pp. 143–4.

[2] This, I should hold, is Hume's implied, though not always fully expressed, point of view.

[3] *Treatise*, I, IV, i; G, pp. 474–5; S–B, p. 183.

[4] *Enquiry*, V, i; G, p. 40; S–B, pp. 46–47.

[5] *Treatise*, I, III, xiv; G, p. 460; S–B, p. 166.

Hume's previous account of arithmetical reasoning,[1] and its falsity is virtually admitted by him when he distinguishes between 'philosophical' and 'natural' relations. As Green has so clearly shown, it is precisely in his failure to consider what is involved in the discursive comparing activity of reason that the weakness of his system lies. Had he realized the problems which are involved in our consciousness of relations, in our apprehension of succession no less than in the apprehension of causality, he would never have attempted to separate completely analytic and synthetic thinking. He would have recognized that the same problems are involved in both. That he did completely separate them, and that he ascribed to analytical thinking a quite secondary role is, however, undoubted. He could not attempt to prove that there is no such thing as rational necessity (for consciousness of it is implied in the proof of its absence); but postulating it in a form for which he could not really account, he seeks to show that owing to the constitution of our experience it cannot be attained in any department of our knowledge of matters of fact. There natural belief takes the place of rational insight.

In the brief summary which I shall now give of Hume's main argument in the *Treatise* and *Enquiry*, my chief aim will be to state the grounds of his naturalistic view of reason, and to show how his philosophy of knowledge culminates in a new theory of belief.[2] I shall first take up Hume's demonstration of the practical value and theoretical irrationality of the ordinary consciousness, and his complementary proof of the practical worthlessness and equal irrationality of the philosophical reinterpretation of it. Thereafter I shall try to show the close connexion between his theory of knowledge and his ethical teaching.

The fundamental assumption involved in ordinary consciousness, that there is permanence and identity in things, is an excellent example of what is in practice an indispensable belief, and yet is incapable of

---

[1] Ibid., I, III, i; G, p. 374; S–B, p. 71. According to this passage, in arithmetical reasoning we possess a standard of perfect precision and certainty, and in applying it we reason according to the constitution of the numbers compared. And even in geometry, though, on Hume's view, we have no such exact standard, we still reason in accordance with the given sensible appearances.

[2] The reader who is familiar with Hume's argument may omit the first part of the summary.

theoretical justification.[1] The vulgar regard their perceptions as the real things, and therefore as continuing to exist while unperceived, and as remaining identically the same even when they have undergone change. Now we have only to close our eyes to annihilate our perceptions, and as the perceptions which appear on opening them again are for us new perceptions, separated from the old by an interval, no proof can be offered that they are the same and have existed throughout the interval. As we know nothing but the distinct perceptions, the assertion of their identity merely on the ground of their resemblance must be purely dogmatic.[2] This, however, is but one defect; there is no contradiction involved, such as we find in the further assertions that each thing is a unity and abides throughout all change. The wax is for us nothing but an aggregate of distinct sensations of smell, sound, taste, touch, and sight; and yet we none the less regard it as a single thing. When placed before the fire, it melts, loses all its previous qualities, and acquires other and different attributes, and we yet regard it as remaining the same identical piece of wax. That is apparently the inevitable procedure of our minds, and results in the union of contradictories. For the thing, which is admittedly a compound or aggregate, is hereby asserted to be one and simple, and that which undergoes transformation to remain the same and identical.

What then, Hume asks, are the causes which make us fall into these evident contradictions? Reason (taken in the ordinary sense) cannot be the force at work, for besides that its whole aim is to avoid self-contradiction, it also demands evidence, and, as we have just seen, none can be obtained. It is here, as elsewhere, a 'blind and powerful instinct', that, demanding no evidence, and ignoring theoretical insufficiencies for the sake of practical convenience, necessitates belief. Take, first, the belief in identity throughout change. If we observe the gradual changes in the wax when it is put before the fire and melts, at no point is there a break. Throughout the processes in which it entirely changes its outward appearance, the mind is led on through a series of such slight and imperceptible

---

[1] *Treatise*, I, IV, ii.

[2] I am concerned only to state Hume's actual position and do not seek either to defend or to criticize it. His philosophy rests on the fundamental assumption that the mind can immediately experience only subjective mental states.

alterations, each change preparing it for a still greater change that follows, that the passage of the mind from first to last is smooth and uninterrupted. The gradual changes accordingly leave a *feeling*[1] of sameness or identity of function in the mind, and this subjective feeling is the sole ground we have for believing in an objective identity in the real objects. And owing to the mind's instinctive propensity to spread itself over external objects, and to ascribe to them any feeling they occasion, it is a ground which constrains the mind to this belief—the changes notwithstanding. Similarly the diverse sensations constituting the wax are so closely associated, no one of them appearing in the mind without immediately dragging the others into consciousness in its train, that the feeling of their mental union inevitably gives rise to the belief in their objective unity.

The philosophers, observing these contradictions, have only made bad worse by seeking rational justification for the beliefs. Finding none in what is experienced, they fall back on fiction, feigning a something which they name substance, behind the sensible qualities and distinct from them, and which they suppose to be simple and unchangeable. In this way, as they believe, the contradictions can be removed, the unity and identity being ascribed to the substance, the change and multiplicity to its states. But the evidence for this philosophical theory (and the demand for evidence cannot in this case be avoided, since it is for the satisfaction of reason that it is propounded) is no greater than what exists for the popular doctrine, namely, a subjective feeling in the mind and not any real connexion perceived to hold within or between objects.[2] The philosophers have simply doubled the sensible reality which alone is experienced, and as the second reality is purely fictitious they are perfectly free to imagine it as will best suit their purposes and cover contradictions. Also, the assumption of the existence of such substances, besides being incapable of proof, is likewise useless. As Hume shows, not a single one of the old difficulties is thereby solved. The problem is

[1] Cf. note to p. 110.

[2] Hume's detailed and very subtle proof of this statement I must omit. It is primarily directed against Locke and Berkeley, and would, from their point of view, be very difficult to meet. This whole section (bk. I, part IV, § ii) is, as Mr. Selby-Bigge remarks, perhaps the most interesting part of the whole *Treatise*.

only pushed back, to reappear, on further reflection, in an uglier form.

> By this means (the feigning of occult substances) these philosophers set themselves at ease, and arrive at last, by an illusion, at the same indifference, which the people attain by their stupidity, and true philosophers by their moderate scepticism.[1]

Hume accounts in a similar manner for belief in the self as an abiding existence. Our ideas are so closely united one to another through the bonds of association, that the easy passage of the imagination along the ideas generates the *feeling* of identity, and this subjective feeling in the mind is again interpreted as denoting actual identity of existence. This belief in the permanence of the self performs an indispensable function in our practical life, and from it, therefore, we cannot desire to free ourselves. But this practical function is its sole function, and upon it no metaphysic of the soul can be based.

All such attempts, however, to give theoretical explanation of what can only be practically justified, rest rather on the principle of causality than on the conception of substance. For it is always this principle that is appealed to, when the right to assert an abiding substance is called in question or when its relation to the sensible is sought. Since the causal relation holds between distinct and separate events, and does not vary with our ideas, it affords another, and equally important, example of a relation that can neither be demonstrated as necessary by reason nor verified as actual in experience. Hume's familiar argument in support of this position need not, however, be stated. The one point that I need dwell upon is the determining influence which he assigns to feeling. Though we have no insight, rational or empirical, into causal action, we are yet, as practical life demands, firmly convinced of its existence. And here again it is a blind but powerful instinct that apart from all evidence irresistibly inclines the mind to this belief. When ideas have been constantly conjoined, they become mentally associated; the presentation of one to the mind (through the workings of that unknown force, association) is necessitated to call up the idea of the other. This determination of the mind, this feeling of necessitated transition, is the original of our

---

[1] *Treatise*, I, IV, iii; G, p. 510; S–B, p. 224.

idea of necessity, causal efficacy and power.[1] It is something that is felt in the soul, not perceived to hold between objects. It is due to that fortunately irresistible instinct which leads us to spread ourselves on external objects and to ascribe to them any internal impression which they occasion in us,[2] that our belief in the causal agency of objects and in the personal activity of the self is thus independent of reasoning and victoriously withstands all the objections that can be raised against it. Only for moments, when we turn away from practical life, can we free ourselves from this belief that we directly apprehend necessary con-nexion and real activity; and only thus, from this detached philosophical point of view, can we recognize that their real nature can never by any possibility be discovered. The conceptually empty and unmeaning notion of causation is only of practical use within experience, never valid as an instrument for the metaphysical explanation of experience.

But one of the most important points in Hume's criticism still re-mains to be stated. Even if we take the term 'cause' as signifying only the customary antecedent, no *inference* to a cause can ever, in any single case, even within experience, be theoretically justified. All that experi-ence has revealed is conjunction in the past, and the inference to similar conjunction in future cases goes upon the assumption that the future will resemble the past.

[1] Some critics seem to hold that Hume has no right to any such feeling. Certainly Hume cannot pretend to be able to explain *how* the feeling is generated, but that does not deprive him of the right to learn from experience that it is, as a matter of fact, generated. His view of reflection must be kept in mind. Just as we learn from experi-ence that the idea of pain or pleasure, when it returns upon the soul, is followed by the new impression of desire and aversion, hope and fear, which may therefore be called impressions of reflection, so also experience teaches us that after events have repeatedly succeeded one another there arises in the mind a feeling of necessitated transition from the one to the other. But the generating causes of this feeling, like the generating causes of our sensations, can never be discovered. Hume adds in the *Enquiry* (vii, i; G, note to p. 56; S–B, note to p. 67) that what is called the feeling of effort, resistance, or animal *nisus*, also forms part of the vulgar conception of causal activity. But since this also is pure feeling, it affords to the mind no *knowledge*, that is, *comprehension* of the nature of activity, and indeed is not, save through customary connexion, capable even of indicating its existence. All feeling is in itself blind and unilluminating, and there-fore can indicate nothing.

[2] *Treatise*, I, iii, xiv; G, p. 461; S–B, p. 167.

If there be any suspicion that the course of nature may change, and that the past may be no rule for the future, all experience becomes useless, and can give rise to no inference or conclusion. It is impossible, therefore, that any arguments from experience can prove this resemblance of the past to the future; since all these arguments are founded on the supposition of the resemblance.[1]

No sufficient evidence existing for the supposition, it must be the outcome of some unreasoning propensity, and that propensity is custom or habit.

For wherever the repetition of any particular act or operation produces a propensity to renew the same act or operation, without being impelled by any reasoning or process of the understanding, we always say, that this propensity is the effect of *Custom*. By employing that word, we pretend not to have given the ultimate reason of such a propensity. We only point out a principle of human nature, which is universally acknowledged, and which is well known by its effects.[2]

This custom by leading us to anticipate the future in accordance with the past, and so to adjust means for the attainment of our ends, brings about the required harmony between the course of nature and the succession of our ideas.

Those, who delight in the discovery and contemplation of *final causes*, have here ample subject to employ their wonder and admiration.[3]

But in this 'custom' something more must be involved than has yet come to light, for the ideas introduced by it are, as we ordinarily say, 'inferences', and not mere suggestions.

If flame or snow be presented anew to the senses, the mind is carried by custom to expect heat or cold, and to *believe* that such a quality does exist, and will discover itself upon a nearer approach.[4]

[1] *Enquiry*, IV, II; G, p. 33; S–B, pp. 37–38.
[2] Ibid., V, I; G, p. 37; S–B, p. 43.
[3] Ibid., V, II; G, pp. 46–47; S–B, p. 55; cf. V, I; G, p. 39; S–B, pp. 44–45.
[4] Ibid., V, I; G, p. 40; S–B, p. 46.

It would, Hume remarks, be quite allowable to stop our researches at this point, taking custom as a natural propensity of the soul conditioning belief; but, as it happens, we can carry our inquiries a step further. The distinction between a mere idea and one that is believed cannot lie in any peculiar idea, such as that of 'reality' or 'existence', that is annexed to the one and absent from the other.[1]

> For as the mind has authority over all its ideas, it could voluntarily annex this particular idea to any fiction, and consequently be able to believe whatever it pleases; contrary to what we find in daily experience.[2]

It follows, therefore, as the sole alternative, that the difference between fiction and belief lies in some sentiment or feeling that accompanies all ideas believed. And to verify that conclusion Hume suggests an experiment.

> If I see a billiard ball moving towards another, on a smooth table, I can easily conceive it to stop upon contact. This conception implies no contradiction; but still it feels very differently from that conception by which I represent to myself the impulse and the communication from one ball to another.[3]

Belief adds nothing to the content of an idea but only changes our manner of conceiving it, rendering it more vivid, forcible and steady, and so causing it to weigh more in the thought, and to have a superior influence on the passions and imagination. All these characteristics we find in a supreme degree in our perceptions; and since perceptions are, apart from inference or evidence, the immediate objects of belief, this view of belief, as being nothing but such vivid and steady apprehension, may be taken as proved.

Perceptions have, however, Hume contends, a further characteristic. They possess the power of conferring upon any ideas that are in any way connected with them a share of their vivacity. Memory-images carry the mind through a connected series of images direct to its present perceptions, and being enlivened by them, take stronger hold upon the

[1] Cf. Appendix to the *Treatise*; G, pp. 555 ff.; S–B, pp. 623 ff.
[2] *Enquiry*, V, II; G, p. 41; S–B, pp. 47–48.
[3] Loc. cit.

mind than does the idea, say, of an enchanted castle. The picture of an absent friend enlivens our idea of him, and also every feeling which that idea occasions. For the same reason the superstitious are fond of the relics of saints and holy men. Now this quality of our perception would also seem to be the cause of belief in an effect suggested by a present perception. The perception of fire conveys to the suggested idea of heat a share of its liveliness, and the idea thereby approximating in force to an impression, the mind necessarily believes in its existence.

Inference, then, instead of being based on the relation of cause and effect and presupposing it, is itself identical with that relation. It is nothing but the custom-bred transition from an impression to an enlivened idea. Just as in his ethics Hume grounds the distinction between moral good and evil not on reason but on certain emotions and passions which are to be found in every man, and which constitute the constant element in human nature; so here in his theory of knowledge he declares the operation of the mind, by which we infer effects from causes, to be, like that of moral judgement, so essential to the subsistence of all human creatures, that it cannot be trusted to the fallacious deductions of our reason.

> It is more conformable to the ordinary wisdom of nature to secure so necessary an act of mind, by some instinct or mechanical tendency, which may be infallible in its operations, may discover itself at the first appearance of life and thought, and may be independent of all the laboured deductions of the understanding.[1]
>
> Nature by an absolute and uncontroulable necessity has determin'd us to judge as well as to breathe and feel.[2]
>
> All these operations are a species of natural instincts, which no reasoning or process of the thought and understanding is able, either to produce, or to prevent.[3]

And, as his whole philosophy is directed to prove, reason can neither explain nor control them.

[1] *Enquiry*, V, ɪɪ; G, p. 47; S–B, p. 55.
[2] *Treatise*, I, ɪv, i; G, pp. 474–5; S–B, p. 183.
[3] *Enquiry*, V, ɪ; G, p. 40; S–B, pp. 46–47.

This new theory of belief is the indispensable complement of Hume's new view of the function of knowledge, and was all-important in determining his philosophical attitude. By his predecessors belief had been regarded as intellectual, dependent on insight, and therefore at the mercy of the philosophical sceptic; whereas, if Hume's teaching is true, it does not result from knowledge but precedes it, and as it does not rest on knowledge, so also it is not destroyed by doubt.[1] By the fortunate construction of our nature,

> the conviction, which arises from a subtle reasoning, diminishes in proportion to the efforts, which the imagination makes to enter into the reasoning, and to conceive it in all its parts. Belief, being a lively conception, can never be entire, where it is not founded on something natural and easy.[2]

As the mind departs further and further from its ordinary attitude, sinking itself in ideas,

> tho' the principles of judgement, and the balancing of opposite causes be the same as at the very beginning; yet their influence on the imagination, and the vigour they add to, or diminish from the thought, is by no means equal.[3]

Thus happily,

> nature breaks the force of all sceptical arguments in time, and keeps them from having any considerable influence on the understanding.[4]

[1] 'Shou'd it be here asked me . . . whether I be really one of those sceptics, who hold that all is uncertain, and that our judgement is not in *any* thing possest of *any* measure of truth and falsehood; I shou'd reply, that this question is entirely superfluous, and that neither I, nor any other person was ever sincerely and constantly of that opinion. Nature, by an absolute and uncontroulable necessity has determin'd us to judge as well as to breathe and feel. . . . Whosoever has taken the pains to refute the cavils of this *total* scepticism, has really disputed without an antagonist, and endeavour'd by argument to establish a faculty, which nature has antecedently planted in the mind, and render'd unavoidable.'—*Treatise*, I, IV, i; G, pp. 474–5; S–B, p. 185.

[2] Ibid.; G, p. 477; S–B, p. 186.

[3] Ibid.; G, p. 476; S–B, p. 185.

[4] *Treatise*, I, IV, i; G, p. 478; S–B, p. 187.

They cannot overthrow our natural beliefs without totally destroying our human nature.

Further, even our doubts as to the validity of our natural beliefs rest, not on the demonstration of the falsity of these beliefs, but only on the proofs of the total absence of evidence for them. It is therefore only one possibility against another, and, in our complete and necessary ignorance as to the nature of ultimate reality, all sceptical arguments against trust in these particular beliefs must equally diminish trust in our sceptical doubts. The appeals to reason for and against natural belief mutually destroy one another

> till at last they both vanish away into nothing, by a regular and just diminution.[1]

But this does not make an end of our difficulties. The natural beliefs which we thus perforce follow, themselves mislead us. And this brings us to the second stage in Hume's argument, his proof, namely, that the philosophical reinterpretation of experience is worthless in practical life, and besides containing all the contradictions of ordinary consciousness possesses in addition certain difficulties peculiar to itself. The philosophical reinterpretation that he has specially in view is the spiritualism and consequent deism of Descartes and his English successors. This line of thought I have already touched upon in stating Hume's criticism of the category of substance, and may now consider it more at length. What we call 'reason', and oppose to our natural beliefs, is in Hume's view nothing distinct from these beliefs; and it is just the *de facto* necessity we are under of following them which gives rise to the philosophical or 'rational' reaction against them. The understanding is nothing but the imagination acting according to its most general and established habits or instincts;[2] and it is because these instincts, when theoretically devel-

---

[1] Ibid.; G, p. 478; S–B, p. 187.

[2] Ibid., I, iv, vii; G, p. 547; S–B, p. 267; cf. I, iii, xvi; G, p. 471; S–B, p. 179. 'To consider the matter aright, reason is nothing but a wonderful and unintelligible instinct in our souls.' The completeness with which Hume equates reason and instinct, and gives a purely naturalistic explanation of both, is well illustrated in the following passage from the *Dialogues*, vii; G, pp. 422–3: 'These words, *generation, reason*, mark only certain powers and energies in nature, whose effects are known, but whose essence is incomprehensible, and one of these principles, more than the other, has no

oped, conflict with one another that the understanding is at variance with itself.[1]

Our two most fundamental beliefs are, first, that the objects we perceive have an independent substantial reality, and secondly, that nothing can come into existence save through a pre-existent cause. Now in acquiescing in the first belief we fly in the face of all the inevitable consequences of the causal postulate. This Hume contends has been proved by Berkeley. When we reason from cause and effect we conclude that neither colour, sound, taste, nor smell have independent reality, and when we exclude all these nothing of all that we apprehend remains as real existence. Thus though no abstract arguments drawn from the universal application of the one belief can destroy the other, the neces-

---

privilege for being made a standard to the whole of nature. . . . In this little corner of the world alone, there are four principles, *Reason, Instinct, Generation, Vegetation*, which are similar to each other, and are the causes of similar effects. What a number of other principles may we naturally suppose in the immense extent and variety of the universe, could we travel from planet to planet and from system to system, in order to examine each part of this mighty fabric? . . . Reason, in its internal fabric and structure, is really as little known to us as instinct or vegetation; and perhaps even that vague, undeterminate word, *Nature*, to which the vulgar refer everything, is not at bottom more inexplicable.' But though Hume in describing the understanding as nothing but the imagination acting according to its most general and established habits, certainly means to emphasize that it is in essence instinctive and contains no objective standard to which reality must conform, he must not be taken as implying that it is therefore identical with imagination in the ordinary sense, and is a source of arbitrary fictions. The imagination constitutes the deepest element in our human nature, and fulfils the same function as Kant's faculty of understanding: it creates the order of nature out of the detached impressions of sense. 'In order to justify myself, I must distinguish in the imagination betwixt the principles which are permanent, irresistible, and universal; such as the customary transition from causes to effects, and from effects to causes: And the principles, which are changeable, weak, and irregular. . . . *The former are the foundation of all our thoughts and actions, so that upon their removal human nature must immediately perish and go to ruin.*'—*Treatise*, I, IV, iv; G, p. 511; S–B, p. 225. Italics are mine. Hume ascribes an equally important function to imagination in the creation of mathematical science.

[1] We may compare Hume's line of argument with that of 'the Prussian Hume', 'the all-destroyer'.

sity of holding both must prevent us from ever being satisfied with either.[1]

Again, it is these natural beliefs that induce idle speculation. The belief in causal connexion being instinctive is unlimited in its pretensions, and leads us, in the pursuit of knowledge, to demand a sufficient cause for all things. But since we have no adequate conception what would be a 'sufficient' cause—Hume further develops this point in his *Dialogues*—either for the world as a whole or for any phenomenon in it, this demand can never be satisfied. In demanding, however, explanation of all things, reason also requires justification for its own demands, and since these rest on blind instinct, for which no theoretical justification can be given, it here again demands the impossible. The demand for 'sufficient' causes is itself insufficiently caused, and in thus insisting on itself it finally brings to light its purely practical function and its non-rational source.

We must, then, draw the 'sceptical' conclusion, that though our natural beliefs are our sole guides they are reliable and legitimate only in practical life. We must limit our inquiries to 'the experienced train of events'.

> Nothing else can be appealed to in the field, or in the senate. Nothing else ought ever to be heard of in the school, or in the closet. The more sublime topics are to be left to the embellishment of poets and orators, or to the arts of priests and politicians. . . . Those who have a propensity to philosophy will still continue their researches; because they reflect, that, besides the immediate pleasure attending such an occupation, philosophical decisions are nothing but the reflections of common life, methodized and corrected. But they will never be tempted to go beyond common life, so long as they consider the imperfection of those faculties which they employ, their narrow reach, and their inaccurate operations.[2]

But this is a more sceptical conclusion than is strictly demanded by Hume's philosophy. Hume in these and similar passages seems to imply that no really definite and final set of opinions can be arrived at. As he

---

[1] Hume's detailed proof is too lengthy to be given. Cf. *Treatise*, I, iv, iv; *Enquiry*, XII, i.

[2] *Enquiry*, XII, iii; G, p. 133; S–B, p. 162.

says in the *Treatise*,[1] we must study philosophy in a 'careless manner', and be as diffident of our sceptical doubts as of our philosophical convictions. On his own showing, however, reason (in its synthetic form) is as necessary as natural belief. It is true that if we seek to reject natural belief in favour of reasoning we are really only rejecting belief in the independent existence of our impressions for belief in their causal dependence—a belief which leads to equally self-contradictory results. But it is also true that if we condemn all refined reasoning, that is to say, all application of the synthetic principles of imagination beyond the sphere of immediate experience, we run into the most manifest contradictions. In either case we entirely subvert the human understanding.[2] The more consistent conclusion would therefore be, that though reason cannot take the place of natural belief, still less overthrow it, its generalizing powers are yet necessary for its interpretation and control. Only through the use of our natural beliefs as universal synthetic principles can we discover their limited range and their merely practical worth. This more positive view of the relation of reason to feeling and instinct is also more in agreement with the conclusion which, as we shall see, Hume comes to in his ethical philosophy.[3]

[1] *Treatise*, I, iv, vii; G, p. 552; S–B, p. 273.

[2] *Treatise*, I, iv, vii.

[3] Hume's view of the relation between natural belief and synthetic reason may profitably be compared with the very different, though analogous, opposition of understanding and reason in the Critical philosophy. Just as reason, on Kant's view, discovers the contradictions involved in the conceptions of understanding when universalized, so reason reveals the contradictions involved in our natural beliefs when these are regarded as theoretically true. Also, while Kant shows reason to be helpless apart from understanding, Hume proves reason to be incapable of acting apart from natural belief. And lastly, to complete the analogy, just as Kant's ideas of reason are simply the categories freed from all limitations, so reason is for Hume nothing but our natural beliefs universalized. It is because, when thus universalized, they conflict and lead to insoluble contradictions that we are forced to recognize their purely practical function. I do not, of course, mean to imply that the views of Hume and Kant are really akin. Each gives so different a meaning to reason that the tendencies of their systems are quite divergent. The following passage from the *Prolegomena* brings out in a striking manner Kant's agreement with Hume, but is a very inadequate statement of Kant's real position. 'The principle of all genuine Idealists, from the Eleatic school to Bishop Berkeley, is contained in this formula, "All knowledge by

I may now, before passing to Hume's theory of morals, consider the difficulties involved in his use of the terms 'illusion', 'fiction', 'propensity to feign', in reference to our notions of body and of causation.[1] Hume's argument rests throughout on the supposition that perishing subjective states are the only possible objects of mind, and that it is these perishing states which natural belief constrains us to regard as abiding independent existences. Such belief is obviously, on the above interpretation, sheer illusion and utterly false.[2] It is due to a propensity to feign. Belief in the existence of body does not, however, necessarily involve this identification of the external world with the world perceived. The philosophical theory postulates the double existence of objects and perceptions; and to an objective world, thus conceived as distinct from our fleeting impressions, the terms fiction and illusion cannot be applied. For if the existence of such a world cannot be asserted, just as little can it be disproved. Philosophers, however, though they have sufficient force of genius to free themselves from the vulgar error, have not sufficient insight to keep them from seeking to justify their own theory at the bar of reason.

> However philosophical this new system may be esteemed, I assert 'tis only a palliative remedy, and that it contains all the

---

sense and experience is nothing but mere appearance, and truth is to be found only in the ideas of pure understanding and reason". The principle which throughout governs and determines my Idealism is: "All knowledge of things from pure understanding or pure reason is nothing but mere appearance, and truth is to be found only in experience".'—*Werke* (Hartenstein), iv, p. 121.

[1] In Hume's teaching in regard to the self (cf. above, pp. 99–101, 109) his argument as to the reality of material body may be taken *mutatis mutandis*, as holding also of the self.

[2] In my account of Hume in *Studies in the Cartesian Philosophy* (chap. vi, especially pp. 247–8, 251–2), I have followed the current view more closely than I am now prepared to do. It was quite impossible for Hume to adopt the position which he suggests in the *Treatise* (I, iv, ii; G, pp. 495–6; S–B, pp. 207–8). An interpretation of this passage, similar to that which I have given in my *Studies*, and open therefore to the objections which I have indicated above, has recently been presented in an interesting manner by Dr. Montague (*Philosophical Review*, January 1905—'A neglected point in Hume's philosophy').

difficulties of the vulgar system, with some others, that are peculiar to itself.[1]

[Though] it pleases our reason, in allowing, that our dependent perceptions are interrupted and different; and at the same time is agreeable to the imagination, in attributing continued existence to something else, which we call objects,

it presupposes the popular theory, and derives all its authority from it. Apart from that theory it can offer no grounds for itself, and therefore can never really displace natural belief by rational judgement.[2]

Now Green, besides ignoring Hume's doctrine of natural belief, misrepresents his position by taking the epithets which concern only the popular theory as applying also to the philosophical. As we have just seen, Hume's utterances from the one point of view are not inconsistent with those from the other. Though the popular belief is an illusion and demonstrably false, the philosophical view, in some one or other of its forms, may be true though it can never be established. And this is all that is required in order to turn the scales in favour of our natural beliefs. They may contain genuine truth though the particular form in which they exist is obviously false. The form which they take is influenced by practical convenience, and theoretical consistency is not, therefore, an indispensable condition of their practical truth. The illusions upon which they rest may the better fit them for their immediate end. And since reason is as incapable of correcting as of displacing them, we must accept them in the crude form in which they result from the instinctive equipment of the human mind. Hume candidly admits that such inquiries raise doubts even in his own mind as to the validity of those natural beliefs which he contends to be unavoidable.

I begun this subject with premising, that we ought to have an implicit faith in our senses, and that this would be the conclusion I shou'd draw from the whole of my reasoning. But to be ingenuous, I feel myself *at present* of a quite contrary sentiment, and am more inclined to repose no faith at all in my senses, or rather imagination, than to place in it such implicit confidence.[3]

[1] *Treatise*, I, iv, ii; G, p. 499; S–B, p. 211.
[2] Here again I can only summarize Hume's argument.
[3] *Treatise*, I, iv, ii; G, p. 504; S–B, p. 217.

But this he regards as simply one illustration of how all reflection upon ultimate questions must inevitably lead to uncertainty and doubt. Such philosophical inquiries are both useless and harmful, except in so far as they lead us to detect the inherent impossibility of all metaphysical construction and so constrain us to resign ourselves to our natural beliefs.

> 'Tis impossible upon any system to defend either our understanding or senses; and we but expose them farther when we endeavour to justify them in that manner. As the sceptical doubt arises naturally from a profound and intense reflection on these subjects, it always increases, the farther we carry our reflections, *whether in opposition or conformity to it.* . . . An hour hence he will be persuaded there is both an external and an internal world.[1]

It is, however, in reference to causation that Hume's most ambiguous statements are made. Inference, instead of being based on the relation of cause and effect, and presupposing it, is itself identical with that relation.

> Necessity is something, that exists in the mind, not in objects; nor is it possible for us ever to form the most distant idea of it, consider'd as a quality in bodies.[2]

> The efficacy or energy of Causes . . . belongs entirely to the soul. . . . 'Tis here that the real power of causes is plac'd along with their connexion and necessity.[3]

Before commenting on these passages I may point out that Hume states as strongly as Green himself the objection to this position which at once suggests itself, namely, that it entirely reverses the natural order of thought and reality, and contradicts the assumption which Hume himself inevitably makes at every turn, even in his proof that we can have no genuine conception of causal agency.

> What! the efficacy of causes lie in the determination of the mind! As if causes did not operate entirely independent of the mind, and

---

[1] Ibid.; G, p. 505; S–B, p. 218. Italics are mine. Cf. *Enquiry*, XII, I; G, p. 127; S–B, p. 155.

[2] Ibid., I, III, xiv; G, p. 460; S–B, pp. 165–6.

[3] Loc. cit.

wou'd not continue their operation, even tho' there was no mind existent to contemplate them, or reason concerning them. Thought may well depend on causes for its operation, but not causes on thought. This is to reverse the order of nature, and make that secondary, which is really primary.[1]

Hume's answer to this objection shows very clearly that he does not mean to deny the objective reality of material bodies or their mutual influence.

> I can only reply to all these arguments, that the case is here much the same, as if a blind man shou'd pretend to find a great many absurdities in the supposition, that the colour of scarlet is not the same with the sound of a trumpet, nor light the same with solidity. If we have really no idea of power or efficacy in any object, or of any real connexion betwixt causes and effects, 'twill be to little purpose to prove, that an efficacy is necessary in all operations. We do not understand our own meaning in talking so, but ignorantly confound ideas, which are entirely distinct from each other. I am, indeed, ready to allow, that there may be several qualities, both in material and in immaterial objects, with which we are utterly unacquainted; and if we please to call these *power* or *efficacy*, 'twill be of little consequence to the world. *But when, instead of meaning these unknown qualities, we make the terms of power and efficacy signify something, of which we have a clear idea, and which is incompatible with those objects, to which we apply it*, obscurity and error begin then to take place, and we are led astray by a false philosophy.[2]

In the next sentence, however, Hume states his position in an ambiguous manner that goes far to account for the common misunderstanding. He proceeds:

> This is the case, when we transfer the determination of the thought of external objects, and suppose any real intelligible connexion betwixt them; *that being a quality, which can only belong to the mind that considers them.*[3]

[1] *Treatise*, I, III, xiv; G, pp. 461–2; S–B, p. 167.
[2] Ibid.; G, p. 462; S–B, p. 168. Italics in last sentence are mine.
[3] Loc. cit. Italics are mine.

Unless that last sentence is carefully interpreted in the light of its context, the words which I have italicized may seem to involve a conclusion which there is nothing at all in Hume's argument to support, and which moreover is in flagrant contradiction with the admissions which he has just made. All that it really says is that causal connexion denotes for us merely a feeling, the feeling of necessitated transition, and that *this, qua feeling*, can exist only in mind. This, I should contend, is the point of view from which the sentences which I have quoted above, in the beginning of the previous paragraph, must be interpreted. Reading their context this seems quite obviously to be their meaning. To take the strongest of his assertions:

> The efficacy or energy of causes is neither plac'd in the causes themselves, nor in the deity, nor in the concurrence of these two principles; but belongs entirely to the soul, which considers the union of two or more objects in all past instances. 'Tis here that the real power of causes is plac'd along with their connexion and necessity.[1]

Now what Hume has here in view is the explanation of our causal 'inferences'. The foundation of such inference is the *de facto* transition from cause to effect, arising from repeated union. *This* transition is in no wise due to the objective nature of either the cause or the effect, but solely to their acquired mental connexion.

> The necessity or power, which unites causes and effects, lies in the determination of the mind to pass from the one to the other.[2]

Hume's contention, therefore, is that the connexion and necessity which ground our 'inferences' can only exist in us; and this does not involve the assertion that objects are incapable of influencing one another independently of mind.

---

[1] *Treatise*, I, III, xiv; G, p. 460; S–B, p. 166.
[2] Loc. cit. This is the sentence immediately preceding that which we are now considering.

The Naturalism of Hume[1]

II

IN the previous article I have considered Hume's theory of knowledge and may now proceed to his treatment of morals. My chief aim will be to show how Hume finds in the facts of the moral life convincing confirmation of his naturalistic view of reason, and so is enabled to develop an ethical theory in harmony with his general philosophy. Up to a certain point Green states very fairly the connexion between Hume's view of reason in his theory of knowledge and his account of its function in his ethics.

> Reason, constituting no objects, affords no motives. 'It is only the slave of the passions, and can never pretend to any other office than to serve and obey them.' . . . It is the clearness with which Hume points out that, as it cannot move, so neither can it restrain action, that in this regard chiefly distinguishes him from Locke. The check to any passion, he points out, can only proceed from some counter-motive, and such a motive reason, 'having no original influence', cannot give.[2]

But since Green has ignored Hume's doctrine of natural belief, and therefore has interpreted him as a thoroughgoing associationist, he very naturally treats as an inconsistency Hume's theory of the disinterested passions. Hume, he asserts, is constrained by his principles to explain all action as due to pleasure and pain.

> Hume's system has the merit of relative consistency. He sees that the two sides of Locke's doctrine—one that thought originates

---

[1] *Mind*, vol. xiv, N.S., no. 55.
[2] Introduction to the moral part of the *Treatise*, p. 48.

nothing, but takes its objects as given in feeling, the other that the good which is the object of desire is pleasant feeling—are inseparable. Hence he decisively rejects every notion of rational or unselfish affections, which would imply that they are other than desires for pleasure. . . . But here his consistency stops. The principle which forbade him to admit any object of desire but pleasure is practically forgotten in his account of the sources of pleasure, and its being so forgotten is the condition of the desire for pleasure being made plausibly to serve as a foundation for morals.[1]

Now so far as I understand Hume's philosophy, it contains no fundamental principle which forbids him to recognize disinterested passions. The mind through natural belief transcends itself in knowledge, and it may similarly through love, sympathy, and benevolence, forget private interests in unselfish affection. If it can be shown that Hume nowhere asserts the object of all action to be pleasure and pain, and that, on the contrary, he constantly maintains that there are many disinterested propensities in our complex human nature, we may conclude that there is no such inconsistency in his ethical philosophy nor any lack of agreement between it and his theory of knowledge.

This part of my task is rendered easy by Professor McGilvary's very convincing article on 'Altruism in Hume's *Treatise*' in the *Philosophical Review*;[2] and I shall make full use of his conclusions, referring the reader to his thorough and detailed examination of the relevant passages. Two points would seem to be established by Professor McGilvary: first, that Hume recognizes passions which are not founded on pleasure and pain; and, secondly, that even in those passions which are founded on pleasure and pain the object of the desire is not pleasure.[3] As to the first, though

[1] Introduction to the moral part of the *Treatise*, pp. 31–32.

[2] May 1903, vol. xii, no. 3.

[3] As Professor McGilvary points out, Lechartier, Jodl, Pfleiderer and Albee all more or less agree with Green in their interpretation of the *Treatise*. Jodl, Pfleiderer and Albee admit, however, that in the *Enquiry* Hume represents human nature as largely moved by unselfish considerations. Gizycki seems to be the only commentator, previous to Professor McGilvary, who regards Hume as maintaining the disinterestedness of sympathy and benevolence in the *Treatise* as well as in the *Enquiry*. Professor McGilvary does not attempt to show the bearing of Hume's ethics on his theory of

pleasure and pain are 'the chief spring or actuating principle of the human mind', passions

> frequently arise from a natural impulse or instinct which is perfectly unaccountable. Of this kind is the desire of punishment to our enemies, and of happiness to our friends; hunger, lust, and a few other bodily appetites. These passions, properly speaking, produce good and evil, and proceed not from them, like the other affections.[1]

These same passions may be artificially roused by ideas of pleasure and pain, but unless they were primarily instinctive, the pleasure and pain would have no existence at all. Hume gives as a list of the instinctive passions—in addition, of course, to such bodily desires as hunger and lust—'benevolence and resentment, the love of life, and kindness to children'.[2] Apparently, therefore, by 'the desire of happiness to our friends' Hume means private benevolence, or as he names it in the *Enquiry* 'humanity and friendship', and by 'the desire of punishment to our enemies' resentment or love of vengeance. In the *Enquiry* Hume adds to the above list, love of fame or power.

> Nature must, by the internal frame and constitution of the mind, give an original propensity to fame, ere we can reap any pleasure from that acquisition, or pursue it from motives of self-love, and desire of happiness.[3]

Hume nowhere states his position in a more forcible manner than in the following passage:

> Who sees not that vengeance, from the force alone of passion, may be so eagerly pursued, as to make us knowingly neglect every

---

knowledge; and it is with that alone that I am here directly concerned. It is undoubtedly the usual purely associationist interpretation of Hume's theory of knowledge that has led commentators to expect from him an egoistic theory of morals.

[1] *Treatise*, II, III, ix; G, p. 215; S–B, p. 439. By the phrase 'produce good and evil' Hume means, it must be noted, 'produce *pleasure* and *pain*'.
[2] *Treatise*, II, III, iii; G, pp. 196–7; S–B, p. 417. Cf. McGilvary, p. 277, note.
[3] *Enquiry*, appendix ii; G, p. 271; S–B, p. 301.

consideration of ease, interest, or safety; and, like some vindictive animals, infuse our very souls into the wounds we give an enemy; and what a malignant philosophy must it be, that will not allow to humanity and friendship the same privileges which are indisputably granted to the darker passions of enmity and resentment.[1]

As regards the direct and indirect passions which are 'founded on pleasure and pain', Green was obviously misled by the ambiguous phrase. It does not mean that these passions have pleasure and pain as their object but only as their efficient cause.

> The mind by an *original* instinct tends to unite itself with the good, and to avoid the evil, tho' they be conceiv'd merely in idea, and be consider'd as to exist in any future period of time.[2]

Hence any pleasant idea, however objective the content of that idea may be, at once inclines the mind to desire it. Feeling is thus the chief moving principle, but anything whatsoever to which it is attached by nature, the happiness of a fellow-creature as immediately as one's own good, may be the end of action. Hume does not, of course, deny that pleasure and pain may themselves be the ends sought, but even in such cases we can distinguish between the pleasure sought as end and the pleasantness of the idea of that pleasure which is the efficient cause.[3]

Now nature both through the instinctive and through the indirect passions has connected feeling with very definite objective ends. And though a double process of association is required to bring the indirect passions into play—and upon this associationist mechanism Hume dwells at great length in the *Treatise*—the associations do not explain the disinterestedness of their action, but from the start presuppose it. As the detail of Hume's associationist explanation of the mechanism of the passions does not specially concern us, I may simply quote the following

---

[1] Ibid.; G, p. 272; S–B, p. 302. I may quote Professor McGilvary's remark on Hume's treatment of love of life: 'Contrary to the usage of Hobbes, Hume does not include the self-preservative instinct in self-love. In this he showed fine psychological discernment. The instinct which prompts us to cling to life has no conscious end in view, any more than hunger has' (p. 277, note).

[2] *Treatise*, II, III, ix; G, pp. 214–15; S–B, p. 438.

[3] Cf. McGilvary, p. 281.

passage in which Professor McGilvary sums up the results of his examination of it.

> There is nothing said of past experience, nothing about the previously ascertained conduciveness of the loved object to my pleasure, for the sake of the re-enjoyment of which I am now doing anything. Association does not begin with self-love and change it into a love for another. On the contrary, it is the *original* qualities of love which make it possible for the double association to work. And one of these original qualities is the fact that love is 'always directed to some sensible being external to us', that is, the original and invariable altruism of love is *presupposed* by Hume's associational explanation; and associations do not produce the altruism. . . . To put it succinctly, we love others because for some reason they please us; but we do not love them in order to get pleasure either from them or from our love for them.[1]

Thus nature, by establishing a connexion between our feelings and certain objective ends, determines us to actions that completely transcend self-love. The distinction between the direct and the indirect passions is not fundamental, and we may apply to both what Hume says of the instinctive passions, that, properly speaking, they 'produce good and evil, and proceed not from them.'[2] Indeed no philosophical writer has ever stated more forcibly than Hume the important ethical principle that pleasure is conditioned by desire and not *vice versa*.

> Whatever contradiction may vulgarly be supposed between the *selfish* and *social* sentiments or dispositions, they are really no more opposite than selfish and ambitious, selfish and revengeful, selfish and vain. It is requisite that there be an original propensity of some kind, in order to be a basis to self-love, by giving a relish to the objects of its pursuit; and none more fit for this purpose than benevolence or humanity. The goods of fortune are spent in one gratification or another: the miser who accumulates his annual income, and lends it out at interest, has really spent it in the gratification of his avarice. And it would be difficult to show why a man is more a loser by a generous action, than by any other

[1] Ibid., pp. 290–1.
[2] *Treatise*, II, III, ix; G, p. 215; S–B, p. 439.

method of expense; since *the utmost which he can attain by the most elaborate selfishness, is the indulgence of some affection.*[1]

So far from thinking, that men have no affection for any thing beyond themselves, I am of opinion, that tho' it be rare to meet with one, who loves any single person better than himself; yet 'tis as rare to meet with one in whom all the kind affections, taken together, do not over-balance all the selfish.[2]

But to return to our central point—the dependence of reason on feeling and instinct—Hume derives from the facts of moral experience evidence in proof of the truth of his naturalistic point of view. There is, he holds, complete analogy between the dependence of reason on natural belief, and its relation to the natural passions. The passions determine our moral sense and the standard of conduct, just as the natural beliefs constitute the only possible ground of empirical inference.

It has already been shown that reason does not produce the passions; and from this it follows that it is equally incapable of governing them. A passion can only be opposed by a counter-passion, and as no passion is produced by reason, none is controlled by it.

We speak not strictly and philosophically when we talk of the combat of passion and of reason. Reason is, and ought only to be the slave of the passions, and can never pretend to any other office than to serve and obey them.[3]

This conclusion is so vital for my purpose that I may state Hume's argument at length.

A passion is an original existence, or, if you will, modification of existence, and contains not any representative quality, which renders it a copy of any other existence or modification.[4] When I am angry, I am actually possest with the passion, and in that emo-

---

[1] *Enquiry*, IX, ɪɪ; G, pp. 255–6; S–B, p. 281. Italics in last sentence are mine.

[2] *Treatise*, III, ɪɪ, ii; G, p. 260; S–B, p. 487.

[3] Ibid., II, ɪɪɪ, iii; G, p. 195; S–B, p. 415. Cf. *Treatise*, III, ɪ, i; G, pp. 235–6; S–B, pp. 457–8.

[4] According to Hume all the passions, both direct and indirect, are ultimate and unanalysable. No passion can through association or any other means be developed out of, or transformed into, any other passion.

tion have no more a reference to any other object, than when I am thirsty, or sick, or more than five foot high. 'Tis impossible, therefore, that this passion can be oppos'd by, or be contradictory to truth and reason; since this contradiction consists in the disagreement of ideas, consider'd as copies, with those objects, which they represent. . . . It must follow, that passions can be contrary to reason only so far as they are *accompany'd* with some judgment or opinion.[1]

Now only in two senses can an affection, when accompanied by judgement, be called unreasonable:

First, When a passion, such as hope or fear . . . is founded on the supposition of the existence of objects, which really do not exist. Secondly, When in exerting any passion in action, we chuse means insufficient for the design'd end, and deceive ourselves in our judgement of causes and effects. When a passion is neither founded on false suppositions, nor chuses means insufficient for the end, the understanding can neither justify nor condemn it. 'Tis not contrary to reason to prefer the destruction of the whole world to the scratching of my finger. 'Tis not contrary to reason for me to chuse my total ruin, to prevent the least uneasiness of an *Indian* or person wholly unknown to me. 'Tis as little contrary to reason to prefer even my own acknowledg'd lesser good to my greater, and have a more ardent affection for the former than the latter.[2]

Thus though a passion may be described as unreasonable when accompanied by a false judgement, even then it is not the passion that is unreasonable but the judgement. And on this account also, reason and passion can never oppose one another. For immediately we discover the falsity of the judgement, passion at once yields to reason. The actions, being recognized as based on false calculations, cease to be the required means for the satisfaction of our desire, and are no longer willed. The restraint which is exercised by the calm emotions, such as sympathy and benevolence, over the violent and transitory passions constitutes strength of will; but owing to the former being more known by their

[1] *Treatise*, II, III, iii; G, p. 195; S–B, pp. 415–16.
[2] Loc. cit.; cf. III, I, i; G, p. 236; S–B, p. 458.

effects than by immediate feeling they have been mistaken for the determinations of reason.

In the section of the *Treatise* entitled 'Moral Distinctions not deriv'd from Reason',[1] and also in Appendix I of the *Enquiry*, Hume repeats and reinforces this argument against the attempt to rationalize morals. Reason is the discovery of truth or falsehood; and truth or falsehood

> consists in an agreement or disagreement either to the *real* relations of ideas, or to *real* existence and matter of fact.[2]

As we have just seen, however, each passion is a unique modification of mind, an original fact complete in itself, and therefore reveals no relations either between itself and other passions or between itself and reality, that can be pronounced either true or false, either contrary or conformable to reason. Each passion imperiously demands the satisfaction of its instinct, and carries no reference to any reality beyond. But though the yielding to passion is never in any single instance contrary to reason, we still judge such satisfaction to be either good or bad, meritorious or the reverse, and in accordance with these judgements control our propensities. Does not that imply the activity of reason?

In treating of this problem Hume states what he regards as being the use of reason in knowledge and in morals. What greatly strengthens, and partly causes, belief in the rationalistic theory of morals is the fact that before deciding upon the merit of any particular action we have to consider all the separate relations, all the circumstances and situations of the persons concerned. Our procedure thus seems to be identical with the process by which we determine the proportion of lines in any triangle by examination of the relations of its parts. The analogy, however, is quite misleading. For whereas the mathematician from the known relations of the parts of the figure infers some unknown relation, in moral inquiries *all* the relations and circumstances must be submitted to us before we can pass sentence of blame or approbation.

> While we are ignorant whether a man were aggressor or not, how can we determine whether the person who killed him be

[1] *Treatise*, III, 1, i; cf. *Enquiry Concerning Morals*, appendix i.
[2] *Treatise*, III, 1, i; G, p. 236; S–B, p. 458.

criminal or innocent? But after every circumstance, every relation is known, the understanding has no further room to operate, nor any object on which to employ itself.[1]

When the whole set of circumstances is laid before the mind, we instinctively feel a new impression, such as exists nowhere outside the mind and therefore can never be discovered in the external circumstances of an action, in its consequences to ourselves or to others, namely, a new and original impression of affection or disgust, esteem or contempt, approbation or blame.

> Here is a matter of fact; but 'tis the object of feeling, not of reason. It lies in yourself, not in the object. So that when you pronounce any action or character to be vicious, you mean nothing, but that from the constitution of your nature you have a feeling or sentiment of blame upon the contemplation of it.[2]

> Thus the distinct boundaries and offices of *reason* and *taste* are easily ascertained. The former conveys the knowledge of truth

---

[1] *Enquiry Concerning Morals*, appendix i; G, p. 262; S–B, p. 290.

[2] *Treatise*, III, I, i; G, p. 245; S–B, p. 469. On the eve of the publication of this third volume of the *Treatise* (16 March 1740), Hume wrote as follows to Francis Hutcheson: 'I must consult you in a point of prudence. I have concluded a reasoning with the following sentences: "When you pronounce any action or character to be vicious, you mean nothing but that, from the particular constitution of your nature, you have a feeling or sentiment of blame from the contemplation of it. Vice and virtue, therefore, may be compared to sounds, colours, heat, and cold, which, according to modern philosophy are not qualities in objects, but perceptions in the mind. And this discovery in morals, like that other in physics, is to be regarded as a mighty advancement of speculative sciences, though like that too it has little or no influence on practice." Is not this a little too strong? I desire your opinion of it, though I cannot entirely promise to conform myself to it. I wish from my heart I could avoid concluding, that since morality, according to your opinion, as well as mine, is determined merely by sentiment, it regards only human nature and human life. . . . If morality were determined by reason, that is the same to all rational beings; but nothing but experience can assure us that the sentiments are the same. What experience have we with regard to superior beings? How can we ascribe to them any sentiments at all? They have implanted those sentiments in us for the conduct of life like our bodily sensations, which they possess not themselves.' Burton in quoting this letter (*Life of Hume*, vol. i, pp. 117–20) points out that the above passage appears in the *Treatise* with no other variation than the substitution of the word 'considerable' for 'mighty'.

and falsehood: the latter gives the sentiment of beauty and deformity, vice and virtue. The one discovers objects as they really stand in nature, without addition or diminution: the other has a productive faculty, and gilding or staining all natural objects with colours, borrowed from internal sentiment, raises in a manner a new creation. . . . From circumstances and relations, known or supposed, the former leads us to the discovery of the concealed and unknown: after all circumstances and relations are laid before us, the latter makes us feel from the whole a new sentiment of blame or approbation.[1]

In the sentences which follow the above quotation, Hume speaks of reason as an ultimate faculty which attains to truth and reality. And in so far as reason is analytic, discovering necessary relations between ideas, it is undoubtedly so. We have learned, however, in the *Treatise* that reason in its more important function as synthetic is exactly on a level with taste and equally incapable of supplying an absolute standard: the judgements to which both give rise are alike relative to 'the particular fabric and constitution of the human species'. Both also are creative faculties. For while the one produces the moral sentiments which condition all action, the other, as imagination, generates those synthetic principles which make human knowledge possible.

So far Hume's theory would seem to assign so minor a role to reason, as practically to eliminate it from the specifically moral sphere. For though it is required to pave the way for sentiment and give a proper discernment of its object, it would seem to play no part at all in determining any one of these objects or their relative value. When we pass, however, to Hume's treatment of the 'artificial' virtues and of the principle of utility upon which they rest, the other side of the truth comes into view, and is quite fairly emphasized. To the question why justice is approved, the only possible answer consists in a reference to its utility. Justice with all the machinery of law and government is necessary for the existence and advancement of society. Justice is indispensable, and therefore is approved. 'Reflections on the beneficial consequences of this virtue are the *sole* foundation of its merit'[2]. Utility

---

[1] *Enquiry Concerning Morals*, appendix i; G, p. 265; S–B, p. 294.
[2] *Enquiry Concerning Morals*, III, 1; G, p. 179; S–B, p. 183.

is the sole source of the moral approbation paid to fidelity, justice, veracity, integrity, and those other estimable and useful qualities and principles.[1]

The boundaries of justice still grow larger, in proportion to the largeness of men's views, and the force of their mutual connexions. History, experience, reason sufficiently instruct us in the natural progress of human sentiments, and in the gradual enlargement of our regards to justice, in proportion as we become acquainted with the extensive utility of that virtue.[2]

But why does justice receive *moral* approbation? If it is entirely based on utilitarian grounds, the approval must be due to reason, and that is contrary to Hume's fundamental thesis. To answer this question we must raise the further problem: Why does utility please? What is good for society as a whole does not necessarily in any particular case coincide with the good of the individual. That he should esteem justice is not therefore self-evident; and his approval really rests on the sympathetic instinct which makes the good of society appeal to him.

The ultimate ends of human actions can never, in any case, be accounted for by *reason*, but recommend themselves entirely to the sentiments and affections of mankind, without any dependence on the intellectual faculties.[3]

Utility is only a tendency to a certain end; and were the end totally indifferent to us, we should feel the same indifference towards the means. It is requisite a *sentiment* should here display the pernicious tendencies. . . . Here therefore *reason* instructs us in the several tendencies of actions, and *humanity* makes a distinction in favour of those which are useful and beneficial.[4]

Or as Hume states the same position in the *Treatise*:

Self-interest is the original motive to the establishment of justice: but a sympathy with public interest is the source of the moral approbation, which attends that virtue.[5]

[1] Ibid., III, ii; G, p. 196; S–B, p. 204.
[2] Ibid., III, i; G, p. 187; S–B, p. 192.
[3] *Enquiry Concerning Morals*, appendix i; G, p. 264; S–B, p. 293.
[4] Ibid., G, p. 259; S–B, p. 286.
[5] *Treatise*, III, ii, ii; G, p. 271; S–B, pp. 499-500.

Even the artificial virtues, therefore, rest on feeling and instinct, and save through them can acquire no moral sanction. Indeed only for convenience in distinguishing them from the more direct virtues can we name them artificial. They are influenced by the reflective activities of reason; but, as Hume remarks,

> in so sagacious an animal [as man], what necessarily arises from the exertion of his intellectual faculties may justly be esteemed natural.[1]

Hume considers, and rejects, the purely instinctive explanation of justice. That justice does not arise directly, like hunger, love of life, or attachment to offspring, from a simple original instinct, is obvious if we consider how intricate and often conventional are the laws, such as those of property, through which justice is realized. There would be required for that purpose

> ten thousand different instincts, and these employed about objects of the greatest intricacy and nicest discernment. For when a definition of *property* is required, that relation is found to resolve itself into any possession acquired by occupation, by industry, by prescription, by inheritance, by contract, etc. Can we think that nature, by an original instinct, instructs us in all these methods of acquisition?[2]

In any case, as Hume very justly adds,[3] we cannot believe that nature creates a rational creature and yet does not trust anything to the operation of his reason. Through the instinctive activities of reason nature adapts the other instincts of man to the complex requirements of social existence.

The remaining problem, how, if virtue is just this feeling of approbation, and every passion carries with it the approval of its own particular end, the control of one passion by another, or the condemnation of any particular passion in its opposition to another, is to be accounted for, lies to a great extent beyond the province of this article, but may be

[1] *Enquiry Concerning Morals*, appendix iii; G, p. 275; S–B, p. 307.
[2] Ibid., III, ii; G, pp. 194–5; S–B, pp. 201–2. Cf. *Treatise*, III, i, ii; G, p. 249; S–B, p. 473.
[3] *Enquiry*, loc. cit.

briefly indicated. Hume regards the social passions upon which the artificial virtues rest as the specifically moral sentiments.

> These principles, we must remark, are social and universal; they form, in a manner, the *party* of humankind against vice or disorder, its common enemy.[1]

> Avarice, ambition, vanity, and all passions vulgarly, though improperly, comprised under the denomination of *self-love*, are here excluded from our theory concerning the origin of morals, not because they are too weak, but because they have not a proper direction for that purpose.[2]

They produce different sentiments in different minds, and the same object will not satisfy more than one individual; whereas the social sentiments are identical in all men, and the same object rouses them in all human creatures. Language is moulded upon this obvious distinction, and invents a peculiar set of terms to express those judgements of censure and approbation which arise from the social sentiments and which are developed in the artificial virtues through considerations of general utility.

> Virtue and Vice become then known; morals are recognized; certain general ideas are framed of human conduct and behaviour. . . . And by such universal principles are the particular sentiments of self-love frequently controlled and limited.[3]

Hume might well have named the artificial virtues the rational virtues, and so without giving up the primacy of feeling, have more completely recognized the regulating power of reason. Each and every passion is in itself, taken generally, perfectly legitimate. Reason can neither justify nor condemn it. But since life, especially social life, demands organization, we learn to govern our various passions in the light of those general utilitarian considerations which constitute the rules of personal prudence and of social justice. The controlling force in such cases is the universal social sentiments upon which the appeal to utility rests.[4] These senti-

---

[1] *Enquiry Concerning Morals*, IX, 1; G, p. 251; S–B, p. 275.
[2] Ibid., G, p. 248; S–B, p. 271.
[3] Ibid., G, p. 250; S–B, p. 274.
[4] Ibid. VI, 1; G, p. 222; S–B, p. 239.

ments are originally weaker than the selfish passions, but are so strengthened both by private affections, such as the love of fame or reputation, and by various social influences, as finally to overpower them. Thus, as Hume explicitly states both in the *Treatise* and in the *Enquiry*, reason and sentiment concur in almost all moral action.

> Both these causes are intermix'd in our judgements of morals; after the same manner as they are in our decisions concerning most kinds of external beauty: Tho' I am also of opinion, that reflections on the tendencies of actions have by far the greatest influence, and determine all the great lines of our duty.[1]

Feeling determines all our ends: reason decides when and how these can best be attained. Though reason is 'only the slave of the passions', it is in this subordinate function as indispensable as feeling. Without displacing the instincts, it enables them to fulfil their human function.

Hume's theory of reason and instinct thus runs throughout his whole philosophy; and the unity to which it enables us to reduce his system seems to me to justify the importance which I have ascribed to it. His sensationalist principle, that all the ultimate data of knowledge are detached impressions, is equally fundamental, but is consistent with the most divergent views of the constitution of our complex experience. Only when we have recognized the important functions which Hume ascribes to feeling and instinct, and the highly complex emotions and propensities which he is willing to regard as ultimate and unanalysable, are we in a position to do justice to his new, and very original, conception of the nature and conditions of experience. Hume may, indeed, be regarded, even more truly than Kant, as the father of all those subsequent philosophies that are based on an opposition between thought and feeling, truth and validity, actuality and worth. Though his real position is positivism or naturalism, it is not of that familiar type which seeks to limit knowledge to material phenomena, but rather is akin to

---

[1] *Treatise*, III, III, i; G, p. 247; S–B, p. 590. Cf. *Enquiry Concerning Morals*, i; G, p. 172; S–B, pp. 172–3. Reason is here used in its broadest sense as including both its analytic and its synthetic form. But as the estimation of the consequences of an action involves reasoning about matters of fact according to the principle of causality, the latter is, even in moral inquiry, the more important.

the broader, more humanistic, philosophy which was developed by Comte in his later days, and which rests the hopes of the future on those sciences which more immediately concern our human nature. For Hume's disbelief in speculative physics and in metaphysics is more than counterbalanced by a belief in the possibility of a philosophical science of human nature, and of the special sciences of ethics, aesthetics, politics and political economy. These, he believes, are sciences which have a sure foundation in human experience.

> So great is the force of laws, and of particular forms of government, and so little dependence have they on the humours and tempers of men, that consequences almost as general and certain may sometimes be deduced from them, as any which the mathematical sciences afford us.[1]

Undoubtedly it is the other, and purely negative, side of his philosophy that has exercised most influence in the past; but more and more attention is being bestowed upon his constructive views, and these are certainly capable of independent development. Even if we reject the dogmatic sensationalism which he shares in common with Kant, this positive side of his teaching may still retain its value. At the same time we must regard it as doubtful whether the attempts that are being made to divorce this teaching from the metaphysical scepticism which serves as its foundation, and to use it in developing an idealistic conception of the universe, are likely to be successful. The *Treatise on Human Nature* may perhaps be regarded as still remaining the best commentary on such theories.

---

[1] *Essays*, iii, 'That Politics may be reduced to a Science'; G, p. 99. Compare also the essay 'Of the Standard of Taste', and those on political economy.

Avenarius' Philosophy of Pure Experience[1]

I

AVENARIUS propounds his philosophy from a standpoint whose originality borders on paradox. While all previous philosophers have regarded experience as awaiting interpretation through metaphysical conceptions, Avenarius holds pure experience to be self-intelligible, and the existing metaphysical theories to be the only facts that call for philosophical explanation. Sometimes he describes his philosophy as the philosophy of pure experience, and sometimes as 'empiriocriticism'. The former title refers to its content, the latter to its method. He claims that, as regards method, it combines and transcends the philosophies of Hume and Kant. The resulting system is as original in its positive teaching as it is novel in orientation. For though in certain aspects it is closely akin to the metaphysical idealism of Spinoza and Hegel, and recently in this country has been employed as a buttress to the Bradleian philosophy, its most competent critic has described it as the latest, and, in the present state of knowledge, the only tenable form of materialism.[2] A system so strangely affiliated is, even apart from its intrinsic merits, sufficiently remarkable to claim attention. In this article I shall state and criticize the main principles of Avenarius' philosophy. But in so doing I shall consider them only from the point of view of the problem of knowledge, and as leading up to

[1] *Mind*, vol. xv, N.S., no. 57.
[2] Wundt: 'Über naiven und kritischen Realismus' in *Philosophische Studien*, vol. xiii, pp. 334–5, 349 ff.

the statement of his theory of the introjectionist argument. That theory, which has been adopted by several English writers, I reserve for detailed criticism in a second article.[1]

The assumptions which determine Avenarius' central problem may, if somewhat freely stated, be expressed in the following manner. Nothing exists save experience; and the fundamental characteristic of the content of experience is space. The self apprehends itself as an embodied existence, and so as spatially related to the objects around it. All its perceptions, thoughts and feelings, have reference direct or indirect either to the body or to its environment. Now the spatial world thus experienced varies together with one particular part of itself, namely, with the brain. And this relation is mutual; change in either involves change in both; they stand in functional relation, varying simultaneously with one another. Since nothing exists save as experienced, and since as experienced it involves change in the brain, the relation must be of this nature. On the other hand, however, objects are causally related to the brain, and by their changes produce changes in it. This causal relation as involving sequence and implying independent self-centred existence holds only in the forward order, and therefore excludes the possibility of simultaneous variation. The fundamental problem of metaphysics is to reconcile these two standpoints, the attitude of pure experience with the standpoint adopted in physics and

---

[1] The following are the titles and dates of Avenarius' works: *Über die Phasen des Spinozischen Pantheismus*, 1868. *Philosophie als Denken der Welt gemäss dem Prinzip des kleinsten Kraftmasses: Prolegomena zu einer Kritik der reinen Erfahrung*, 1876. *Kritik der reinen Erfahrung*, vol. i, 1888; vol. ii, 1890. *Der Menschliche Weltbegriff*, 1891. 'Bemerkungen zum Begriff des Gegenstandes der Psychologie' in *Vierteljahrsschrift für wissenschaftliche Philosophie*, vol. xviii (1894), vol. xix (1895). A very useful summary of the *Kritik* is given by Emil Koch in the *Archiv für systematische Philosophie*, vol. iv (1898). Petzoldt has published (1900) the first volume of his *Einführung in die Philosophie der reinen Erfahrung*. It gives an admirable account of Avenarius' position as embodied in the *Kritik*. Its value is, however, seriously impaired by its strange neglect of the *Menschliche Weltbegriff*. It does not seem to contain a single reference to that work, nor consequently to the more purely metaphysical aspects of Avenarius' philosophy. Petzoldt's second volume appeared in 1904, but I have not been able to consult it. An excellent and detailed criticism of Avenarius' philosophy is given by Wundt in the articles above referred to. Carstanjen has contributed an article on Avenarius to *Mind*, N.S., vol. vi.

physiology. How can the whole vary simultaneously with a part of itself, and with a part which is causally dependent for its changes upon its relations to the rest of that whole? Avenarius will have nothing to do with the solution offered by subjective idealism—that our experience as purely subjective may vary simultaneously with those brain-states which real external objects have produced. That solution rests on a dualism which Avenarius denounces as ungrounded and absolutely false. Our experienced world is reality, and its functional relation to its own component, the brain, must therefore be reconcilable in some other manner with the equally undoubted causal relations of that brain to the objects external to it.

Avenarius' detailed analysis of the natural point of view, of the attitude, that is to say, of pure and complete experience, and of its relation to the scientific, I shall now proceed to state. As far as possible I shall avoid the technicalities of Avenarius' special terminology.

I with all my thoughts and feelings find myself in the midst of a spatial environment.[1] This environment is composed of manifold elements which stand in relations of dependence to one another. Within it I also find my fellow-men. They interfere with the common environment, altering certain parts of it and maintaining others, and of all their actions they through words and gestures reveal the intention and reason. In everything they agree with myself. I accordingly believe that they are beings like myself, and that I am myself a being like them. The spatial world which thus includes both myself and others is for ordinary consciousness a something given, existing, familiar, known, lasting on in thought, constantly rediscovered as fact, and in all its repetitions remaining the same.

This natural consciousness is composed of two elements which from a logical point of view are of very different value, namely, of an experience and of an hypothesis. The experienced—*das Vorgefundene*—includes, as has just been said, the bodies of my fellow-men. The hypothesis lies in the interpretation which I give to the movements of my fellow-men, in the interpretation that they are *expressive*, that is, that they are dependent on feeling and will. This hypothetical element can be eliminated. I can, by an effort, think of my fellow-men as being merely

[1] *Der Menschliche Weltbegriff*, § 6 ff.

automata, extraordinarily complex but without thought and feeling. Our reason for rejecting this attitude is not its unnaturalness or its unfruitfulness. Apart altogether from the difficulties of consistently developing such a view, there is a valid reason for regarding it as false. For, if the elimination of the hypothesis is suggested by its formal logical character as hypothesis (in distinction from experience), its retention is enforced by its actual agreement with experience. In the sole case in which through personal experience I am acquainted in all its relations with the movements of that mechanism which is named 'man', I find it in definite relations to thoughts, feelings, volitions, etc. The denial of the hypothesis therefore involves a theory, equally hypothetical, which in its content is further removed from my own experience than the hypothesis itself. And, since the content of my assumption is the matter of another individual's experience, though the hypothesis introduces a duality or plurality, it does not cause a dualism in the philosophical sense. Nothing is assumed which is not or cannot be experienced either by myself or by others.

The proof that the natural consciousness involves no dualism demands, however, a fuller analysis of its various elements. The first distinction which Avenarius notes is that between things and thoughts.[1] Here, again, there is duality but no dualism. The portrait of a friend which is before me is comparable with the appearance of my friend which I recall in thought. I can note that the features, etc., are the same or different, and can state the outcome of the comparison as similarity or the reverse. If we interpolate the image between thing and thought we have a series the members of which are comparable with one another. And being, as the natural consciousness admits, thus relatively comparable with one another, there cannot exist that absolute heterogeneity between thoughts and things which some philosophers have asserted. The chief difference between them is, indeed, merely one of time. The sense-experience of, say, a tree, is a *first* experience; the tree as it reappears in thought or image is a *second* experience. Were the two absolutely different experiences we could no longer speak of the image as the reappearance of the original experience, and yet at the same time

[1] *Der Menschliche Weltbegriff*, § 19; *Vierteljahrsschrift*, vol. xix, 'Bemerkungen', pp. 2–3, § 121.

we should have to make it dependent for its occurrence on what, as absolutely different from it, could never account for it.

Avenarius' next distinction is between what he names the absolute and the relative points of view.[1] Both may be adopted without desertion of pure experience. In the absolute point of view the self is left out of account, the parts of the environment being apprehended in and for themselves. A tree, for instance, is then apprehended as existing in space in definite relations to other things, as changing with the seasons, and as being in all these relations and changes independent of the presence of the self. It may even be known as having been planted before the self was born. The world thus experienced is apprehended as having a past that survives itself in thought and a future that anticipates itself in knowledge, and similarly as having spatial limits that may be transcended in imagination and thought. On the other hand, from the relative point of view the tree is considered not in and for itself, but in itself and for me. It is then perceived that my apprehension of it varies together with it. If its branches are bent or broken my perceptions vary accordingly. Further knowledge, however, reveals that the perception depends not only upon the tree but also upon particular parts of the 'self', namely upon the sense-organs, nerves and brain. Experience reveals these relations of dependence just as it reveals the tree. When the causal series between the tree and the brain-state is not completed, when, for instance, it is interrupted by injury to the nerve-fibres, the self can have no apprehension of the tree. The perception depends, therefore, only mediately on the object, and immediately on changes in the nervous system. And the relative point of view therefore reveals three relations of dependence: (1) between the tree and its perception; (2) between the tree and the nervous system; (3) between the nervous system and the perception. For all three the same formula holds: if the first term be changed the second undergoes corresponding changes. But only in form (2) is the relation causal or physical, and so a special case of the law of the conservation of energy. The two other forms (1 and 3) are logical functional relations.

Much of Avenarius' best work has consisted in developing a new view of the nature both of mental and of physiological processes, and so

[1] *Der Menschliche Weltbegriff*, § 21.

in restating the parallelist theory in a thoroughly original manner. He was dissatisfied with the use made by the traditional psychology of the distinction between knowing, feeling and willing, and also with the mental atomism of the associationists. The fundamental characteristic of the mental life is, he holds, that it falls into more or less distinguishable series which in their general features are of a fixed and universal type. Each series originates in a feeling of pain, opposition, or uncertainty. The mind then desires or strives or wills to remove this unpleasant experience; and as a consequence the series of mental experiences sooner or later, through complex mental processes or through simple habitual actions, as the case may be, terminates in the feeling of rest, successful action, and certainty. 'We feel lightened and exalted, satisfied and freed.' Such series, which are repeated as often as mental experience occurs, Avenarius has named 'vital series'.

Avenarius conceives the brain-processes as being of an exactly analogous character.[1] He makes no assumptions as to their special nature; in particular, he rejects as hypothetical, or at least as needless for his purpose, the picture-mechanism of cells and fibres upon which the associationists rely. His only postulates are that the brain, as a living thing, requires both nourishment and exercise, and that in response to the stimuli of a hostile environment it strives to maintain a 'vital maximum'. Practically, however, he makes the further general assumption that it is capable by internal organization and outward action of progressively increasing its possible maximum. The ideal maximum would be reached in complete adaptation to an all-comprehensive environment. Physiological processes therefore correspond in type to the mental series. A vital disturbance is either cancelled by other internal changes or removed by a motor response. The stimulus, however, which starts the series need not be, and usually is not, merely injurious. Work is as necessary as nourishment, activity as indispensable as rest. Through response to stimuli the brain organizes more and more complex vital series which by enabling it to maintain itself with greater ease in the given environment release energy for more extended activities. In determining, by general dialectical argument, the various types to

---

[1] When the series are physiological he calls them *independent* vital series, and when mental, *dependent* vital series. His reason for this will appear shortly.

which such vital series must conform, Avenarius professes to have sketched the programme of future physiological research.

From this point of view Avenarius states the parallelism of psychical and physical in quite a fresh light. He frees the doctrine from dependence upon any particular set of views as to the constitution and working of the nervous system, and yet brings the two series more closely together than had ever been done on any previous theory. Indeed, just on this account, he maintains, his view is not properly describable as parallelism. For, while parallelism implies dualism, the relation which he himself traces between the mental and the physiological series is of the same nature as that which exists between the factors in a mathematical function. There is a point for point correspondence which is, he claims, absolutely complete. In this logical functional relation there is no more dualism than exists between the premisses of an argument and the conclusion in which they result.

One very important feature of his position remains for consideration—a feature which is very puzzling to any reader who seeks to approach it from the point of view of the *Menschliche Weltbegriff*. Petzoldt's suggestion[1] that Avenarius formulated his theory of vital series through examination of mental experience, and then interpreted the brain-processes in the light of such experience, is undoubtedly correct. None the less Avenarius maintains as the fundamental principle of his *Kritik* that the only hope of a scientific treatment of mental experience lies in the development of physiology on the lines which he has sketched. Only through a scientific understanding of the brain in its relation to environment can we acquire knowledge of the ultimate nature of experience as a whole. This part of his philosophy appears to have been formed previous to the views developed in the *Menschliche Weltbegriff*, and to be uncritically based on the scientific teaching prevalent in his day.[2] Being convinced of the closed nature of the physical world, as

---

[1] *Einführung in die Philosophie der reinen Erfahrung*, vol. i, p. 93.

[2] This assertion seems to be justified, though of course Avenarius, like Mach, seeks to vindicate his position by reference to the supreme principle of simplicity or economy (cf. Carstanjen in *Mind*, N.S., vi, p. 466). As everything within the physical world can, he contends, be explained in accordance with the principle of the conservation of energy, the introduction of spirit or any other 'metaphysical' factor is needless and

obedient in all its changes to the principle of the conservation of energy, he asserts as ascertained fact, that consciousness can neither intervene to modify a brain-process nor emerge from it as its effect. In this respect he is a thorough-going parallelist. The body as an automaton conditions the most complex actions in the same complete manner as the merely reflex. All human activity, the highest as well as the lowest, thought as well as bodily action, can on its physiological side be interpreted in the same manner as the reflex functioning of the headless frog.[1] The nature of brain-processes must therefore be determined without any reference to the accompanying mental activities; and as scientific method is limited to the domain marked out by the principle of the conservation of energy, only through this prior determination of the brain-processes can the mental life, which runs a parallel course, be brought within its sphere. The analogies which are established between the cerebral and the mental series co-ordinate them in the closest manner, and in their particular nature are fitted to apply throughout the whole range of mental experience. The brain of an individual is, in Avenarius' technical phraseology, the 'empiriokritischer Substitutionswert' of that individual.[2] Since everything which happens to, or is experienced by, the individual is adequately represented by corresponding processes in the brain, the brain can be substituted *functionally* for the individual. Exhaustive knowledge of the one yields completed knowledge of both. Stated in terms of Avenarius' monistic view of experience, this amounts to the assertion that experience in all its concreteness, that is, as mental, varies in exact correspondence with this particular part of itself, and can therefore be explained through it. This is the line of argument developed in the *Kritik*. In the first volume Avenarius analyses the independent vital series, and in the second volume applies his results in explanation of the conscious life.

---

therefore illegitimate. But the belief that the principle is actually sufficient seems to be due to an uncritical extension of results gained in purely physical inquiry to the more complex phenomena of life and consciousness. Cf. *Philosophie als Denken der Welt gemäss dem Prinzip des kleinsten Kraftmasses.*

[1] Cf. *Kritik*, vol. ii, p. 486, note 153.
[2] *Der Menschliche Weltbegriff*, § 158.

To revert, now, to Avenarius' distinction between the absolute and the relative points of view. His position requires to be carefully interpreted, and would seem to be as follows. All complete experience involves the relative point of view. Though the absolute standpoint states nothing which is not true, and though in experience we apprehend objects as independent of the self, we never experience them save in relation to the self. The absolute standpoint is therefore reached only by abstraction from complete experience. Further, Avenarius refuses to recognize any such thing as the perception *of* an object. The only reality that can exist is experience, and experience has the two inseparable aspects, inner and outer, psychical and physical, perception and object perceived, thought and object thought about. But to avoid the misleading connotation of these familiar terms, he names the two aspects 'character' and 'content'. To the variable aspect of character belong feeling, perceiving, conjecturing, believing, knowing, etc., the form, whatever it may be, in which we experience anything. As content, on the other hand, he classifies everything which is felt, perceived, conjectured, believed, known, etc. In the relation, character–content, each aspect may vary independently of the other. On the one hand, we may perceive, believe, know, one and the same content; on the other hand, we may take up the same mental attitude to very different things at different periods of our lives. Since experience as character may itself, however, become content of experience, the difference between the two aspects is in the end only relative.

This distinction of subjective and objective aspects must not be confused with the very different distinction between self and not-self.[1] As character or immediacy is a universal aspect of *everything* experienced, the self and its constituents cannot be experienced more immediately than the not-self. The environment is not given *to* the self. The ego does not find objects before it.[2] The self as well as the not-self is located in space. They are equally objective, and must be apprehended in exactly the same manner as spatially related within the unity of objective experience. The self differs from other contents in space only through

[1] Cf. *Der Menschliche Weltbegriff*, §§ 138 ff.

[2] Cf. *Der Menschliche Weltbegriff*, §§ 143 ff.; *Vierteljahrsschrift*, vol. xviii, 'Bemerkungen', pp. 145–6, §§ 22 ff.; pp. 151–2, §§ 40–41; p. 406, § 81.

its greater richness and manifoldness, especially as regards the inter-relations of its thoughts. Though the self is in the same space with its environment, thoughts which have outlived the environment which they previously constituted form one whole with it, and so stand in highly complex spatial and temporal relations to one another and to the environment which is present here and now. These thoughts, however, as has already been pointed out, have the objectivity that belongs to every content, and are therefore experienced in the same manner as any sensible object in space. Everything in the self, and accordingly the self as a whole, is experienced as having the same kind of existence as its spatial environment. Here again, therefore, as in the distinction between characters and contents, there is duality but no dualism. While the opposition of characters and contents is a distinction between aspects inseparably involved in every single experience, the opposition of self and not-self is a distinction of kindred groups of concrete contents within the field of objective experience. Avenarius' view of the self is obviously determined by the same naturalistic intention as that of Hume. But while Hume contends that we can know nothing of the ultimate nature of the self, Avenarius seeks to prove that there is nothing in the self which cannot be known by a possible extension of our present experience.

The brain is experienced as independent in the same sense as 'material' bodies.[1] Everything, in fact, which is not character is experienced as permanent existence. Avenarius therefore contrasts the dependent characters with the independent vibrations of the nervous system. The characters are dependent not merely in the sense of existing only when and as experienced by the individual, but also as involving the actual existence of the corresponding nervous states in his body at that particular moment. The subject-matter of inquiry remains, however, objective throughout: all we have to do with is, on the one hand, the causal relation of objects to one another and to the nervous system, and on the other the functional relation of states of the nervous system to the complete experience which includes this whole spatial environment with all its causal relations within itself. Throughout we are dealing with reality,

---

[1] The brain can itself be brought within the experienced field by opening the skull and making a suitable arrangement of mirrors. Cf. *Der Menschliche Weltbegriff*, § 129.

and with a reality in which there appears no dualism, and therefore no insoluble problems. The only possible questions are questions which can be solved by a possible extension of experience. Insoluble problems only arise when the true and natural and primitive attitude is departed from, and such departure is in all cases due to that illegitimate process to which Avenarius has given the name, introjection.

But consideration of this falsifying process of introjection I must defer until I have stated more completely Avenarius' own view of reality. To illustrate the truth of his assertion that there is nothing which need lead to radical alteration of pure experience, and that all questions which are insoluble from its point of view are problems which involve illegitimate assumptions, Avenarius takes the following crucial instance.[1] Two individuals, one of whom is red-blind, apprehend an object as being numerically the same for both, and name it cinnabar. They agree that the number of vibrations which it communicates to the ether is such and such. They also agree that these vibrations are independent of their presence or of their apprehension of the cinnabar. But in regard to the colour they differ: the cinnabar is red to one, black to the other. Now, since these statements as to the colour of the cinnabar contradict one another, both cannot be true, and we seem forced to the conclusion that one or both experiences must be false and therefore merely subjective.

As we have already observed, two points of view are possible without desertion of pure experience. From the absolute point of view, each individual describes reality just as he finds it. But since this, as in the above instance, often leads to contradictory assertions, we are frequently forced to reinterpret it in the fuller light of the relative point of view. We preserve the simpler attitude so long as it works; when it breaks down we correct its conclusions from the more concrete standpoint. Taking into account the relation of the cinnabar to the self we observe that only when the vibrations caused by it affect the nerve-endings, and thereby the brain, do we perceive the coloured cinnabar. Though all observers apprehend the same cinnabar, each apprehends it in relation to a different self, and therefore, it may be, differently. There is, indeed, no fundamental difference between the contradictory perceptions of

[1] *Der Menschliche Weltbegriff* (Anmerkung 58).

colour and the varying apprehensions of shape and size at differing distances. In both cases there is difference in the spatial relations and therefore in the causal processes involved. That this difference lies in the one case within the body and in the other case partly outside it is no fundamental difference.

But, it may be urged, this pretended solution is really an admission of the truth of the objection. Throughout the argument spatial arrangement has been assumed to possess a reality that can be accurately defined and which is known as conditioning the apprehension of colour or shape. Since the nature of the vibrations in ether is recognized as constant while the colour is individual, the former alone supplies the means of determining the nature of the cinnabar *as it is in itself*. In a similar manner our knowledge of the actual size of an object enables us to neutralize differences of subjective appearance.

Now there are here involved two distinct questions. First, the more general problem, which of the many qualities of bodies afford the most economical and effective means of scientifically describing them and of determining their causal relations to one another. Science has answered that question by showing how all qualitative differences are best explained by reference to the spatial and quantitative. And that has been achieved through preservation, with the least possible change, of the absolute standpoint of pure experience. The attitude carries with it no assertion as to the reality or unreality of the secondary qualities. The problem of natural science consists in following out to ideal completion (a completion possible only in thought though always in terms of actual experience) of those quantitative relations which are given us as holding between objects in space.

The second problem, that which alone concerns us in this inquiry, is as to the significance of the relative standpoint which in certain cases requires to be adopted even by the scientist, and which constitutes that modification in the absolute standpoint which I have referred to above as being the least possible. Does the relative standpoint imply that the vibrations which condition colour may be distinguished from colour as reality from appearance, in the same sense in which it may be said that the difference of the white colour of my paper before the perception of a red card from the green colour of the paper after the perception resolves itself into the distinction between a really white and an apparently green object? Such a statement must involve one or other of the three following positions:[1] (1) If the cinnabar communicates a certain rate of vibration to the ether, and the sense-organ stimulated by these vibrations is completely normal, then the cinnabar *is* red; but if the organ is abnormal it *appears* different, for instance, to the red-blind black. (2) If the cinnabar communicates a certain rate of vibration to the ether, it depends on the special nature of the sense-organ whether the cinnabar *appears* red or black. (3) If the cinnabar by means of ether vibrations stimulates our nervous system and thereby causes the sensation of red or black, then these colours, and colours in general, are quite incomparable with their cause, and accordingly are not properties descriptive of the cinnabar as an actually existing thing, but only of its *appearance*.

No one of these three positions is tenable. As regards the first position, the statement that the cinnabar appears but is not black to the red-blind observer is contrary to fact. The statement can only be made by a normal individual who in setting himself at the point of view of the abnormal observer still retains his own. In describing the abnormal as unreal, he illegitimately assumes that difference of standpoint (and that in this case means for Avenarius different constitution of the nervous system) should involve no difference in the content apprehended; in other words, that the object exists out of relation to the self, and that it has a particular nature and colour in and by itself. The second position involves the same fallacy in an aggravated form. The illegitimate interpretation first made by the normal observer of the object of the abnormal observer is, by a further confusion, extended to the object of his own observation. It therefore misrepresents normal perception as completely as the first position misrepresents the abnormal. The third position, while equally untenable, brings the determining assumptions— and they are of course those involved in the process of introjection— more clearly into view. We may, in the first place, note that even if colour is an effect of which ether-vibrations are the cause, that does not justify us in describing it as appearance. An effect is equally real with its cause. Before colour can be described in that way it must be set in

[1] Loc. cit., § vii.

opposition to something actual, and that is only possible through introjection. The objects apprehended must be regarded as merely representations in our heads, as effects produced by the real external objects. These external objects will constitute reality: the representations will be mere appearance. It is then only a question of consistency how far this view is to be carried—whether the ether, the object and the whole spatial environment including the brain itself, are not also merely representations in us, or rather representations in the representation of my head 'Vorstellungskopf in meiner Kopfvorstellung.'[1]

While still deferring consideration of the process of introjection, the following observations may be made.[2] When it is asserted that an object produces a perception in us, it is assumed that it acts on the sense-organs and brain, and also upon that inner something, soul or consciousness, which introjection adds. What now is meant by 'acting on'? It covers the conception of physical causation. There is a continuous causal relation between the object and the resulting process in the brain. This causal relation will not, however, carry us from the brain-state to consciousness. For when followed further it only leads back again through the muscles to the external world. The empirical fact that our apprehension of the object varies together with the brain-state has led to the quite illegitimate assumption, for which there is no evidence, that it likewise is an effect caused by the object. We transform the merely logical functional relation, according to which our world as a whole and in all its parts varies together with changes in this particular part of itself, into a causal relation between our world conceived as an effect and the brain as its external cause. We duplicate the one given reality into an external world and its internal representation.

The most, then, we can ever do is simply to describe what we actually find as constituting reality.[3] From the absolute standpoint we describe the object just as it is presented, and from the relative point of view, while considering it as a term in a relation whose other term is the self, we must also still describe it just as it exists for us. In the latter case, however, the observer no longer asserts without limitation 'the cinnabar

---

[1] Loc. cit., § viii.
[2] Loc. cit., §§ ix–xi.
[3] Loc. cit., § xii.

is red' (or 'is black', as the case may be), but 'to my eye, or for me, it is red'.[1] By this limiting addition the contradictions involved in the absolute standpoint are removed. So long as the errors of introjection are avoided, this relativism is perfectly unambiguous, and it is also the only possible or consistent attitude. But when misled by a dualistic distinction between the absolute and the relative, between appearance and reality, we ask: What is the object in and for itself?—we raise an unreal, because self-contradictory, problem. And it does not matter whether in answering this question we take up a positive or an agnostic attitude. The two statements—'The object in and for itself is neither red nor black'; 'The object in and for itself we do not and cannot know' —are alike untenable.

The sole remaining question, properly stated, is not how the brain, viewed as an external and independent reality, is related to consciousness as something distinct from the brain and dependent upon it, but why our experience as a whole should vary together with one particular part of itself. And, as we have seen, Avenarius seems to hold that this problem is on a level with the question, why the three angles of a triangle should vary together with one another. The laws of logical functional relation between experience and the brain, when discovered, are ultimate facts, beyond which nothing remains to be known. Even the suggestion of the problem implies unconscious reminiscence of dualistic metaphysic. In his *Kritik der reinen Erfahrung* Avenarius, as I have also already indicated, has formulated the laws which he conceives as holding between the brain and the world which includes it, that is to say, the laws according to which the brain as a reacting agent either neutralizes or uses for its self-maintenance the stimuli which are constantly arising from its own internal changes and from the spatial world within which it lies. In accordance with these laws it progressively adapts itself by internal organization to a more and more comprehensive environment, and so preserves itself through change in relative equilibrium. And as there is a logical functional relation between the states of the brain and our experience as a whole, these laws express the ultimate truth regarding the self in its relation to reality.

I cannot here enter upon Avenarius' 'physiology of knowledge'

[1] Loc. cit., § xiv.

beyond indicating in the briefest manner how he applies his biological laws in explanation of experience as a whole. I may cite his theory of protective concepts. When the brain is unable to adapt itself to certain stimuli it drains them off through channels (*Schutzformen*) specially organized for the purpose. In so doing it sacrifices energy, not for the sake of increasing its resources, but merely in order, as far as possible, to preserve itself unchanged in this hostile environment. Similarly, when the mind meets with facts which conflict with its dominant concepts, it invents *Beibegriffe*, that is to say, modifies its concepts in such a way as to neutralize the conflict in the simplest possible manner and with the least possible change in its accustomed attitude.[1] The concepts, or attitudes of mind, with which the facts of experience conflict are, according to Avenarius, in all cases ultimately due to that process of introjection which has given rise to the animism of primitive man. The spiritualism which results from the animistic conceptions of the soul and of God leads by its own disintegration, as these conceptions are progressively modified to fit the facts of experience, through agnosticism back to naturalism.[2] But further consideration of this view of animism, the understanding of which, and of Avenarius' view of its relation to introjection, is absolutely essential for a clear conception of his philosophy, I must defer until the next article. Some preliminary criticisms may now, however, be passed upon Avenarius' general position.

Most readers of Avenarius' *Menschliche Weltbegriff* will probably agree that, however convincing as criticism, it is tantalizingly illusive in its positive teaching. So long as we seek to interpret his theory of experi-

---

[1] Avenarius' test of truth is the immanent idealist criterion, viz. the degree to which a suggested idea harmonizes with the rest of our experience. The statics and dynamics in which this criterion results are described with remarkable subtlety in what is one of the most interesting parts of the *Kritik* (vol. ii, pp. 258–97).

[2] The following concrete instance may be quoted as illustrating Avenarius' view of the transition from spiritualism to agnosticism: 'A single inconceivability—as, for instance, in philosophy the relation of divine omniscience to freedom of the human will, or in daily life an undeserved affliction or an unusually terrible death-agony—is "solved" by reference to the *universal* "incomprehensibility of God's essence and will" or to the *universal* "unknowableness" of his providence . . . the same result is attained by substitution of the "insufficiency and incompetence of the human faculty of reason" ' (*Kritik*, vol. ii, p. 281. Cf. pp. 296–7).

ence in the form in which it is avowedly presented, namely, as genuinely realistic, it eludes all clear comprehension: its whole meaning seems to be exhausted in negation of the subjectivism which it overthrows. It is only when we translate Avenarius' technical terms into more familiar language that we discover where the real source of the mystification lies. Avenarius has diverted attention from the defects of his position by directing his main attack against the very weakness which is fatal to his own theory. Thereby he surprises the reader into admissions which he could never have elicited by direct argument, and which are indeed inconsistent with the central tenets of his philosophy. The general criticism which I shall seek to justify is, therefore, that Avenarius' true metaphysical position appears only in the physiology of the *Kritik*, and that, though his attempt in the *Menschliche Weltbegriff* to defend that crudely realistic position, and to restate it in a tenable form, has resulted in a most interesting and valuable criticism of subjective idealism, that realistic position itself involves the theory which he rejects. Owing to his refusal to recognize any metaphysical distinction between appearance and reality he cannot escape the position which he so successfully attacks. For, though he asserts character and content to be inseparable, in admitting, as he was bound to do, that content can vary independently of character, he relapses into the dualism which cuts off all possibility of escape from the subjectivist *impasse*.

At starting Avenarius formulates as self-evident, requiring no detailed analysis, the far-reaching distinction between character and content; and by a quite illegitimate use of it he establishes that view of the self which is all-important for his naturalistic philosophy. By identifying subjectivity with character he is enabled to treat subjectivity as an aspect that colours, quite indifferently, any and every objective content, and therefore as yielding nothing that can constitute the self as a self-centred reacting agent.[1] The same consequence is reinforced by his classification of such different experiences as feeling, desire or volition, and knowledge, under the general heading of character. The whole problem of the nature of characters and of their relation to contents, the problem,

[1] Even desires and feelings are *found* or *given* in the same manner as any other experiences. Each has its twofold aspect of character and content. Cf. references given above, in note 2, p. 147.

that is to say, of the relation of subject and object to one another, is dismissed in the most casual manner in a few short paragraphs. And having thus assumed the right to treat subjectivity as a universal aspect of all possible experience, he has no great difficulty in establishing a purely naturalistic view of the self as merely one group of concrete contents within the field of objective experience. Throughout the *Kritik*, and indeed in all cases in which he is not directly engaged in defending his monistic view of experience, he practically equates the self with the brain. As the brain is an agent that reacts upon its environment and yet at the same time is an object existing in space, it very conveniently combines his two conflicting views of the self—as subject or character when it is felt as active and as self or content when it is experienced as object. In this way he is enabled in the *Kritik* to adopt, from a physiological point of view, that subjective and active standpoint which in his *Menschliche Weltbegriff* he by implication entirely negates.

Throughout the whole discussion the vagueness of the term experience stands him in good stead. Sometimes it means experiencing and at other times the experienced, the latter meaning being emphasized when the nature of the self is in question. These two meanings of the term experience practically coincide with his important distinction between the absolute and the relative standpoints; and these two points of view are not in his philosophy really reconciled. For when he allows as legitimate the demand that experience be ideally completed in thought, he makes an admission which he cannot successfully combine with his assertion that nothing exists save in relation to the self. The ideal completion of given reality which results from the analysis of material bodies into elements which no human senses can apprehend, or from following the earth back to a time when no human being existed upon it, is, strictly, not a completion of experience but only of what is experienced. It completes only one of the two aspects which Avenarius has asserted to be inseparable. It leads us not only to what has not been experienced but to what can never by any possibility be experienced by beings like ourselves. But here again the ambiguities of the term experience come to Avenarius' rescue. He argues that thought is as genuine a form of experience as sense-perception, and so in the end falls back on the time-worn argument of subjective idealism, that thought and reality are inseparable, because reality can only be conceived in thought, and thought involves the presence of the thinker.[1] Not, therefore, any original and profound re-establishment of realism, but only the restatement in its crudest form of the familiar position of subjective idealism is the final outcome of Avenarius' positive speculations. He entirely fails to solve the central problem which he so suggestively propounds. There are in his system two objective worlds, and therefore two brains; the world (and also, it may be, the brain) apprehended in sense-experience, and the world, including the brain, as scientifically reconstructed in thought. The first as subjective varies not with the brain as a part of itself but with the brain as scientifically conceived.

In spite of all disclaimers,[2] Avenarius' whole treatment of the relation between consciousness and the brain reveals his secret retention of the extreme parallelist position. In his frequently quoted statement, that the brain is not the seat, organ or supporter, of thought,[3] he rejects the only terms which we possess for defining their connexion. The truth which he seeks to emphasize, namely, that ascription of consciousness to the brain involves confusion of two distinct and contradictory standpoints, is certainly of fundamental importance, but his statement of it is exaggerated, and compares somewhat unfavourably with that which has been given by other writers, as, for instance, by Fechner forty years earlier in his *Zend-Avesta*.[4] Avenarius' own term for describing the con-

---

[1] *Der Menschliche Weltbegriff*, Anmerkung 58, § xiv; *Vierteljahrsschrift*, vol. xix, 'Bemerkungen', note 2 to p. 144. Avenarius' statement of the same argument in materialistic terms (resulting from his equation of the self with the brain) in the 'Bemerkungen' (*Vierteljahrsschrift*, vol. xix, pp. 136–43, §§ 176–88) is significant of the opposite, and conflicting, trend of his system. Its idealism is in conflict with the underlying materialism.

[2] Cf. *Vierteljahrsschrift*, vol. xix, 'Bemerkungen', pp. 13–14, §§ 147–8.

[3] 'The brain is not the dwelling-place, seat, producer; it is not the instrument or organ, not the supporter or substratum, etc., of thought. Thought is not the inhabitant or commander, not the other half or side, etc., but neither is it a product; it is not even a physiological function, or merely some state of the brain' (*Der Menschliche Weltbegriff*, § 132). Cf. 'Richard Avenarius' by Carstanjen (translated by H. Bosanquet) in *Mind*, N.S., vol. vi, p. 472; Taylor, *Elements of Metaphysics* (Methuen, 1903), p. 315.

[4] First edition, vol. i, pp. 410 ff.; vol. ii, pp. 313 ff. Fechner has given a careful statement of the sense in which such terms as seat, organ, etc., may legitimately be applied to define the relation of consciousness to the brain. Cf. vol. ii, p. 345.

nexion holding between mind and body, viz., logical functional rela-tion,[1] is only satisfactory if parallelism expresses the ultimate and com-plete truth; and at the present time there are many signs that even as a provisional working hypothesis it no longer proves adequate to the needs either of physiological or of psychological research. The formula is also open to the serious objection that it exaggerates the kinship of the two parallel series. Avenarius' contention that the relation holding between them is of the same nature as that between the factors of a mathematical function has no sounder foundation than the quite general analogies derived from his biological interpretation of the vital series. These analogies fail to bridge the gulf which still remains between the purely quantitative attributes of the brain processes and the qualitative characteristics of the mental life.[2] By his own admissions, too, the relation cannot be a 'logical' one. For if that were its nature, the relation would hold in both directions, and we would not be limited to 'deduction' of the mental from the material, but would likewise be able to reconstruct the brain-processes from our knowledge of mind.

As further evidence that Avenarius' distinction between his own position and that of parallelism is a distinction without a difference, I may quote the passage in the *Bemerkungen*,[3] in which he speaks of sub-jective experience as 'Etwas, das Eines mit dem vorgefundenen Bewegten ist, das unauflöslich mit ihm verbunden ist, wie Form und Stoff, und das auch selbst nie ohne Form und nie ohne Inhalt ist und doch immer in anderen Formen und mit anderen Inhalten und zugleich immer in Uebereinstimmung mit dem Gesetz der Erhaltung der Energie'. Though the position expressed in this passage may appear Spinozistic (and Avenarius was of course greatly influenced by Spinoza), it must be borne in mind that his philosophy allows of no metaphysical distinction between appearance and reality, and therefore necessarily remains at the parallelist point of view which Spinoza transcends. In so far as Avenarius' philosophy deserts the parallelist position it must tend towards materialism. A parallelism of the physical and the psychical,

---

[1] Cf. *Vierteljahrsschrift*, vol. xix, 'Bemerkungen', pp. 17–18, §§ 153–6.

[2] Cf. Wundt, *Philosophische Studien*, vol. xiii, pp. 356 ff.

[3] *Vierteljahrsschrift*, vol. xviii, p. 154, § 46. For the sake of accuracy I quote it in the German.

conceived as distinct existences and as standing in functional relation, is the final outcome of his metaphysical speculations. The monistic conception of experience which he unfolds in the *Menschliche Weltbegriff,* from which he criticizes subjective idealism, and upon which he professes to re-establish a scientific realism, he has failed to reconcile with the naturalistic philosophy of his earlier *Kritik.*

The interest and value of the *Menschliche Weltbegriff* is, however, by no means lessened when we thus recognize its sturdy idealism as being spoken out of the mouth of its convinced opponent. The bankruptcy of materialism is dramatically represented in its whole-hearted welcome of the old gods disguised under strange names. Idealism has found a prophet in the enemy's camp. Further confirmation of this interpretation of Avenarius' philosophy will be gained in the next article from an examination of his theory of the introjectionist argument.

Avenarius' Philosophy of Pure Experience[1]

II

IN the preceding article I have sketched the general philosophical position from which Avenarius propounds his theory of the introjectionist argument, and may now proceed to the consideration of that argument in itself. Avenarius has given two very different statements of it, one in *Der Menschliche Weltbegriff*, and the other in four articles entitled 'Bemerkungen zum Begriff des Gegenstandes der Psychologie' in the *Vierteljahrsschrift*.[2] I shall start from the latter as being the more definite. Avenarius' teaching is that though the attitude of pure experience is perfectly consistent with itself, there inevitably arises at a very early stage of mental development that falsification of experience to which may be given the name introjection. It consists in a false interpretation of the experience of others which by a backstroke necessitates a similar, and equally false, interpretation of our own experience. When we look at another person we observe that the objects which he perceives lie outside him, and, arguing that the perceptions of them are in him and not outside him, we feel compelled to conclude that he does not apprehend the real external objects but only subjective images or counterparts. As this interpretation is applied by me to the experience of all other persons and is applied by all other persons to me, I feel compelled to apply it to my own world, and accordingly conclude that I do not perceive the outer objects but only their inner copies. There must

[1] *Mind*, vol. xv, N.S., no. 58.
[2] Vol. xviii, p. 150, §§ 35 ff.

be two external worlds, the actual world in space and the apparently real but merely subjective world of each separate observer.[1] Such an argument is, as Avenarius contends,[2] obviously false. It rests on the assumption that the objects which I immediately experience as outside the body of another person are the real objects which that other person apprehends only indirectly through mental copies. That is to say, on a realistic interpretation of my own experience I base an idealistic interpretation of the experience of others. This contradiction becomes explicit when I am compelled to extend the conclusion thus reached to my own experience, for in so doing I destroy the premiss upon which the whole argument rests.

Now I have not the least intention of seeking to defend such a form of argument. Also, I do not question that in all subjectivist thinking a perpetual alternation between the realistic and the idealistic attitudes is inevitable. In one form or another the realistic assumption is always tacitly made; and that assumption undoubtedly has its origin in the realistic attitude which we spontaneously take up towards the sensible world of immediate experience. Avenarius, in tracing the presence of this self-contradictory assumption through all the various forms of subjective idealism, has rendered a genuine service to philosophy. What I call in question is his assertion that subjective idealism not only logically implies, but finds its originating cause in, this false inference. It is to be observed that Avenarius has given no ground for the assumed necessity of the introjectionist argument save only the spatial externality of objects to the bodies of those who perceive them; and that seems to me insufficient to account for desertion of the realistic attitude of ordinary consciousness. No one at the standpoint of pure experience can fail to observe this spatial externality, and, so far from finding it a stumbling-block and a source of problems, must surely recognize it as necessary for the very purpose of knowledge. We cannot in looking through a window see an external landscape unless the landscape actually exists outside the window, and just as little can we in looking out upon the external world through the eyes—and that is what primitive and un-

[1] Vol. xviii, p. 154, § 46.
[2] Ibid., §§ 47 ff.

reflective man conceives himself as doing—see that world unless it is actually there outside the eyes. Avenarius insists that the realistic attitude of pure experience is a perfectly satisfactory one. From its point of view any and every possible experience can be consistently interpreted. But if so, why should one of the most universal of experiences, the experience, namely, that objects are always external to the body of the observer, or at least, as regards the parts of his own body, to the organ through which they are apprehended, inevitably lead the mind to draw self-contradictory conclusions? Why should such inconsistent conclusions be drawn from a consistent experience?

Dr. Stout in his article on introjection in Baldwin's *Philosophical Dictionary* has quoted a passage in which Herbart has anticipated Avenarius' argument. 'A child sees a dog run whimpering from a stick which is raised to strike it. Immediately the child locates (*hineindenkt*) the pain of the blow in the dog; but as a *future* pain, for the dog is not yet struck. He also locates the stick in the dog, for the dog runs away from it; not, however, the real stick for it is outside the dog, but the stick *without its reality*, that is the image of the stick. . . . For an image is distinguished from the object represented by the fact that though not possessing its reality it yet resembles it in every other respect. In this way, then, the child is led to ascribe the representation (*Vorstellung*) of the stick to the dog and to distinguish it from its object. The child now possesses a representation of a representation, a very easy but indispensable step in the development of self-consciousness.'[1] This is exactly Avenarius' argument, but the more concrete form of statement enforces the obvious objection that no child ever does argue in this way. A child would never dream of thus setting a mental copy of the stick inside the dog. The mind must become thoroughly sophisticated by reflexion on philosophical problems before it can be brought to admit, even as a possibility, that the world immediately experienced is a merely subjective copy. The child feels no difficulty in regarding objects as immediately apprehended by all observers. Just as various spectators may look out of different windows upon the same external landscape, so, the child holds, may animals and men look out through their eyes upon the actual

[1] *Psychologie als Wissenschaft*, § 133.

real objects that constitute their common environment. The observers are different and so accordingly are their apprehensions or experiences, but the immediate contents of these experiences are the identical real objects. There is, of course, much difficulty as to how the child conceives the distinction between the objects and his experience of them, and as to what is involved in the implied distinction between mind and body,[1] but even granting the possibility of the most various interpretations of these terms, it remains true that the child does not conceive the objects apprehended as being representative images or copies of external bodies. The statements of Herbart and Avenarius are therefore in flagrant contradiction with the facts. Realism is the fundamental characteristic of the standpoint of primitive man and of the child-mind, and the considerations which lead to subjective idealism, even in the Cartesian form, are quite beyond their range of vision.

The true originating cause of subjective idealism seems to me to be physiological.[2] Subjective idealism was not definitely formulated until the physiology of the nervous system had been developed by Descartes and his contemporaries; and the fundamental reason which inclined them to subjective idealism may perhaps be stated in the following simple manner. So long as the eyes can be regarded as windows through which the mind can look out, every observer may directly apprehend the real external objects. But when it is discovered that the eyes are not exits but always only entrances, that they are not passages through which the mind may issue out but only channels through which currents pass into the brain, the mind then appears to be shut off from direct communion with the external objects, and to depend for all its knowledge on mental images which in a mysterious manner accompany the brain-states. These physiological considerations apply as directly to my own experience as to that of others, and so, on the same identical grounds, I may infer that both my own experience and that of other men, though an apparently immediate apprehension of an external

---

[1] Cf. below, pp. 167–8.

[2] So far as subjective idealism appears in Greek philosophy, as for instance in the philosophy of Democritus, it involves, and would seem to be due to, physical and physiological considerations.

world, is purely subjective. Avenarius explicitly disavows this explanation.[1] Nowhere, however, does he consider it, much less refute it.

I should further contend that the subjectivist position is not a falsification of the attitude of naïve realism but a necessary step on the way to its correction. Subjective idealism may not itself be true, but the facts upon which it is based suffice to prove that naïve realism is certainly false. In the end Avenarius' own theory breaks down because of its irreconcilability with these physiological facts. As I have tried to prove in the previous article, he only escapes them by inconsistently accepting the extreme subjectivism involved in the parallelist position.

To revert, however, to my previous line of argument. Avenarius seems to have confused two quite different mental attitudes, the attitude of animism which in its full and unchecked development is found only in the primitive and savage mind but which in a modified form is still the attitude of the child-mind, and that subjective idealism which was first definitely formulated in the time of Descartes. As these two attitudes are fundamentally different, he was bound to fail in any attempt to trace them both to a common root in introjection. Being, however, profoundly impressed by Tylor's treatment of animism in *Primitive Culture*, and following Tylor in his exaggerated view of the part which animism plays in the development of theological and philosophical thought,[2] he very naturally tried to connect the Cartesian dualism, which is the stumbling-block of all naturalistic systems, and which is therefore in a very especial sense the *bête noire* of his own philosophizing, with the animistic theories of primitive man. That dualism had previously compelled Avenarius to develop his naturalistic system on idealist lines.[3] The relief which he felt in escaping both idealism and dualism by

---

[1] *Vierteljahrsschrift*, vol. xviii, 'Bemerkungen', p. 419, § 116: 'Dieselogisch unberechtigte Deutung der Abhängigkeit der "Farben", "Gefühle" u.s.w. vom Gehirn ist nicht der *Grund* der Introjection, sondern ihre *Folge*'.

[2] Cf. previous article, p. 154.

[3] The stages in the gradual development of Avenarius' philosophy are clearly marked in his published works. The above interpretation of animism, together with a somewhat immature statement of his later doctrine of pure experience, is presented in *Philosophie als Denken der Welt*, but from a point of view indistinguishable from subjective idealism (cf. §§ 115 ff.). In the *Kritik* this subjectivism is rejected in favour of realism. His doctrine of introjection, as the explanation both of animism and of sub-

readoption of the realistic attitude of natural science and physiology he has described in his introduction to the *Menschlicher Weltbegriff*.[1]

I may now turn to Avenarius' earlier statement of the introjectionist argument in the *Menschlicher Weltbegriff*. His articles in the *Vierteljahrsschrift* enter upon the problem of introjection only in so far as that is necessary in order to refute the current conception of the data of psychology, and to vindicate that view of its province which has been advocated in this country by Ward and Stout. As the current conception was based on subjective idealism, the theory of introjection required to be formulated only in its connexion with idealism. No direct reference is made to animism,[2] or, save very briefly, to the attitude of ordinary consciousness. In *Philosophie als Denken der Welt* and in the *Kritik* Avenarius had, however, traced all the false conceptions of dualistic metaphysic to primitive animism; and the problem which still remained for solution, and which he set himself to solve in the *Menschlicher Weltbegriff*, was that of accounting for, and removing, the various dualisms (between inner and outer, soul and body, mind and matter, God and the world, etc.) into which the unity of pure experience had thus been resolved. This involved explanation of the transition from pure experience to animism and from animism to subjective idealism; and by interpreting his introjectionist argument, here propounded for the first time, now in a wider and now in a narrower sense, he sought to make it yield an explanation of both these vitiating transformations of experience. With the elimination of all introjection, both animism and subjectivism, and together with them every vestige of dualism, would, he claims, entirely vanish, leaving that pure experience out of which through introjection they originally emerged. To eliminate

---

jectivism, appears, however, only in the *Menschlicher Weltbegriff*. Finally, in the *Bemerkungen*, Avenarius restates the introjectionist argument, and also develops more explicitly certain aspects of his naturalistic system.

[1] Pp. ix–x.
[2] Except in a very significant note (*Vierteljahrsschrift*, vol. xviii, *Bemerkungen*, pp. 153–4) which seems to indicate consciousness of the unsatisfactory manner in which introjection and animism had been connected in the *Menschlicher Weltbegriff* (cf. § 56).

introjection is to overthrow both agnosticism and spiritualism, indeed every philosophy which asserts that there are realities which cannot be completely known or problems that cannot be completely solved by ideal completion of the existing sciences. The kind of completion which Avenarius would regard as satisfactory has already been indicated in the previous article.[1]

The introjectionist argument is stated in the *Menschlicher Weltbegriff*[2] in much the same manner as in the *Bemerkungen*, but is developed to a very different conclusion.[3] The conclusion now drawn is not that the world perceived is a mental copy of external reality but only that the perception of external objects is in the mind. Since the object which another person perceives is seen by us to lie outside him, we infer that there exists in him the perception of it. 'Thus in consequence of introjection [we] find on the one side the parts of the environment as "things", and on the other side individuals who "apprehend" the "things"; that is to say, "things" on the one hand and "perceptions of things", or, more shortly, "perceptions" on the other.'[4] As the voice of each individual comes from within him, and as each individual locates certain feelings in organs which are as a rule inside the body, the perceptions are regarded as forming an inner world. This conclusion seems all the more inevitable as these perceptions are not discoverable on the outside [*am Aüssern*] of the body.[5] The inference may therefore be stated as follows: All other persons have an outer world which they perceive or experience and each has an inner world which consists of these perceptions or experiences. The introjectionist argument is then completed through application to the self. I have an outer world which

---

[1] Cf. previous article, pp. 147–50.

[2] §§ 38 ff.

[3] The two views do not seem to have been distinguished by previous writers. The statement of the theory given by Ward (*Naturalism and Agnosticism,* vol. ii, p. 172) is somewhat indefinite. Taylor (*Elements of Metaphysics,* pp. 81, 299) is more explicit, but though apparently basing his statement on the *Menschlicher Weltbegriff* seems to have read into it the view of the *Bemerkungen*. Stout, on the other hand, bases his statement entirely on the latter.

[4] *Menschlicher Weltbegriff,* § 43.

[5] Ibid., § 45.

I perceive or experience and an inner world which consists of these perceptions and experiences.

Many objections to this argument at once suggest themselves. In the first place, the distinction between objects and perceptions of objects must be present in our own experience before we can infer its presence in the experience of others. Dr. Ward has stated that 'the essence of introjection consists in applying to the immediate experience of my fellow-creatures conceptions which have no counterpart in my own'.[1] But if the self has no conception of inner experience or of perception as something distinguishable from the objects apprehended, it could not invent the distinction by any amount of reflexion upon the spatial externality of objects to the bodies of others. Also, it is not clear why the spatial externality of objects to our own body should not in itself, without this roundabout argument through other selves, suffice to direct our attention to so fundamental a distinction as that between objects and the perception of them. But since Avenarius admits as original and primitive the distinction between characters and contents, that is to say, between experience or perception and the contents experienced or perceived, he can only mean that the introjectionist fallacy consists in transforming distinguishable aspects into separate worlds, the insepar- able aspects of experience into two kinds of experience.

To that the reply is that neither primitive man nor the child does thus oppose inner and outer. Here again Avenarius is interpreting the words 'inner' and 'outer' in terms of the later subjectivism of reflective consciousness. The distinction between inner and outer, between per- ception and object perceived, is not in itself illegitimate and false. Everything depends upon the particular manner in which it is viewed; and when Avenarius interprets the spatial metaphor and the localization of perceptions within the body in a quite literal fashion he is guilty of ignoring the subtleties of a highly complex and very vaguely defined position. The language which he employs to express the distinction has been created in the course of philosophical inquiry and as such is thoroughly misleading. Primitive man and the child do not use so general a term as perception or experience. They say 'I *see* the object' or

---

[1] *Naturalism and Agnosticism* (1899), vol. ii, p. 172.

'I *touch* it', and thus always keep in view that complexity of relations by which soul and body, mind and object, are interconnected. And no better illustration of this fact could be obtained than the animistic conception of the soul as depicted by Tylor. As Tylor has shown, and as Avenarius himself admits, the soul is not pictured by primitive man as consisting of inner experiences, nor even as the subject or bearer of such experiences, but as a duplicate of the body, itself possessing sense-organs and therefore related to objects in the same manner as the physical organism. Animism is a form of naïve realism, and indeed its extremest form, and just for that reason it always makes use of spatial metaphors, conceiving the inner body as related to the outer body as an individual is related to the house which he inhabits or the clothes which he wears.[1] It is not the dualizing of experience, but the duplication of one of the objects experienced, that constitutes animism.

Avenarius' assumption that experience has been at some point in the long past of the human race, and is at some stage in the life of each child, pure experience, and that this primitive experience has been vitiated in both cases by a supervening process of introjection, aided in the case of the child though not of course in the history of the race by current thought and language, has no sufficient ground either in anthropology or in child-psychology. We may get back to a stage at which the child does not distinguish self and not-self, inner and outer, but the differentiating process by which its confused experience is articulated through these distinctions does not seem to be vitiated at some particular stage in its development, but rather constantly to advance towards a more and more definite, more and more exact, appreciation both of the opposition between self and not-self and of their interrelations. At no stage is the development describable as a transition from a consistent and true experience to an impossible or illegitimate dualism. If at certain stages duality, such as that of soul and body in the animistic theories, is unduly emphasized, it can be said with equal truth that in the preceding stages the duality was unduly ignored. A duality that leads through animism to the idealism of Plato can only be reckoned an illegitimate development of thought by those who, like

---

[1] Cf. *Menschlicher Weltbegriff*, § 59.

Avenarius, advocate a purely naturalistic interpretation of spiritual experience. His attempt to give logical and conclusive proof of its illegitimacy by his theory of the introjectionist argument has certainly failed. In so far as introjection goes beyond the distinction between my experience and the experience of others, that is to say, beyond the hypothesis implied in the attitude of pure experience,[1] it is not involved in animism. For, as we have just seen, though animism modifies the attitude of pure experience, the opposition which it develops is not between inner experience and the outer world, but only between an inner and an outer body. Also—to indicate a further important point— animism in its development is not determined by the introjectionist argument. For it does not originate in any fallacious inference from others to the self, but spontaneously arises as the natural explanation of a very special set of concrete phenomena—those of sleep, dreams and death. As Tylor has by reference to these concrete facts accounted for it in a satisfactory manner, a second explanation is quite superfluous.

Avenarius' conception of the part which animism has played in the development of thought is as unsatisfactory as his attempted explanation of its origin by means of introjection. His position is entirely motived by the desire to trace all the higher conceptions of religion and philos- ophy back to the animistic belief in visions of the dead, and so to con- demn them as *Aberglaube,* as 'the shadow of a shade'. From this point of view Avenarius seeks to interpret the progress of philosophy as an inevitable development of animism through more and more subtilized forms of spiritualism back to naturalism. Philosophy, as it develops the conception of spirit, passes by completion of the dualism between it and all the objects of possible experience into agnosticism, and agnosticism, by elimination of the spiritualistic opposition of appearance and reality which it has unconsciously retained, returns to the naturalism of pure experience.[2] The various conceptions of spirit, including that of the

---

[1] Cf. previous article, p. 141.

[2] *Menschlicher Weltbegriff,* § 55 (cf. *Kritik,* vol. ii, p. 281, pp. 296–7). According to Avenarius this desertion of the attitude of pure experience and consequent develop- ment through spiritualism and agnosticism back to naturalism is not only inevitable, but also fruitful as leading to a naturalism which is conscious of its own meaning and so can never again be tempted to transcend possible experience. Fechner states in a less

unknowable, are the *Schutzformen* or *Beibegriffe*[1] through which the human mind has sought to maintain its inherited beliefs in face of the contrary evidence of pure experience. They are progressively modified to fit the facts as these become more fully known, but the completion of the adaptation coincides with their complete elimination. The following passage from Tylor's *Primitive Culture* may be quoted as the source from which Avenarius probably gained his point of view: 'The animism of savages stands for and by itself; it explains its own origin. The animism of civilized men, while more appropriate to advanced knowledge, is in great measure only explicable as a developed product of the older and ruder system. . . . As we explore human thought onward from savage into barbarian and civilized life, we find a state of theory more conformed to positive science, but in itself less complete and consistent. . . . The soul has given up its ethereal substance, and become an immaterial entity, 'the shadow of a shade'. Its theory is becoming separated from the investigations of biology and mental

---

exaggerated and much more satisfactory manner a similar, though opposed, view of the development of knowledge (*Zend-Avesta*, 1st ed., vol. ii, pp. 87–96). He shares Avenarius' belief in a primitive state of pure and true experience. Though the starting-point of human experience is the '*unaufgeschlossenes Ei des Glaubens*', in which the whole truth of the Universe is contained in germ, 'it was so unstable that it yielded to every idle suggestion, so uncertain of itself that it fell victim to every deceptive appearance, so little capable of grasping the parts simultaneously with the whole, that every attempt to enter more fully into the parts caused it to lose the meaning of the whole. . . . And so reality divides and subdivides itself without ceasing, becoming always clearer and more intelligible in detail, and always more meaningless [*todter*] and self-contradictory as a whole' (*Zend-Avesta*, loc. cit.). While Avenarius regards the completion of this development as involving a return to that attitude of pure experience which he believes to have preceded animism, Fechner with more historical justification identifies both the primitive and the final attitudes with animism. 'The axiom of the forms of knowledge', formulated by Avenarius in the *Kritik* (*Vorwort*, p. vii) and emphasized in his earlier *Philosophie als Denken der Welt*—that scientific forms of knowledge are in all cases developments of the pre-scientific—does not by itself in any way justify his naturalistic conclusions. It is accepted by Fechner, as well as by all idealist writers. This is one of the many points in which Avenarius' view of the development of knowledge reveals kinship with the Hegelian philosophy.

[1] Cf. previous article, p. 154.

science, which now discuss the phenomena of life and thought, the senses and the intellect, the emotions and the will, on a groundwork of pure experience'.[1]

Avenarius' treatment of animism has been approved in most unexpected quarters,[2] and on that account I have dwelt upon it at greater length. But surely if we were called upon to make a choice between Avenarius' condemnation of animism as the source of all false metaphysics and Fechner's idealization of it as containing the germ of a final philosophy, we should be compelled to side with the latter. Animism is not the source of the distinction between soul and body but only the first and crudest attempt to comprehend and define their interrelations. To say, as Tylor and Avenarius both do, that the real grounds for the conception of the soul lie in primitive thinking, and that all later attempts to develop it fail to strengthen the grounds upon which it was adopted by the savage mind, is a grotesque misrepresentation of the history of human thought. Some distinction between self and not-self is present from the very start of human experience, and the philosophical value of animism may perhaps be regarded as chiefly consisting in the definiteness which it gave to that more primitive distinction—a definiteness which enabled it to take hold on the human mind and so ultimately to become a subject of scientific reflexion. As an opposition between soul and body it may or may not be tenable, as containing the germ of the distinction between mind and matter, thought and extension, it is indispensable for clearness in philosophical thinking. Avenarius' attempt to remove the distinction by contending that with the advance of knowledge it has ceased to exist even as a problem has resulted in his own case in a one-sided materialism. In overcoming the opposition of the subject and object he very seriously misrepresents it. When, on the one hand, he identifies the opposition of subject and object with the distinction between character and content, by using these new and quite

[1] E. B. Tylor, *Primitive Culture* (Murray, 1871), i, pp. 452–3. I have not been able to find any authoritative statement as to the extent of the influence which Tylor's treatment of animism exercised on Avenarius. But that it was decisive in determining Avenarius' conception of the main stages in the development of philosophy, and of human thought generally, seems fairly obvious.

[2] Cf. Ward in *Naturalism and Agnosticism*, vol. ii, p. 172.

general terms, and by describing character and content as inseparable aspects of every experience, he escapes the duty of analysing the varied and complex forms in which they are related in special cases. And when, on the other hand, he identifies the opposition of subject and object with the distinction between self and not-self, in analysing the self into its varied factors he ignores the aspect of character or subjectivity which is the fundamental feature whereby a self is distinguished from all other objects.[1] To this separate treatment of these allied distinctions we may ascribe both the misleading plausibility and the complete failure of his attempted re-establishment of a scientific realism.

In conclusion I may sum up my criticisms of Avenarius' theory of the introjectionist argument. He gives two quite distinct and conflicting statements of it. Both cannot be true, and, as I have tried to show, both are in some degree false. If introjection is interpreted in the wider sense as covering the distinction between inner and outer, perceiving and perceived, it is a quite legitimate distinction, and one which has been formulated by Avenarius himself as the relative opposition of characters and contents. Animism, as the recognition of this duality and a first attempt to define it, is not so much the source of the subsequent errors of philosophy, as the beginning of its positive development. And lastly, animism does not originate in the introjectionist argument but in the interpretation of a very special set of concrete phenomena. Avenarius, therefore, has not succeeded in proving either that introjection in this abstract form is a fallacy or that its concrete embodiment in animism is the ultimate source of metaphysical error. If, on the other hand, introjection is identified with subjective idealism, it is undoubtedly a fallacy, involving that self-contradictory alternation between the realistic and the idealistic attitudes which Avenarius has so acutely and suggestively analysed. As a title for this particular fallacy the term 'introjection' is entirely satisfactory. When Avenarius, however, presents the introjectionist argument as the generating cause of subjective idealism, his thinking is evidently perverted by a false view of the development of knowledge. He has again been misled by his confusion of animism with subjectivism, and so has been compelled to represent the latter as a

---

[1] For a fuller treatment of this important point, see previous article, pp. 147–8, 155–6.

universal illusion of the human mind. Such a view is refuted both by the facts of anthropology and by the actual history of philosophy. Subjectivism is a purely philosophical development which is based on physical and physiological considerations and which did not take definite form until modern times.

Subjectivism and Realism in Modern Philosophy[1]

IN this paper I have a twofold object in view: First, to state the arguments which seem to prove that subjectivism is in all its various forms incoherent and untenable; secondly, to present for discussion that particular form of realism which seems to contain most promise of a satisfactory solution of the complex problems involved.

Let me define precisely what I intend to signify by the term 'subjectivism'. I take it as being interchangeable with the phrase 'subjective idealism'. It appears in varying forms in Descartes, in Spinoza, and in Leibniz, in Locke, Berkeley, and Hume; in short, in every one of the chief pre-Kantian philosophies. But however variously interpreted in the different systems, it is determined by the fundamental assumption, that the objects immediately apprehended in sense-experience exists only in the mind of the individual observer, and that they are numerically and existentially distinct for each observer. According to Descartes, they represent real material bodies; according to Berkeley, they reveal the world which is abidingly present to the mind of God. What is fundamental in this position is not, therefore, the particular view adopted of the causes of our mental experiences,—the difference in this respect between Descartes and Berkeley is by comparison unimportant, —but the interpretation given to mental experience itself.

If we leave Arnauld and Reid out of account, as not sufficiently thoroughgoing, we may regard Kant as being the first to question the underlying assumption of the subjectivist position. In so doing he was led to formulate what has been named 'objective idealism'. Each indivi-

[1] Read before the American Philosophical Association, at Cornell University 27 December 1907.

dual, through subjective processes, constructs a world which is permanent and which is the same for all observers. The mental processes are
distinct for each observer; the objects immediately apprehended are
identical for all. But though the historical value of the Kantian idealism
can hardly be overestimated, we cannot accept it as a genuine solution
of the special problems involved. It is, I should say, impossible to
extract from Kant, and still more impossible to gather from Hegel, any
coherent account of how consciousness stands related to the brain;
why it is that the world apprehended varies for each observer together
with this small and insignificant portion of itself. Objective idealism
has, in the past, been parasitic. It has lived on the weaknesses of its
opponent. It has taken the refutation of subjectivism as equivalent to its
own establishment. And as a consequence, objective idealism has made
practically no headway except among those who have devoted themselves to the study of pure metaphysics. It has yielded no fruitful
orientation for scientific research. As a practical standpoint, subjectivism
has retained its hold over those who are chiefly occupied in physics,
physiology, and psychology, and who accordingly do not have
constantly before them the logical and metaphysical difficulties to which
it gives rise.

Even within the sphere of the positive sciences the subjectivist position does not, however, prove really satisfactory. As a working hypothesis it fairly well satisfies the needs of the physiologist; but as a
view-point in physics and psychology it hopelessly breaks down.
Accordingly, within recent years, workers in physics and in psychology,
but especially in the latter, have occupied themselves in seeking some
other standpoint. And as they strive to develop this substitute out of
our detailed knowledge, through study of those very facts which have
hitherto been the stumbling-block of all objectivist theories, there is
good hope of a successful issue.

The two most courageous and thoroughgoing attempts to establish
realism have been those of Avenarius and of Bergson. Avenarius is
probably the most original thinker that Germany has produced within
the past forty years; Bergson is the leading constructive philosophical
thinker in France at the present day. Both are primarily psychologists,
and both have been impelled to develop a realistic philosophy through

their detailed study of the actual facts of our concrete experience, As they substantially agree in the criticism which they pass upon subjective idealism, I may state that criticism before proceeding to consideration of their constructive views.

The contradiction inherent in subjective idealism consists in its view of our mental states as standing to objects in a twofold simultaneous relation: cognitively, as their apprehensions, and mechanically, as their effects. The first is a relation of inclusion, the second is a relation of exclusion. By viewing ideas in terms of the first relation, the subjectivist reaches his starting-point, namely, the real material body acting on the material brain, and through the brain generating or occasioning the mental state. The object is separated from its effect by a large number of intermediate links which bear no resemblance to it, save in that they are physical processes in space. The facts, therefore, which prove that the mental state is a mechanical effect of the real object justify no assertion as to its internal resemblance to that object, and so inevitably undermine the view of mental states from which the argument starts. If the subjectivist conclusion is accepted, there can be no ground save only the *deus ex machina* of a pre-established harmony for retaining our primitive belief in the objective validity of the mental state.

The first view of mental states, as cognitively related to objects, must be accepted as valid if the subjectivist argument is to have a starting-point; it cannot be valid if the subjectivist argument is correct. Either, therefore, the subjectivist must establish his position without assuming the ultimate truth of his starting-point, or he must recognize the truth of that starting-point as proving the falsity of his conclusion.

This argument has in one form or another been so frequently stated, and in spite of its simplicity seems to be so cogently valid, that as a rule subjective idealists now recognize its truth. They therefore endeavour to start from facts which involve no realistic assumptions. And, in so doing, they propound their argument in a new form, as the argument from relativity. Even while remaining within the field of consciousness, our perceptions can, they contend, be proved to be subjective, numerically and existentially distinct in the mind of each observer. Sense-perceptions are, as is easily shown, conditioned by the individual circumstances, view-point, and previous experience of each observer. They vary proportionately with changes in the relation of our bodies to the objects, as when objects alter in apparent size and form according to their distance from us. Or they may vary in correspondence with variations within our bodies, as when what is red to the ordinary observer is grey to the colour-blind, or as when objects are seen double upon displacement of one eyeball. And in all cases the exact nature of the variations can only be discovered in and through determination of the influence exercised by objects on the brain. The perceptions vary independently of the objects apprehended, and directly only with the brain-states. They are conditioned, mediately by objects, immediately by the brain-states which these objects cause.

These, then, are the undeniable facts. They can neither be called in question nor ignored. They constitute the problem which awaits solution. How, now, are they interpreted by the subjectivist? He may argue in either of two ways. If he believes that our mental states carry us to a trans-subjective reality, he will argue from this conditionedness of our perceptions to their subjectivity. He will contend that, as our perceptions vary directly only with the brain-states, they must be effects distinct from the real objects and separately existent in each individual mind. But, obviously, in so arguing the subjectivist falls back upon the realistic interpretation of experience. The argument from relativity reduces to the previous argument from causal dependence of experience upon the brain.

The subjectivist may, however, take a very different line. He may entirely give up the belief in a trans-subjective world, and consequently in the existence of a material body and brain. He may contend that we know and can know nothing but sensations, that sensations remain the sole possible objects of all our thoughts. And from this position he may then argue that the objects immediately known are subjective for a twofold reason: first, because they are sensations; and secondly, because they vary from mind to mind.

The first reason is that objects are known only as sensations and therefore as subjective. Now, without questioning the contention that objects are known as sensations, we may dispute the inference drawn from this assertion. Psychologists have come to recognize that 'sensation' is a thoroughly ambiguous term. It is used with two very different meanings, as process of apprehension and as object apprehended. If sensation is mental process, then for that sufficient reason it must fall on the subjective or mental side. But if, on the other hand, sensations have to be regarded not as mental processes, but as objects revealed in and through such processes, this argument will fall to the ground. Though red is known only as sensation, it is undoubtedly an objective content. Similarly, a sound or an odour or a taste is an object apprehended by the mind, and is therefore distinct from the processes through which such apprehension is brought about. Nothing but confusion can result from employing the term 'sensation' in both these conflicting connotations. The ambiguity is very similar to that which makes the term 'experience' so serviceable to certain contemporary schools of philosophy. It may be said that the two aspects—process of apprehension and object apprehended—are inseparable; but even granting that, they are none the less distinguishable. And a name that is adequately descriptive of the one aspect cannot rightly be applied to the other.

Now the subjectivist argument, that objects are known only as sensations, and therefore as subjective, makes use of this fundamental ambiguity. Only by interpreting sensations as signifying objective contents, can it justify the assertion that objects are known as sensations; and yet, only by regarding sensations as mental processes, can it legitimate the inference that they are therefore subjective. The ground of the argument involves one interpretation of the term 'sensation', the conclusion implies the other. It is open to us to propound the counter-argument. Since sensations are distinct from mental processes, objects which are known as sensations cannot be mental or subjective. This is the meaning now ascribed to the term 'sensation' by such psychologists as Ward, Stout, and Alfred Binet. They limit it to denote objective content. Binet admits that there is no contradiction in speaking of an object both as sensation and as material.[1] He also points out that there is no reason why sensations, so regarded, may not have permanent existence. That is to say, the use of the term 'sensation', when thus clearly defined, decides nothing either for or against realism.

This, however, brings us to the second argument. Sensations vary from mind to mind, and for that reason must be numerically and

---

[1] *L'Âme et le corps*, pp. 13, 63.

existentially distinct for each observer. Now if by sensation is meant mental process, there is no question. Mental processes are undoubtedly subjective; they take place separately in the mind of each conscious being. But if by 'sensation' we mean content apprehended, the conclusion does not follow. The same identical objective content may be differently apprehended by different minds. The subjectivist tacitly makes the impossible assumption that if we apprehend real objects in sense-experience, we must apprehend them in their intrinsic, absolute nature, and that, on a realistic theory, sense-perception must therefore be identical with scientific knowledge. If realism proceeded on any such assumption, it could, of course, be condemned as an absurdity from the very start. The difference between subjectivism and realism consists not in the acceptance or rejection of any such underlying assumption, but only in this, that the subjectivist seeks to explain the varying sensations in terms of themselves, the realist by equating them with variations in the totality of the complex conditions, both subjective and trans-subjective, which are therein involved.

The mere general fact, therefore, that such variations do occur is by itself no conclusive proof either for or against any one theory of knowledge. The variations constitute a problem to which subjectivism and realism remain as alternative explanations. This argument may therefore be rejected as invalid. By itself it proves nothing, and would never have been put forward had not the subjectivist been already convinced on other grounds that the objects of mind are purely mental. These other unexpressed grounds would seem ultimately to reduce to the physiological argument which I have already considered.

The belief that sensations are mechanically generated through brain-processes is, so far as I can discover, the sole originating cause of subjective idealism. Other arguments may be employed to develop the position, but they cannot be regarded either as causing or as justifying it. The subjectivist who seeks to ground his position on the facts of relativity is still chiefly influenced by the physiological standpoint which he professes to reject.

Thus it matters not from which side the subjectivist may approach the facts. He may start with the physicist and physiologist from material bodies and the material brain, or with the psychologist from our immediate mental experiences; in either case he lands himself in the same quandary. He can only prove mental states to be subjective by proving them to be externally related to objects as their mechanical effects, and yet this can only be done by simultaneously interpreting the mental states in the cognitive terms which justify the realistic standpoint. This perpetual alternation between realism and idealism is as contradictory as it is unavoidable.

Now, if we accept this criticism of subjective idealism, and at the same time hold fast to the fundamental fact upon which that criticism is based—the fact, namely, that any view which regards mental 'states as effects generated or occasioned by the brain must render impossible the understanding of their representative function—we are brought to the view propounded by Avenarius and by Bergson, that the brain is in no sense the seat or organ of the conscious life, that its function is purely motor and never cognitive. It differs from the spinal cord only in degree of complexity. It is not the material substrate of consciousness, but only the motor instrument through which it actively intervenes in the material realm.

That the body is the instrument and not the necessary substrate of the mind has often been propounded as a pleasing speculation, as for instance by William James in his Ingersoll Lecture on the immortality of the soul. It is a very different matter, however, when Avenarius and Bergson strive to work it systematically into the web of our scientific knowledge, urging that it is the only feasible interpretation of the empirical facts. Both are led to its adoption by the requirements of the detailed psychological inquiries in which they are engaged. They possess a genuine interest in cerebral physiology and are thoroughly acquainted with its established results.

As regards Avenarius, it must be admitted that in his mouth the contention means very much less than at first sight appears. He developed his realistic theory comparatively late in his philosophical development, and never thoroughly succeeded in bringing his general metaphysic into harmony with it. He oscillates between parallelism, on the one hand, and materialism, on the other; that is to say, between a view which entirely separates mind from matter, and a view which denies the existence of anything but matter. Avenarius meant, indeed, to develop a view very different from either of these two familiar standpoints. For in both of them, as he has been careful to show, subjectivism is necessarily in some degree involved. He does not, however, seem to have succeeded in establishing the realistic philosophy whose programme he has sketched. His criticism of subjectivism is remarkably thorough, and, as it seems to me, entirely successful. But he fails to provide a satisfactory substitute.

With Bergson matters stand very differently. He rejects parallelism and materialism with equal emphasis. No one can possibly accuse him of coquetting with either. His words may, therefore, be allowed their full weight. He means everything that he says when he contends that the brain has no cognitive function. Moreover, he has developed his position in considerable detail. In his *Matière et Mémoire* he has shown how the facts known regarding brain-localization, specific energy of the nerves, Weber's law, and the like, can all be satisfactorily interpreted from this point of view. His philosophy has, therefore, the unique value of establishing a new possibility, one that has not been developed by any preceding thinker.

I shall conclude by indicating—I can do no more than indicate—the chief consequences which Bergson's position entails. In the first place, it involves our giving up the attempt to explain the genesis of our knowledge. Our starting-point is the world of material bodies in space. The problem is not to account for consciousness of it, but to explain why we know it in the form relative to our individual position and practical needs. By right it is knowledge of true independent reality; in actual fact it is limited in extent, permeated with illusion, and largely personal.

Secondly, Bergson does not mean to imply that physiology and psychology have gone off on an entirely false scent, and that, in seeking to explain the mind through study of the nervous system and brain, they are looking for light where none is to be found. It is from the physiological point of view that Bergson propounds the fundamental problem of his philosophy. As he recognizes, and indeed insists, the world perceived varies together with that special portion of itself which we name the brain. Accordingly, all knowledge of the organization of either casts light upon the nature of both. The more fully we understand the manner in which the brain reacts upon the external world, the better shall we comprehend the nature and meaning of the conscious life. The subjectivist explanation of this functional relation is that the brain-processes are either the sufficient or the occasional cause of the mental states. Bergson's explanation, on the other hand, is that ordinary consciousness is essentially practical. The orientation of the healthy, unsophisticated mind is exclusively towards action. Therein it harmonizes with the brain, which by its changes determines the possible actions through which the body may adapt itself to its material environment. The stimuli coming from objects to the various sense-organs prepare the reactions, potential or actual, whereby the body adapts itself to them. By controlling the reactions thus caused the mind can intervene in the material realm. The mind can only act through the bodily mechanisms thus placed at its disposal. It is limited by the motor instrument which conditions all its activities. And since the activity even of scientific or philosophical thinking depends upon sensuous instruments, such as language, this limitation reaches even into the purely theoretical domain.

Thirdly, mind and body must be regarded as standing in a one-sided relation of interaction. The mind controls the body. The body, on the other hand, while not itself acting on the mind, limits and defines all mental activities, even those which seem to be of an exclusively cognitive character. Thus the mind in sense-experience develops only those perceptions which are necessary for action, and develops them in that particular form which best enables them to fulfil their practical function. Ideas which can gain no purchase on the body can form no integral part of our real life, and therefore, though possible to the mind, will not appear within the conscious field. Inefficacy is equivalent to unconsciousness. In this manner the limitation of our sense-experience to the immediate environment in which the body stands, and also the various illusions, convenient though false, which characterize the visual field, may one and all be explained. They reveal the transformations which our consciousness of the real world undergoes in order the better to gain control over the material body.

Fourthly, though this position involves a pragmatist attitude towards ordinary consciousness, it implies an anti-pragmatist view of knowledge as a whole. True knowledge consists in emancipation, within the theoretical domain, from the tyranny of practical needs.

These, then, are the chief consequences which follow from Bergson's position. His philosophy is a detailed and very definite contribution towards the establishment of realism. It makes a bold frontal attack upon all the main obstacles which stand in the way of a realistic interpretation of sense-perception. As I have already said, it has the unique value of establishing a genuinely new standpoint from which to approach the problem of knowledge. We have, it seems to me, no right to put forward realistic theories of our own until we have discussed and definitely come to terms with this highly elaborated system. For myself, I can neither accept nor reject it; but it seems to me to afford better promise of further light than any theory yet presented. If this paper will in any measure serve to draw the attention of others to Bergson's works, it will have been written to good purpose.

How far is Agreement Possible in Philosophy?

IN this brief paper I shall try to indicate a possible line of answer to the questions[1] formulated in the programme of discussion arranged for the coming meeting of the Philosophical Association.

The term 'science' is currently employed in two very distinct senses. It may mean thinking that is as rigorous, as enlightened, and as competent as our present knowledge of the factors involved in the problems dealt with will permit. All philosophical thinking, worthy of the name, may be presumed to be of this character, and as such will fall under the rubric of science in this broader meaning of the term. It will be grouped with mathematics and physics as well as with sociology, politics, and psychology. But the term is also employed, and as I think more advisedly, in a narrower sense to denote those disciplines in which there is a working agreement as to principles, methods, and results. By universal admission philosophy has not in the past been of this character.

Are we then to conclude that all knowledge worthy of the name is science, and that we can have no knowledge save in those regions where science has gained secure footing? Such a question answers itself. We cannot defer having convictions in ethics and politics until the scientific expert is prepared to enlighten us upon the duties of life. And as history proves, we would not possess even the existing mathematical disciplines if non-scientific, tentative theorizing had not seemed to our ancestors a legitimate and worthy form of attainable knowledge.

The nature of the distinction between science and philosophy may perhaps be interpreted somewhat as follows. Science deals with the isolable, philosophy with the non-isolable problems. Each science has

[1] Cf. *Journal of Philosophy, Psychology and Scientific Methods*, vol. ix, no. 22, p. 615.

been brought into existence through the discovery of a method whereby some one problem or set of problems can be isolated from all others, and solved in terms of the factors revealed within a definitely limited field of observation and analysis. Science is successful specialization. Galileo founded the science of dynamics by demonstrating that it is possible to discover the laws governing the behaviour of bodies independently of any solution of the many metaphysical problems involved in the determination of the causes of motion. Newton transformed Descartes' speculative cosmology into a scientific system by a further extension of the same procedure. Darwin's triumphant achievement was similar in character. He successfully segregated the problem of the preservation of variations from the question, with which all that is speculative in biology is so inextricably bound up, of the nature of the causes determining their origin. Such methods of specialization prove acceptable to other workers in the same field, and their application leads to a growing body of generally accepted teaching.

It is frequently urged that science succeeds where philosophy has failed. But that, as history can demonstrate, is an entirely false reading of the actual facts. The sciences, when not simply new sub-divisions within an existing science, and sometimes even then, are always the outcome of antecedent philosophizing. The coming into existence of a new science means that the earlier 'unscientific' speculations have at length succeeded in forging conceptual weapons sufficiently adequate for the steady progressive solution of the problems dealt with. The creation of a science is consequently the justification of the relevant previous theorizings. But the objection will at once be restated in altered form. Philosophy, it may be said, is of value only in proportion as it becomes science, and it has already been displaced from every one of the fields of knowledge. Induction from observed facts has been substituted for *a priori* reasoning from fictitious premises. Philosophy, so far as it continues to exist in any form distinct from science, is on this view merely the attempt to formulate solutions while our insight is still such as not to justify them. In the absence of the disciplinary rigour of observed fact, it freely indulges the caprice of temperament, and employs the arts of the special pleader to justify conclusions antecedently adopted.

Such objections, I take it, only show that even in devoted students of science the old Adam of circumscribed outlook may still survive. The above attitude is merely the modern representative of the kind of objection that greeted the beginnings of speculation even in ancient Greece. And to any such sweeping criticisms the history of philosophy is sufficient reply. It is still what it has always been, the history of genuine insight in the making. For reasons entirely understandable Hegel is of evil repute with the majority of scientists. But surely in the field of the historical disciplines his influence has been fruitful to a quite remarkable degree. The list of historians and sociologists who have profited by his speculations would overflow the limits of many pages. I need only mention, as outstanding instances, Ranke and Zeller, Renan and Strauss, Proudhon and Karl Marx. Or to cite the work of an earlier thinker: Leibniz not only shares with Newton the honour of discovering the differential calculus, he also formulated that programme of a universal logic which has since been developed by Boole, Peano, Whitehead and Russell, and which has in consequence made so beneficial an eruption through the hard crust of the more traditional logic. The difficulties which we find in defining the present relation between science and philosophy would not seem to be due to any diminution in the influence which philosophy is exerting either upon science or upon general thought. They are largely caused by its more delicate and sensitive adjustment to the varied and complex needs of our modern life. It has learned to formulate its theories in more adequate terms and so can bring its influences more subtly and persuasively to bear. The interplay of influences is closer and more complicated than ever before.

The tasks of philosophy vary, indeed, with the needs of the age, and for that reason are all the more inevitably prescribed. The very certainty and assurance which the sciences have acquired in their several fields constitutes a new menace to the liberality of thought. The frequent unreliability of the expert in matters of practice is universally recognized; his dogmatism in matters broadly theoretical is less easily discounted, and may in the future prove insidiously harmful. Philosophy is still needed in order to enforce breadth of outlook and catholicity of judgement. It stands for the general human values as against excessive pretensions, whether in science, in religion, or in practical life, for the past and the future as against the present, for comprehensiveness and leisure as against narrowness and haste. The individual philosopher may not, of course, possess these qualities, but he at least lays claim to them, and is supposed to have earnestly striven to embody them in his own person, when he professes to give a theory of life that is genuinely philosophical. And though, perhaps, at some time in the very distant future philosophy may overcome the differences between itself and science, this is not a possibility which we can anticipate in any precise or even imaginative fashion. What truly concerns us is rather to define the actual relation in which, under present conditions, the two types of theoretical inquiry would seem to stand to one another.

All the most important distinctions, even those that are most fundamental, are ultimately partial and in some degree relative. I am not concerned to maintain that the isolation of scientific problems is ever quite complete or that the sciences do not from time to time themselves become metaphysical. I also recognize that philosophy does in some measure experimentally employ methods of partial isolation within its own field. But in this brief paper I can take account only of the broader features of the intellectual landscape. Should these be properly surveyed, the description will yield an outline that no minuteness of detail need essentially modify. Science and philosophy may have community of origin, of logical structure, and of ultimate destiny; and yet may be most fruitfully interpreted in terms of their differences. The fact that mountain ranges have been ocean beds and may become so again does not affect the truth and utility of our modern maps.

That brings me to the second part of my question. What is philosophy *in its distinction from* science? Philosophical knowledge, I should contend, differs from the scientific in its incapacity to answer any one of its problems without anticipating, in broad outline, the kind of answer that has to be given to all the others. That is to say, it deals with all those problems for which no method of successful isolation has yet been formulated. The present position of logic may serve as an illustration. There is as great divergence regarding logical questions as there is in regard to ethical problems. And the reason would seem to be that the theory of the judgement and of the nature of universals has never yet been successfully segregated from the general body of philosophical doctrine. Bertrand Russell's analysis of deductive reasoning is inspired by his rationalist epistemology, just as Mill's counter-theory is based on his sensationalist metaphysics. This is still more obvious when we come to such problems as the nature of consciousness or of our moral vocation. They involve considerations which reach out into all departments of life. They are humanistic problems, and carry with them into their theoretical treatment all the complexities and difficulties of a practical, ethical, and religious orientation towards life. They bring into play the whole man as well as all the sciences. The various philosophical problems cannot be treated as so many separate issues and their solutions combined to form a comprehensive system. That would result in what Faguet, in speaking of Voltaire, has described as 'a chaos of clear ideas'. The specific characteristic of philosophical reflexion is that in dealing with any of its problems it must simultaneously bear in mind the correlative requirements of all the others. Even when it finds its chief inspiration in some one specific field, it may do so only in so far as the insight thereby acquired can be shown to be supremely illuminating in other spheres.

But if the residual problems can only be solved in terms of a general philosophical standpoint, how is this latter to be attained? The answer—lack of space must excuse dogmatism of statement—lies in recognition of the manner in which the past history of philosophy predetermines, consciously or unconsciously, our present-day problems. Philosophy is to be found only in the history of philosophy, and each new system fulfils its mission in proportion as it yields an enlightening reading of past experience, a genuine analysis of present conditions, and in terms of these a prophetic foreshadowing of its own future development. The results of scientific research sum themselves up in definite principles and in prescribed methods. To that extent the scientist can dispense with the study of history. But this does not happen in philosophy, and the place of those principles and methods has therefore to be supplied by such guidance as the individual thinker can extract from the past development of the philosophical problems.

There are, of course, two paths, apparently independent, upon which philosophical truth may be sought. It may be discovered through direct historical study. It was largely so in the case of Comte and of Hegel.

Or it may come through concentration on the present-day problems as in Spencer and Karl Pearson.[1] But in neither case is the procedure such as to completely dispense with the alternative method. It is easy to decipher the interpretation of past thought which underlies Spencer's or Pearson's thinking. It is some such hag-ridden reading of history as we find in Buckle's 'Civilization in England'. We can similarly single out the contemporary influences which controlled and directed the historical studies of Comte and Hegel. The alternative is not really between historical and systematic treatment of our philosophical problems, but only in both classes of thinkers, between the more competent and the less competent, between intellectual mastery and unconscious preconception.

My meaning will be made clearer if I draw attention to the obvious fact that the history of philosophy cannot be written once and for all. It has to be recast by each generation to suit its own needs, to harmonize with its increased insight and altered standpoint. Ultimately every independent thinker must reinterpret it for himself. It is no less plastic to new interpretations than the present reality with which our analytic thinking deals. An adequate solution of philosophical problems and a valid interpretation of past systems must develop together. They mutually condition one another.

This practically amounts to a reassertion, in a more special form, of my previous contention that the problems of philosophy, as co-ordinating and humanistic, are non-isolable. They differ from the problems of the positive sciences, not only in the complexity of their data, but also in the impossibility of adequately treating them by any method exclusively analytic. They likewise demand an orientation towards history, and the application of the insight thereby acquired.

Proof of this may be found in the perennial character of the three fundamental types of philosophical thinking; naturalism, scepticism, and idealism. All three are in this twentieth century as vigorously assertive, and as eagerly supported by competent thinkers, as they have ever been in past time. While developing *pari passu* with the general body of human knowledge, they stand in a constant relation of interaction and mutual aid. Each in the struggle for self-maintenance compels

[1] It is significant how few examples of 'unhistorical' philosophy can be cited.

the competing systems to develop on fresh lines, meeting new objections by modification of their former grounds; and in this process each progresses largely in proportion as it can profit by the criticisms rendered possible by the two opposing standpoints. The debt which modern agnosticism owes to the transcendentalism of Plato and to the phenomenalism of Kant is only to be matched by that which Plato owed to Heraclitus, and Kant to Hume. Present-day idealism is largely indebted for more adequate formulation of its views to the mediating function which naturalism has exercised in the interpretation of scientific results. Any system, therefore, which is accepted as most satisfactorily solving our present-day problems will have to be viewed as that towards which previous philosophies of every type have gradually converged.

The history of philosophy can, indeed, be written from any one of the three standpoints in such manner as to demonstrate that all past thought has been contributory to its ultimate strengthening. The grouping, interrelation, and valuation of historical facts will vary in the three interpretations, but the entire content of each will be reinterpreted by both the others. The sceptic, for instance, can not, without self-stultification, without the tacit admission of the inadequacy of his philosophy, recognize the possibility of a *separate* history of scepticism. He must sweep into his historical net the positive teachings of the idealist thinkers; he must be able to assign a value to the mystical temperament, and to assimilate the results of the so-called positive sciences. In other words, his history must be a history of philosophy as a whole. Thus the type of system which a philosopher propounds determines, and is determined by the interpretation given to the history of philosophy. Only in proportion as he consciously realizes this, does he look before and after, and show the philosophic mind. And if we may argue not only from the past to the future, but from the character of the present situation to the remedy for its confusions and defects, surely we may conclude that no one of the three standpoints has yet outlived its usefulness. Would not the liberality of thought and the progressiveness of philosophy be seriously endangered if any one of the three were to be permanently suppressed, and could no longer gain supporters willing to yield to it their whole-hearted devotion?

This contention may be further developed by reference to the influence exercised by temperament. That its influence is very considerable cannot be questioned. Frequently it is of an entirely legitimate and beneficial character, aiding in clarity of judgement. A pessimistic temperament may render a thinker more sensitive to the facts of evil, and more willing to recognize them for what they truly are. The mystic's firm personal footing in immediate experience may conduce to a more acute and open-minded recognition of radical defects in the mediating labours of idealist thinkers. No doubt in both cases the advantage will be counterbalanced by corresponding limitations which the temperament will impose; but that need not prevent us from recognizing the quite invaluable role which it frequently plays.

But it is one thing to recognize the psychological value of varying temperaments; it is quite another to view them as *justifying* the conclusions to which they may lead. Philosophy is an enterprise no less rigorously intellectual than science itself. In dealing with the immediate experiences of religion, of art, and of social and individual life, it must aim exclusively at theoretical interpretation. Such feelings can be relied on only in proportion as they are found to possess some cognitive significance. Even if we might assume that the various temperaments tend to generate specific types of philosophy, it would still have to be recognized that each must justify its preference by arguments that can be intellectually tested. But the assumption is surely contrary to all experience. Does not each of the three types of philosophical system meet the needs of all possible temperaments? The Marxian socialist is frequently mystical and idealistic in the enthusiasm of his materialistic creed; and many idealists are of the exclusively logical cast of mind. And as a rule temperament, it would seem, chiefly displays itself in some such manner. It does not so much determine the type of system adopted, as lend to it the emotional atmosphere in which it is suffused.

The really fundamental reason why equally competent philosophical thinkers may arrive at diametrically opposite results is not, I believe, to be looked for in temperament, but rather in the complexity of the problems, and in the limitations which personal experience, necessarily incomplete and differing from one individual to another, imposes upon us. Owing to the multiplicity of the elements which we are called upon to co-ordinate, omission of certain factors and the distribution of emphasis among those that are retained, are all-important in determining the outcome. This, of course, affords temperament its supreme opportunity. But in ultimate analysis it is not temperament itself, but the complexity of the data that makes this situation possible at all. And the sole escape from the perverting influence of subjectivity lies in progressive intellectualization of the experiences which generate and support it. Recognition of temperament as a universally present and subtly illusive psychological influence does not in any wise conflict with the ideal demand for a rigorous enforcement of impersonal standards. If thinkers can sincerely differ in so radical a fashion, ought we not rather to argue that the material which awaits scientific treatment, and which meantime can allow only of the tentative insight entitled 'philosophy', must be rich in significant data, and on fuller knowledge will deepen and revolutionize our present theories?

The criticisms passed upon current systems for their lack of agreement would apply equally well to the pre-Socratic philosophers, and yet, arbitrary as their conflicting views may at first sight seem, there is surely no more fascinating period in the whole history of human thought. For we there find truth in its manifold aspects coming to its own through the devious channels of opposing minds. The pre-Socratics co-operated through their very diversity more fruitfully than they could possibly have done had they all belonged within a single school. What is purely arbitrary, merely temperamental, due to ignorance or confusion, is gradually eliminated, while the really fruitful problems and the truly helpful methods are retained and developed.

The willing acceptance by the individual of mutually irreconcilable beliefs, i.e., pluralism within the individual mind, is the 'happy despatch' of philosophy. The co-operative pluralism of divergent thinkers may, on the other hand, prove its salvation. Though logical consistency is a far from reliable guide in the affairs of life, it must none the less be accepted as a valid criterion of truth. The only field of legitimate pluralism lies outside the individual mind in the sphere of historical development, and in the encouragement, in our present-day thinking, of everything which favours individual reaction. For we have to recognize that while mutual agreement may perhaps be the ultimate goal, it cannot reasonably be looked for in the near future. The situation does not allow of it. Should it come about, by the tyranny (it could be nothing else) of a dominant school, such as that of the Hegelian philosophy in Germany in the beginning of the nineteenth century, philosophy itself would cease to fulfil its critical function, and the scientific philistine would deserve, for the greater good of his generation, again to reign supreme. When experts in science contrive to be of one mind, benefits result to society at large; but when metaphysicians consent to agree, philosophy may safely be counted as being on the decline. Science is able to discover more or less final truth, and so all scientists may unite to voice a common rejoicing; but philosophy with its merely tentative and always inadequate formulations must regard each step forward as a challenge for criticism, and as a call for counter-emphasis upon omitted facts. The duty of scientists is to arrive at mutual agreement upon fundamentals; the best service which one philosopher can do another is to supply effective and damaging criticism. No doubt such a mode of statement exaggerates the differences. But it is these that seem to me chiefly relevant.

I do not wish to argue against the formation of groups or schools. Thinkers tend to group themselves according to affinities. In the difficult task of developing a novel theory against the damaging onslaughts of ingenious and forceful opponents who will always have the advantage of deriving ready-made weapons from the armory of established and therefore more fully elaborated philosophies, the sympathetic backing of an understanding group is certainly a helpful and legitimate support. But such agreement does not, I think, require to be artificially fostered. It comes about of itself, and frequently in the most unlooked-for fashion. When consciously sought, as it was in France under Cousin's domination of university teaching, it may all too easily prove dangerously harmful. Even when more or less unified groups exist, a member of one group may learn more from the members of opposed groups than from those of his own school.

Science, Bacon has declared, is a discipline in humility of mind. But, surely philosophy is so in even greater degree. It is not gregarious like science—not even in conferences, for we meet only to learn from our mutual differences. Philosophy still pursues, in tenor of its ancient ways, a life solitary and itinerant, devoted to problems which may be illusive and refractory, but which seem to it to make up by centrality of interest for anything they may lack in definiteness of detail or in finality of statement. We here find one of the most striking manifestations of the influence of temperament. The scientist has a liking for the one type of problem, the philosopher for the other. May both continue to flourish to their mutual benefit! Probably the best aid to their mutual understanding lies in a frank canvassing of what in the present situation would seem to be their ineradicable differences.

This indicates my answer to the last of the questions in the discussion programme. The point of view which inspired the elaborate organization of last year's discussion[1] seems to me to involve an impossible ignoring of the radical differences between scientific and philosophical inquiry. Though both interesting and valuable as an experiment, it seemed to me, on trial, to have proved self-defeating. That did not happen through any fault of the committee on definitions; their difficult task was, I think, most admirably executed. But the initial agreement which they sought to establish was really impossible. Science may start from agreed principles and defined terms, since it has behind it a body of universally accepted knowledge from which such principles and definitions may be obtained. But it is just upon the question of how to define ultimate terms that all our philosophical disputes really turn. Such imitation of scientific procedure would therefore seem to be altogether impossible. The formulations given, whether of terms or of postulates, have to be lacking in precision in order to allow of use by differing disputants. And being indefinite they are ambiguous, and so defeat the very purpose for which they are formulated.

The committee's discussion programme for the coming meeting seems better calculated to achieve the purposes which our Association has in view. It does not assume that we can start from points of agreement; it aims only at better mutual understanding of our points of difference, in the hope that we may—for such is in almost all cases the sole outcome of friendly discussion on such fundamental topics—thereafter be more clear minded in regard to our own tenets, and better

[1] *Journal of Philosophy, Psychology and Scientific Methods,* vol. viii (1911), no. 26, pp. 701–6. (Report of the Committee on Definitions of the American Philosophical Association.)

appreciative of the more inward aspects of our opponents' positions. Our purpose is increased understanding of what are almost certain to continue to be our lines of divergence, and not what, as I have argued, would under present conditions be a most undesirable consummation, mutual conversion to a common standpoint. Reciprocal enlightenment is surely more likely to descend upon us when each uses his terms in the individual manner that most naturally expresses the trend of his thought.

The Middle Ages, the Renaissance, and the Modern Mind

THE coloured windows of the Gothic cathedrals and the dazzling lights of Dante's *Paradiso* are no mere accidental expressions of the medieval spirit. It demanded bright and gorgeous colouring for the expression of its intense emotional life. The *Romance of the Rose,* the story of *Abelard and Heloïse*, the ideals of chivalry and the love poetry of Provence are as truly medieval as are the lives of the saints, so full of fervour and poetry, or the magnificent Latin hymns. Dante fainting at sight of Beatrice is medieval in the intensity, the almost morbid intensity of the medieval spirit. The fine-spun, over-subtle distinctions of scholastic philosophy are indeed frequently pedantic, but it was a pedantry largely due to love of traditional forms which were closely knit into the general mind and sanctioned by the emotional life which they expressed and nourished. Frequently, too, it was due to a love of symbolism, of the word as more than the thought, of language as an instrument of power and not merely of expression, valuable for its emotional suggestiveness as well as for its intellectual content. The Holy Mass of the Roman Church, symbolic in its every word and action, is a no less typical creation than is Gothic architecture. All the best medieval thinking is impassioned thought, emotionally charged with love and fear. It was spiritually intense, with all the high lights and deep shadows of a vivid inner life. To realise how greatly the modern mind has been enriched by its medieval inheritance we have only to compare the work of Michelangelo with that of Phidias and Praxiteles. We speak of the emotional atmosphere of Michelangelo as being not Greek but modern— yes, modern, but only if that term is taken in its widest sense as including the medieval, and as opposed only to the ancient or classical.

Owing to the present-day predominance of science over art, we are apt carelessly to assume that ignorance of mind and poverty of soul must go hand in hand. No conclusion is more false. Anthropologists would seem to be working round to the view that imagination is the faculty which more truly than reason distinguishes man from the animals. The power to form free images has been a chief agency enabling man to emancipate himself from the given environment and to subordinate it to his needs. It is to imagination also that religion and the arts are in large part due. Inspired by fitting standards of value, it can interpret the universe and human life more adequately than the more enlightened generation which has no recognized controlling values through which to master and appropriate its accumulated body of knowledge. The periods of enlightenment and the periods of spiritual greatness, as manifested in the arts, in religion, and in social life, by no means coincide. As a rule, standards of value make their appearance in the general life long prior to any possibility of their theoretical establishment. And so it would seem to be in the development of the European mind. Modern values which have called for a reconstruction of life not yet completed, were, it would seem, first brought into existence under the stimulus and discipline of medieval conditions.

An alteration of emotional values is an infallible sign, both in the development of the individual and in the history of humanity, of radical transformation in the structure of life, and is laden with consequences as far-reaching as any that can be caused by additions to our knowledge. Now, in the Middle Ages the European scale of emotional and spiritual values was not only extended and enriched, but was profoundly altered in its standards. And I shall strive to maintain that the chief contribution of medieval life to modern civilization exactly consists in this deepening and transvaluation of the standards of judgement. But, as I have said, I shall indicate only indirectly, through criticism of the defects of the classical tradition, in what this contribution consists.

In the transition to modern standpoints two very distinct sets of causes were contributory: on the one hand, the new discoveries, geographical and scientific, and, on the other hand, the revival of Greek and Hebrew studies. Of the first set of causes much might be said. I shall single out for consideration only the new astronomy. The entire scheme of medieval theology rests upon the assumption that the earth is the sole planet inhabited by a race of beings similar to man. The discovery, therefore, that the stars are suns identical in nature with our own, and therefore presumably surrounded by planets similar to the earth, was most disconcerting. It is not surprising that Giordano Bruno, the philosopher of the Copernican system, should have been condemned by the Church. If it was to burn any heretic, it could not have chosen a more fitting victim. His philosophy demonstrated very clearly the necessity for a radical reconstruction of Church dogma.

But we must distinguish between the religious attitude and its theological interpretation. And in terms of this distinction we may say that though the Copernican astronomy dealt the death-blow to the traditional theology, it has strengthened the higher and deeper elements in the religious consciousness, and has favoured the elimination of its more compromising features. The religious consciousness and the Ptolemaic cosmology hardly seem to harmonize. Who has not felt in reading Dante the almost grotesque character of the cosmical setting which the current astronomy compelled him to give to the sublime mysteries of his Christian Faith? It was excellently suited to his realistic imagination, but it was incongruous with the conceptions which he was seeking to body forth.

Calvin was no scientist, and held to the traditional cosmology, but in cutting away from the medieval theology those doctrines which seemed to him inconsistent with the teaching of the Old and New Testaments, he developed a religion which at its best breathes the very spirit of the new astronomy. The Calvinist teaching almost demands a Copernican astronomy as the only appropriate setting for human life, the fitting manifestation of a Divine Being before whose perfection, as Calvin delights to insist, even the cherubim faint with fear and shade their eyes. What I mean will become clear if we take a passage from the opening chapter of Calvin's *Institutes:*

> Very remote from the divine purity is what seems in us the highest perfection. Hence that horror and amazement with which the Scripture always represents the saints to have been impressed and disturbed, on every discovery of the presence of God. For when

we see those, who before his appearance stood secure and firm, so astonished and affrighted at the manifestation of his glory, as to faint and almost expire with fear, we must infer that man is never sufficiently affected with a knowledge of his own meanness, till he has compared himself with the Divine Majesty. Of this consternation we have frequent examples in the Judges and prophets; so that it was a common expression among the Lord's people: 'We shall die, because we have seen God.' . . . And what can man do, all vile and corrupt, when fear constrains even the cherubim themselves to veil their faces? This is what the prophet Isaiah speaks of: 'The moon shall be confounded, and the sun ashamed, when the Lord of Hosts shall reign'; that is, when he shall make a fuller and nearer exhibition of his splendour, it shall eclipse the splendour of the brightest object beside.[1]

The new astronomy has been one of the abiding sources of the ineradicable differences between Greek and modern interpretations of life. It has tended to confer upon modern modes of thinking something of that spirit of moral intensity and religious humility which are so characteristically medieval. It has brought us into closer sympathy with, and better understanding of, the Hebrew attitude of mind—the attitude of inspired humility, which teaches that fear, or to use a less misleading term, reverence, is the beginning of wisdom. Not a craven fear that swamps the mind, but a fear that searches the spirit, steadying it to clearer vision, and awakening it to consciousness of the serious issues of life.

But I turn to the second main set of causes, generative of the Renaissance, the revival of Greek, and in minor degree of Hebrew, studies. The Renaissance in its earlier periods largely consisted in a twofold attempt to restore antiquity. The majority of the humanists were chiefly interested in classical antiquity, but others, among whom we must count Reuchlin and Erasmus as well as Calvin, were much more concerned in penetrating to the sources of the Christian tradition. The *Hebrew Rudiments* of Reuchlin appeared in 1506. Erasmus published his edition of the Greek New Testament in 1516, and his editions of the Christian Fathers appeared in succeeding years.[2] Calvin,

[1] Allen's translation.

[2] Cf. Bacon, *Advancement of Learning* (Cassell, 1905), bk. I, iv, s. ii: 'Martin Luther, conducted (no doubt) by a higher providence, but in discourse of reason, finding what

who came in the second generation of the Reformation movement, when it could first hope to succeed in adequately formulating to itself its philosophy of life, especially concerns us, and I may briefly dwell upon the influence which he has exercised.

Calvin is a modern, and belongs to the modern world. He was a very competent humanist, and his first work was a commentary on Seneca's *De Clementia*. But his historical significance is due chiefly to his sympathy with what we may call medievalism, to the fact that he reformulated medieval ideals in austere and noble form, and that he successfully carried them forward as living forces into the modern world. Professedly what he sought to do was to return to Christian antiquity, and to restore it in its pure and pristine form. What he actually achieved was to formulate the strictly medieval view of human life and destiny in the most unrelieved and definite manner. This success was due to his elimination of ecclesiastical and secondary considerations of every kind. His teaching is the teaching of St. Paul, as interpreted by St. Augustine. In this respect it is analogous in character to the Jansenist movement, which in the seventeenth century and within the Roman Church generated the noble group of the Port Royal. It makes everything rest upon the doctrine of original sin, and views that doctrine not as a mere dogma, referring to a long-past historical event, the sin of our first parents, but as a correct and literal reading of human nature as it presents itself in each and every man. It declares that man is defective in will-power, and is enslaved by passions and desires which in the most insidious fashion flatter his human pride and conceal from him his weak and evil state. I may cite the passage which in the *Institutes* immediately precedes that above quoted:

> It is plain that no man can arrive at the true knowledge of himself, without having first contemplated the divine character, and then descended to the consideration of his own. For such is the native

a province he had undertaken against the bishop of Rome and the degenerate traditions of the Church, and finding his own solitude, being no ways aided by the opinions of his own time, was enforced to awake all antiquity and to call former times to his succour to make a party against the present time: so that the ancient authors, both in divinity and in humanity, which had long slept in libraries, began generally to be read and revolved.'

pride of us all, we invariably esteem ourselves righteous, innocent, wise, and holy, till we are convinced, by clear proofs, of our unrighteousness, turpitude, folly, and impurity. But we are never thus convinced, while we confine our attention to ourselves, and regard not the Lord, who is the only standard by which this judgement ought to be formed. . . . The eye accustomed to see nothing but black, judges that to be very white, which is but whitish, or perhaps brown. . . . Thus also it happens in the consideration of our spiritual endowments. For as long as our views are bounded by the earth, perfectly content with our own righteousness, wisdom, and strength, we fondly flatter ourselves, and fancy we are little less than demigods. But if we once elevate our thoughts to God, and consider his nature, and the consummate perfection of his righteousness, wisdom, and strength, to which we ought to be conformed, . . . what strangely deceived us under the title of wisdom will be despised as extreme folly; and what wore that appearance of strength will be proved to be most wretched impotence. So very remote from the divine purity is what seems in us the highest perfection. Hence that horror and amazement with which the Scripture always represents the saints to have been impressed and disturbed, on every discovery of the presence of God.

Thus at the very time when the Greek spirit, in its freedom and self-assurance, was gaining converts on every side, Calvin reformulated the alternative interpretation of life. His theology is, like all the best medieval thought, genuinely mystical. It is Augustinian, and that is to say medieval, in the intensity of its emotional force. It is intense in exact proportion to its self-restraint, and to the narrowing of the channels in which it is made to run. Not expansiveness but sincerity and intensity are its ideals, not self-realization but self-mastery, not happiness but discipline for the sake of a supreme perfection entirely transcendent of anything immediately attainable in a present successful and happy life. It would contrast the face, pale and drawn, of the Christian saint, in his never-ceasing combat for a surpassing perfection, with the ideal of health and competency, of success and achievement, to which the classical spirit pays all its homage. The one is preoccupied with the fact of inevitable failure for all who are living the religious life, who are aiming at ideals which transcend their powers and induce a perpetual humility of soul. It emphasizes man's natural weakness, his lack of inspiration and lack of power. The aim of the other is health of body and social efficiency, and these being under favourable conditions readily attainable, it feels justified in maintaining that normal human powers are entirely adequate to all appeals that may be made upon them. It is, of course, to some reconciliation of these divergent ideals— and it is useless to refuse to recognize that they constantly diverge and often conflict—that the modern spirit aspires.

Now, as I have just said, the Renaissance was, at starting, largely historical in its interests. These historical interests originated, however, in the belief, entertained by the Renaissance scholars, that in returning to the past they were returning to the sources of all true life, secular and religious, and were therefore preparing the way for a better under-standing of present conditions. Like so many reformers, they meant 'forward', though their cry was 'back!' Their historical interests were only secondarily historical; they were really pragmatic in aim.

For this, and for other reasons into which I need not enter, the historical interest gradually receded, and in place of the watchword, 'return to antiquity', was substituted the rallying-cry, more adequate because more truly expressive of the actual tendencies, 'return to nature and to reason'. And not until towards the end of the eighteenth century and the beginning of the nineteenth, did any genuinely historical interest re-emerge. The seventeenth and eighteenth centuries were centuries of unhistorical thinking, centuries that had no real under-standing of their own roots, and in which therefore tendencies all too frequently brought about their own destruction by entering into con-federacy with forces radically inconsistent with the essential values for which they themselves stood. This is especially true of the Reformation churches during those two centuries. They failed adequately to represent and enforce the ideals which were entrusted to their keeping. Many of their most influential leaders lost touch with their sources, and were dragged at the chariot wheels of an overwhelmingly victorious classical tradition; with the consequence that they shed off from their Faith just those tenets which gave it meaning and a solid foundation in the psy-chology of the human mind. The English Deists, for instance, actually attempted to establish Christian theology upon the doctrine of the essential goodness of human nature. This was just the sort of theology to appeal to the poet Pope, to Voltaire and to Rousseau; and in their hands it became a European force. But it is the desertion of everything for which the Protestant reformulation of medieval values had professed to stand.

When I thus maintain that in the intellectual realm the Protestant churches proved false to the medieval traditions which were in their keeping, and so became a negligible influence in the philosophical field. I employ the word 'intellectual' in order to mark an important limitation. For, of course, the various evangelical movements, such as Wesleyanism in England and Pietism in Germany, had a profound influence on the general life, and preserved the medieval values in an active though submerged form. But they generated no leaders intellectually capable of rendering them a force in the sphere of philosophical reflection.

The very fact that medieval sympathies were in intellectual circles in abeyance, and that the churches which stood for medieval ideals were in the main without important intellectual influence—this situation enabled the classical tradition to develop a new vitality, and to inspire, under the altered modern conditions, a genuinely original, and astonishingly fruitful, interpretation of life. The main stages of its development appear in Francis Bacon, John Locke, the English Deists, Voltaire, the French Encyclopedists, and Rousseau. Francis Bacon strikes a note never before sounded. He was not himself scientifically trained, and in many respects, especially owing to his ignorance of mathematics, he radically misinterpreted the methods and ideals of the new science. But he prophetically expounded, in speech of magnificent power, a new vision of human possibilities upon the earth. He taught that knowledge, scientific knowledge, is power. In virtue of his intelligence man has a creative capacity, to which no limits can be prescribed, a power of subordinating nature, and of taking the destiny which hitherto nature has controlled into his own hands. If, as it seemed to the archaeologists of that time, the Greeks may be said to have created the arts, the moderns, according to Bacon, were destined for the still greater task of recasting the entire economy of human life.

The beginnings of the next step appear in John Locke. Bacon's vision had been limited to the material conditions of human existence. Locke applied the same free and forward-looking analysis to its political and educational aspects. And the seed which he sowed, slowly maturing, came to sudden flower in what have very fittingly been named the Enlightenment philosophies, the philosophies of the Encyclopedists and Rousseau. They taught that by the radical recasting of social institutions and by the development of new and better educational methods, human life may be transformed into something very different from and immeasurably superior to, all that it has hitherto been. The future will be related only through contrast to the past. As Godwin, an enthusiastic supporter of this teaching, declared in his *Political Justice:* 'Nothing can be more unreasonable than to argue from men as we find them, to men as they may hereafter be made.' The entrance of this philosophy upon the stage of history was celebrated by the great drama of the French Revolution, which was at once the offspring of its aspirations, and the proof of its almost demoniac powers. It released energies which at once transformed it from an academic philosophy into a world-force. The Enlightenment is well named, and deserves more credit than we, who have profited by its labours, and can criticize its earlier manifestations, are usually prepared to admit. Its influence seems to me even more fundamental and far-reaching than that which has been exercised by the evolution-theories propounded by Darwin. It is the specifically modern standpoint. It is the type and norm of every philosophy which seeks to justify its methods and doctrines by the future rather than by the past. It is also the legitimate offspring of the classical tradition. For it expresses, under the altered conditions of modern life, and in view of the powerful weapon which modern science has placed in men's hands, the same free self-assurance that inspired the Greeks in the upbuilding of their civilization. It expresses the same conviction of the supreme value of intellectual enlightenment as the chief agency of human progress.

I should like especially to emphasize the humanitarian character of the eighteenth-century Enlightenment. An extremely significant feature of its humanitarianism is its comparative independence of any very real interest in moral ideals. Anyone who identifies humanitarianism and morality would seem to rule himself out from understanding the movements of history. For many of those who are genuinely human-itarian in their instincts and sympathies—Voltaire is the supreme instance, Diderot is another—are almost completely non-moral in matters of the inner life. And many who are deeply spiritual are ex-tremely indifferent to questions of social reform.

The cause is not far to seek. The spiritually ambitious value nothing so highly as the disciplinary tutelage of affliction and hardship. The only argument they will readily listen to is that inequality, poverty, and oppression are so excessive as to remove all possibility of moral reaction. The more secularly minded, on the other hand, themselves locating the entire meaning of life in happiness, and its material conditions, vividly appreciate, and cannot so easily condone or excuse, the glaring in-equalities.

This explains many things. It partly explains why the Middle Ages, spiritually so ambitious, should stand notorious in history for the insensitiveness of their political and ecclesiastical rulers. It also in part explains why the humanitarianism through which the nineteenth century is so strongly marked off from all preceding times should be due much more truly to classical than to Christian sources, and why the Christian churches should as a rule be so very dilatory in recognizing that the spirit which inspires the demand for the removal of abuses and inequalities is that which is inculcated in the Gospels. It explains why, for instance, the doctrine of natural rights—a doctrine of very composite origin, issuing from Stoic teaching embodied in Roman law—why that doctrine, theoretically so unsound, historically so beneficial, should have found many of its chief supporters among the anti-religious, and, as in Diderot, non-moral philosophers of the eighteenth century. It also suggests the reflection that a materialistic age may very easily contrive to conceal from itself its spiritual poverty by exclusively emphasizing its humanitarian activities. Here, as elsewhere, the Christian and the classical traditions have each something to teach the other.

Before passing to my next main point, let me briefly indicate what would seem to be one of the chief defects of the Enlightenment philos-ophies, their inadequate appreciation of the truth involved in that most characteristic and fundamental of all the medieval tenets, the doctrine of original sin. The various Enlightenment thinkers one and all start from

Locke's doctrine that the mind of the new-born child is a *tabula rasa,* a sheet of white paper, upon which society and the educator may inscribe whatever they please. There are, they taught, no inborn tendencies that set a limit to the possible transformations which human nature may be made to undergo. I have already quoted Godwin's dictum: 'Nothing can be more unreasonable than to argue from men as we find them, to men as they may hereafter be made.' They one and all trace man's evil conduct to the perverting influence of *external* causes. The explanation of the Deists and of Voltaire was that all moral evil is ultimately traceable to superstitions invented by priests for their own private ends. In place of this absurdly inadequate anti-clerical explanation Rousseau substituted the theory which has had so important an after-history—that evil is due ultimately to economic causes, reinforced by the perverting influence of the arts and sciences. But even that explanation is one which modern psychology cannot accept. Let me quote the words of a thinker who cannot be regarded as a benighted medievalist, Thomas Huxley:

> With all their enormous differences in natural endowment, men agree in one thing, and that is their innate desire to enjoy the pleasures and to escape the pains of life. . . . That is their inheritance (the reality at the bottom of the doctrine of original sin) from the long series of ancestors, human and semi-human and brutal, in whom the struggle of this innate tendency to self-assertion was the condition of victory in its struggle for existence. That is the reason of the *aviditas vitæ*—the insatiable hunger for enjoyment—of all mankind. . . . The maxim "Live according to nature" has done immeasurable mischief. . . . It has furnished an axiomatic foundation for the philosophy of philosophasters, and for the moralizing of sentimentalists. . . . The pertinacious optimism of our philosophers hid from them the actual state of the case. . . . The logic of facts was necessary to convince them that the cosmos works through the lower nature of man, not for righteousness, but against it. . . . The theory of evolution encourages no millennial anticipations. . . . The cosmic nature born with us, and, to a large extent, necessary for our maintenance, is the outcome of millions of years of severe training, and it would be folly to imagine that a few centuries will suffice to subdue its masterful-

ness to purely ethical ends. Ethical nature may count upon having to reckon with a tenacious and powerful enemy as long as the world lasts.[1]

Thus Locke's doctrine of the *tabula rasa* has given place to a sounder psychology which, if less optimistic, is no breeder of idle dreams, and need not make us any the less determined upon all possible furtherance of practicable reform. It emphasizes the fact that man's future is not a natural destiny but a moral vocation, and that in face of the moral dangers by which the higher civilization is constantly menaced, what is most called for is training and discipline in self-mastery; and so, while leaving us profoundly altered in our social aspirations by eighteenth-century optimism, restores the key for the understanding of medieval attitudes—of their moods of despair as well as of their spiritual ambitions —and indeed enables us to begin to divine what it was that the medieval moralists were after when they spoke eulogistically of fear. It was because they did not trace evil chiefly to the bodily appetites. (That is the defect in Huxley's distribution of emphasis). The flagrantly sensuous life can be satisfying only to the vulgar-minded. The supreme source of evil according to medieval teaching is *pride*—pride in all its various and esteemed forms, emulation, desire for human affection, loyalty to this or that party or institution, and the like. It is this constant and insidious body of highly respectable temptations, and the deadening of the spiritual faculties which the yielding to them may produce—this sense of the danger of allowing the heart to become set upon anything short of the highest—this was the source of the haunting fear by which the finest spirits of the Middle Ages were spurred to the never-ceasing combat of spiritual endeavour. Surely I am not wrong in saying that such a mood, while extremely unclassical, and almost unknown in the typical representatives of the eighteenth century, is by no means foreign to the modern mind. Tolstoy, for instance, a genuine modern, is profoundly medieval, and not at all Greek, in many of his spiritual traits.

And now I am brought to the last main point upon which I shall dwell. As I have argued, the seventeenth- and eighteenth-century

[1] *Evolution and Ethics* (1894, Eversley series), pp. 27 ff.

Enlightenment thinkers, in losing all appreciation of the Middle Ages, severed the roots of their culture, and cut themselves off from all possibility of any genuine comprehension of the tendencies which were sweeping them along. I shall now briefly trace, in bare outline, the interesting and circuitous routes by which the Christian and medieval tradition, secluded within the unenlightened church organizations, formed other channels of expression for itself, and so forced its way back into the intellectual life of the nineteenth century.

It was in and through the various tendencies that together compose what is usually called the romantic movement (a most unfortunate and inadequate title, but one which we must employ, as no satisfactory substitute has been suggested) that the modern mind resumed contact with its medieval sources. Let me recall some of the many events for which it stands. Mallet, a Genevan, who had gone to reside in Denmark, unearthed the romantic history and discovered the ancient literature of the Scandinavian countries. One of Mallet's works was translated into English by Bishop Percy, and by it he was inspired to form his epoch-making collection of old English ballads and poetry. His *Reliques of Ancient English Poetry*, published in 1765, has justly been described as 'the Bible of the Romantic reformation'. It was a chief cause of Sir Walter Scott's early awakened interest in the past, and it likewise influenced Herder, the father of German Romanticism. Prior to Percy's *Reliques* in 1760 Macpherson had published his impudent but inspired forgeries, which were almost universally accepted as an ancient epic of the Celtic race. Jakob Grimm, the founder of Germanic philology, was directly inspired by a body of Celtic students—Celto-maniacs, as they were called—with whom he became acquainted while on a visit to Paris. He returned to Germany to collect the folk-lore, fairy-tales, and dialects of the German people. He published the first volume of his epoch-making *Deutsche Grammatik* in 1819. The romance of the Middle Ages was first studied by Thomas Warton and Richard Hurd, who in 1762 published his *Letters on Chivalry and Romance*. Hurd was also one of the first to appreciate the beauties of medieval architecture, hitherto denounced as barbarous and Gothic.

Thus new and wonderful worlds full of imaginative appeal were opened out to the astonished gaze of a generation which had lost all knowledge of its own past, and which was already weary of the arid and purely intellectual dogmas of the Enlightenment philosophies.

An immense impetus was given to this historical interest in the romantic past by the discovery that the sacred language of the Hindus, a language rich in a very noble sacred literature, is akin to the languages of Western Europe. This discovery worked powerfully on men's imagination and inspired the most enthusiastic study not only of Sanscrit and the Vedas, but of all the accessible sacred writings of the Oriental peoples. And in due course the Bible, especially the Old Testament, was re-read with renewed interest and a deeper human understanding. The Bible soon became one of the chief sources of romantic inspiration.

That, however, was in large part also due to the influence of a work, now seldom read (and not indeed very readable, save for occasional passages) which played an important role in the opening decades of the nineteenth century—Chateaubriand's *Génie du Christianisme*, published in 1802. As a European influence, awakening the mind of his generation to a keen and sympathetic interest in medieval life and ideals, Chateaubriand preceded Scott, whose *Waverley* was not published until 1814. Hitherto Christianity had been associated, in the minds of the 'Enlightened', with the abuses and intolerance, and with all that was most odious and degenerate in the surviving medieval Church. Chateaubriand imaginatively depicted and sympathetically portrayed all that is sublime, generous, or tender in the teaching, history, and ideals of the Church. And the enthusiasm with which his message was welcomed marked the extent to which it opened out fresh sources of thought and feeling, and satisfied needs which had been starved on the scanty spiritual fare of the intellectual philosophies.

This interest in the past, though at first largely literary and imaginative, soon became genuinely historical, and finally scientific. It led, by easy and natural stages, to the creation, not only of history strictly so-called, but also of the historical sciences of philology, of comparative religion, of the development of social institutions and of morals. The historical and genetic method came more and more to be the method almost universally employed in the various human sciences. This method finally, through Cuvier, Lamarck, Lyell, and others, invaded the geological and biological sciences, and in the hands of Darwin gave rise to the modern evolutionary science of biology; and its astonishing success in this department powerfully reinforced the hold which it had already obtained in the human disciplines.

The romantic movement has undoubtedly inspired many extremely reactionary tendencies. No movement that looks upon the Middle Ages with admiration and sympathy could help doing so. But in the main its influence has been on the line of genuine progress—deepening our thought, enriching the emotional and spiritual life, and enabling us more wisely to direct those humanitarian enterprises upon which, thanks largely to the eighteenth century, the modern mind is immovably set. We have only to think of Edmund Burke in the field of political theory, and to compare him with such as Montesquieu, to realize that, profound and impressive as the latter undoubtedly is, and reactionary as Burke could often prove, a new and deeper way of thinking is making its appearance—one that in its reverence for tradition and for the organic processes that transcend the scope of the designing intelligence vindicates something very valuable in medieval attitudes, too valuable to be ever again lost. The state is an organic growth, which, like language, is capable of being altered only in accordance with *indemonstrable* laws inherent to itself. I say *indemonstrable* laws, for romanticism, at its best, culminates in a very genuine empiricism. Just as in social matters it would emphasize the analogy between the development of social life and the development of language, so in the field of logic it would stress the analogy of the work of art. The significance of a work of art is always bound up with the special detail of its uniquely individual character; and only through patient study, specially directed upon it, can its meaning be deciphered. If all reality be interpreted in this fashion, only a genuinely empirical method can be regarded as adequate. The sweeping generalizations, and the correspondingly wide deductions, of enlightenment theory seem to the romanticist a caricature of genuine thinking. The Encyclopedists, in ignoring the specific characteristics of the individual (and they were always speaking about man and humanity in the abstract), turn their backs upon the source of all true insight.

For this reason romanticism, in its best forms, has proved extremely favourable to the cultivation of the sciences. It is inspired by the conviction that the details of nature and of history are pregnant with mysteries more marvellous than any which the discursive understanding or mere fancy can possibly divine, and are therefore worthy of the most laborious study. And yet, being, if I may so name it, a visionary empiricism rooted in the sense of wonder, it has discountenanced the uninspired accumulation of mere detail. It has insisted upon the indispensableness of that element of hypothesis or theory, of meaning and significance, which is so underestimated in the philosophies of Bacon and Locke.

Romanticism has also, in equal degree, proved favourable to the philosophical disciplines. For the great scientific periods and the great philosophical periods have always, for very good reasons, more or less coincided. The period when the mathematical sciences were getting on to their feet was also the period of Socrates and Plato. The Middle Ages, second-rate in philosophy, are negligible in the matter of science. The eighteenth-century thinkers were, with very few exceptions, theorists, in the bad sense of that term; and they one and all followed Voltaire in denouncing metaphysics as idle, incompetent, and altogether fruitless. Nineteenth-century thinking, in becoming historical and genuinely empirical in method, led to a rejuvenating of the philosophical sciences. What Hegel, for instance, set himself to do was to rationalize romanticism, to develop the logic which its higher empiricism presupposes. And this task he fulfilled with a wealth of historical knowledge and with a wonderful felicity of illustration, in his doctrine of what he named the *concrete* universal. That is why he inspired so many of the foremost historical students of his time—Renan and Strauss, Proudhon and Karl Marx, Michelet, Taine, Ranke, Zeller, and a host of other less distinguished scholars. The measure of Hegel's success is, I should say, the degree in which he profited by the fruitful influences of the romantic movement. The extent to which he failed was determined by his retention, in spite of his deeper tendencies, of the excessive rationalism of the Enlightenment philosophies. He professed to be able to rationalize history in the light of his doctrine of logical dialectic. The result is all too frequently a flagrant violation of the fundamental romanticist principle, that only by mastery of significant detail can ultimate meanings be even approximately discerned.

But the tasks of philosophy, as formulated by Hegel, still remain the central tasks of present-day speculation. This may be seen even in the current popularity of the Bergsonian metaphysics. In his stressing of creative activity and of what he names intuition, Bergson would seem to incline as unduly towards an extreme romanticism as did Hegel towards an excessive rationalism. Bergson is, however, a comprehensive and genuinely philosophical thinker, for he at least valiantly strives to transcend the oppositions and half-truths of those thinkers who, inspired exclusively by classical or by medieval ideals, are therefore unready to look for inspiration impartially, as occasion may offer, to both of those great traditions. The really great nineteenth-century philosophical thinkers have sought, at least in aim and purpose, even, for instance, such as Auguste Comte, to fulfil the high ambition of the medieval and early Renaissance thinkers, that of vindicating the unity of all past human endeavour, the ultimate working together of classical and Christian influences to the upbuilding of a civilization in which both alike may find their completion and justification.

I may conclude by briefly restating my main thesis. The task of the Renaissance thinkers was that of combining, in a more adequate synthesis than was possible in the Middle Ages, the two great traditions upon which our European civilization rests, the Christian and the classical. In the fifteenth and sixteenth centuries the two sets of influences acted and reacted upon one another in the most complex fashion. Both are prominent in Michelangelo, and even in Calvin. But in the seventeenth and eighteenth centuries the medieval forces failed to maintain themselves in the intellectual field, with the consequence that the classical tradition acquired a predominant influence and generated, under the altered conditions of modern life, a genuinely new and profoundly fruitful interpretation of life, in what have very fittingly been named the Enlightenment philosophies. To them our humanitarianism, our belief in reason and in reasoned foresight, are in large part due. But towards the end of the eighteenth century the inevitable reaction began to appear. The medieval forces which had been driven underground, and which had actively survived only in such popular movements as Wesleyanism and Pietism, or in the corresponding movements within the Roman Church, but which, as it would almost seem, had accumulated upon themselves, rather than weakened, in the prolonged and unfavouring age of reason, now formed new channels of expression for themselves, and so forced their way back into the intellectual life of the nineteenth century. The complex of connected tendencies thus set agoing have been very inadequately named the Romantic movement. Through it the modern mind resumed contact with its medieval sources. And so at last, for the first time since the sixteenth century, or, to be more accurate, since the middle of the seventeenth, the two opposed interpretations of life, the Christian and the classical, more adequately represented and more convincingly maintained, stood face to face, clamant for thinkers sufficiently Catholic to comprehend both, and to take up afresh, enriched by all the accumulated gains of the intervening centuries, those tasks to which such Renaissance scholars as Mirandola, Reuchlin, and Erasmus had in the early periods of the Renaissance so courageously devoted themselves, of reconciling, and, in view of modern circumstance, of reformulating, the two great traditions upon which our civilization historically rests.

The Moral Sanction of Force

WHAT part may legitimately be assigned to brute force in human affairs? Does the State rest upon force or does it rest upon moral sanctions? Or if both are necessary, under what conditions may the State apply force in the furtherance of its ends? This is ultimately the question by which we are faced, when we endeavour to discover what changes the occurrence of the present war is making, or has already made, in our understanding and interpretation of life. I have deliberately chosen the words brute force in preference to a milder term, such as coercion. For though brute force has seldom to be applied in its cruder forms, it would seem that under certain circumstances no other kind of coercion is capable of taking its place. For though the coercive power of public opinion is a valuable restraint upon individual vagaries, it is helpless against a group sufficiently large to set its own standards and to satisfy its own social needs. When such organized rebellion refuses to temporize, challenging the established powers, brute force in all its crudity is frequently the only arbiter. Under what circumstances, and on what grounds, is this appeal to force, whether within the State or between States, morally justifiable?

There is a further question, and I should like to indicate its bearings before I proceed to my main theme. This more fundamental question is the problem of evil in human affairs. Probably the greatest controversy which history records is that which raged over so many centuries between the Pelagians and the Orthodox party. The Pelagians traced all evil to misuse of the freedom of the will. Each man is the Adam of his own soul. Evil exists because this, that, and the other man have fallen short of their duty. The Orthodox, on the other hand, claimed that the universality of evil, the fact that no one is free from it, points to a common origin for the sinfulness of the whole race. Evil has a deeper source than individual misconduct. That the individual is individually

214

responsible, is the great truth emphasized by the Pelagians. That all men, and not merely this or that man, are sinful is the hardly less significant fact which the Orthodox endeavoured to reconcile with the existence of individual guilt. The Pelagians were satisfied with one of these two great truths; the Orthodox insisted upon the retention of both.

I should maintain that unless we are willing to adopt the Orthodox position, restating it no doubt in altered terms, we cannot hope to understand the part which brute force plays, and rightly plays, in human affairs. Brute force is indispensable; it has to be employed. It is a name for a weapon by which alone evil in certain forms, under certain conditions, can be withstood and eradicated. These forms and conditions which make brute force indispensable are partially traceable to individual misconduct, but also, and in greater degree, to the circumstances under which human life has to be lived. The Orthodox standpoint is more pessimistic than the Pelagian; but that is not to say that it is therefore more likely to be false. All the great religions have been extremely pessimistic as to man's present life, and not over-sanguine regarding his future destiny on this terrestrial globe.

This old-time controversy has its present-day counterpart. Our Pelagian contemporaries, when a disaster occurs, whether it be a mining disaster or a railway catastrophe or a war, are mainly bent on discovering the individual or individuals who can be regarded as criminally responsible. Those of us who represent our more Orthodox forefathers, while willing to recognize this factor of individual negligence or guilt, are chiefly concerned about the conditions which make it possible for the individual agent to cause such widespread evil. Again, our Pelagian contemporaries take so optimistic a view of our human powers, that they regard as an insult to human nature any suggestion that men need to be guarded against themselves, that the threats and penalties of the law, the supporting and constraining power of public opinion, or the manifold other external influences which society brings to bear upon the individual, are in any degree necessary to the living of the higher life. Laws, on their view, exist only for the criminal; the good citizen would obey them whether they were enforced or not. The truer view, however, seems rather to be that social institutions are created by men to counterbalance their natural weaknesses and fallibility. In creating them the human race creates instruments of coercion in the hope that by their aid it may be raised above itself. Necessity is the mother of all good things; and among the best of its gifts is the freedom which can be acquired only under its stern discipline. As Goethe has said, natural strength and crutches come from the same hand. Man can be all that he ought to be, only when advantage is taken of the artificial aids which society can supply for enabling him to guard against his weaknesses, and to supplement his natural strength. The individual needs the constraints of society, imposed when necessary by main force, in order that he may live up even to the generally recognized standards of virtue and attainment. Should, for instance, the individual find that one of his besetting weaknesses is laziness, he will, if he be wise, place himself in situations, incur obligations, which will constrain and compel him by a given time to perform tasks that would probably lie unfulfilled if he relied only on his native strength of will to push him at them.

What I have sought to suggest—I can do no more than suggest it—by these preliminary remarks is that when I make a plea for brute force in political and international affairs, I do not do so in order to prove that might is right, but in the interests of morality itself. The moral sanctions are independent of force, but just for that very reason they can justify us in the employment of it. The chief task of civilization *on its political side* is so to develop the institutions and instruments through which force is applied, that the higher spiritual interests of mankind may, by their aid, be safeguarded and secured. Beyond the field of brute force lie, of course, the instruments of moral coercion, public or international opinion, religious influences, and the like. These are superior in moral value, and ultimately are creative and regulative even of the instruments of brute force. But, as I should maintain, they require for their development the favouring environment supplied by a political order which, when challenged, is found to be capable of securing itself by the successful employment of armed force.

I may now proceed to my main theme. We would all of us, surely, gladly see the time when war with its attendant horrors would no longer be a possible part of human life—when some other means than brute force would arbitrate between disputing nations. We are therefore sympathetic towards the pacifist ideal, and very willing to have the pacifists make good their indictment of war. But when they claim that war can be eliminated in the near future, and that this is likely to be the last great war, many of us feel extremely doubtful of their analysis of the situation by which we are faced. We feel that the assumptions in terms of which the pacifists proceed may, unless corrected, lead to a tragic misdirection of energy, and to the baulking even of legitimate hopes. That is to say, we may approve the end which the pacifists have in view, and yet be constrained to condemn their methods of approach.

The pacifists would seem to formulate their philosophy of life by reflection solely upon society while in a state of profound peace, or, as I should prefer to express it, while in a state of *apparently* profound peace. That is to say, they construct a philosophy of life in which war finds no place, and then proceed to apply this philosophy in the interpretation of war, with the inevitable result that war seems to them an irrelevant and barbarous interruption to civilized life, an anachronism, something that need not exist, and ought not to exist. Civilization, they argue, tends to the elimination of force, and to the substitution of higher sanctions in place of force. The occurrence of such a war as that which is now raging means, they therefore conclude, nothing less than the utter breakdown of European civilization. Such a point of view seems to me quite perverse and thoroughly mistaken. The general thesis which I wish to maintain is that civilization tends, not to the elimination of force, but to such modifications in the established organs and institutions through which force is applied that might and right may more and more be made to coincide. Joseph de Maistre has said, in his usual extreme and paradoxical manner, that two things are indispensable to the existence of a State, a priest and an executioner—that is, the statesman and the soldier, a representative of the spiritual interests and a representative to enforce and conserve the executive power. In the absence of the one the State is without guidance; if the other be lacking, it is at the mercy of its least enlightened members and of all external foes. In the perfecting of both, the tribunals of justice and the instruments of coercion, and in the solving of the many problems involved in their harmonious co-operation, lies the chief task of civilization on its political side.

But these remarks are rather general. Let me state my position in more specific terms. When it is said that this war means the breakdown of our civilization, the implication is that a state of peace, into which considerations of force do not enter, represents the normal situation, and that when war occurs it breaks in upon a civilization to which it is wholly alien, with the true spirit of which it conflicts, and the higher conscience of which it outrages. In opposition to that view I shall maintain that we live in a continuous state of war. Our civilization cannot be understood save by recognizing that the appeal to force is something quite fundamental to it. Is it true that war is something incidental, and that the occasional outbursts of war are of the nature merely of interruptions to a state of peace in which the appeal to force plays no essential part, in which, in fact, it is displaced by appeal to higher and more equitable sanctions? What is the actual situation *in time of peace*, first within the State, and secondly in the relation of States to one another?

Does civilization tend within each State to the elimination of force, i.e. of compulsion? Surely not. On the contrary, it consolidates and extends compulsion, so that it applies over an ever wider field with a constantly increasing effectiveness of control. Civilization brings it about that compulsion is less often questioned, and that there is less and less temptation to question it, and that it is as a matter of fact less frequently challenged, but not any the less insistently enforced. The State at great expense organizes a police force to compel the criminal to cease from his evil ways, and to compel the discontented to obey the laws. The State at great expense organizes courts of law to compel citizens to act justly by one another. Each railway and tramway company has at great expense to provide conductors to make sure that their customers do not attempt dishonestly to withhold their fares. Or, to take cases of a different type. Parents are compelled to treat their children with humanity and are compelled to educate them, or at least to allow them to be educated. Employers must compensate their employees in case of injury. The individual must contribute to the cost of the State in proportion to his income, and so forth. The number of things to which the individual is compulsorily constrained has steadily increased as civilization has advanced. There is an immense amount of human labour which would be saved if the individual could be his own guardian

—if, for instance, to choose a minor but obvious example, a box at the entrance to each tramway car were all that were necessary to secure payment of fares. It is not the criminal, it is the average good citizen, that lays this enormous burden of vigilance and expense upon the shoulders of society. The cost of militarism, the cost of maintaining order in international relations, is by comparison very slight, that is, if we count in all the innumerable ways in which the guarding against fraud, greed, incompetence, and especially laziness, enters into the price of the necessary and ordinary comforts of life. In order that the ten commandments may be obeyed, the State must expend a high percentage of its manhood and its wealth. This expenditure is required in order to secure, by the compelling arm of the law, ultimately either through bodily duress or through the exacting of indemnities, that might and right will coincide. The organization of social instruments of coercion is no less indispensable in modern society than in the simpler days when the King's highways had to be guarded against the breakers of the law. One effect of the social legislation represented by Factory Acts, or by the recent Insurance Bill, has been to create an army of inspectors with policing functions. Each extension of the activity of the State involves an extension of the field of coercive interference with the life of the individual. The cost of this policing organization has increased, not diminished, as civilization has advanced.

Further, were it not for the existence of the army, the police force would have to be immensely larger than it now is. There is no existing country that has not from time to time to employ the military in the defence and maintenance of social order. Thus, in the railway strike in England in the summer of 1911, it was the decision of the Liberal Cabinet that the transport trade of the country must not be even temporarily interrupted, and that if necessary the army would be employed to run the railways, that brought both capitalists and trade unionists to reason, and averted what might well have turned into civil war. Only the English army and navy can make Home Rule possible for Ireland, should Ulster opposition continue in strength. Within the past year American troops have been employed in the State of Colorado. Democratic government means control by the majority. Minorities must, *if necessary*, be coerced. It will be objected that, since the problem of democracy is to make might and right coincide, the appeal to force is merely incidental to those transition stages in which law is being readjusted in such manner as will remove the grievances that inspire to rebellion. That may at once be granted. The task of the State is so to organize itself that it will never thwart interests spiritually superior to those which it itself protects. For we may observe that, though warfare within the State is a much rarer thing than in more barbarous centuries, though it is more deliberately entered into, and morally, on the average, of a much worthier type, the right to rebellion remains one of the inalienable rights of which a rational agent can never be deprived. What civilization has done—and it is a very great achievement—is to raise to a higher level the reasons which lead to and precipitate the appeal to arms. Civilization brings it about that the causes of rebellion cease to be those of mere self-interest, and reduce to the more spiritual conflicts that result from divergence of ideals. He would be a bold man, and would underestimate the part which competing philosophies of life, and the conflicts of imaginative ideals, are likely to play in the coming centuries, who will venture to prophesy that civil war will never again occur in a State governed on genuinely democratic lines. Should the modern State come to be organized upon centralized socialistic lines, we can very well conceive that its tyranny, though enthusiastically supported by a majority within the State, and all the more on that account, should become just as intolerable as that which was exercised by the Catholic Church in the Middle Ages. Meantime, despite the segregation of classes, widespread discontent, and a disheartening lack of clearness and of agreement as to the ends and purposes of life, rebellion remains so rare an occurrence as it now is, largely because those who would resist the verdict of the law must do so with weapons in their hands.

If this be the condition of affairs within each separate State, what are we to expect in the intercourse of nations with one another? The members of a State live in a common atmosphere; they have common traditions and common ideals, and a multitude of common interests—at least there is much more of this community of interest between the individuals of a nation than there is between nations regarded as units. If, as I have argued, the individuals of a State cannot so trust one another as to dispense with the appeal to force, can we hope to dispense with it in international relations? In view of such argument, the pacifist will probably modify his mode of statement, and will reply that he does not mean to profess that force can be dispensed with, but only that it can be legalized and made to proceed in the prescribed channels which human foresight and human justice are able to provide and ordain. That is to say, the problem of international relations can be tackled and solved in the same fashion in which the problems of personal relations have been approached within each several State. Just as litigants are not left to fight out their personal differences, and are not permitted so to do, so nations must be compelled to submit their differences to an impartial tribunal, and to accept the verdict at which it may arrive. Force may not be employed by an interested party. It can be justly exercised only by a deliberately established court of appeal that will act in conformity with impersonal and non-national standards of right and justice.

Let us bring this proposal to the test of facts. How are international disputes settled *in time of peace*? By diplomacy. How does diplomacy act? By mutual interchange of views to discover and to define the points of difference, by mutual interchange of views to find whether a compromise of the conflicting claims satisfactory to both parties be feasible. If such be discoverable, well and good; the threatened conflict has been averted and the dispute settled by mutual consent. But if the differences remain outstanding, if no compromise be possible without some sacrifice to which one or other side is unwilling to consent, what then? Under present conditions what decides? In those cases which concern only profit and loss of a measurable amount, as in regard, say, to fishery rights, neither party is likely to desire war, and resort to arbitration is the obvious solution. But in issues which have to do with more vital and far-reaching interests, such as may involve a radical alteration in the mutual relations of the two nations, this solution would seem to be impossible. In such questions, for instance, as whether Japan should or should not be allowed entry into Australia or into Canada or into the United States; whether Russia may or may not establish a fortified base on the east coast of Asia facing Japan; whether Germany may or may not extend its Baghdad railway to the Persian Gulf and towards Egypt;

whether the Monroe doctrine is to be maintained, and European Powers forbidden to colonize in South America. These are questions, it will be noted, in regard to which compromise is practically impossible. In the end it is a matter of yea or nay. One or other side must, on the main issue, give way, and give way absolutely.

Secondly, they are questions in regard to which no court of arbitration could decide. For in regard to such issues there are no principles upon which a tribunal could proceed. The question is not as to whether a particular claim is just or unjust. The appeal to justice, though relevant, is entirely inconclusive. For instance, in the question whether or not the Japanese are to be excluded from all parts of the earth in which they are not already settled—and that is ultimately the question as to whether or not intermarriage is to be encouraged between those of the yellow and those of the white race—there is no moral or legal principle which will enable us to decide the one alternative to be just and the other unjust. If we are Orientals we shall probably take the one view, if we are Westerners we shall probably take the other. But we can quite well conceive an individual, even though striving to decide in accordance with the golden rule of Christian ethics, taking either view of the case. In law courts, the judges and juries make their decisions in accordance with the established laws of the land. Their task is merely that of interpretation. International tribunals, on the other hand, would be required, in dealing with such vital issues as those above cited, to decide upon their principles as well as upon their application. Each judge, however impartial he might be, however he might rise above the prejudices prevalent in the country which he represents, would merely be expressing his private opinion on a matter too complicated and difficult to permit of scientific or legal demonstration. A majority of such private opinions would thus, under the most ideal conditions, be all that could be hoped for.

Thirdly, we cannot, considering the paucity of nations, obtain a tribunal that on such issues will really be impartial. If it be a question that divides East and West, the composition of the court, according as it has a majority of Orientals or of Westerners, will predetermine its verdict. A tribunal in which the European continental powers had a clear majority would probably decide against the Monroe doctrine; a tribunal in which England had the balancing vote would probably decide for it. Individual differences within the State affect so small in number in comparison with the millions who go to compose the State that an impartial jury can in most issues be easily obtained. There is not a sufficient number of States, and the crucial issues are so ramifying in their influence that a decision at once definite and impartial would seem frequently to be impossible in international dealings.

Fourthly, a self-respecting nation cannot, in such questions, any more than in moral matters, relieve itself of the responsibility of judging for itself. It cannot have the broader outlines of its future destiny determined, or even in any essential degree controlled, by the opinion of outside Powers. Must not the American people, for instance, decide for itself whether the maintenance of the Monroe doctrine is essential to the welfare of the American continents? If it so judges, can it self-respectingly consent to have the issue decided by a majority vote of other Powers?

I may now return to my main thesis. Upon what basis, *in time of peace*, do international relations rest? The answer, as it seems to me, is as follows. The *status quo* is maintained by force. Many nations feel aggrieved that the *status quo* is what it is. Peace exists only because they do not feel prepared to challenge the forces which those who favour the *status quo* are able to employ in its defence. The diplomatic representatives of different nations, in all really vital issues, do or do not win out in international disputes according as the countries they represent have or have not adequate military forces at their disposal. Many pacifists speak as if armies and navies lie useless when not engaged in war. As a matter of fact they are what alone give weight to the arguments of diplomacy when vital issues are at stake. *It is the armies and navies that decide under what conditions, and in favour of what nations, peace will be maintained.* That is my meaning when I argue that our civilization rests ultimately upon the appeal to arms. When war occurs it is due, not to a breakdown of that civilization, but to the fact that some one nation has made up its mind that the forces to which it has hitherto yielded must now be challenged. Throughout the period of peace it has been constrained by the threat of force; war is simply the challenging of the forces that have hitherto held the competing interests in temporary equilibrium.

What, then, are the conclusions at which we would seem to arrive? If it be true that the task of civilization is to co-ordinate and direct the tribunals of justice and the instruments of coercion that might and right will coincide, any solution that looks to the elimination of force instead of to the just application of it is unpractical, and involves a false reading both of past history and of present conditions. It is not the will to abolish war that is most lacking. Even though all statesmen and every voter were sincerely desirous of abolishing war, it would not necessarily for that reason be preventable. So long as men value the spiritual goods of life more highly than life itself, they must still regard even the horrors of war as lesser evils than certain others that might arise if men were unwilling to make the necessary sacrifices. What is most needed, in order to achieve the elimination of war, is knowledge of the ways and means by which a substitute method of employing force may be provided. In other words, the solution must be analogous to that which has been employed in the case of duelling. Duelling, which is merely the last surviving and most refined form of the blood-feud, could not, any more than other forms of individual revenge, be abolished until the State had established tribunals through which the powers withdrawn from the individual could be otherwise exercised. These civil courts have taken over the right and the duty, which they withdraw from the individual, of coercing and punishing those who refuse to respect the rights of others. Now, it is just because the problem of war is only to be solved on lines analogous to those which have afforded a solution of the problem of individual revenge that it proves so baffling and difficult. The abolition of duelling has been rendered possible in and through the creation of the modern State; and that, as we all know, has involved the overcoming of a multitude of difficulties. The obstacles that lie in the way of the creation of a universal or of a European society which may be entrusted with the right and the duty of applying force seem even greater. As already argued, there can be no impartial international tribunals, because all judges and juries would, in view of the ramifying character of the questions which they would be called upon to decide, be parties to the issues at stake. Also, there are no guiding principles sufficiently relevant to the matters in dispute and sufficiently definite to dispense with legitimate differences of private opinion. While, therefore, we may strive by pacifist propaganda to strengthen the will to abolish the evils of war, let us not fall victim to the Pelagian fallacy, blinding ourselves to the complexity of the situation by which we are faced. If we are to be led out of our necessities, we must first recognize them.

I cannot more fitly conclude this paper than by appealing to the authority of a writer whose labours in the field of international law are likely to bear fruit in the near future. 'Man is not wholly irrational, or entirely bereft of what reason he possesses as a citizen, when he deals with interests which transcend the limits of State existence; and I consequently see no ground for doubting that what his partial and fitful reason has accomplished in municipal jurisprudence may be gradually accomplished in international jurisprudence. Extravagant hope is as inimical to steady and orderly activity as groundless discouragement, and it is hard to tell which of the two has acted most prejudicially on the progress of international jurisprudence. After ages of honest and on the whole intelligent effort, the freedom of the individual has as yet been only very imperfectly protected from the inroads of despotism on the one hand and anarchy on the other; and it is vain to hope that the freedom of the State can be secured by a single spasmodic throe of international reason. But if it cannot be accomplished by reason at once, it cannot be accomplished without reason at all.'[1]

[1] James Lorimer, *Studies, Law, National, International* (Edinburgh 1890).

Whitehead's Philosophy of Nature

THE examination of Whitehead's philosophy of nature must be a co-operative task in which mathematicians, physicists, and philosophers take their respective shares. Owing to my ignorance of mathematics and of physics, there is much in his works in regard to which I am unable to form any competent opinion. On the other hand, there is also much which is likely to be almost equally puzzling to those who are innocent of philosophy; and it is to these latter portions of his teaching, in so far as they can in any degree be separately dealt with, that I shall confine my attention.

Whitehead's teaching, on its critical side, is directed to showing that the fundamental concepts usually employed in the physical sciences rest on certain assumptions which may seem to have behind them the prestige of science, but which really have been foisted upon science, partly through the influence of mental habits acquired under the stress of practical needs, and partly through the influence of speculative doctrines that obtained currency among the early Greek thinkers, and that have held the field ever since. As language has also been moulded in terms of the dominant ways of thinking, it too plays an important part in the maintenance of these false views.

Happily, science does not depend, for its fruitful development, upon the successful elaboration of a philosophy of nature. The experimental verification of hypothetical deductions, especially when the verification is by means of the most precise quantitative measurements, keeps the working scientist upon the path to truth, or else warns him when he has strayed therefrom. And since he very rightly lays comparatively little stress upon the logical perfection of his procedure, he holds somewhat loosely to his fundamental concepts, modifying them freely, in this or that regard, as need arises. By such hand to mouth methods, he can usually, in a sufficiently satisfactory manner, meet all the immediate

226

needs, both practical and theoretical. There can be little question, however, that fundamental concepts and postulates do exercise considerable influence; they certainly do so, when, as in philosophy, we endeavour to envisage nature in its broader features, and in its relation to the purposes of human life.

The account which Whitehead gives of what may be called the traditional or classical philosophy of nature, that is, of the view of nature which underlies the Newtonian physics, is as follows. The physicist ordinarily regards himself as concerned with the adventures of material entities in space and time, and accordingly has interpreted the course of nature as being the history of matter. More particularly defined, the attitude is this: the physicist conceives himself as perceiving the attributes of things, and the things which have these attributes as being bits of matter. He further conceives these bits of matter as capable only of moving in space; and so has come to believe that a complete description of the aggregations and motions of which they are capable would constitute an adequate solution of all the problems with which natural science has to deal.

But in carrying out this theory it has been found that bits of matter, i.e., corpuscles or atoms, do not suffice to account for all the phenomena, and the concept of ether has therefore been introduced. Ether is, however, Whitehead maintains, only the conception of matter over again. It too is conceived as occupying space, and its constituent parts are again regarded as capable only of motion. It is matter attenuated into what are supposed to be its sole indispensable properties. As Lord Salisbury has remarked, ether would appear to be simply the substantive of the verb to undulate. The minimal requirements for the possibility of undulation are space, and as involved in the conception of motion a something, which need not otherwise be discriminable from nothing— a something that moves. Ether is not, therefore, a new type of entity, but merely a re-dressing up of that matter whose deficiencies it is supposed to make good.

Whitehead formulates an alternative to this philosophy of nature. In place of the substantial, material entities, persisting through time and moving in space, he would substitute as being the ultimate components of reality, a very different set of entities; and these he would describe as being events. Nature, he declares, is at each moment an all-comprehensive event within which we discriminate constituent events; and, as he adds, behind the notion of an event we cannot penetrate by any amount of analysis. Analysis of an event at most only reveals within it still other events of smaller duration; it does not enable us to resolve the notion of an event, in the alleged manner of the traditional physics, into an abiding substance and its merely transitory states. Events are the ultimate constituents of reality; and it is in terms of them that we must explain all those appearances of permanence and of abiding structure which are no less characteristic of nature than is its transitoriness. The permanences in nature are in all cases conditioned by events, and cannot, therefore, be employed to render events more intelligible than they are when conceived simply as events.

As already suggested, events, as experienced or known, are never limited to the instantaneous present. Like a melody, they have duration, and within this duration, we can always discriminate constituent events of shorter duration. However far the analysis be carried, we never arrive at point-instants, but only at durations which have themselves a time-span, and so within themselves allow of a distinction between the earlier and the later components of which they are made up. For the same reason, since physical events are never merely in time, but always constitute the four-dimensional continuum of space-time, they are likewise endlessly analysable in their spatial aspect. The notion of point-instants can be accepted only as an ideal limit, arrived at by the 'method of extensive abstraction'.

A street accident is an instance of what Whitehead means by an event. Its occurrence may occupy, say, thirty seconds: within that period the constituent events which make up the accident can be discriminated. We have seen the man hit by the vehicle; we have seen him fall; and the wheel of the vehicle pass over his body. But if so, are we not, in describing the accident as an event, really using that term, in a merely popular manner, to cover what is in itself a series of events? To this criticism Whitehead replies that it is just as legitimate or illegitimate to name the accident as a whole an event as to describe in that way any one of its constituent events of shorter duration, such as the man's being hit or falling. These also are really series of events. For even if we limit the term event to what we can experience, as we say, at a single instant, we find that this is determined by the nature of our senses, and by the span of our consciousness. The retinal processes being of a chemical nature cannot discriminate stimuli that fall upon the retina at a shorter interval than one-eighth of a second; and accordingly the maximum number of discriminable events that we can experience through sight in thirty seconds is two hundred and forty. But as science can demonstrate, by means of indirectly obtained evidence, there are immensely more than two hundred and forty events in a street accident, they have to be numbered by millions; and even so, we should not reach a point-event. So far from reaching reality by such a process of limiting down the duration of events, we find that the further we proceed the more of reality we leave out, and that we have made this sacrifice to no effect, since what is left over still continues to preserve those objectionable features—duration in time and extension in space—the features that started us off on the wild-goose chase, to escape them.

Accordingly, Whitehead admonishes us, we had just as well begin by recognizing what we are constrained in the end, willy-nilly, to recognize, that events have duration. Nature is not in clock-time but in duration; and duration exists only in slabs, be the slabs longer or be they shorter. To this cause, he argues, is due that 'unexhaustiveness [which] is an essential character of our knowledge of nature'.[1]

But if this be the situation, why has the scientist found it necessary to seek always for the simple, resolving the complex into its smaller constituents both temporal and spatial? Why has the scientist been constrained to invent all those instruments of precision, the clock, the balance, the thermometer, the microscope and the like, whereby finer and finer discriminations in time, space, and quantity in general are obtained? Why are these instruments indispensable, if analysis, however far we carry it, only lands us face to face with the same unsolved problems as those from which we start?

In reply to this objection, Whitehead develops one of the most interesting and valuable parts of his argument—an explanation, in terms of his theory, of why it is that all natural science, as he fully recognizes, is directed to the endeavour to explain the complex in terms of the laws

[1] *The Concept of Nature* (Cambridge, 1919), p. 14.

and nature of its simpler constituents. This, however, is a part of his teaching upon which I shall not dwell.

There is another, and much more fundamental, objection which has to be met. On the traditional view what now exists has always existed; matter once there is there for good and all; the transitory shapes and forms which time carves out of it are alone new; what is new is transitory, and what is abiding never really changes. Matter is thus conceived as a kind of stuff or material, abidingly there, and always being re-made over, thrifty nature making it down, as it were, like a parental garment, for the younger generations:

> Imperial Caesar, dead and turned to clay,
> [May] stop a hole to keep the wind away.

This view Whitehead summons us to give up, as no longer tenable. But before we can do so, a seemingly insuperable difficulty must be overcome. Popularly we distinguish between things and events. We do not conceive a street accident as a thing or object; and if we tried to do so, we should not succeed; it refuses to stand still. But now Whitehead appears to be asking us to consider a table or a chair as an event; and that, surely, is equally impossible; they refuse to get under way. An abiding thing stands in essential contrast to the events which may happen to it.

To this difficulty Whitehead has a twofold reply. In the first place, he gets some little amusement out of his readers by seeming to question whether the difficulty is a genuine one. Is it true, he asks, that a street accident is an event, and that what we call a thing is not? Take Cleopatra's Needle as it stands on the Embankment in London. It is true that the street accident happens and is done with, whereas Cleopatra's Needle is there day and night, year in, year out, looking down, in abiding contrast, on the stream of traffic that flows by it on the river and on the roadway. But there was a time when there was no Cleopatra's Needle either on the Embankment or in Egypt; it is disintegrating with fabulous slowness, but still continuously, and there must come a time when it will no longer be there. In this regard the difference between it and the street accident would seem to be merely one of time-span. Ultimate difference there appears to be none.

But this is only Whitehead's way of awakening the reflective reader to a better appreciation of his difficulty. For, as Whitehead proceeds to emphasize, there is a quite radical distinction between events and things or objects. And he enumerates objects as being of three types: sense-objects, such as a sound or a colour; perceptual objects, such as a chair or living organism; scientific objects, such as molecules, atoms, and electrons. There is, he recognizes, a fundamental distinction in nature between all such objects and events. An event is unique; it happens once, and it cannot happen again; once it is over, it is done with. By a thing or object, on the other hand, we mean just that which can be met with at different times, which can appear and disappear, and yet remain the same identical being. Otherwise expressed, the distinction is this: an event cannot be recognized; since every event is unique, and can occur only once, it cannot recur, and so allow of its being recognized as something experienced at some previous time. Since, however, we do recognize objects as previously experienced, there must be some ultimate distinction between them and events.

At first sight there may appear to be an easy way of escape from this conclusion. Though the same event never recurs, events may none the less be uniform in type, and so may resemble one another. May we not therefore recognize events, in the sense of recognizing the type to which they conform; and may we not do so though there is no self-identical sameness in the sense of recurrence? If I meet a man whom I have never seen before, I cannot, of course, recognize him as an individual but I certainly can recognize him as being a man. I can recognize in him a standard type, though I cannot recognize in him recurrent individuality.

But what do we mean by fixity of type or standard: what do we mean by resemblance? All such phrases, in which the terms type, pattern, structure, occur, involve the notion of permanence in some form, and consequently imply that which is irreducible to the non-recurrent uniqueness of events.

The distinction between objects and events is indeed fundamental; the only question is as to how the two types of existence are to be conceived as standing to one another. According to the traditional standpoint, it is space and time on the one hand, and abiding particles on the other, that make events possible; the events are the adventures which befall the particles. The alternative method of procedure is that which Whitehead advocates—so to recast our fundamental modes of conceiving natural existence as to recognize that space and time are abstractions, not prior-existing conditions making events possible, and that it is equally illegitimate to conceive matter or ether as a kind of stuff, extended in space and with parts movable in space-time. What we alone immediately experience are events, not detached events standing in serial order in time, but events that always overlap and so together constitute the one total durational event that is nature at any assignable period. Our problem is to explain how, this being so, the distinction between events and objects comes to be drawn, how it is possible, and what it involves. We know space and time only as elements involved in events; we know so-called objects only in and through events. How, then, out of a matrix of continuously changing events, do those relatively isolable aspects of reality, space and time, and those relatively permanent things which we call objects, ever come to emerge? And once they have through our intellectual discriminations come to emerge, what kind of ontological status do they possess?

Obviously such a standpoint demands a very complete transformation of the conceptual foundations of the natural sciences. To borrow a metaphor from Whitehead, 'recourse to metaphysics is like throwing a match into a powder magazine'. Since metaphysical matches are frequently rather poor in quality, usually when this is done nothing very particular happens. But when the fuse is of the kind manufactured by Whitehead, the trouble is rather that too much happens; 'the whole arena is blown up'. However, this arena, according to Whitehead, was a structure of unhappy design; and when it is demolished, what is left is the true natural world as it has always existed, and such as we shall know more adequately when viewed through the spectacles which he is ready to supply. We shall then realize that nature is falsely apprehended, when interpreted primarily in terms of the conservation of mass and energy, that is, when we regard it as a kind of self-winding clock, the character of which has been determined once and for all, and which marks time in more senses than one; and that we should rather conceive nature as an historical being, that is, as a process which at each and every moment is 'creatively advancing into novelty'.

Even if it were feasible to discuss within the limits of this paper the many difficult problems of scientific methodology to which this very novel manner of envisaging nature at once gives rise, I am not qualified to do so. There are just two points, of a more purely philosophical character, upon which I shall dwell: first, Whitehead's criticism of the fallacy which he entitles 'the bifurcation of Nature'; and secondly, that view of the function of reason which, as it seems to me, Whitehead's interpretation of nature illustrates and reinforces.

When Whitehead tells us that all present-day natural philosophy is vitiated by the fallacy of bifurcation, he means that it commits us to a quite untenable division of the components of objective nature into two diametrically opposed types of existence, the material and the mental; or to employ a more adequate pair of terms, the physical and the psychical.

That some such dualism is, upon the traditional view, quite inevitable, first came to be appreciated in the seventeenth and eighteenth centuries, owing to the development of the transmission theories of sound, of light, and of heat. Physically, sound has been found to be conditioned by wave-movements in air. Physically, light and heat have turned out to be conditioned by vibrations in ether. Sound, heat, and colour, having been thus found to bear not the least resemblance to their physical counterparts, they must, it was argued, be mental creations, psychic additions to reality.

The doctrine which Whitehead thus entitles the bifurcation of nature, and which largely coincides with what is more usually termed the doctrine of representative perception, has in the past two centuries had all the prestige of science behind it. Philosophical thinkers, from time to time, have raised objections to it; but so long as the results of science seemed to support it, these criticisms passed idly over men's heads. Now, however, that Whitehead, in the name of science, is telling us that for the sake of science itself the doctrine must be eradicated from our thinking, some headway may as last be made.

Galileo, being the first to formulate the standpoint of modern physics, was also the first to distinguish between the primary and the secondary qualities of bodies. All the secondary qualities, he taught, are non-objective; in so far as we apprehend objects in terms of them, we apprehend them falsely.

The main reason which constrained Galileo to adopt this position is quite fundamental, and was already evident to the early Greek thinkers. The mythological stories relating to the Gods proceeded on the assumption that creation and annihilation are real occurrences; and the Greek philosophers at once recognized that so long as this assumption is made the nature of things must remain opaque to the human understanding, and that no scientific knowledge can be possible. Accordingly they set themselves to formulate an account of the real which would not be committed to any such postulate. But this task, as they found, is not at all an easy one. For if there be anything that is fundamental in our sense-experience, it is the fact of qualitative change. A hot object becomes cold; that is to say, heat vanishes out of existence and cold, a something which did not exist before, takes its place. When, therefore, we recognize such an occurrence as coming about, are we not admitting the fact of annihilation and creation just as truly as when we accept any of the stories of the doings of the Gods? What, then, they asked, is to be done? Just what Galileo did, some two thousand years later, though less definitely and less persuasively, since the science of dynamics had not yet been established. We must, it would seem, recognize that bodies are in themselves neither hot nor cold; that all such qualities are appearances, mental entities. Nature consists of matter and motion, and of nothing else; and both matter and motion are alike ingenerable and indestructible. There is a fixed and abiding amount of matter, and a fixed, abiding amount of motion. The particles of matter move about in space, but none of them ever either come into existence or pass away. Motion is similarly ingenerable and indestructible, though, as essentially non-static, it is always in process of altering its distribution, playing, as it were, a never-ending game of musical chairs with the physical particles.

When this philosophy of nature is adopted, the way is clear. Qualities do not exist in nature, and therefore qualitative change has not to be reckoned with by the physicist. There is no longer any difficulty in conceiving how a hot body becomes cold. When the body is, as we say, hot, its particles are vibrating violently; when it becomes, as we say, cold, its particles lose some of their motion to other particles. Nothing has occurred save only a redistribution of the same total amount of motion among the same ever-abiding particles.

From the point of view of physics, this has proved a very satisfactory position. But, then, look at it from the other end! Consider the unhappy quandary in which the psychologist and the philosopher are placed! They have still to reckon with qualitative change, and to reckon with it in a peculiarly aggravated form. All that is constant in nature is alleged to be physical; and what remains as mental is, so far as can be seen, constantly coming into being and then passing away into nothingness. For, though the psychologist is more than willing to model his behaviour on that of the scientist, he cannot do so in this particular respect. The physicist has got rid of the problems of qualitative change by shouldering them off into the mental realm; but the psychologist cannot do likewise, and shoulder them off in turn on to someone else. There is no further realm, no intellectual Hell, so to speak, into which they can be cast. The psychologist is up against them; and they stare him down. If, therefore, the fields of mental philosophy are to be thus treated as a kind of dumping-ground for all those happenings which are too discreditable to be allowed as belonging to physical nature, then only outside the bounds of philosophy, only in the strictly physical domain, will knowledge be possible.

But why, it may be urged, should we be surprised to find it so? The world is a sufficiently strange place, and this may very well be the nature of its strangeness. Why not accept the subjectivity of the secondary qualities, and in the manner of the old-fashioned epiphenomenal view of consciousness reconcile ourselves to the futility of mind, as incapable of inserting itself into the closed system of nature. That even so large a section of experience as the strictly physical can be successfully rationalized, is this not even more than we could antecedently have reasonably expected? Because, as miraculously ·happens, science is possible, does it at all follow that philosophy must be so likewise?

To these questions there is, however, an answer—whether sufficient or not, time alone can prove. Had any such pusillanimous attitude been maintained toward physical nature, the difficulties which have lain in the way of scientific insight would never have been overcome. When problems, within the realm of physical nature, have proved insoluble, the reason has invariably been found to lie in some false assumption for which we ourselves, and not the problems dealt with, are responsible.

The probabilities, therefore, so far as known, are in favour of White-head's conviction that a view of nature which leads to such an intellectual *impasse*, is hardly likely to prove ultimately tenable.

To repeat: the reason why the physicist bifurcates objective nature into physical and psychical components, and counts the secondary qualities as belonging to the latter class, is that he is unable, by means of his physical principles, to explain either their coming to be or their ceasing to be. Indeed, from his point of view, it would be more satisfactory if they did not exist at all. So far as he can discover, they make no difference in the behaviour of the bodies in which they are found. A red billiard ball acts on a white ball in precisely the same manner as a green one. Indeed, only so is the game possible, as fair and square between the players. Where the colours do come in, to make a difference, is solely in the behaviour of the players: the colours enable them to identify which ball is which. The colours, that is to say, first come in just where, through the intervention of life, or at least of consciousness, reality displays that degree and kind of qualitative complexity which marks the limit beyond which, on the traditional view, no scientific knowledge, at least of the explanatory type, is any longer possible. Since, it is argued, the behaviour of physical entities is completely accounted for in the absence of the secondary qualities, these qualities must fall outside physical nature, and must, like consciousness, be irrelevant to it.

But is not a very large assumption being here made? Do the actual methods and the positive results of physical science constrain us to any such attitude? Are not Galileo's teaching and the similar teaching of Descartes determined by misunderstanding of what it is that physical science is really doing? In particular, are we justified in assuming that science is yet in a position to explain the behaviour of bodies? It does so to the extent that it establishes certain correlations which we presume to be causally determined; but the causal determinations, if there, are never themselves brought to view. This may be taken as having been proved, once for all, by David Hume. Thus, in studying the manner in which—to keep to Hume's own illustration—one billiard ball moves another, all that the physicist can do is to define the correlations between changes in the shape and stopping of the one ball and corresponding changes of shape and motion in the other ball. But if this be all that is done, and if the physicist, as is undeniable, can establish similar correlations between the secondary qualities and their physical and physiological antecedents and accompaniments, what right have we to exclude colours, sounds, etc., from the physical domain? By means of these correlations the secondary qualities are as inextricably bound up with the other items in objective nature as are the primary. Thereby we do not, indeed, explain how it is possible that they should occur; but does that differentiate them from any other of nature's happenings? Are we not justified in holding that colours are as truly physical as are the bodily organs of sight, and sounds as truly physical as are the organs of hearing? These organs are telepathic; they discharge their functions by enabling us to apprehend what exists in places where our organisms are not themselves located; and they do so in and through the secondary qualities. We cannot observe a distant object save as it is outlined against a background; and this is only possible through colour variations. In the absence of colour, as in the dark, the eyes are as good as non-existent. Similarly, if there be no sounds, the ears are entirely useless. To treat the bodily organs as strictly physical, and the qualities of colour and sound as purely psychical, is surely to substitute for nature's complex but unitary workings the crude and incredible simplicities of a cast-iron dualism, the sole justification for which is the supposed adequacy of the Newtonian physics, and the supposedly closed character of the physical system as therein conceived.

The traditional philosophy of nature certainly proceeds in strict accordance with the logic of its own avowed principles. On the traditional view nature, at any chosen time, can have only instantaneous existence. In the sequence of its events, only one event at a time, and that in the order of the sequence, can be allowed as existing. Now physics teaches that at least two complete air-waves of the same length are required for the possibility of a musical sound. But since each single wave, or rather each instantaneous state of each wave, alone exists at any one moment, it is impossible for the sound to exist as a physical entity; and we must, it would therefore seem, conclude that it belongs to the only other type in which reality is known to exist, namely, the psychical. If nature can exist only as the instantaneous, everything which, like sound, involves the telescoping or integrating of successive events must be psychically conditioned. The same argument applies to colour. Red, according to physics, integrates the happening of millions of events in ether, and is therefore patently incapable of having physical existence in an instantaneous time.

But does not this desperate expedient of bringing in the mind, as the supposed creative source of sound and colour, fail of its purpose? In face, on the one hand, of the many correlations which have been established between the secondary qualities and their physical and physiological accompaniments, and on the other hand of the absence of any similar known correlations in the psychical sphere, is not such procedure suspiciously indicative of some radical defect in the assumptions which are being made, and especially in the assumption that outside the mind only that can exist which exists in an instant?

Let us take, as our illustration, a melody, such as the song of the nightingale. Is it impossible that such a melody should exist as an item in physical nature? The melody, as extending over a sequence of events, demands for its apprehension as melody certain mental processes, namely, those which make possible recollection and anticipation. Must not the melody, therefore, as an integration of the non-instantaneous, be classed as itself mental?

Beyond all possibility of questioning, processes of recollection and anticipation do thus condition our *awareness* of the melody. The melody, as a whole, is apprehended in and through such processes, and they form a sequence. But because these processes condition the *awareness*, it does not follow that the melody which surprises and delights us when the awareness thus reveals it, must itself be similarly conditioned. That view, Whitehead maintains, originates in a false view of time. On his doctrine of duration, the melody takes its place alongside the secondary qualities as a possible item in objective nature. The song of the nightingale can belong to the objective order; only our awareness of it need be reckoned as mental.

The difficulties which arise in connexion with this question centre, you will observe, in and about Whitehead's fundamental distinction between events and objects. Most of Whitehead's readers must have wished that he had dwelt upon this distinction at greater length, and in particular that he had stated more explicitly his reasons for classing sounds, colours and the like, as being objects, and not events. The major part of his argument is designed to show that the reasons assigned for classing sensa as mental are quite inconclusive, and that certain of these reasons are demonstrably invalid. But we can accept this part of his teaching, and therefore can count sound and melodies as being items in objective nature, and yet not feel committed to the further contention that they are persistent and recurrent objects, and as such condition recognition.

There are, of course, many good reasons why this part of Whitehead's teaching should present special difficulty. He is here treating of that most troublesome of all logical problems, the possibility and status of universals. The question, however, as to whether sensa can be classed as objects is capable of being discussed in and by itself; and that Whitehead has nowhere done in any detail. The objections to the position which he is maintaining are many and obvious. He would seem to be adopting, in regard to sensa, that very view which he denounces in regard to matter. He would seem to be contending that sounds never come into existence nor pass out of existence. Consequently, on Whitehead's view, I may be using some of the self-identical vowel or other sounds of which Julius Caesar availed himself during his campaign in Gaul. Their having been heard in Europe, and that so many centuries ago, need be no obstacle to their also being present here with us *in propria persona*. Indeed, Whitehead is prepared to go even farther, and to maintain that since sounds are objects and not events, the same sounds can be in more than one place at a time; they can, for instance, be in all parts of this room at once. But most of us, probably, will, until better evidence is shown, continue to hold to the more usual contrary view, namely, that sensa are events, and, like other physical happenings, are non-recurrent. We shall hold that the sounds which Caesar heard, when he or others spoke, were heard but once, and, like the slabs of duration which they constituted, can never again appear within the historical series.

But let us follow the further stages in the argument in which Whitehead defines more precisely his distinction between events and objects. Events, he tells us, make their entry only in order to take their exit. They perish, for good and all, in the very time of their occurring.

An object, on the other hand, has, so to speak, an immortality which enables it to survive not only the mental events in and through which it is experienced, but also the physical events in and through which it obtains its diverse locations in time and space. And if a melody be an object, this must likewise be true of it. We have heard the song of the nightingale; we hear it again years after, and say: 'There it is again, the same melody that I heard before.' Is this only a manner of speaking; or does the melody really have the immortality which Keats so fancifully ascribed to the bird that voices it? The traditional view has a very definite answer to this question. The nervous system of the nightingale has a fixed type of structure, handed down from generation to generation. Hence the uniformity of its behaviour; only so is it able to delight us in this twentieth century as it delighted the Greeks in classical times. It is not the melody which persists, but a type of structure in nervous matter, physically conditioned.

But it is precisely upon this position that Whitehead proceeds to train his heaviest artillery. So long as the argument concerns only the secondary qualities and such entities as a melody, there are so many difficulties, and so little specific evidence, that decisive conclusions can hardly be looked for. The situation undergoes change, and as it would seem very decisively in Whitehead's favour, when we limit the discussion to the physical field, as ordinarily conceived. For it is in this domain that his view of duration, if accepted, most clearly displays its revolutionary character. The traditional physics will not countenance persistent melodies, but it does believe in what, as Whitehead is prepared to show, are more or less in the same class therewith, namely, persistent electrons, atoms and molecules. These, Whitehead argues, cannot exist, any more than the secondary qualities, if nature be viewed as instantaneous.

Whitehead takes as an example the molecule of iron.

> Consider a molecule of iron. It is composed of a central core of positive electricity surrounded by annular clusters of electrons, composed of negative electricity and rotating round the core. No single characteristic property of iron as such can be manifested at an instant. Instantaneously there is simply a distribution of electricity and Maxwell's equations are required to express our

expectations. But iron is not an expectation or even a recollection. It is a fact; and this fact, which is iron, is what happens during a period of time. . . . There is no such thing as iron at an instant, to be iron is a [consistent and recurrent] character of an event. Every physical constant respecting iron which appears in scientific tables is the register of such a character. What is ultimate in iron, according to the traditional theory, is [not iron but] instantaneous distributions of electricity; and this ultimateness is simply ascribed by reason of a metaphysical theory, and by no reason of observation. In truth, when we have once admitted the hierarchy of macroscopic and microscopic equations, the traditional concept is lost. For it is the macroscopic equations which express the facts of immediate observation, and these equations essentially express the integral characters of events. But that hierarchy [the macroscopic referring to what is integrated and the microscopic to the instantaneous] is necessitated by every concept of modern physics —the molecular theory of matter, the dynamical theory of heat, the wave theory of light, the electromagnetic theory of molecules, the electromagnetic theory of mass.[1]

This view Whitehead extends to the living organism. The organism must, he maintains, be interpreted in the same general manner as atoms and molecules. By its existence it demonstrates the physical reality of certain rhythmic functionings which, as such, are incapable of being enclosed within the instantaneous. As rhythmic, they presuppose duration as truly as does a melody. 'Life is too obstinately concrete' to be located in an instant, even if at the instant it be spread over a space. For this reason, living organisms, for their definition, demand synoptic as well as analytic treatment. In so far as they are complex, analysis is required to determine the precise nature of their complexities; but in so far as they are rhythmic, these complexities are subordinate to, and determined by, the unities which they constitute. When, therefore, the extreme mechanists endeavour to view the unity of the organism as something which can be exhaustively accounted for as a resultant of the interactions of its parts, they would appear to be developing a very fruitful scientific technique into philosophical consequences which it need not imply.

[1] *An Enquiry Concerning the Principles of Natural Knowledge* (Cambridge, 1925), pp. 22–23.

The behaviourists, in unfaltering devotion to a strictly logical consistency, are prepared to go even farther, and to deny the effective existence of anything that can properly be entitled consciousness. Behaviourism—may we not say?—is the *enfant terrible* of this way of thinking.

Whitehead completes his indictment of the traditional philosophy of nature, by showing that there are yet other items which the classical physics itself recognizes and which yet can find no foothold in the world so conceived. As Whitehead shows by detailed argument, this is true of such factors as velocity, acceleration, momentum, stress, mass, and kinetic energy, and even of so seemingly ultimate a feature as that of contact. Such factors are, indeed, made use of by the classical physics, just as are the secondary qualities; otherwise physics could not get along at all. But, as Whitehead maintains, it does so, in each case, only by inconsistently doing violence either to its own principles or to the facts as it has itself defined them. If, therefore, the secondary qualities are to be ejected from the system of instantaneous nature, so much else must follow on their heels, that, in consequence of these migrations, physical nature will become so shadowy and unsubstantial that quite palpably the title 'reality' will belong more properly to what lies outside it than to what it itself continues to include. 'The ideal [is that] of all nature with no temporal extension, . . . of all nature at an instant. But this ideal is in fact the ideal of a nonentity'[1].

Is not this, indeed, the reason of what surely is a highly paradoxical situation: namely, that if we wish to discover, in these modern times, a whole-hearted adherent of Bishop Berkeley's view of the function of science, as consisting merely in the determination of the coexistences and sequences of our sensations, we have to search for him in the ranks of the students of the natural sciences? In Karl Pearson and in Ernst Mach—the latter of whom has exercised considerable influence upon Einstein—the wheel has gone full circle. Nature, for them, has come to be located, together with the secondary qualities, merely and exclusively in the subjective experiences of this and that individual. The fundamental concepts of science, whether of mass and energy or of molecules and electrons, are, they declare, merely working fictions, and can be justified only by certain practical services which they discharge.

[1] *The Concept of Nature*, p. 61.

The remedy, according to Whitehead, lies in a radical revision of our fundamental assumptions. We may not thus pick and choose among nature's components. We must keep to nature, explaining it in terms of itself, and not of any outside entity, such as mind. The type of problem with which science, properly understood, will have to deal will then no longer be: how a billiard ball causes the mind to see red or green; but the problem: when red is found in nature, what else is found there in addition. Under guidance of this question, we shall no longer discuss the causes of knowledge, but the coherence of the known. The understanding which we shall seek is an understanding of relations within nature, not of relations between nature and a something called mind, supposed to lie outside it.

> All we know of nature is in the same boat, to sink or swim together.[1]

> For us the red glow of the sunset should be as much part of nature as are [its] molecules and electric waves. . . . It is for natural philosophy to analyse how these various elements of nature are connected. . . . We are instinctively willing to believe that by due attention more can be found in nature than that which is observed at first sight. But we will not be content with less.[2]

To describe any of the items of nature as mental in character is not only to deprive them of their legitimate birthright, but in mockery to offer, as substitute, what in this connexion is a quite empty and meaningless title. This device of bringing in the animal and human mind as a supposedly creative source of new entities, really avails nothing in rendering intelligible the occurrence of these entities, or the part which they unquestionably play in animal and human behaviour.

Thus nature, as envisaged by Whitehead, is extraordinarily different from nature as defined in terms of the classical physics. While less tidy, with all sorts of loose ends, it is allowed to have more content; and in proportion as it has become more bewildering, just thereby it has come more and more to resemble the reality which faces us in experience. In view of the amazing diversity of the items which, on Whitehead's view,

[1] *The Concept of Nature*, p. 148.
[2] Op. cit., p. 29.

compose nature—the tastes as well as the textures of foods, the roar of the lion and the song of the nightingale as well as the labyrinthine structures of the inner ear, the gorgeous coloration of the peacock's tail as well as the rods and cones of the retina—nature, thus envisaged, will at every turn, to the great benefit of our open-mindedness, force upon our attention the immense gaps, not merely in our detailed and established theories, but also even in our most conjectural interpretations of nature's doings. We may allow the imagination to suggest all manner of possible possibilities beyond the actualities which we are in position to verify; but we shall not thereby succeed in comprehending, even distantly, in bare outline, how these gaps can be bridged—not at least if, as we ought, we insist upon retaining belief in the continuity which is so fundamental, and, as we have good grounds for believing, so universal a feature of all reality.

On the traditional view—only a generation ago Tyndall and Huxley were speaking of atoms as the foundation stones of the universe—the ultimate constituents and the possible types of combination are supposed to be already more or less known; and for science it only remains to determine the particular ever-changing combinations which occur in this and that space at this and that time. On Whitehead's view, on the other hand, even nature's most usual and seemingly ordinary features are but hieroglyphics which bear a wealth of meaning beyond all that we have yet succeeded in discerning.

> The materialistic theory has all the completeness of the thought of the middle ages, which had a complete answer to everything, be it in heaven or in hell or in nature. There is a trimness about it, with its instantaneous present, its vanished past, its non-existent future, and its inert matter. This trimness is very medieval and ill accords with brute fact. The theory which I am urging admits a greater ultimate mystery and a deeper ignorance.[1]

> We are apt to fall into the error of thinking that the facts are simple because simplicity is the goal of our quest. The guiding motto in the life of every natural philosopher should be, Seek simplicity and distrust it.[2]

[1] *The Concept of Nature*, p. 73.
[2] Op. cit., p. 163.

We have to remember that while nature is complex with timeless subtlety, human thought issues from the simple-mindedness of beings whose life is less than half a century.[1]

All that one can hope to do is to settle the right sort of difficulties and to raise the right sort of ulterior questions, and thus to accomplish one short step further into the unfathomable mystery.[2]

These considerations, and especially this last phrase 'the unfathomable mystery', bring me to my second main question, which I must treat more briefly. You will have observed the many respects in which Whitehead's terminology resembles that of Bergson's. Like Bergson, he regards the traditional philosophy of nature as false and distorting; like Bergson, he substitutes duration for the instantaneous present; like Bergson, he speaks of nature as an historical being, and as at every moment creatively advancing into novelty. He also agrees with Bergson that we must start from something directly experienced, and that in proceeding to know it we must do so by widening the field of this experience, not by leaving out more and more of it. Is then Whitehead also committed to Bergson's attack upon discursive reason as incapable of yielding insight into reality, and as finding its proper sphere not in the realm of theory but in the catch-who-catch-can scrimmages of practical life? The question almost answers itself. Whitehead has none of Bergson's deep-rooted antipathy to that surely very admirable, if for purposes of transportation very expensive and troublesome, aspect of reality which we entitle space. According to Whitehead, reality is in space no less assuredly than it is in time; and he therefore regards the analytic procedure whereby the physicist explains the given in terms of its simpler components as resulting in genuine knowledge, and not in distortion of what is intrinsically simple and unitary. Indeed he insists that we should give as literal an interpretation as possible to physical theories regarding the existence and structure of molecules, atoms and electrons. Also, though Whitehead does not believe in a material ether, he does hold that we are committed to acceptance of an ether of events. With this appreciation of analysis, Whitehead holds, however, to much

[1] *An Enquiry Concerning the Principles of Natural Knowledge*, p. 15.
[2] Op. cit., p. viii.

that is more or less distinctive of Bergson; and I shall therefore conclude by considering how far Whitehead's teaching is compatible with an unqualified and whole-hearted belief in rational criteria. This is not a question upon which he has expressed himself in any explicit manner; but it can, I think, be answered in the light of his other utterances.

Those who depreciate discursive reason, in the manner of Bergson, consider that it is too inflexible, too logical, to allow for the freakishness of life, and for the strange and seemingly irrational contingencies of which nature and history offer so many examples. Logic seems out of place when we are faced, as we constantly are, by contingency, factualness, historicity.

Take, for example, the fact that Great Britain is an island and is not triangular or equilateral, but grotesquely shaped. Its being an island, with this specific irregular shape, has largely determined the history of England and Scotland. Yet it is strictly factual. Geology can, indeed, give an explanation of these facts; but the explanation consists in running them back to a body of contingencies more primitive but equally factual, and which are as little capable of rational justification as the present distribution of sea and land.

This is typical of all the fundamental facts and conditions of human existence. We cannot by means of reason establish their necessity. The most that we can do is to determine their actual nature and the consequences that follow therefrom. And so doing, we generally succeed in finding that, under the conditions prescribed, a rationality or order appropriate to them, determined by them, gradually discloses itself—an order which is richer and more wonderful than any that unassisted, that is, discursive, reasoning could ever have anticipated, even if called upon to invent what it would desire to discover. It is not, indeed, the task of the human mind to prove the rationality of the universe or any part of it. It is for the universe, on detailed study, to reveal the kind of rationality which does, as a matter of fact, belong to it. Ahead of detailed study, we do not know what, in reference to any specific subject-matter, we ought to mean by rationality. Taken abstractly, in general, we mean by rationality merely that which is at once in harmony with the relevant appearances, and which when formulated in terms of human speech, and thereby embodied in judgements, does not involve direct logical contradictions. But clearly this definition of the rational is purely formal; it is empty of all specific meaning. It does not in the least prefigure what detailed study is likely to disclose—as in physiology, the crossing of the nerve-trunks which makes us leftbrained, or as in grammar the irregular verbs, or as in political history the British Constitution. What the rationalist can alone be required to stand for is the conviction that reality, if known in its details and in all its manifold aspects, will be found to justify itself in face of the claims to which it has given rise in *any* of its embodiments. The rational is for us a problematic concept, and only by empirical inquiry, in proportion as such inquiry is successful, can it be progressively defined in its relevant detail.

To all of this Whitehead would, I think, whole-heartedly agree; while Bergson, on the other hand, would desire to make certain provisos. For they differ fundamentally, not only in those respects which I have already enumerated, but also in one other respect which is even more fundamental, namely, that Bergson denies the validity of universals, whereas Whitehead allows them a large and prominent place in his philosophy. According to Bergson there is no fixed structure or constancy in nature to balance, in any reliable manner, the creative processes whereby it advances or emerges into novelty. The gates of the future are so wide open that we have no ground for asserting anything to be either possible or impossible prior to its actual entry into the realm of the actual. It is, Bergson tells us, an illusion that there is, in addition to the actual, any such thing as the possible. When the future has, through creative activities, been rendered actual, it casts back into the past the mirage of its own possibility; and so leads us, if we be not careful in observation, to believe that, had our previous experience been more extensive, we could have anticipated the future prior to its arrival. But if this be the situation, if we cannot know how far the actual will continue to behave as it has hitherto done, and if, indeed, our one certainty in regard to the future is that it must differ from the nonrecurrent past, must not some other guide than reason be set in the seat of authority?

To these queries the answer can be made that if with Bergson we deny the existence of universals, if types and patterns are but artificial schemes devised by our analytic and merely anthropomorphic reason, if under the stress of our merely practical need for rhythms and recurrences we are reading them into the ever-changing, freely creative processes of nature, and if, therefore, nothing not already existent can be regarded as being either possible or impossible, then certainly such rational criteria cannot be relied upon as a source of theoretical insight. For a vision of the genuinely and independently real we shall have to look to some other source.

But if, on the other hand, we recognize with Whitehead that universals, that is, recurrent rhythms and patterns, are as important and essential a factor in nature as is the uniqueness of its transitory, non-recurrent events, then the possible at once comes into its own, and reason is therewith reinstated in authority. For is it not, above all else, with the possible that reason, *qua* reason, is primarily concerned?[1] And that not because reason is detached from, or indifferent to, the actual, but because only through study of the possible can the actual, in its many concealed aspects, come to be known.

What, for instance, does the scientist do when he makes an experiment? Constructing an hypothesis, in the light of his acquired experience and knowledge, he conceives a situation which has never been actualized in nature, or which at least has never been disclosed to him or to others in actual experience. This situation he sets about producing with the artificial aids which his laboratory supplies; and according as its outcome is or is not in accordance with his predictions, he confirms, modifies, or rejects his hypothetically inferred conclusions. The possibilities which he thus hypothetically entertains may, more often than not, be akin to the mirages of which Bergson speaks; but ever and anon he finds that by their means he has entered more deeply into the constitution of the real. Through study of possibilities he discovers for himself fresh data by reasoning upon which he can make further advances in the building up of knowledge.

Even when the hypotheses fail, they frequently, in failing, yield data which, if not positively, at least negatively, mark out the boundaries between the true and the false. They afford clues, by further reflection upon which possibilities of a more genuine character may be brought into view.

[1] I have here profited by recollections of Stout's unpublished Gifford Lectures.

Without attempting to enter into the difficult problems which centre round the question as to the nature of universals—and recognizing, as I have said, that on this point Whitehead's own statements are too brief to be altogether satisfactory—it is surely clear that experience does reveal to us actual universals. Particulars resemble one another; they recur, and can be recognized. There is permanence of patterns and types; reality has a structure. But this being granted, the possible at once comes into its own. Every universal has possible, as well as actual instances, and the possible instances are, in many cases, in experimental science as in the moral, social and political fields, even more important to us than the actual instances. They are possible only in so far as they are instances of *actual* universals. Our knowledge of them is to that extent empirical. In considering them we are still dealing with reality. We are justified in giving to them the eulogistic title of possibilities, in that they are genuine modes in which the actual, granted the other required conditions, can come to be. Their basis is factual, being found in the present and in the past. In arguing to them we are still arguing in the light of, and under the guidance of, experience.

The reason why, though actually possible, they are merely possible, is that besides the conditions which make them possible, they demand other conditions not yet actual. Whether these other conditions are themselves possible is one of the questions which we have to settle in the process of considering them. To take, for instance, practical possibilities: in deciding whether we ought to guide our conduct, personal, social, or political, in such manner as to realize certain possibilities, we are deciding two questions which, however difficult, may be quite within our competence. One is as to the possibility of the supplement of conditions required for converting the possibilities into actuality; the other is as to the value of the possibilities thus sought, and the costs of their achievement. Neither question can be entertained, and neither can be solved, save through the instrumentality of reason; and it is in these two types of enquiry that reason proves itself the indispensable ally of all our specifically human activities. Human activities, whether theoretical or practical, are certainly creative; but that which at once inspires and directs them comes from study of the possibilities disclosed to us in experience of existing universals. Experience fructifies reason; and reason clarifies experience into the anticipation of all that it involves for its greatest possible, and most ideal, extension. The greater constructive thinkers, like Plato, are, as a rule, rational empiricists, or if we please, empirical rationalists. Only thus, they believe, can reliance on reason be harmonized with the prevailing contingency and factualness and historicity of all that is fundamental in human experience, alike in the natural or in the spiritual domains. Reality is full of the unexpected. As Montaigne wisely remarks: 'Unknown truths are improbable.' But the unexpectedness of the real reveals itself in its universals, no less than in its particulars; and to this extent, even in its wildest vagaries, may come within the scope of our reasoned predictions. As the speculations of Einstein are now demonstrating, science can correctly predict the seemingly incredible. Through insight, genuinely rational in character, it can anticipate the actual prior to its occurrence.

Thus Whitehead, notwithstanding the revolutionary character of his philosophy of nature, is not called upon to question any of the positive results of the natural sciences, nor to condemn any method of inquiry which the natural sciences now fruitfully employ. What he alone questions are the limitations which certain representative scientists, in philosophizing upon their results, have sought to impose upon scientific procedure, and by which they have sought to deprive the natural world of a considerable proportion of its observed features. Thus while he recognizes a larger measure of mystery in the proceedings of nature, he does not depart from the rationalist position, that, while we can hardly expect that the human race will ever have advanced so far on the path of knowledge as to have banished mystery, none the less only by the employment and continuous improvement of appropriate methods can we hope to define in what precise manner the features which remain as mysterious have to be reckoned with as actually present.

The Nature of Universals[1]

I

THE position which I shall adopt is that universals, expressive of genuine identities and not merely of similarities, are necessary to knowledge. This position can be, and has been questioned. But for the purpose of these articles I shall ask to be allowed to assume its truth. The sole question which I shall discuss is what, granted the necessity of universals, we ought to mean by them. After statement of the main problem, I will endeavour to develop a positive standpoint, first through criticism of the teaching of Bradley and Bosanquet, and secondly by way of comment upon the recently published views of Cook Wilson and of Stout. All of these writers propound some type of idealism; and being myself of that persuasion, I can best define, by their aid and by reference to them, such reasons as I have found, in this and that regard, for differing from them.

The position ordinarily adopted by those who believe in universals is that universals are either qualities characterizing a number of distinct particulars or relations recurring in a number of different situations. Thus if it be asserted that A is red and that B is red, what, on this view, is meant is that though the things A and B are distinct and spatially separate, one and the same identical character is found in both. It is as against this fundamental thesis that the outstanding difficulty in regard to the nature of universals—the difficulty which has given rise to so endless an amount of discussion—at once presents itself. By what right are things and characters thus differentially treated? The red that is seen in A is spatially separate from the red that is seen in B. If spatial separation justifies us in regarding A and B as numerically distinct, why not

[1] *Mind*, vol. xxxvi, N.S., no. 142.

also in the case of the characters? What justifies us in saying that though A and B are numerically distinct, the red thus seen in two places is none the less identical in both?

The usual reply is somewhat as follows:[1] There is, we seem justified in saying, an essential difference in the meaning of our statements according as they refer to concrete things or to characters. A concrete thing cannot be in two places at the same time. Characters or qualities, on the other hand, differ from concrete things precisely in this respect. No amount of spatial separation and no amount of multiplication can destroy the identity of the colour. The reds may, indeed, be spoken of in the plural, as being locally separate and as two in number; but these ways of expression, correctly interpreted, apply, it can be said, only to the concrete things which are thus coloured, not to the colour itself. When we say 'A is red and B is red', we are applying one and the same predicate to both, and what we are asserting is that the same specific colour belongs to these two spatially separate things. We have made no assertion, and so long as our statements mean what they claim to mean, we have no right to assert, that the colours themselves are separate in the sense in which the things are separate. Qualities, unlike concrete things, 'spread undivided, operate unspent'.

The implications of this general thesis can be further defined. When two different things are said to be, in this or that respect, identical, their differences, whether spatial or temporal or in sensible characters, are not, of course, being denied. That would destroy the whole point of the assertion made. What we are maintaining is that different things, notwithstanding their admitted differences, are in this and that respect the same; or in other words, that sameness can exist together with difference and is not in any way destroyed by it.

> We [may] not [be able to] say how far it extends, or what proportion it bears to the accompanying diversity; but sameness, so far as it goes, is actually and genuinely the same.[2]

However much [the] diversity may preponderate, however

[1] Cf. G. E. Moore, *Relativity, Logic and Mysticism* (Aristotelian Society, 1923), pp. 105–6.
[2] F. H. Bradley, *Appearance and Reality*, 2nd ed. (London, Swan Sonnenschein & Co., 1908), p. 351.

different may be the whole effect of each separate compound, yet, for all that, what is the same in them is one and identical.[1]

These quotations, when thus taken in isolation, are, of course, by no means unambiguous. The view for which I shall later argue is that though conditions (surroundings, etc.) may make a thing *lose* a given character, at any given time the character is either there, unmodified, or not there at all. This, I presume, would be the position of Moore and Johnson, but not of Bradley and Bosanquet.[2]

Further, just as the abstract thesis, in and by itself, says nothing as to the amount of sameness that persists in and through diversity, so also it leaves entirely open the question as to what the sameness will or will not bring forth. Sometimes the identical character involves the diverse things in active community. This happens when two souls meeting are, by their identity, drawn together. But it does not happen (at least not in the same direct manner) when they are sundered in time. This is still more obviously so in the material world, as ordinarily interpreted in the physical sciences.

> In Nature sameness and difference may be said everywhere to exist, but never anywhere to work. This would, at least, appear to be the ideal of natural science, however incompletely that ideal has been carried into practice. No element, according to this principle, can be anything to any other, merely because it is the same, or because it is different. For these are but internal characters, while that which works is in every case an outward relation.[3]

Sameness and difference are, indeed, indispensable for those processes of identification and discrimination through which the external relations are discovered and formulated. But this only reinforces the contention that sameness and difference, while omnipresent in Nature and necessary to our knowledge of it, are not, in themselves, directly operative. The diverse interpretations of which these statements allow may again be noted. For Bradley they suggest a *criticism* of natural science; those, on the other hand, who have a different metaphysics can accept the negative

---

[1] Op. cit., p. 352.
[2] Cf. below, note to p. 257.
[3] Op. cit., p. 353.

criticism as only drawing attention to what we should in any case have expected.

Indeed, this would seem to be the point at which such thinkers as Bradley, Moore and Johnson diverge from one another, taking fundamentally different views as to the nature of the consequences to which they believe themselves to be committed in the acceptance of these positions.

Thus when we propound to Bradley the question: Can two numerically distinct things, A and B, have common predicates? his answer is twofold. If, he says, we are talking about existences in space and time— and that is what so far we have been doing—then we are moving in the realm of appearances, a realm in which any statements that can be made are contradictory of one another and ultimately of themselves. If two distinct things, A and B, are in any respect identical, then to that extent each transcends itself and is the other. In the realm of appearance, not only may such self-transcendence be allowed as occurring, it is, Bradley declares, the fundamental characteristic of appearance as such. It is the very nature of a finite appearance so to behave. Its 'what' is loosened from its 'that'; its existence is incompatible with its nature; it carries us beyond itself to what is other and different. The problem, therefore, as Bradley conceives it, is not as to what, in face of the separateness of things in space and time, we should mean by universals; but how such separateness—in other words, how finite centres—can exist in appearance, when a single indivisible Absolute has to be allowed as alone real. Bradley does not claim to be in a position to answer this question, but only to have shown the necessity of propounding it. Self-transcendence, and the external relations in which alone it can find expression, are, he argues, what constitute appearance; and if, as he further argues, all such relations can be proved to be self-contradictory, there is no option save to postulate a Reality in which content is never loosened from existence, and in which self-transcendence is therefore neither possible nor required. This is why Bradley has been so ready to adopt the view of universals as being identical in their various instances; it is because he has no belief in the real separateness of the latter.[1] If A and B are not

---

[1] Cf. Bosanquet, *Essentials of Logic,* 2nd ed. (Macmillan, 1895), vol. ii, p. 279. 'I quite see for myself that [identity in difference] must go "in the end", that is to say,

really what they would seem to be, separate and distinct, there need be no obstacle in the way of our holding, on the contrary there must be every reason for holding, that the 'red' is identically the same in both.

This, then, being Bradley's attitude—that the separateness of things in space and time is merely appearance, and that the question how the existence of identical characters can be reconciled with this separateness is consequently an unreal problem—it is not surprising that he pays little further attention to it, and while still occasionally making reference, always in a depreciatory manner, to 'abstract' characters, gives his whole attention to the type of identity which, by contrast and in the manner of Hegel, he entitles the 'concrete universal'.[1]

This doctrine of the 'concrete universal' has, ever since Hegel, played so prominent a part in the idealist philosophies that, as I have just suggested, it has almost entirely displaced the problem from which I have started. Accordingly I shall have to employ the remainder of this and a second article in its discussion. I shall then, however, be in a position, in a third article, to return to the main problem in the precise form in which I have stated it above, and with the advantage of having meantime defined certain of the main issues involved.

Bradley makes the transition from the abstract to the concrete universal in a very abrupt, offhand manner, which has the effect of concealing from his readers the numerous, highly questionable assumptions upon which he is proceeding.

> To deny [that a sameness can exist together with difference] is to affront common sense. It is, in fact, to use words which could have no meaning. . . . If you will not assume that identity holds throughout different contexts, you cannot advance one single step in apprehending the world. There will be neither change nor

in any experience for which objects are self-contained, and cease to transcend themselves. . . . Undoubtedly the Real is self-complete and self-contained. But I insist on the words "in the end".'

[1] Cf. F. H. Bradley, *The Principles of Logic*, 2nd ed. (Oxford, 1922), vol. i, p. 188. 'The *abstract* universal and the *abstract* particular are what does not exist. The *concrete* particular and the *concrete* universal both have reality, and they are different names for the individual.'

endurance, and still less, motion through space of an identical body; there will be neither selves nor things.[1]

In other words, Bradley is here maintaining—a contention fraught with far-reaching consequences, and calling therefore for the most careful and considered argument—that the main evidence in proof of universals lies not in characters common to separate existences, but in the self-identity of each thing, whether in and through motion, or in and through qualitative change, or in and through the diversity of its constituent attributes. It is this latter type of identity which, in contrast to the former, he entitles 'the concrete universal'.

This method of distinguishing between two kinds of universals is especially bewildering in view of Bradley's assertion that universality is, by its very essence, abstract.

> Identity obviously by its essence must be more or less abstract; and when we predicate it, we are disregarding other sides of the whole. We are asserting that, notwithstanding other aspects, this one aspect of sameness persists and is real.[2]

At first we may be tempted to think that Bradley must be distinguishing between universality and identity. That, however, is not his intention. For by the abstract universal he means an identical character found in separate particulars, and by the concrete universal the identity wherein a thing or self expresses itself through its changes and in the diversity of its constituent characters. The two types of universal mark out these two types of identity: identity of character or quality in differing things and the self-identity of a single continuing existence.

In passing, we may note that when universality is thus equated with identity, relations, not being readily reducible to either type of identity, tend to be left out of the reckoning.[3] Bradley does, indeed, frankly

---

[1] *Appearance and Reality*, pp. 347–8.

[2] *Appearance and Reality*, p. 351.

[3] This is one main reason for Bradley's very sceptical teaching in his doctrine of the judgement. A judgement, as he interprets it, never asserts a relation. When we say, 'This tree is green', we are not asserting of an *appearance* that it stands to greenness in *the relation of* substance to attribute. What, according to Bradley, we are alone ultimately asserting is that 'Reality, *i.e.*, the Absolute, is *such that* appearances are so

recognize that relations resemble characters in being universals. The relation of being 'to the right of' is the same relation however many be the situations in which it is found. But both characters and relations he groups together under the heading of the 'abstract universal', and as such they share in a common neglect. His all-absorbing interest is in the other type of identity, the lesser and greater perfections of which are, as he believes, so many degrees in which human experience, achieving truth, proceeds towards the 'Absolute'.

Bosanquet has given a fuller treatment both of the abstract and of the concrete universal; and I shall adopt his exposition as the basis of my discussion. Let us consider—it will not involve much repetition—his statement of the relation of the two types of universal to one another. The universal, he states, is in both forms an identity in difference. To take first the abstract universal: things, in order to be similar, must be in some respect identical. If two substances be red or spherical, then to the extent of their redness or sphericity, they are the same. Such identity is, however, compatible with any amount of difference in other regards.[1] Notwithstanding such identity the substances may differ in

---

apprehended'. The 'such that', which on this view is alone ultimately asserted, is not itself a relation but a quality. Bradley entitles it a 'latent quality', meaning that, though postulated as real, it is not itself known. Similarly, when we assert that 'A is to the right of B', we are not asserting the *reality* either of the appearance A or of the appearance B, and accordingly we are also not asserting the *reality* of the spatial relation. In the 'Absolute' there can be no relations. To assert a relation is, by implication, to define reality in terms of what is peculiar to appearance, and therefore other than itself. As to Bradley's acceptance of Bosanquet's restatement of his doctrine, I shall have more to say later. In anticipation of my argument, I may here state the point of view from which my criticisms are made. The furthest that I can go in agreement with Bradley and Bosanquet is to formulate the ultimate implication of the propositions as: 'There is an actual situation of which "The tree is green" (or "A is to the right of B") is a partial description'.

[1] I say in *other* regards: for if Bosanquet, as he would frequently seem to do, goes further than this (cf. above, p. 253), and maintains that a character is never indifferent to differences, and therefore never remains precisely the same in different instances (*e.g.*, that humanity is different in each of its instances, *i.e.*, that we never find 'common' features among men) then he is coming very close to the position of Cook Wilson and Stout, that the universal is a name for the totality of the instances.

their spatial and temporal relations, and in most (though not in all) their other characters. Such forms of identity Bosanquet therefore entitles abstract universals. They do not subordinate to themselves the differences among which they are found. A substance that is red may be cinnabar and therefore heavy, or a child's balloon and therefore light. A spherical substance may be of any kind of material. The identity is in each case *indifferent* to the varying circumstances; the substances have through possession of it only that *superficial*—so Bosanquet regards it— type of unity represented by a class. Should we view objects in terms of this kind of universal, the most incongruous conjunctions will be brought about; things really connected in their essential features will be grouped apart, while the classes actually constituted will yield no insight into the diversity which each displays. It is by contrast to the abstract universal, as thus depicted, that Bosanquet defines the concrete universal as being always individual. As already stated, Bosanquet would frequently seem to be maintaining that identity is never indifferent to differences, *i.e.*, that there are no *common* qualities, and therefore no universals of the abstract kind. If he be held to strict account in these statements, criticism will have to take an even more radical line than I have been following. We should then have to ask: Can Bosanquet in any way account for the fact that we *do* use this kind of universal?

Now when Bosanquet describes the concrete universal as being the individual, he does not, of course, merely mean that every individual embodies universals, and is not cognisable save by means of them, namely, as being light or heavy, as this or that type of element or compound, as inorganic or organic, as non-personal or personal, and so forth. He means so very much more than this, and is using the term 'universal' in a manner so contrary to ordinary usage, that at first we are apt to interpret his statements as merely figurative in character. He means, however, precisely what he is saying when he declares that the individual, *qua* individual, is a universal, and is more genuinely so than its abstract counterpart.

> Most people have some sort of schema which helps them to handle their philosophical ideas. The traditional schema of the universal . . . was, I suppose, extent of area. The greater uni-

versal included the wider surface, and was more abstract. The schema I should now use would be more like a centre with radii, or simply a subject with attributes, the greater universal having the more or more varied radii or attributes, and being therefore the more concrete. Such a schema is particularly in harmony with taking an individual as designated by a proper name for the example of a universal.[1]

The criticism which, as we have just noted, Bosanquet passes upon the abstract universal is that while it represents an identity which is found among differences, it is indifferent to these differences, and would seemingly remain what it is even if they were quite other than they are; or if this is going too far, we are at least, he argues, within the truth in saying that it affords us no aid in understanding these differences. An individual, on the other hand, such as Julius Caesar, is dominant in the determination of circumstance. Even when events happen to him through merely external causes, they are put to such use, and have such consequences, as his personality can alone render understandable.[2] Not that his personality is antecedent to, or is indifferent to, the course of events. In this type of existence it is equally true that if the differences are as they are the identity must be what it is, and that the identity being what it is the differences have, from the start, been constrained to reckon with it, and in the degree in which it is dominant, to conform.

This being Bosanquet's reason for describing the individual as a concrete universal, the nature of the contrast between the concrete and the abstract universal can be further defined in the two following ways:

(1) The abstract universal is adjectival to its differences (white to the different things that are white); whereas in the case of the concrete universal the reverse relation holds; the differences are adjectival to the identity (as being so many expressions of its constitution). The abstract universal is either a quality in an object or a predicate in a proposition; the concrete universal is a self-conditioning being and is itself the subject of all the propositions into which it enters.

---

[1] *Essays and Addresses*, pp. 166–7.

[2] Bosanquet, it may be pointed out, tends to ignore (what presumably he would not deny) that this is quite as true of everything else. If a body is, e.g. spherical, what happens to it will depend on this fact as well as on what things come in contact with it.

(2) The abstract universal is instrumental to knowledge; through it, used as a predicate, a subject is apprehended. But since, in each such application, it is (on Bosanquet's view) determined to a fuller, more specific meaning, it is to the subject-term, i.e., to a universal of the concrete type, that all meaning and significance must ultimately be traced. All knowledge is knowledge of the individual—the individual that may not be opposed to the universal but is itself the type of all universality which is not merely abstract. As above indicated, I am not at present raising the question whether, on his principles, Bosanquet can justify even such partial recognition of 'the merely abstract'.

So far Bosanquet's method of argument is straightforward and unambiguous. It suggests, however, one obvious objection; namely, as to the legitimacy of the terminology which is being employed. It has, of course, been usual to define the universal as 'the one in the many', meaning by 'the many' numerically distinct particulars. But what, we may well ask, are we being committed to, when required to interpret 'the one in the many' in this other very different sense which renders it applicable to each particular thing or self? If the original meaning of the term 'universal' involves its distinction from the term 'particular', can this meaning, by any legitimate process of analogy, be so extended as to render the term synonymous with the particular? A term cannot signify its own opposite, not even if that opposite be a counterpart which it presupposes for its own completion. The term 'husband' does not signify 'wife', though each term has meaning only in and by reference to the other.

Bosanquet has taken account of this objection, and indeed welcomes it as affording an opportunity of defining his position more precisely. Though he has stated that Julius Caesar is a very serviceable illustration of what should be meant by a concrete universal, it is no part of his contention that each and every particular existence is so in equal degree. There are two points of view from which a finite being can be regarded, and to mark the difference in these points of view Bosanquet requests permission to differentiate much more definitely than is customary in ordinary speech the meanings to be attached to the terms 'particular' and 'individual'. A finite thing in so far as it excludes other finite things is, as we may agree, very suitably entitled finite—and a *particular* finite at that; and as such it is correlative to the universal, being that which participates in but is none the less to be distinguished from it. But the same finite thing in so far as it subordinates diversity, and change, of content to the maintenance and expression of an abiding unity, displays to us a very different aspect of its being, and one which is less apt than its particularity to receive sufficient attention. The prevalence of 'natural kinds' with their repetitious instances, and the sharp-cut outlines whereby each such instance seems to segregate itself off from the rest of reality, mark out the 'particular' in too obvious a manner to be overlooked. It is unmistakable, as being at once in this and that character similar to certain others, and as in its existence exclusive of all others; and as being, therefore, in these respects, an instance of this and that abstract universal. It is only in proportion as we pass beyond the merely physical domain that the other aspect of finite being comes into anything like corresponding prominence; and even then it is so much more difficult to envisage, and there is consequently such constant temptation to assimilate it to better known types on lower planes, that it is very necessary to have a term exclusively appropriated to denote it; and in Bosanquet's view no term is so suitable for this purpose as the term 'individual'. The term 'individual' then signifies that combination of diversity with unity which, as we have seen, is what Bosanquet means by the concrete universal. The abstract universal applies to things considered only in their aspect as so many resembling but mutually exclusive particulars; the concrete universal is a name for each thing in its other aspect, namely as exhibiting a complex internal constitution.

It is in order to make quite unambiguously clear the kind of universality intended, that Bosanquet has selected as its type and exemplar, in the person of Julius Caesar, a self-conscious and rational being. The sharpness of the boundaries of Caesar's physical organism is obviously secondary in significance compared with the inclusiveness of his spiritual nature. He is a Microcosm in communion with the Macrocosm. The Macrocosm is *the* Universe, but each Microcosm is *a* Universe; and though still finite, and therefore still in another aspect a particular, may without unduly violating the properties of language—so Bosanquet maintains—be fittingly entitled a universal. Working back from this obvious instance, we shall then be in a better position to detect some corresponding aspect of individuality even in those existences in which on first view it is seemingly lacking. The term 'individual', when thus employed, is not synonymous with the term 'particular', but rather its opposite counterpart; and it is therefore easily understandable that while the particular has by general admission to be distinguished from the universal, conceived as abstract, the same particular in its aspect as individual can none the less be identified with the universal, conceived as concrete.

My statement, however, of Bosanquet's teaching in regard to the concrete universal is not yet complete even in outline. For we have still to consider the alternative form in which he expounds it, namely, by contrasting the abstract universal, not only as hitherto with a concrete individual, but also with what is signified by such terms as organism, world, cosmos, and (above all) system. Each of these latter terms refers to a complex which consists of members such that while distinct from one another, nevertheless, just by virtue of the features which render them distinct, they contribute to the unity of the whole. Accordingly, here also, the unity is a unity different in type from that which is generated when an abstract character, employed in and by itself, brings together its heterogeneous embodiments into the superficial unity of an aggregate or class. And since the unity of an articulated system, like that of an individual, is sameness *by means of* difference, it also is concrete.

The statement of this second antithesis, taken by itself, is again straightforward and unambiguous. The differences between a group or class and an organism, cosmos or system (which Bosanquet treats as differences between the *unity* of a class and the unity of an organism or system), are certainly sufficiently important to call for their careful discrimination. Up to this point, therefore, though I am largely out of sympathy with Bosanquet's general teaching, I have no difficulty in following his argument, or indeed in allowing, granted his general point of view, the legitimacy of his procedure. If it is to be possible for us to believe in the kind of Absolute to the exposition of which the philosophies of Bradley and Bosanquet are so single-mindedly devoted, this doubtless must be on some such lines as those suggested. But after long-continued struggles to disentangle the reasons which Bosanquet assigns for the next following stage—unfortunately he never explicitly distinguishes the stages—in his argument, I find myself settling into the conviction that they are such as do not allow of clear and un-ambiguous statement.

The stage in Bosanquet's argument to which I am referring comes at the point when he proceeds, under cover of the phrase 'individual system' (which, so far as I can see, can only mean single system), to run together his two pairs of contrasted terms—the abstract universal and the individual on the one hand, the abstract universal and system on the other—by identifying system with individuality. I say system with individuality, and not reversewise; for it is individuality which alone remains, as an ultimate category of thought when his argument is complete, system being treated as a relational, and therefore as ultimately a self-contradictory, type of unity. Of course, if we agree with Bradley and Bosanquet in regarding relational thinking as being by its very nature self-contradictory, any and every type of system will have to go by the board, and along with it must likewise go all finite centres and therefore every form of individuality save that of the Absolute. Short, however, of such ruthless procedure, possible only to those who can believe in a supra-relational Absolute, typified by feeling, I do not see how this last and all-important stage in Bosanquet's argument can be carried through.

To disentangle Bosanquet's argument, so far as I have been able to disentangle it, I will first consider his treatment of the abstract universal, and then proceed to comment on his identification of the concrete universal with the individual and with system.

I may recall the kind of evidence by which Bosanquet endeavours to exhibit what he describes as being the superficial character of the abstract concept, namely, the artificiality and meaninglessness of the groups which it generates. When a single character such as white is selected, it crops up in the most diverse quarters and in the most hetero-geneous of bearers; and the significance of its presence, as regards the *other* properties of the concrete things, is therefore minimal in amount. The things cannot indeed be known without it, but because the predicate is true of so many different things, no one of these things in its *specific* nature is thereby understood. It is an identity, but rather in spite of the differences than in and by means of them, and is not therefore of any great service in knowing the differences.

There are various comments to be made upon the above statements. In the first place, it is by no means clear by what right Bosanquet should thus identify the abstract universal with the class-concept. In so far as the abstract universal is some one character, it is indeed applicable as a predicate to any and every concrete existence in which the character is found; and we may, if we please, describe this range of application as being a class. Our purpose in selecting the character need not, however, be classificatory;[1] we may be investigating the character in and for itself; and it may be in the very variety and heterogeneity of its embodiments that we obtain the needful data. Thus in studying weight, metals and feathers, as in Galileo's experiments with falling bodies, afford just the kind of variations which are most helpful. Soap bubbles and mother of pearl have each made their contribution towards the understanding of the constitution of light and of the colours which it conditions. To depreciate such universals as weight and colour, because of the extreme diversity in, and seeming lack of all connexion between, the things in which they are found, is not therefore legitimate. On the contrary, their presence in objects otherwise so fundamentally different is testimony to the pervasiveness of the agencies and conditions to which they are due, and consequently to their importance in the nature of things.

Bosanquet pursues the abstract universal with such unwavering malignity of purpose that it is not surprising to find him, in another section of his writings,[2] also denouncing it for the quite opposite reason that in its most typical forms it generates classes which, so far from exhibiting a haphazard diversity, are characterised by the monotonous uniformity of their recurrent instances. Though Bosanquet has himself made no comment on the manner in which he thus condemns the

[1] Cf. Bosanquet's own statements, *Logic*, vol. ii, p. 198. 'It is usual to treat of classification as one special form, among others, of logical thought. I am unable to regard it in this light. It appears to me to be merely an external consequence, reappearing in every kind of universal, of the relation between universal and differences. The nearest approach to pure classification is therefore to be found in superficial arrangements destined merely to facilitate reference, in the dictionary, the index, the Linnaean system.'

[2] Cf. *The Principle of Individuality and Value* (Macmillan, 1927), pp. 32 ff.

abstract universal for two quite opposite reasons, doubtless, if asked, he would have replied that such opposite defects are naturally to be expected as a consequence of the merely external relation in which the abstract universal stands to its differences. What he is concerned to emphasize is that in the repetitious character of the instances, when they are repetitious and not merely diverse, we have an illustration of—as he expresses it—'the difference of principle' between the concrete and the abstract universal. The one, he says, signifies a world, the other refers to a class; and whereas 'it takes all sorts to make a world; a class is essentially of one sort only'.[1] The one is based on the uniformity of mere repetition; the other, in proportion as it is true to type, leads us in thought towards the unity of an ordered and variegated system.

This also is a mode of contrasting the two types of universal which is, I should say, much more misleading than helpful. If we take as our example of a universal one that stands comparatively near to the concrete particulars, e.g., the concept of the Death's Head beetle, it certainly represents, like the class Ford car of the year 1925, a standardized type that repeats itself without significant change in each of an immense number of particular instances. The feature of monotonous repetition is at a maximum. If, however, we choose a class-concept higher in the biological hierarchy, and which is therefore more definitely abstract, and therefore presumably a more adequate illustration of the nature and function of the abstract universal, we can no longer say that while it takes all sorts to make a world, a class is essentially of one sort only. The universal 'beetle' covers some half-million different species that vary among themselves in colour and shape, in organs and instincts, in their environments and in their consequent modes of life, and yet none the less, in all these multitudinous variations, maintain a type of structure which justifies the common appellation. Just as a world may or may not be a macrocosm of microcosms—the most marked feature of the mechanical world of the traditional physics is its uniformity of structure—so a class may or may not be a type of types. In any case it is *not* in proportion to its abstractness but to its closeness to the concrete that it reduces to a uniformity of simple recurrence.

The question as to the nature of the class-concept is so central in this

[1] Op. cit., p. 37.

enquiry that it may be well, at this point, to consider Bosanquet's own very carefully considered statement as to the manner of its formation. It is no doubt true that concepts, as vulgarly employed, tend to be vague and indefinite, '*merely* abstract', in proportion as they are of wider application. The meaning, for instance, which the ordinary man attaches to the term 'beetle' contains little else than the features of smallness and of general resemblance to the few types of beetle with which he happens to be familiar. It is either too particularized or else is empty of quite specific content, and accordingly in both respects is unreliable as a guide to identification. It covers instances to which the true conception is not applicable, and excludes others which properly come within its range. In logical discussion, however, we can deal only with precisely defined concepts; we are not concerned with the fact that owing to negligence, ignorance, or vagueness of mind, they very frequently, as actually employed, fail to conform to this requirement. Now when the issue is so defined, Bosanquet has no hesitation in dissociating himself from the view that abstraction proceeds merely by omission. The example which Bosanquet himself takes is the relation of the concept 'animal' to the concept 'man'. The former concept is not formed simply by omission of certain qualities which differentiate man from the other animals. There is, for instance, something corresponding to rationality in animals, namely, intelligence. The counter-view that, while man is guided by reason, animals are ruled solely by instinct, is quite unscientific. Further, even if rationality could be regarded as peculiar to man, it would still remain true, Bosanquet maintains, that in man animality is profoundly modified from what it is in the beasts, indeed that it also varies, though in a different, less profound, manner, in each of the families of the animal kingdom. Accordingly, in forming the concepts 'man' and 'animal' we can neither merely omit the characters which vary in their instances nor proceed by simple inclusion of those that are strictly uniform.

> Therefore the notion or abstraction which is to include both men and animals must on the one hand provide for a variable animality; must be considered, that is, not in the light of a fixed mark, but as a scheme of modifiable relations; and must, on the other hand, find room for some reference to intelligence, and not simply strike

it out as a mark in which the kinds to be classified are not the same. *Prima facie* then the content of the superior class-conception is made up of the very same elements as those of the conception nearer to individual reality, only that it must represent each attribute schematically, by limits of variation, instead of embodying a fixed system of amounts or values.[1]

I reserve, for later consideration, in my third article, the question how far Bosanquet is justified in maintaining that the wider concept, though more schematic, ought, when properly constructed, to be more complex, not less complex, than that which applies over a narrower area. It would, however, be misleading, in this connexion, to omit all reference to so distinctive a part of his teaching.

> Humanity, considered as a wider, and therefore as a deeper, idea, may have more content, as well as more area, than French-manity. We do not really, in thinking of humanity, omit from our schematic thought all reference to qualities of Greek, Jew, English, and German, and their bearing and interaction upon one another. It is only that we have been drilled to assume a certain neatness in the pyramidal arrangement by which we vainly try to reduce the meaning of a great idea to something that has no system and no inter-relation of parts, but approaches as near as possible in fixity to the character of a definite image, though far removed from such a character in the impossibility of bringing it before the mind.[2]

As Bosanquet further contends,[3] it is sometimes advisable to include in the concept properties that are absent in certain of the particulars or subclasses to which it applies, taking the property as present in them all but as having in these latter a zero value. This is what has to be done when, for instance, the straight line and the circle are taken as the limiting cases of the ellipse. Similarly, instead of saying with Keynes[4] that intension is 'increased when we pass . . . from man to negro', it is surely, as Bosanquet maintains,

---

[1] Bosanquet, *Logic*, vol. i, pp. 58–59.
[2] *Essentials of Logic*, p. 96.
[3] *Logic*, vol. i, pp. 63–64.
[4] *Formal Logic*, p. 36, n. 1, cited by Bosanquet, *Logic*, vol. i, p. 58.

better to take it that the negro has qualities which are distinctive
variations within the qualities of man, and which are compatible
with his falling short of the full intension of man as such.[1]

Such, then, are Bosanquet's own avowed views regarding the
doctrine that abstraction proceeds merely by omission.

> The idea of abstraction thus implied is altogether wrong. The
> meaning of a genus-name does not *omit* the properties in which
> the species differ. If it did, it would omit nearly all properties.
> What happens is that the genus-idea represents the general plan
> on which the species are built, but provides for each of the parts
> that constitute the whole, varying in the specific cases within
> certain limits.[2]

When, however, Bosanquet is seeking to justify his doctrine of the
concrete universal, he allows his own avowed view of the abstract
concept to fall into the background. Setting abstract universals in
unfavourable contrast to concrete universals, it is upon their indifference
to differences that he alone dwells. In proportion as they are 'merely
abstract' they are, he declares, emptier in content, and so the less helpful.
And for genuine understanding we must, therefore, he argues, look to
universals of a different type, those which he has chosen to eulogise as
being 'concrete'.[3]

For two reasons the term 'concrete', as a title for the class-concept,
however it be formed, is, I shall argue, illegitimate. Were there two
possible ways—by abstractive omission and by constructive analysis—of
forming a *genuine* class-concept, the two might doubtless be conveniently
so contrasted. 'Concrete' is certainly the correlative opposite of 'abstract'.
But by Bosanquet's own showing there is no such opposition; all concepts alike have a content, and the wider concept (when not wrongly
formed) may have the richer content. There being, therefore, no
universals of the '*merely* abstract' type with which 'concrete universals'

---

[1] Loc. cit.

[2] *Essentials of Logic*, p. 95.

[3] Cf. especially Bosanquet's address on 'The Philosophical Importance of a True
Theory of Identity' in *Essays and Addresses*, pp. 162 ff.; and *Principle of Individuality and
Value*, pp. 31 ff.

can be contrasted, the reason which has been given for using the term 'concrete' is no longer available. But the term is also inapplicable for a second reason, namely, that though universals, in proportion as they are abstract and so apply to a greater variety of subclasses, will, on his view, if properly formed, have a greater complexity, this complexity must also at the same time, in the same proportion, be more schematic, and will therefore be further from the concrete in every usual sense of that term. Further, because of this last reason, even if the term concrete were allowed as a synonym for the term 'complex', the phrase 'concrete universal' would still not be applicable to the individual.

Bosanquet, in his desire to justify the terminology demanded by his absolutist metaphysics, and so to represent the 'abstract' in the required depreciatory manner, is also driven to another device. He describes an abstract statement as being a 'bald generality'.

> We are often told that the individual cannot be made by a combination of universals. It is true that it cannot be made by a combination of generalities, but the reason is that it is itself the superior and the only true type of universal.[1]

> The most general knowledge . . . must obviously be the least instructive, and must have its climax in complete emptiness.[2]

Bosanquet adds indeed that

> from the very beginning (in the development of knowledge) this conception is untrue. Even the baldest generality has its value in the differences of context which it includes and which it illuminates.[3]

This does not, however, prevent him from continuing to speak, in the very next paragraph, of 'the abstract generalization' and to declare that

> a body of knowledge, if understood in the sense of a body of highly abstract rules and inferences, must be said *prima facie* to depart from what is given in experience, and truth, if taken in a similar sense, to abandon fact.[4]

---

[1] *The Principle of Individuality and Value*, p. 40.
[2] Op. cit., p. 34.
[3] Op. cit., p. 32.
[4] Op. cit., pp. 32–33.

The same alternation of view occurs in a more considered form in his *Logic*, in his distinction between two kinds of generalization—*generalization by mere determination* and *generalization mediately by hypotheses*.[1] In the former case the general is given, being a part in a presented whole. Merely in selecting and defining it, we have already completed the work of generalization.[2] The general, in *this* sense, is therefore analogous to an abstract character such as 'colour'. Though, like all concepts, it has its own field of possible application, it is not strictly a class-concept. Its generality is a quite secondary consequence of its being a fundamental and therefore pervasive feature of some section of the natural world. On the other hand, generalizations, in the full and proper sense of the term, proceed with great indirection. What they seek to formulate is not present in the data as initially presented, and is not discoverable merely by an extension of the range of direct observation or testimony. This is why such generalizations can only be constructed with the aid of hypotheses, and why the total data thereby brought into view must be in some degree capable of systematic interrelation.

> Inductive analysis can never make full provision for the application to fresh cases of a principle which it discovers, except in as far as it discloses the nature of a comprehensive *individual* system of Reality within which other individuals fall.[3]

> Thus, *e.g.*, in an anthropological hypothesis about the past of the Hellenic race a considerable portion of the history of Europe is ultimately involved, and the data bearing on it are inter-related and elucidated.[4]

Now such generalizations are obviously akin to universals of the schematic type; and like them, however little capable of being arrived at by processes merely of selection and omission, are none the less highly abstract; and indeed are more appropriately so named than those more casually formed. Yet, as just stated, Bosanquet still continues to speak depreciatingly of generalization, as proceeding always by omission; and

---

[1] *Logic*, vol. ii, pp. 163 ff.
[2] Op. cit., p. 164.
[3] Op. cit., p. 169. Italics in text.
[4] Op. cit., p. 164.

the impression which he conveys to his readers is that when the concrete universal and the individual are thus shown to stand in the same relation of contrast to the abstract universal, they are thereby being shown to be equivalent terms.

> The key to all sound philosophy lies in taking the concrete universal, that is, the individual, as the true type of universality.[1]

> The ultimate tendency of thought . . . is not to generalize. . . . If its impulse is away from the given it is towards the whole. . . .[2]

Bosanquet's twofold attitude—alternately rejecting and accepting the 'merely abstract'—is so patently inconsistent that I may be suspected of having given an unfair representation of his procedure. But as a matter of fact—at least so it seems to me—all that I have done is to set side by side statements which do not occur together, but always in different connexions, in his logical and metaphysical writings. That they should thus have been kept apart, not of deliberate design, but as the natural consequence of his accustomed ways of thinking, and that he himself should have been so unaware of their inconsistency,[3] is not really surprising, if we bear in mind the historical sources of the teaching to which he is here making himself heir.

The doctrine of the concrete universal is, of course, Hegelian in origin; and its formulation was in considerable degree influenced by Kant's distinction between understanding and reason[4]—a distinction which has tended to perpetuate in idealist thinkers the belief in a twofold employment of the intelligence, one appropriate to the uses of ordinary life and of the positive sciences in dealing with appearances, and another better suited to yield insight of a metaphysical character. Anyone who adopts such a standpoint must come, almost inevitably, to recognize two kinds of Logic, and while denouncing one of them as superficial—

---

[1] *The Principle of Individuality and Value*, p. 40.

[2] Op. cit., p. 55.

[3] That he had, however, an uneasy awareness that something was wrong, is, I think, shown by his constant use of the word 'mere' as a prefix to 'abstract' and of 'mere' or 'bald' or 'simple' as a prefix to 'generalization'.

[4] Cf. Bosanquet, *Logic*, vol. ii, p. 85.

or, as Bosanquet has entitled it,[1] 'low-grade thought'—none the less to tolerate its teaching as being necessitated by the exigencies of life on the human plane.

This is very much what we find to be Bosanquet's attitude. Though the whole trend of his logical teaching is to exhibit human thinking as uniform, alike in its methods and its criteria, whatever be the level upon which it is working, and though he has therefore to denounce the shortcomings of 'the merely abstract' universal, he still allows it as existing, and by means of its deficiencies—especially its alleged attempt to segregate identity from difference—justifies the search for a quite opposite, non-abstract type of universality, that which contains and dominates its differences. His argument would require radical restatement, and the positive portion of his teaching would have to be more independently developed,[2] were he to admit, as in view of his logical teaching he ought to have done, that a universal (unless improperly formed) is never merely abstract, not at least if it is a class-concept; and that when it is not a class-concept, but signifies a single character, it only does what it ought to do in selecting out, and having as the body of its content, this one special factor. Bosanquet himself would then have realized that in representing individuality as the pattern and true type of universality (properly conceived) he is not merely contending that there are two forms of universality, a higher and a lower, but is really propounding a quite impossible thesis, namely, that solely in the individual, in proportion as it is truly individual, is *universality* to be found.

Any adequate discussion of this fundamental issue must, however, lead to the raising of certain other wider considerations. These I shall endeavour to deal with in my second article.

---

[1] *Knowledge and Reality*, 2nd ed., p. 193.

[2] We may here apply to Bosanquet's procedure what he has himself observed in another connexion. 'A change of the name by which a *whole* region of phenomena is designated is seldom a serious matter. . . . It is thus that a consistent materialist and a thorough idealist hold positions which are distinguishable only in name. But to leave a category standing, and yet to transfer the greater part of its contents to some other place in a system, is a disturbance of the *status quo* that must always demand the most careful scrutiny.' *Knowledge and Reality*, 2nd ed., p. 7.

The Nature of Universals[1]

II

IN my previous article[2] I have referred to Bosanquet's view that the
wider concept ought to have the richer content, that triangularity,
for instance, expresses itself in 'being equilateral', 'being isosceles',
'being scalene' (just as Julius Caesar expresses himself in crossing the
Rubicon and in writing his *De Bello Gallico*), and that triangularity is
therefore a more complex, not a less complex, concept than that of any
of its three species. Bosanquet is committed to this view by his doctrine
that identity is never indifferent to its differences, and cannot, therefore,
be abstracted from them. Does he not indeed maintain that the most
notable feature of the so-called 'abstract universal' is that, being a bare
identity, it is not a one in many, and therefore not a universal at all?
In other words, Bosanquet's fundamental position is that there is no
identity 'common' to different things or to different situations; the
differences penetrate into the identity; it is an identity only in and
through the differences. Since the differences are thus necessary to it,
it cannot be known apart from them; and further, since the differences
can never be exhausted, it is an identity which is never more than
partially known. Ultimately there is only one identity, that of the
Absolute; and it is, as such, co-extensive with the differences which
constitute it. My discussion of Bosanquet is therefore so far incomplete;
one of his main theses is still left undiscussed. That, however, will be
one chief purpose of this article, and especially of my third, concluding
article. Both in criticizing Bosanquet's teaching, and in discussing the problem in systematic fashion, I shall argue, in support of

[1] *Mind,* vol. xxxvi, N.S., no. 143.
[2] pp. 257–8, 267.

a directly opposite standpoint, that all universals are abstract in character, and can be quite adequately defined in independence of their varying embodiments.

Much of the trouble is, I think, traceable to the central position occupied in the philosophies of Bradley and Bosanquet, as in that of Hegel, by the category of identity in difference. It intrudes into every discussion; every problem is made to conform to the terms which it prescribes; and consequently any distinction which cannot be so treated is neglected or denied; or if it is too obvious a distinction to be ignored, it is described as a difference merely of degree and not of kind. This practice does indeed give a certain massiveness and consistency to their thinking; but it is also, as it seems to me, the source of many artificial difficulties and of much confusion.

Bosanquet's procedure in this regard, stated in its simplest terms, would seem to consist in the following four steps: (1) No distinction is made between the two main forms of identity—identity of a character as found recurring in numerically distinct particulars and the self-identity of each continuant thing or self. (2) Identity, taken in this wide sense, as covering both the recurrent and the continuant, is defined as being a meeting-point of differences, i.e., as being a one in the many, and therefore as being a universal. (3) The universal, thus regarded, is treated as appearing in two forms, according as the identity does or does not contain and dominate the differences. In the one case it is a concrete universal, and in the other it is abstract. And since there is no such thing as pure identity, having meaning apart from *all* difference, the distinction is ultimately treated as being one of degree and not of kind. (4) Identity which contains and dominates its differences is then easily shown—the definition of identity as being always a meeting-point of differences approximates it more to the continuant than to the recurrent —to have as its exemplar an entity such as Julius Caesar, and therefore to be definable as being the individual.

This is a highly condensed statement of an argument which is never presented quite in this bald fashion. None the less there is, I think, no unfairness in thus summarizing it. I should especially draw attention to the fateful consequences of the first and third steps, and to the manner in which the third follows from the first. In them Bosanquet treats what are ordinarily regarded as differences in kind—between the identity of a recurrent character and the identity of a continuant thing, or self, between the abstract and the concrete—as being differences merely of degree. Further, it is his equating of the two kinds of identity in the first step which alone makes possible, and indeed inevitable, the conclusion drawn in the third. This being so, we should have expected that Bosanquet would have given very special attention, and have devoted much careful argument to establishing, beyond all possibility of question, the legitimacy of treating these two forms of identity as differing merely in degree—degree of complexity, comprehensiveness, and unity. I have, however, looked in vain for any such proof; and the omission is, I presume, traceable partly to the influence of Hegelian terminology and ways of thinking, and partly to Bosanquet's own personal metaphysical preoccupations. Owing to these causes, the assumption is so fundamental in all his thinking that it has served rather as a self-evident assumption than as a conclusion. This is why I have stated acceptance (not proof) of the assumption as being the first step, and as being that from which all the other steps follow in an orderly and logical sequence. By such methods there is, I believe, no possibility of dealing in any satisfactory manner with what, as it seems to me, is much more fundamental in our thinking than identity in difference, namely, *relatedness within a system* (this is a criticism which I shall presently be stating more at length); but subject to this proviso, and granted Bosanquet's fundamental assumption, the argument proceeds in a quite consistent manner.

It is, however, in Bosanquet's illustrative material, much more than in his abstract dialectic, which is not his strong point, that the movements of his thought can be most clearly discerned. Let us take, therefore, a simple, very typical example of his method of dealing with a situation in which individuals stand in relation to one another. He is discussing the nature, within the situation created by the family, of a man's relation to his son; and to illustrate his view of it he applies one of his favourite illustrations of identity in difference, and therefore also of universality, namely, the coincident part of two outlines.

> A man's relation to his son . . . is like the case of the two outlines (which partly coincide). The two men are bound together by certain facts known to both of them, certain sentiments and

purposes; all of which they both share, but in regard to which each of them has a different position from the other, apart from which difference the whole identity would shrink into nothing.[1]

In other words, the two men, when thus 'related', are not really two but so far one. They participate in a common identity, and to the extent of their doing so they are adjectival to it and not it to them. So far their differences are differences in and of the identity; and as such they make the identity to be no mere identity but concrete and universal. It is in this strange direction that Bosanquet is moving when he suggests that a family, being more comprehensive and more differentiated, is a more perfect exemplar of what should be meant by the individual than is any one of its constituent members. That it maintains its unity in and through diverse personalities with varying gifts and temperaments and of both sexes, is, in Bosanquet's eyes, further evidence of the truth of his contention. For it is, he holds, in the overcoming of the merely external relations of time and space, whereby particular personalities are, in seeming, so sharply sundered, that the power of the concrete universal is most significantly shown. This point of view Bosanquet has developed mainly in its application to the State. The relation of the State to the citizens composing it he compares to the relation in which the universe stands to finite centres.

> The treatment of the State . . . is naturally analogous to the treatment of the universe. . . . The State is a name for a special form of self-transcendence, in which individuality strongly anticipates the character of its perfection.[2]

We are now in a position to consider some of the other aspects and consequences of Bosanquet's central doctrine—that the concrete universal coincides with the individual, or to take the doctrine in its other, but exactly equivalent formulation, that individuality, with its two correlative requirements, comprehensiveness and unity, is, in its varying degrees, the sole criterion of truth and reality.

In stating this doctrine, Bosanquet, we may observe, is constrained to widen in two different ways the meaning ordinarily given to the term

---

[1] *Essays and Addresses*, p. 172.
[2] *The Principle of Individuality and Value*, pp. 311, 316.

'individuality': first, in the manner which we have already considered, by equating it with universality (itself, in turn, equated with identity in difference), at the expense of the usual meaning of both terms; and secondly, by so insisting on the thoroughgoing interdependence of the identity and the differences, that the term 'individuality' becomes applicable only to the *universe considered as an individual* (the 'Absolute'). It is the second point which now concerns us.

Bosanquet defines the individual as the 'self-contained, the self-consistent, the self-dependent'.[1] 'All finite individuals', he states, 'differ in their degree of these characteristics.' Other epithets which he similarly employs are 'self-existent',[2] 'self-expressive'.[3] Obviously, to define the individual in this manner, and to insist as Bosanquet does upon these terms being taken in a quite literal fashion, is to beg the main issue. We are then assuming, from the start, that individuality is a character not of creaturely beings but only of the Absolute. The best of reasons can, indeed, be given for refusing to apply any of the above terms, interpreted in the manner in which Bosanquet interprets them, to the finite individual. The self, for instance, so far from being self-contained, in the fashion suggested, finds its very being to consist in the apprehension and appreciation of that which while other than itself it finds to be in some way necessary to itself.

> Thus a man, we may say, is not what he thinks of, and yet he is
> the man he is because of what he thinks of.[4]

For the same reason, and also for other reasons, the self, in proportion as it comes to know itself, finds how completely it is dependent upon what is different from itself and not controlled by itself. As Bradley also emphatically states, 'the Ego is a derivative product'.[5]

---

[1] *Logic*, ii, p. 253.

[2] Op. cit., p. 254.

[3] Op. cit., p. 255.

[4] Bradley, *Appearance and Reality*, p. 302.

[5] *Appearance and Reality*, p. 321, 321 n. Cf. also Bosanquet's own statements in another connexion: 'Our minds, if they could be visualized . . . would look like bits of machines or organs of organisms, fragmentary and incomprehensible till the whole were supplied to which they respectively belonged, each with its driving

Bosanquet, it may be observed, has not gone the length of defining the individual as the all-containing as well as the self-containing. That would have been too flagrantly out of keeping with the nature of the individual ordinarily so-called. Yet it is a descriptive epithet which is applicable equally with the others, to the one true individual, the Absolute, and which is, therefore, so far on all fours with them.

Another term which Bosanquet employs in an unusually wide sense, with the effect of again reducing a difference of kind to a difference merely of degree, is the term 'concrete'. He applies it not only in its ordinary sense to whatever is not completely analysable into a number of universals, but also as virtually equivalent to the much wider terms 'complex' and 'comprehensive'. A concept or a universal is, he declares, concrete in proportion as its content is complex. Constantly he speaks of a concrete unity when obviously he means simply a complex unity. Concreteness is thus treated like individuality as being a matter of degree and as being found in its perfection only in the Absolute. The finite in proportion to its finitude is at once non-individual and non-concrete.

As a result, the correlative term 'abstract' is also used in a quite unusual manner, namely, as being equivalent to the less comprehensive, and to the incomplete, and therefore as covering the partial no less than the abstract ordinarily so-called. The concrete being a name for the Whole, or rather for whatever in its degree approximates to the Whole, the abstract becomes a title for anything and everything partial, no matter what kind of a part or what kind of a whole we may have in view. Thus an adjectival characteristic of an object, the human hand, the entire human organism, and a self-conscious being such as Julius Caesar, are all alike on occasion described by Bosanquet as being abstract— the adjectival property as depending on that to which it belongs, the human hand as existing in and through the human organism, the human organism as belonging to the order of Nature, and Julius Caesar as being a citizen of Rome. Similarly, Bosanquet regards a universal as being less abstract and more concrete in proportion as its content is

bands or nerves or wireless aerials hanging loose around it, all senseless and self-contradictory apart from the inclusive structural system.' (*Proceedings of Aristotelian Society*, 1917–18, p. 486).

more complex and inclusive. In becoming more universal it also, indeed, becomes more schematic. But Bosanquet has to ignore this feature; and judging it by its increasing complexity alone, he describes it as therefore more concrete.

The impossibility of dispensing with the abstract, *in the character in which it contrasts with the individual and therefore contrasts also with the partial*, is sufficiently demonstrated by the straits to which Bosanquet is reduced in the attempt to do so. We find him constantly contrasting what he entitles the '*merely* abstract' with what though covered by the phrase 'concrete universal' is really the genuinely abstract. For, as I have pointed out, the term 'concrete' as thus applied to a universal signifies that it has an articulated or structural content—a content which, though thus complex, is always, in proportion to its universality, schematic in character, and therefore always still unavoidably abstract in nature. But an actual passage from Bosanquet's *Logic*[1] will illustrate more effectively than much indirect comment the shifts and devices of language to which he is driven in his attempt to discount the abstract and the relational in favour of concrete individuality. Bosanquet is speaking of our idea of the Orchid which covers some '433 genera and probably about 6,000 species'. I italicize the words and phrases which are specially significant, and in certain cases I also add in brackets the terms that would ordinarily be employed.

> The determinate idea is abstract, indeed, as all thought is abstract, but nevertheless it may have a content which is *concrete* [complex], and in the example before us we have such *concrete* contents. These, therefore, bear the morphological character of *individuality* [complex structural unity], by which alone even the unique object named by a proper name is made recognisable, persistent, and so universal. Compared with such an individual subject the Generic subject has lost unique reference; but it has gained abstract significance, with which the proper name was incompatible. And it is in virtue of this significance, the significance of *individual self-completeness* [schematic articulation of type], that the Generic subject persists as an identity through the differences which form its attributes. Now the *individuality* [articulated schematic pattern

[1] Vol. i, pp. 213–14.

or type] *when reduced to a content* [surely a very strange phrase], is not single, but exists in instances. Thus, in attaching differences to *the individually characteristic content as such* [the schematic type as such] the judgement goes altogether beyond the synthesis of differences in an actual individual subject, and affirms such a synthesis mediately of a number of subjects, which may be taken as endless seeing that its limit is at this stage not held essential and not enquired after. Such a judgement which treats a *concrete individuality* [complex systematic unity or articulated pattern] as an abstract universal, and extends its incidents to all individual instances, may be described as an *analogical judgement* [italics in text]. And this is the fundamental nature of the ordinary Generic assertion.

Bosanquet, in the succeeding paragraphs,[1] proceeds to distinguish between contents which are 'merely abstract as not sensuous, and contents which are abstract as not concrete'.[2] Such generic concepts as that of the Orchid are, he declares, abstract in the former but not in the latter sense.

They are ideas of totalities, *existences complete in themselves.* . . . We have thus a character or complex of attributes which is *at once general and individual, abstract in thought and concrete in content.*[3]

When, therefore, we form a judgement in which such a subject occurs, e.g., 'If Orchid, then insect-fertilized', it is analogical, i.e., it does not merely apply to instances and yet also is not simply a statement of a relation of necessary connexion. Its subject is a *concrete* universal, that is to say, *an individual;* and what the judgement expresses is

a perception or presumption that the content enunciated in the judgement is bound up with *the characteristic individuality* [the schematic pattern or type] which forms the immediate subject. . . . The judgement that pronounces what is involved in this content and what is not rests on the presumption of *the individual* [systematic] *unity of the content* [complex], and on the capacity of

[1] Op. cit., p. 214.
[2] Op. cit., p. 209. Cf. p. 223.
[3] Op. cit., p. 214.

discerning from the *structure* of this unity aided by empirical knowledge of instances what is essential to it and in what degree.[1]

I find no cause to question anything in these passages save what seems to me to be their strangely perverse, forced, and misleading terminology. The ultimate purposes which are at work in leading Bosanquet to adopt this terminology, notwithstanding its obvious drawbacks, come out more clearly in a later passage to the following effect:

> Rose in the abstract does not exist. But it is a *concrete universal* [*i.e.*, approximates in type to an individual such as Julius Caesar] which has power, in the context of the real world to which we refer it, to dictate the epoch, place and quantity of its *individual*[2] *embodiment*.[3]

A schematically formulated type or pattern may, if we please, be said to possess individuality (what Bosanquet elsewhere[4] in contrast to the individual calls 'mere individuality'), i.e., a nature of its own which allows of certain variations in its instances and is incompatible with others. But when, as in the case of the orchid, the type is a biological order, it presupposes a certain kind of physical environment, and for its fertilization is dependent on certain species of insects. That is to say, it belongs to a system of which the inorganic part, in a certain stage of stellar and geological development, is a necessary precondition, and within which it and other types of organism mutually determine each other's existence. It is therefore on all fours with such entities as man and humanity; and we shall be in a better position to decide how far Bosanquet is justified in treating it as a concrete universal, and so as having an individuality analogous to that displayed by Julius Caesar, if we follow him in his further discussion of the logical status of these latter concepts.

There is, first of all, the question as to how 'man' and 'humanity'

[1] Op. cit., pp. 214–15.

[2] As Bosanquet, on the same page, speaks of '*individual* actual roses', I am unable to decide whether he here uses it as equivalent to particular or in his own special sense, or simultaneously in both senses.

[3] Op. cit., p. 227.

[4] *Logic*, i, p. 229.

stand respectively to one another, with the corresponding question as to the relation between 'orchid' and the 'orchidean order', 'rose' and 'the rose family'. Bosanquet does not regard them as equivalent terms; and is at considerable pains to define carefully the distinction between them. He takes the distinction in each case as being that between the generic and the corporate. In the generic judgement the subject (rose, orchid, man) is not, he says, a real or a single individual, but 'a mere individuality'. Thus in the judgement, 'The rose has perigynous flowers', we are 'treating the individuality of all roses as one by analogy':[1] we mean that actual roses have the attribute in question.[2] Similarly, in the judgements, 'Orchids are insect-fertilized', 'Man is by nature social'. On the other hand, the judgement which has a corporate subject (the rose family, the orchidean order, humanity), is not true of any and every individual singly 'but only of the kind taken as an individual'.[3] 'The rose family is a descendant of x, a divergence from y, and a transition towards z.' 'The Orchidean order includes 433 genera and probably about 6,000 species.' 'Humanity is the object of worship to Positivists.'

When Bosanquet here alleges that the subject in each of these latter judgements is 'a real and a single individual, and not a mere individuality',[4] he is making at once a very significant admission and a highly questionable statement. In saying that the schematic pattern, represented by the generic concept 'rose' is 'a *mere* individuality',[5] he is virtually admitting that its being complex and systematic does not render it any the less abstract. Secondly, though the rose family is indeed *real* enough and is a single *family*—in the botanical sense of that term, as signifying a certain distinguishable vegetable stock of which the continuous evolutionary history is more or less known—it is surely misleading to describe it as being 'a single *individual*'.[6] Similarly with the other

---

[1] Op. cit., p. 229.

[2] Op. cit., p. 227; cf. pp. 199 ff.

[3] Op. cit., p. 229.

[4] Op. cit., p. 229.

[5] Here, as elsewhere, Bosanquet by addition of the word 'mere' directly *reverses* the meaning which he more usually attaches to the term. Cf. op. cit., p. 135, 'Individuality or Absoluteness'; and vol. ii, p. 257, 'All finite individuals fall short of true individuality'.

[6] Cf. op. cit., vol. i, p. 229.

judgements: the orchidean order is an *order;* humanity is a title for the human *race.* To entitle families, orders and races 'individuals', simply because (so far as I can follow the argument) they are highly articulated complexes, is surely to bring endless confusion into our logical discussions, and quite unnecessarily to burden ourselves with a cumbersome and unnatural terminology, as in the passages above quoted. Highly important and significant judgements can, indeed, be passed upon such entities, but this is not in the least incompatible with their being, at the same time, non-individual. A family, a clan, a nation, the human race, a political organization, has in each case the complex type of unity and the kind of existence appropriate to its own special nature. However a family, through community of affections, sentiments, customs, and the like, may be welded into a unity capable of withstanding the stresses and strains of the personal frictions and of the divergent interests of its members, and indeed to anticipate these by so moulding the individuals by prearranged influences as to create in them the favouring qualities of character, it is not thereby brought nearer in type to the individual. The ideal for a family is other than the ideal for an individual; and this is especially so as regards the kind of unity after which each has to strive. In saying this, I am not, of course, making any statement that Bosanquet would care to question; but these are none the less truths which he does seem to ignore.

As regards humanity, Bosanquet has himself drawn attention to these considerations. The term 'humanity', as he very properly recognizes,[1] takes account of the consequences that do or may follow from the inter-relation of the various communities of men—international law, with its many possibilities is an instance—and so has a corporate aspect which makes it more than the concept 'man'. But as he states elsewhere,[2]

> it is really very hard to show [it as possessing] a centre of identity. You can do something with an ideal human nature embodied in an individual, or with a national consciousness and history; but is there anything at once definite and valuable that links together all humanity, as such, including the past?

[1] Op. cit., i, p. 59.
[2] *Essays and Addresses*, pp. 174–5.

The concept of humanity, like our concepts of the orchidean order and of the rose family, does indeed refer to a single entity, but like them has no meaning apart from the physical—and in the case of humanity also the spiritual—Universe within which they have made their appearance, and in terms of which their present nature, their past history and their future destiny can alone be understood. No finite entity, a family or race just as little as any individual, is knowable in and by itself. Everything finite functions as a part in a wider whole, and only through understanding of the context can itself be understood. This is why Bosanquet is so justly emphatic that only in wholeness, which he entitles individuality, are truth and reality to be found. And in reply to what I have just said, it might therefore be argued that his terminology, however unusual and inconvenient, and however little in harmony with the genius of the English language, is at least so far consistent with the main trend of scientific teaching, and especially with that of the biological sciences.

The implications of Bosanquet's position will, I think, become clearer, if we consider this objection somewhat in detail. How far do the considerations which can be drawn from the part played by system, and by systematic interconnexion, in all scientific knowledge, support, and how far do they conflict with, Bosanquet's adoption of individuality as being the criterion of truth and reality?

As we have already seen, Bosanquet's sole argument for equating individuality and system is that both exhibit the same fundamental contrast to the 'merely abstract'—that in both alike the unity is achieved in and by means of differences and not, as in the abstract, independently of them. This argument is, however, suggested rather than directly propounded; and obviously does not establish the conclusion required. To do so, it would have to be supplemented by proof of what is the really essential point, namely, that there is only one way in which, in and by means of differences, genuine unity can be achieved—the unity of what in being system is at the same time individual.

Here, it would seem, is the crucial point of divergence between those idealists who follow Bradley and Bosanquet towards Absolutism, and those of us—I speak as an idealist—who find ourselves unable to do so. There are two alternative attitudes which can be adopted towards the problems of Logic. If we model our beliefs on the lessons of human experience and of the sciences, there would seem to be overwhelming evidence against the view that the wider whole is always a higher type of unity than any of the individuals which go to constitute it, and therefore against the view that system and individuality are only different degrees of one and the same ultimate type. System, so far as any available experience shows, is not a certain form or degree of a kind of wholeness which appears also in the individual. We have, for instance, no empirical evidence that the physical system within which organisms occur is itself an organism. It is seemingly a system so highly unified that a child's shifting of the sand on the sea shore alters the centre of gravity of the Milky Way. But this is precisely because the unity of the physical order is not of the more complex kind exhibited by an organism, but one that we may legitimately regard as lower in type. For what constitutes the individual, as Bosanquet is always insisting, is just his power of dominating circumstances, and his consequent capacity of self-protection against outside influences. Whereas the Milky Way is at the mercy of the child's spade, it is the privilege in some degree even of the lowliest organism to be able selectively to favour certain agencies at the expense of others. This is a characteristic of the organic and of the individual on every level on which they are found. They are selectively adaptive; and such selective adaptation presupposes an environment which is not itself self-variable (at least not in the same degree), and which is therefore, in its relative fixity, a sufficiently stable field for the acquisition of the habits and methods of response suited to the needs of each different type of living thing. Accordingly, from this point of view, there can be no ground for regarding the Universe as less perfect because one of its realms is purely physical. This does not prevent even that realm from being organic, in the etymological sense of the term, to what is other than itself. Its dignity may indeed consist in the services which it renders to what we are entitled to call the higher forms of existence. But even so, we should not be required—not at least on any empirical evidence—to consider it as other than strictly physical.

There is, of course, a second method whereby the advantages of the higher types of existence may be conceived to be more widely extended throughout Nature than human experience and the physical sciences have yet shown themselves in position to disclose. If we care, with Gustav Theodor Fechner, to be boldly speculative as to questions in regard to which the available evidence is so scanty as to allow of little more than sheer conjecture, we can argue that since in each human being unitary consciousness is physically conditioned by some eleven thousand million distinguishable neurones, embedded in a more or less homogeneous substance and elaborately interconnected, under the dual control of the cerebral hemispheres, there can be no objection of *principle* against our believing that parts of the physical world, while (in certain cases) conditioning lower forms of life, may likewise be organic to a form of consciousness which is higher than any that we experience in ourselves. The Earth, as a whole, has itself, it may be, a higher and more godlike mode of existence than any of its creatures—being related to man and other living organisms somewhat as we are ourselves related to the phagocytes in the blood—its richer and more comprehensive consciousness having a 'here' and a 'now' in which day and night, sunset and dawn, summer and winter are always simultaneously present, and to which the poles and the tropics are alike contributory. That the Earth, unlike the higher animal organisms, has no nervous system, is, as Fechner ingeniously contrives to argue, in and by itself, no conclusive counter-objection.

I have made this passing reference to Fechner's speculations, mainly in order to point out that even if, for the sake of argument, we accept them as suggesting genuine possibilities, we do not thereby succeed in showing that all existence has in itself life. What is suggested is not simply that physical nature is more widely organic to life and consciousness, but also that however and wherever life and consciousness present themselves, even should they they occur in forms higher than that of the human race, they are presumably, like the lower and better known forms, conditioned in their existence by an enormous complexity of contributing non-conscious factors, only part of which need be regarded as organic in constitution. So long as the analogies upon which the argument has proceeded are kept in view, they can yield no evidence in support of the contention that what physically environs organisms is itself an organism. And if it be urged that there is a yet wider whole which can be so described, we pass to a different sphere of enquiry, and the kind of considerations dwelt upon by Haldane and other biologists, important as they are in their own field, have then comparatively little relevance.

But in any case, even were the circumstantial evidence of a different character, neither Bradley nor Bosanquet would be willing to rest their position upon any such basis. The use which Bosanquet makes of vitalist teaching, in regard to the animal organism, is really only to illustrate the same main point as he illustrates by reference to Julius Caesar—the manner in which the unity of the individual dominates the processes which go to constitute it. What in Bosanquet's view, as in that of Bradley, can alone decide the issue are the considerations by which they profess to have shown, on strictly metaphysical grounds, and by processes of purely dialectical argument, that individuality, conceived as a supra-relational type of unity, is our sole clue to truth and reality; and by this belief they are irretrievably committed to a very different and much more sceptical view of the function of Logic—indeed to an attitude towards its problems which is the direct alternative to that which we have just been considering. Logic, they declare, is being wrongly treated so long as it continues to be modelled upon the methods which have been found successful in solving the theoretical problems of practical life and of the sciences. Properly regarded, it is not a methodology of science, but a morphology of knowledge, i.e., a study of the various forms, less and more adequate, but all of them imperfect, wherein the individuality that is our sole clue to truth and reality manifests itself in the realms of appearance.[1] On this view, the methods

---

[1] Perhaps the most notable example of the manner in which absolutist Metaphysics intervenes to determine Bosanquet's logical teaching is the very strange argument by which he supports his contention that the disjunctive judgement is the highest and most perfect form of our knowledge. When, he argues (*Logic*, vol. i, p. 331), a universal enters as a whole (as the individual always does) into each difference, so far each difference excludes all the other differences. 'A man's having a hand does not interfere with his having a foot. But a man's having a feeling in his hand does begin to make a claim on the universal, the man himself, which is to a certain limited extent incompatible with his having a feeling in his foot or elsewhere. And when we come to consider such acute interest or feeling as occasions the absorption of the whole mind in the perceiving or suffering member, then it is true to say, "The man perceives or feels *either* with eye *or* with ear *or* hand *or* foot", as the case may be.' It is difficult to

and criteria actually made use of by the sciences are of a quite different character, and can be allowed no more than a merely practical value as being temporary, and partially (though, in view of their metaphysical falsity, very surprisingly) successful expedients. Even our criterion of scientific truth is, they further argue, so describable. Since the metaphysical criterion is not itself directly available in actual practice, we have, they maintain, to content ourselves with those forms of individuality which are interpretable *in terms of relation*. This, in turn, means the substituting for individuality the conception of a *system* at once all-comprehensive and internally coherent—an ideal that is practically efficacious, but philosophically untenable.[1]

Joachim, in drawing attention to this alleged conflict between Metaphysics and Logic, propounds the following dilemma.

> . . . *either* current Logic must be superseded by a new Logic working within a hypothesis which Metaphysics can accept; *or* it must be recognized that Logic, as a partial science based on a fictitious assumption, formulates conclusions which are not merely *provisional* only, but also of necessity to a large extent false.[2]

---

make out what such argument can be taken as proving, save only this, that for Bosanquet the Absolute is so completely Individual that the *conjunctive* relations characteristic of system, and system itself, can have no kind of ultimate reality.

[1] Cf. Bradley, *The Principles of Logic*, 2nd ed., vol. ii, pp. 489–90, 'The crown of our wishes may never be grasped. . . . Nay, I will not deny that this ideal may itself be a thing beyond the compass of intellect, an attempt to think something to which thought is not equal, and which logic in part refuses to justify. I will not pass this sentence, nor will I gainsay it. But one thing I will say. . . . It does represent that which, because it is absent, serves to show imperfection in all other achievements, takes away our rest in all lesser productions, and stirs our reason to a longing disquiet. There has come into us here, shut up within these poor logical confines . . . a vision of absolute consummation . . . which in other shapes has perplexed and gladdened us; but which, however it appear . . . is at bottom the notion of a perfected individuality.' When in the immediately preceding paragraph Bradley attempts to define more precisely, in the general terms that are alone available, how such perfected individuality is to be conceived, he has still to employ the term 'organism' and twice the term 'system'. The passage is otherwise strongly reminiscent of Hegel.

[2] *The Nature of Truth*, pp. 119–20.

Joachim follows Bradley and Bosanquet in tracing the conflict to the distinction made use of in Logic, between knowing and the known. May it not, with greater justice, be traced to a much less fundamental and more remediable cause—the assumption that ahead of detailed enquiry, and independently of all empirical evidence, we are justified in treating Reality as being of the absolutist type, and therefore as not being compatible even with so essential a distinction as that between the knower and the known?

But I cannot here attempt to discuss the many issues involved. Already we have been carried sufficiently far from the subject in hand. I need only point out that this latter view of Logic is obligatory only upon those who accept the questionable assumptions upon which it is based. Does it not assume the ultimate self-contradictoriness of all relational thinking; and is not this an assumption that neither Bradley nor Bosanquet has succeeded in substantiating? Does it not also rest on their equally sceptical account of the nature of all judgement, as asserting, not what is articulated in the terms of its content, but only instead a non-relational, transformed, and so far unknown Reality?[1] It is only by means of such doctrines—and I can see no obligation to accept either of them—that system can be alleged to be an imperfect form of a kind of unity that is more perfectly achieved in the Individual. Bosanquet can hope to make good his position only by showing that system

---

[1] Cf. in my previous article, note 3 to p. 256. Bosanquet's critical restatement of Bradley's doctrine of the judgement does not, I think, alter it in the essential point to which I am here referring. Bosanquet recognizes that every proposition is as categorical as its elements permit. Even a hypothetical judgement (which is to be distinguished from a 'broken-backed sequence', asserting not a coherence but merely a given conjunction) is affirmed only within an actual system; and to affirm the hypothetical as necessary is to affirm the system as fact. But, as Bosanquet adds (Logic, vol. i, pp. 90, 275), there remains the question 'how and in what way it is capable of existing; in other words, what is the kind and degree of its individuality'. Thus the metaphysical criterion, which has always to be applied, does not allow him to regard system as other than an imperfect, relational form of a non-relational Absolute. Accordingly in the end Bosanquet still retains Bradley's formula: 'Reality is such that . . .' (cf. op. cit., p. 73), and in spite of himself, has to regard all judgements, in ultimate analysis, as being 'illustrative' rather than 'enunciative' of Reality. As to what Bosanquet is suggesting, when he states (op. cit., p. 276) that 'the real Ground, when made explicit, takes us into the province of the disjunctive judgement', cf. above note 1 to p. 287.

originates in, and is the expression of, what is Individual; and this not in any pluralist Leibnizian fashion, but in the manner which leads him (as it has also led Joachim) to eulogize the teaching of Spinoza as an invaluable propaedeutic to all true philosophy.

I may now sum up the conclusions which I have reached through criticism of the doctrines of Bradley and Bosanquet. These conclusions are mainly negative. First, there are two fundamentally different meanings of the term 'identity', on the one hand in its application to the continuant, as found in things and in selves and in all change, and on the other hand in its application to what I may call the recurrent, as found in characters recurring in a number of distinct particulars and in relations recurring in a number of different situations. The problem of universals, I have argued, bears only on the latter, and not on the former type of identity. Secondly, the universal is in all its various forms abstract. It can never appropriately be described as being either concrete or individual. Thirdly, it is not identity in difference, but relatedness within a system, which is the more ultimate category. And lastly, as regards Bradley's and Bosanquet's general attitude towards the problem of Logic: in the process of establishing their doctrine of the concrete universal, they profess to have shown on dialectical, purely *a priori*, grounds, that Reality is not apprehensible save in terms of criteria which Logic is not able to justify but which it must none the less accept, and that when Reality is so interpreted it has to be envisaged in the absolutïst manner. As against such argument, I propose to maintain that the only criteria available either in Metaphysics or in Logic are of a strictly *formal* character—we must not say *merely* formal, since this precisely is their peculiar merit, as rendering them applicable in all types of situation. Ultimate issues, whether between absolutism and pluralism, or between idealism and naturalism, must be settled more on empirical than on *a priori* grounds.

The Nature of Universals[1]

III

THE attitude of Cook Wilson and of Stout in regard to the nature of universals—that is, of the abstract universal—affords a curious and interesting contrast to that which I have been considering in the preceding articles. For whereas Bradley and Bosanquet have no manner of doubt as to the identity of recurrent qualities, and have difficulty only as to the real separateness of the numerically distinct things in which they appear, Cook Wilson and Stout envisage the problem in the diametrically opposite manner. So far from having any doubt as to the separateness of things, they extend this separateness also to their qualities. The qualities, they declare, are as particular, and therefore, as regards their existence, as numerically distinct from one another as are the things in which they are found. The red in A is no less distinct in its existence from the red in B than A itself is from B. A quality, in other words, is never a universal; and the belief in universals, if it is to be upheld, must therefore be formulated in other than the customary terms. This, at least, is what, on first impressions, Cook Wilson and Stout would seem to be maintaining; how far such first impressions are the whole truth, I shall discuss later.

In certain respects the new formulation is somewhat reminiscent of Hegelian teaching.

> Just as it is the very nature of the universal to be a unity which must take specific forms (number *as such* must be odd or even), so also it is its nature to be particularized. The universal is the universal of particulars, and its reality cannot be separated from them any more than its unity can be separated from its species.[2]

[1] *Mind,* vol. xxxvi, N.S., no. 144.
[2] Cook Wilson, *Statement and Inference*, vol. i, p. 335.

Or as Cook Wilson restates this thesis:

> Differentiation or different species of the genus, and individualiza-
> tion or the individuals, are nothing outside the nature of the uni-
> versal and therefore do not require to be reconciled with it. The
> universal as genus is not something in the specific universals with
> the differentia added to it as something outside it, so that the two
> together constitute the species (as though the species agreed in the
> genus only and differed in something which was not of the nature
> of the genus). . . . The individual or particular has not the
> universal *in* it and something also beside the universal to make it
> particular. As the whole nature of the species is covered by the
> genus-universal, so the whole nature of the particular is covered
> by the universal.[1]

So far, though with a very different meaning attached to the terms,
Hegel might concur. But Cook Wilson discloses the extent of his
divergence when he proceeds to add: '[Universality] is a *unique* kind of
unity';[2] and explains in what the unity consists.

> The total being of the universal is not its unity and identity in
> particulars, but the whole of the particulars as the particularization
> of this unity.[3]

A standpoint somewhat similar to that of Cook Wilson has been
developed by Stout; and his statement being much more explicit, I
shall use his version as the basis of my discussion.

According to Stout, the universal is one quite special type of unity
among others. It is 'the unity of a class or kind as including its members
or instances'.[4] Further, we may not, in the manner prescribed by the
customary view, regard the class or kind as a derivative consequence of
the possession by its instances of a common quality or a common
relation. Qualities and relations, Stout maintains, are as particular as
the things which they characterize. Each billiard ball has its own

---

[1] Op. cit., p. 335–5.

[2] Op. cit., p. 336.

[3] Op. cit., p. 338.

[4] 'The Nature of Universals and Propositions' (*Proceedings of the British Academy*,
vol. x, p. 3).

particular roundness, separate and distinct from that of any other ball. When we say that roundness is a character common to all billiard balls, the phrase 'common character' is elliptical. What we are really saying is that each of them has a character (roundness) which is a particular instance of this class of character. Abstract names are not singular but general terms. Shape stands for all shapes as such, and roundness for all round shapes as such.

So far Stout's position, that qualities are as particular as the concrete things which they characterize, and his consequent reduction of the universal to being a name for a class of particulars, would seem to be pure nominalism. This, however, is only one half of his doctrine. The nominalists substitute resemblance for identity. Classification, they hold, depends upon an antecedent apprehension of resemblance; and the class signifies merely those particulars in which such resemblance can be detected. According to Stout's view, on the other hand, particulars are not said to belong to the same class because they are recognized as similar; they are declared to be similar because they are recognized as belonging to the same class.

> Agreeing with the nominalist that characters are as particular as the things or substances which they characterize, the inference I draw from the thesis is not that there are really no universals, but that the universal is a distributive unity.[1]

When we say that A is red and that B is red, though we have no right to allege that the red in A is identical with the red in B, none the less we do assert *identity*, namely, that the two reds are identical in *kind*, i.e., are instances of the same *class*.

Clearly, what is most distinctive, if also most debatable, in Stout's position is his doctrine of distributive unity. Distributive unity is, he holds, an *a priori* category, and indeed the most fundamental of the categories. Nothing can be apprehended save as in instance of a class. Such apprehension is not, however, based on, and the result of, the apprehension of resemblance; on the contrary, it enters into and pre-conditions the latter type of experience. Particulars can be apprehended as similar only in so far as, and because, they have been apprehended as

[1] Op. cit., p. 7.

belonging to one and the same class. Consequently, for this reason, if for no other, identity, he argues, cannot be displaced by similarity.

Stout has also, as against the nominalist position, three other arguments.

First, resemblance, being a relation, presupposes like all other relations, a complex unity within which the terms of the relation, and the relation itself, fall.[1] In the case of resemblance, this unity is the distributive unity of a class. And since apprehension of this unity is the *fundamentum relationis* employed in the apprehension of resemblance, the resemblance cannot be the ground for our assertion of the unity.

Secondly, even the most extreme of nominalists employs the terms 'all', 'every', 'any', 'some', and the indefinite article.[2] Yet obviously, the meaning of these words cannot be stated adequately in terms of resemblance.

> Consider the example 'all triangles'. It may be said that this means all shapes that resemble each other in a certain respect. But such formulas presuppose that the word 'all' has a meaning of its own that cannot be reduced to relations of similarity. It is precisely the concept of distributive unity which remains unexplained.[3]

Thirdly, what can the nominalists mean when they speak of 'resemblance *in a certain respect*'? They cannot be referring to single qualities indivisibly present in the members of the class, as, e.g. in the case of triangles 'being enclosed by three lines'. Their nominalism consists precisely in the denial of any such qualities.

> Hence in the mouth of the nominalist the answer can only mean that the figures must resemble each other inasmuch as they are all triangles—inasmuch as they are all members of the class 'triangular figures'. This is plainly a vicious circle, when what requires to be explained is precisely the meaning of the words 'class' or 'kind'.[4]

---

[1] Op. cit., p. 6.
[2] Op. cit., p. 5.
[3] Op. cit., pp. 5–6.
[4] Op. cit., p. 6.

Stout thus places himself between two fires: he has to defend his doctrine of distributive unity against the nominalists, and he has also to maintain, as against the customary view of universals, that this distributive unity is not determined by possession of common characters. The crucial point evidently consists in the view to be taken of similarity and of its relation to the unity of the class. We have just considered Stout's reasons for regarding as inadequate the nominalists' attempt to treat similarity as an ultimate, unanalysable feature, and as being by itself a sufficient basis of classification. Let us now consider his method of disproving the opposite view that similarity is partial identity, and that it is the occurrence of the same identical character in a number of instances which determines that they should form an actual class. Stout's procedure, if I have understood him rightly,[1] is first to distinguish between two senses of the term 'similarity', and then to show that while one of the two senses may seem to support the orthodox view, and to be inconsistent with his own, both senses must be interpreted in the same way, namely, in the terms which his doctrine prescribes.

The distinction which Stout draws between two senses of the term 'similarity' (or 'resemblance'), a narrower and a wider, is as follows. Things or characters, so far as they can be discerned by direct comparison to be similar, *pro tanto* fall within one class. Thus men can be classed as white, black or yellow. Two shades of red can be classed as red. In all such cases there is a certain respect (or respects) in which the things or characters agree, and which can be discerned by direct inspection of the separate things or characters. When thus discovered, it is the ground of the particular things or characters being so classed. They belong, in each case, to the same class in so far as they are thus similar. This is similarity in the narrower sense.

In the other and wider sense of the term, things or characters are declared to be similar in so far as they are known to belong to the same class; and they need not agree in any respect at all save in thus belonging to the same class. This happens whenever a non-distributive type of

[1] I must make this proviso, as I am here going beyond Mr. Stout's published statements, in reliance upon what I have gathered from personal discussion and from correspondence with him; and may very easily, therefore, be giving an incorrect or inadequate account of his position.

unity is the basis of a class, e.g., the class 'parts of this chair'. The legs, the castors, the constituents of the upholstery, etc., may be of the most different materials, shapes and functions. None the less they are so far similar in that they all agree in being parts of the chair. And quite evidently in their case, we do not know them to be members of one and the same class because of a prior knowledge of their similarity. Their belonging to the same class exhausts, or may exhaust, the extent of their similarity.

This latter sense of the term 'similarity' is, Stout maintains, highly important. Is it not in this wide sense, for instance, that colours are said to be all similar to one another? There is, Stout claims, no common character discernible in all colours; and therefore no evidence of similarity obtainable by direct comparison. Red and green, for instance, do not have any quality which is discernible as common to both. If, however, by indirect methods, we can discover grounds for referring all colours to the same class, we shall be justifed in asserting them to be *pro tanto* similar, in the wider sense of the term 'similar'. The class 'sensible quality', to take another example, is not based on a character common to sounds and colours, and discovered in both by direct inspection. Our grounds for so classifying sound and colour are more indirect; and the two sets of sensa are to be regarded as similar in so far as they have to be so classed, not *vice versa*.

Our method of classing what is similar in the narrower sense would thus seem to conform to the orthodox view, and our method of classing what is similar in the wider sense to conform to Stout's view. Stout accordingly sets himself to show that both, and not merely the second, support his general thesis. And he does so, if I have understood him rightly, by contending that it is only because each of the separate characters compared has, prior to the comparison, already been apprehended as an instance of a certain kind, and because on later comparison the kind is found to be the same, that the characters are said to be similar—similar here signifying 'being instances of the same kind'. If it be the case that in order to be able, through processes of comparison, to recognize two red things as being *both* of them red, we must have already identified *each* as being red, the two senses of the term 'similarity' will no longer be distinguishable in the manner alleged.

In explanation of this contention he points out that a class of characters is not constituted in the same way as a class of *things*.

> A thing belongs to a certain class, only because a character of a certain kind is predicable of it. But we cannot, without moving in vicious circle, go on to say that characters themselves can belong to classes or kinds, only because other kinds of characters are predicable of them. What I maintain, therefore, is that qualities and relations belong to classes or kinds just because they are qualities and relations. Characters *as such* are instances of universals, and this fact is just what makes so plausible the false statement that they are themselves universals.[1]

This, I presume, would be Stout's answer to the objection that his view must refute itself by leading to an infinite series.

> If two things can never have a common character, they cannot both have the common character of having instances of the same colour; they can only have instances of this character. So that they cannot even have instances of the same colour, but only instances of having instances of the same colour and so on *ad infinitum*.[2]

This objection assumes that, on Stout's view, a class of characters is formed in the same way as a class of things. Were it so, as Stout has himself pointed out in the passage quoted above, his position would be untenable, and the objection would hold. But if, on the other hand, distributive unity be, as he contends, the most fundamental of all the categories, and if belonging to a kind or class be therefore an inseparable feature of any and every known character, the objection must be due to sheer misunderstanding. If no character can be known save as an instance, no infinite series can be required in order to find an instance. It may, of course, be that Stout is not justified in his view of distributive unity as being a fundamental category, involved in the apprehension of each and every character; but that would be a very different objection; and the raising of it is not compatible with the objection as actually made.

[1] *Relativity, Logic, and Mysticism* (Atistotelian Society, Supp. vol. iii), p. 116.

[2] F. P. Ramsey, *Universals and the 'Method of Analysis'* (Aristotelian Society, Supp. vol. v, p. 17).

The criticism which, as it seems to me, should be passed upon Stout's position is that so far are the two senses of similarity from being reducible to the second and wider sense, that on the contrary this second sense, on closer scrutiny, turns out to be reducible to the first and narrower sense. We may take Stout's own instances. The members of the class 'parts of this chair' need not be similar in the sense of all agreeing in any such properties as shape, colour, or kind of material. But they do agree in what surely can be called a common character,[1] namely, that they all function as parts of this chair. This is a common character which can be possessed by things which are extremely diverse from one another, and which just by means of their diversity are in a position to constitute a non-distributive unity.[2] And in virtue of this common character they are so far still, in spite of their diversity, similar to one another in the narrower sense of the term.

But these points can be even better illustrated by reference to Stout's other example, that of colour. His argument proceeds on the assumption that his readers will be willing to agree—he refers to Johnson[3] as also making this assumption—that the various colours have no character in common. Red and green are not, he maintains, partly different and partly the same, as would be required if in addition to their differences they possessed a character in common; the various colours are all similar to one another solely because they belong to the distributive unity of the class 'colour'; their similarity is only in the wider sense of the term, and not at all in the narrower sense. Now surely these statements are open to challenge. How have the diverse colours come to be referred to the same class, and therefore to be included under the same general term, if they have no character in common, save only that of belonging to the class? This latter characteristic they cannot be found to possess prior to our classification of them; and it cannot therefore be the ground on which we base the classification.

In the case of the chair we have a prior-existent non-distributive

---

[1] Otherwise Stout would be gaining his conclusion only by means of a very arbitrary limitation in the use of the term 'character'.

[2] The more complexly articulated the non-distributive unity the greater is the diversity required in its constituents.

[3] Cf. W. E. Johnson, *Logic*, vol. i, p. 176.

unity, and by direct experience can learn how all the diverse constituents, in spite of their diversity, or rather just by virtue of it, exercise a common function, that of contributing to compose it; and Stout, I presume, would endeavour to deal with the colours in a similar manner. He would point out that just as the parts of the chair all agree in exercising an identical kind of function, that of contributing to constitute the chair, so all colours agree in exercising, within the extensive field of visual sensa, the function of defining outline and so of defining shape.[1] Any and every visual sensum[2] which discharges this function we can

---

[1] The fundamental fact of experience, it may be noted, is not colour but colours. Had there been only one colour, we should not have required a special name for it; the visible and the coloured would have coincided, and differences of shape would not have been possible visual experiences. Johnson declares (*Logic*, vol. i, pp. 173 ff.) that when red, green, and yellow are classed as colours (primary adjective), this is not done on the ground of any partial agreement (secondary adjective), but on the ground of 'the special kind of difference which distinguishes one colour from another'. If the difference here referred to is their capacity to delimit one another, this, I should say, is a 'secondary adjective' common to them and to every other colour. But if so, the contrast which Johnson draws between the two propositions, 'Red is a colour' and 'Plato is a man', on the ground that the latter, but not the former, is based upon an adjectival predicate, will not hold. Abstract names (adjectives), it will follow, can be divided in the same way as concrete substantive class names into singular and general; and the new distinction between determinable and determinates will, in this connexion at least, be superfluous. In his method of formulating this last distinction, Johnson almost seems to be vieing with supporters of the doctrine of the concrete universal. Colour, he contends, is a single and positive content and is, 'metaphorically speaking, that from which the specific determinates, red, yellow, green, etc., emanate; while from shape emanate another completely different series of determinates such as triangular, square, octagonal, etc.'. The process of emanation he illustrates by reference to the manner in which 'the determinable' 'less than 4' generates '3' and '2' and '1' in the sense that the understanding of the meaning of the former carries with it the notion of the latter. This, as he points out, does not happen in the case of a substantive class-name, such as 'the apostles of Jesus'. Certainly this class-name does not, even in Bosanquet's view, generate 'Peter and John and James, etc.'. But does 'colour' generate the specific colours, or 'number' the specific numbers, or 'shape' triangularity and the conic sections? Are they (i.e. the specific colours, numbers, etc.) not generated by the system, natural or conceptual, by which each 'determinable' is conditioned, and from which it gains whatever meaning it may initially have?

[2] It is important to note that, on Stout's view, the less general can be apprehended (i.e. recognized as of this or that kind) only through discrimination within a wider,

entitle a colour. But if so, does it not also follow that in exhibiting this common character the various colours so far resemble one another in the narrower sense of the term, and not merely in the wider sense?

There is also a further respect in which this holds true. In referring us to the non-distributive unity of visual experience, Stout would seem to be overlooking the very essential difference between such a unity and that of a chair. In dealing with the latter, he is in a position to argue that we discover the identity of function in the constituents not by examining each part separately but by noting how they together make up the unity of the whole. When we class white things as being white, we do so by noting how *each* thing has a quality of the kind in question; but in the case of the chair the fact of their exercising a common function is ascribed to each only indirectly through our study of the whole which they compose. Now whether the extensive field of visual sensa be or be not describable as a non-distributive unity does not really arise. It is only by direct observation of the various colours, and by observing how each in contrast with some other, is capable of defining outline, that we are justified in concluding that in virtue of this common characteristic they can all be ascribed to a single class. In forming the class 'colour' we have really proceeded much in the same manner as when by direct inspection we class different shades of red as being red. Indeed it is probable that observation of resemblance between adjacent shades and the ascription of such resemblance to other shades more dissimilar but still traceably continuous with them has played a considerable part in leading us to group all colours, however diverse—including the greys, as well as the colours strictly so called—in a single class. That the other method cannot, however, be dispensed with, is evident when we consider that our only means of deciding whether two shades of red are or are not the same shade is to set them side by side, and to note whether they are or are not distinguishable, i.e., capable of defining outline as against one another.

To sum up this argument: even where a distributive unity has its source in a non-distributive unity, such as that of a chair, the instances

---

previously apprehended kind, and always ultimately in terms of the category of distributive unity.

of the distributive unity have a common character, though as being functional it is compatible with, and indeed demands, diversity in the particulars which it characterizes. It is the non-distributive unity, and it alone, which determines the nature and limits of the class. Within this class, however, possession of a common character (contributing to this chair) still renders the members similar in the first sense. In the case of colour, the common character is again functional (and so far is compatible with absence of *other* common characters), but in this case is arrived at by the method of direct comparison of the several colours *with one another*. It consists in the capacity, exhibited by these varying sensa, of outlining and being outlined in a visual field. In all respects, therefore, it illustrates similarity of the narrower type.

If these statements are justified, it will follow that there is no such thing as similarity in the wider sense, i.e., no similarity which consists simply in belonging to a distributive unity. Nothing will belong to a class save in virtue of the possession of a certain *kind* of character. In other words, it will be kind or type or pattern that will be alone ultimate: distributive unity or class will be derivative, a consequence of the existence of kind, type, or pattern. 'Kinds', will be definable in terms of characters, more schematically in proportion as more numerous subspecies intervene between them and the particulars of which they are the kinds, and less schematically in proportion as such subordinate variations of kind have not to be reckoned with. Thus while colour has to be defined, in the more general terms, as what can outline and be outlined in a visual field, red is defined in more special terms as what can show up outline as against both orange and purple. A special shade of red requires for its determination yet more specific conditions.

If kind, and not class, be the really ultimate concept, it will further follow that a universal is not correctly defined in the manner of Cook Wilson and of Stout as 'the whole of the particulars as the particularization of its unity' or as 'the unity of a class as including its members or instances'. To regard the universal in this extensional manner is to follow Hegel in his contention that the universal contains its particulars, and is not simply what characterizes them.[1] Mr. Farquharson traces

[1] Cf. Cook Wilson, *Statement and Inference*, vol. i, p. 336: 'The individual or particular has not the universal *in* it and something *also* beside the universal to make it

Cook Wilson's doctrine to the influence of Green.[1] If this be so, it will explain much that is otherwise difficult to understand in Cook Wilson's modes of expression, and more especially the lack of coherence with his otherwise very un-Hegelian teaching. How far, in this matter, Cook Wilson may have influenced Stout in turn, I do not know; but in any case Stout likewise treats the universal as being concrete. For though he recognizes that it can have, when not merely collective, possible as well as actual instances, the possible instances are, he maintains, determined by the universal, and are therefore as much its instances as are the actual instances—the universal consisting in the totality of them all, regarded as a unity. Hegel's idealism has frequently, in his left-wing disciples, transformed itself into materialism. Here we should seem to have his logical doctrine of the concrete universal transforming itself into something very closely approximating to nominalism.

But if similarity in the narrower sense be alone allowed as possible, will it have to be interpreted in accordance with the orthodox view? And will Stout's doctrine that characters are particular be no longer tenable? Or is there any alternative? Before attempting to answer these questions, it may be well, at this point, to consider the objections which can be urged against the orthodox view—the view that when A and B are declared to be red, the quality red is as a quality universal, and is one and the same in both.

We have already considered[2] the first and most obvious of these objections, namely, how, if A and B are spatially separate, the red in the one can be identical with the red in the other. If spatial separation justifies us in regarding A and B as numerically distinct, why not also in the case of the characters? What justifies us in saying that though A and B are numerically distinct, the red thus seen in two places is none the

---

particular. As the whole nature of the species is covered by the genus-universal so the whole nature of the particular is covered by the universal. . . . The expression "particularization of the universal" has been used instead of particular, or particulars, in order to emphasize the fact that the nature of the individual is nothing but what belongs to the universal itself. Particularization is of it and in it as much as differentiation.'

[1] Op. cit., p. 344 note.   [2] p. 252 (in first article).

less identical in both? The usual reply, as we have seen, is that though a concrete thing cannot be locally separate from itself, characters differ from concrete things precisely in this respect. No amount of spatial separation, and no amount of multiplication can destroy the identity of the colour.

This way of meeting the objection is virtually to assert that a character cannot vary in the amount of its existence; or in other words, that, owing to its being a universal, quantitative predicates are not applicable to it. For, obviously, if a character is always identical with itself, it cannot be increased in amount by the number of things in which it is found; and it will therefore follow that there would be just as much colour in existence as at present, were there only one coloured thing and no more, just as much green in the world if there existed only one blade of grass. For the same reason there must be just as much colour in a small surface as in a large one, in half a blade of grass as in a whole blade. Otherwise, were there more, the more could not be identical with what is there prior to the increase. A character, it is argued, cannot be multiplied, though the things which own it can; and though the things which possess it can be large or small, it itself does not vary in amount. This view will have to be made good in reference to all other characters, sound, heat, weight, etc.; and meantime its seemingly paradoxical consequences may be counted, not indeed as disproving the orthodox view, but as a very serious difficulty, of which it must give a more adequate account than any yet rendered.

A second objection, which is closely connected with this first objection, has been very forcibly stated by Stout. When it is alleged that what is really the same indivisible quality can *appear* in different places and times, advantage is being taken of two quite different senses of the word 'appear'. We say that something may appear to be what it is not, meaning that it may *seem* so to do. We also say that something appears, meaning not that it seems to exist, but that it actually exists, namely, *as an appearance*.

> In this [latter] sense, nothing can really appear except what really is, and really is as it appears. I may, in double vision, have two images of a single candle flame. There then appear or *seem* to be two candle flames, whereas in fact there is only one. But the visual

presentations not only appear or seem to exist and be separate. Both they and their separation really appear, are really presented or given, and must therefore really exist. It is only because the images really exist and are really separate that there appear or seem to be two flames.[1]

And as Stout therefore concludes, if qualities of separate things really appear separately, and if the separation is a genuine appearance, they must really be separate and not merely seem to be so. Those who, like Bradley and Bosanquet, do not believe in the ultimate separateness of finite existences may, from their point of view, cope with this objection; but it is otherwise with those who have adopted a pluralist standpoint.[2]

A third objection is that if characters are the same in the different things in which they appear, they might well be expected to be more

---

[1] *The Nature of Universals and Propositions*, p. 8.

[2] A really adequate discussion of Stout's doctrine of universals would have to take account of a further argument (op. cit., pp. 8 ff.) which he regards as one of its main supports, namely, that substance is nothing apart from its qualities, and that its particularity must therefore consist in the particularity of its qualities; or otherwise stated, that if there is an ultimate plurality of substances, characters, as such, cannot be universals. I have not attempted to discuss this very important argument, because, not finding myself in sufficient agreement with it, the questions which it raises, especially as to the nature of substance, could not have been dealt with save by entering upon questions outside the compass of this article. For similar reasons, I abstain from dwelling upon an argument which I should myself regard as supporting the view of certain so-called characters as particulars, but which will have cogency only for those who can agree with the assumptions upon which it proceeds—the argument, namely, that at least certain factors which are usually treated as characters, those which are sensa (colours, sounds, 'heats', etc.), are events, and for this reason alone must be regarded as particular. Each event may be an event of a certain type, but as an event it will be itself particular. I do not wish to suggest that all qualities—this, of course, would be impossible—must ultimately be of this kind. Relations are certainly not events; and if relations are instances of universals it will follow that universals cannot all be conceived as types of events. Some qualities may be so describable and others not. When Whitehead (*Concept of Nature*, pp. 18–19) says that predication is 'a muddled notion', he is, I take it, referring to the predication of properties, and is really asserting that the categories of quality and of substance are muddled notions. 'The predication of properties veils radically different relations between entities. Accordingly, "substance", which is a correlative term to "predication", shares in the ambiguity.'

operative than, by agreement, they are found to be.[1] This, like the first objection, is a difficulty which calls for further explanation than is usually given. It is hardly a sufficient reply to say that this can only be a difficulty to those who regard universals as existing in the manner of concrete things.[2] For those who make this reply seem, as a rule, to be assuming that the only alternative is the drawing of some distinction between the existent and what they entitle the subsistent. Thus we find Dawes Hicks stating that though it is 'an intricate and perplexing matter' to explain what exactly should be understood by the 'subsistence' of universals, he is none the less convinced 'that not only have we no reason for assuming that the realm of being is coincident with the realm of existence, but that we may be perfectly certain it is not'.[3] This, like other statements in reference to the subsistent, I find myself quite unable to understand; and if a theory of universals can be propounded which does not require us to resort to any such doctrine, that, I should claim, will itself be an argument in its favour.

Such, then, are the main difficulties which lie in the way of a view such as Stout's on the one hand, and of the more customary view on the other; and I shall now endeavour to explore the possibility of an alternative to them. Can universals be defended, while asserting that qualities are as particular as the things in which they appear, and while yet denying that the unity of the universal is the merely distributive unity of a class? In the recent discussion on *Universals and the 'Method of Analysis'*,[4] Mr. Joseph, in maintaining that the distinction of particular and universal is not that of substance and attribute, suggests as a reason for the mistaken identification the fact that language does not have distinct names for a particular quality and the universal of which it is an instance. In order to indicate a particular quality we have therefore to indicate the thing or things which possess it; and it may seem that the things are alone

[1] Cf. above, p. 253 (in first article).

[2] Cf. Dawes Hicks, in *Relativity, Logic, and Mysticism* (Aristotelian Society Supp. vol. iii), p. 127.

[3] Loc. cit.

[4] Aristotelian Society, Supp. vol. v, pp. 8–9. I presume that Joseph is maintaining some such general standpoint as that of Cook Wilson. How far he agrees with Stout, he does not indicate.

particular, and that the character, as a character, is universal. For this reason, also, the linguistic form of the proposition allows of either mode of interpretation. 'A is red and B is red' can mean either, as on the orthodox view, that A and B have one and the same identical character 'red', or it may mean that A and B have a character of the same *kind* 'red'. But why, it may be objected, do we bring in the word character at all? It does not occur in the assertions made. Why therefore make the statements cumbersome by introducing it? Why not take the propositions as given, and so as stating simply that both A and B are red? The reply is that when we do so, we leave the question which we are discussing unanswered, and that the propositions therefore continue to be ambiguous. No one questions that A and B are in some sense instances of red. On any and every view, as to the nature of the universal, this will be agreed.[1] The question is as to the nature of the red itself. Is it, *as a character*, particular or universal? Or in other words, is a predicate the same as a character, and are both universal? To answer this question, the formulation of the proposition must be made more explicit than is necessary for the purposes of ordinary speech.

As I have stated, it is not even enough to say that A is an instance of red; the statement is still ambiguous as an answer to our question, for it can still be interpreted in either manner. We may mean that *the concrete thing* A is an instance of red, i.e., that it is the subject of which red is a character. But again no one is concerned to question this. The sole question at issue is as to the nature of the *character*. Is it, *qua* character or quality, a universal, or is it a particular instance of a universal, i.e., of a kind or type? To raise the question therefore involves the bringing in of the term 'character'.[2]

The fact that in every case, alike as regards characters and as regards

---

[1] Cf. Stout, *The Nature of Universals and Propositions*, p. 13: 'On any view, the division of substances into classes is in some way dependent on a corresponding distinction between their adjectives. It presupposes that, in some sense, a plurality of things share in a common character. The only question is, what is meant by their sharing in a common character? I take this to mean that each is characterized by a particular instance of a general kind or class of characters.'

[2] Cf. Cook Wilson, *Statement and Inference,* vol. i, p. 349: '. . . in the sentence "this flower is blue", "this flower" is not a particular of "blueness", . . . the true particular of blueness is the *colour* of the flower, not the flower itself.'

relations, there is only one name, and that if a distinction exist between a character or relation as particular and as universal, it receives no recognition in language, may perhaps be taken as a point in favour of the view that the distinction is not required and is not even possible; but by itself the absence of a linguistic distinction does not prove that this is so. The question under discussion is a strictly philosophical one and as such does not emerge on the non-metaphysical plane. So far as modes of linguistic expression are concerned, we are free to take either view.

To return now to my main question: can we distinguish in every character and in every relation between their existence as particulars and the type of which they are particulars? The fact that while adherents of the orthodox view declare every character and relation, however specific, to be universal, Cook Wilson and Stout have yet found reason to interpret them in the diametrically opposite manner, so far suggests that the *via media* is at least worth exploring. We cannot, I think, hope to justify a distinction between characters, as being some of them particular and some universal. Consider, for instance, the case of a character such as red. Even the most specific shade of red can appear in different places and at different times; and if such separateness of appearance is to be evidence of multiplicity and therefore of the existence of a kind, with instances, it will follow that no distinguishable characters, however specific, are incapable of being so regarded. Nor can we argue that while characters are all alike in being either all of them particular or all of them universal, this need not be true of relations. We might be inclined to take such a view, on observing that concepts, in proportion as they are general, tend to be more predominantly relational (or schematic) in nature. It is so in the case of 'colour': the property which marks it off from other types of sensa, its capacity for defining outline in a visual field, is a highly relational type of character. The evidence, however, for the particularity of relations is the same, neither greater nor less, as for the particularity of characters. The relation 'to the right of' appears in different places and at different times, just as does a character, and there seems no reason for believing that what holds of characters (if it does so hold) is not likewise true of all relations, namely, that they exist as particulars.

The view which I am suggesting, as an alternative to the customary view, may therefore be stated in the following terms: that corresponding to *every* character and to *every* relation there is a kind or type of which the character or relation is an instance. If this assertion, and the distinction which it presupposes, can be justified, the universal will be a name for the kind or type, and not for the class or totality of the instances. It will be by its very nature an abstract, never a concrete universal. It will signify what cannot indeed *exist* save in its instances, but as universal will not signify these instances, either severally or in their totality. By a universal we shall always mean simply a type, that is to say, a kind or pattern, which is, or conceivably can be, repeated. The universal, in other words, will be a name for the recurrent. Now, by general admission, what recurs can never be either a continuant or an event. It cannot be a continuant, because though a continuant can come back into our experience, it does so not as recurrent but simply as continuant. It is the experiences of it—that is, as I should argue, the type or kind of experiences—which alone recur, not itself as experienced. Nor can the recurrent be an event. An event, being a one-time occurrence, also, as such, does not allow of repetition. The only remaining factors in existence, in addition to continuants and events, are characters and relations. These are admittedly, in *some* form, recurrent. On the traditional view, they are regarded as universals; every quality and every relation, it is contended, is capable of appearing in different times and places, and in connexion with numerically distinct things. While dissenting from this view, and agreeing with Cook Wilson and Stout that qualities and relations are, as existences, always particular, I shall argue that none the less each is apprehensible only as a 'so-and-so', as a 'such', and that what is recurrent in them is exclusively a type, kind, or pattern.

Cook Wilson draws attention[1] to the distinction between a proposition such as 'This flower is a hyacinth', and the proposition, 'This flower is blue'. In the former proposition, 'this flower' is a true particular of the universal 'hyacinthness' (A-ness) in this sense that there is nothing in its nature as a particular (A), which is not comprised in its having the quality A-ness.[2] In the other proposition 'this flower' is not a particular

---

[1] Op. cit., pp. 149, 348 ff.

[2] The influence of Hegelian teaching, presumably as handed on by T. H. Green, is here particularly evident.

of 'blueness', since blueness does not cover its whole nature. The true particular (A) of blueness (A-ness) is in this case the *colour* of the flower, not the flower itself. Arguing from this distinction, Cook Wilson maintains that it is wrong to say that 'Circularity is a universal'. He does not question that circularity is the universal of which all circles are the particulars. But he none the less contends that it is illegitimate, or at least misleading, to say that it is a universal. For this assertion, he claims, can only mean that while circularity is itself a universal, it is at the same time in its whole nature determined as a particularization of another universal, namely, of 'universalness', i.e., that one universal is a *particular* of another. (Different universals can have a universal common to them, Cook Wilson explains, but not as particulars of this common universal, only as differentiations of it.) But surely the proper analogy upon which to interpret the proposition, 'Circularity is a universal' is the proposition, 'This flower is blue'—regarded in the manner in which Cook Wilson himself regards it. We should then interpret the former proposition as asserting that circularity has a character of the type, being a type, and is therefore correctly describable as being *in this respect* a universal, and indeed as having *in this respect* its *whole* nature determined thereby— that is to say, if I am correct in maintaining that being a type is precisely, neither more nor less than, being a universal. Similarly, when Cook Wilson contends[1] that 'universalness' is not a true universal, on the ground that a universal must have some definite quality,[2] I should reply that 'being a type' is the exact equivalent of 'universalness', and is the required quality.[3]

There are two chief difficulties which call for consideration. First, if all characters and relations exist as particulars, and only types can be general or universal, how is it that types can be truly predicable of characters? And secondly, in what do types, in their distinction from particulars, consist? If types are admitted to be universals, and also to allow of differences in the degrees of their generality, are we not,

---

[1] Op. cit., p. 351.

[2] Cf. below p. 311.

[3] The separate typescript, which Mr. Farquharson has given as § 148 (op. cit., pp. 344–8), seems to be an earlier, less successful attempt to formulate the above argument, as given in § 149.

under the title 'type' or 'universal', virtually asserting, what we have professed to deny, that characters can exist as universals?

As already stated, I am maintaining that a particular cannot be apprehended save as an instance of a universal, i.e., as a 'so-and-so', as a 'such'. Recognition, I shall argue, is fundamental in all knowledge—meaning by recognition, not what is popularly so-called, namely identification of a continuant as previously experienced, but apprehension of an existence as a 'such', as being of a kind, type or pattern. An alternative mode of formulating this same thesis is to claim that the judgement or proposition is the unit of thought, and that the distinction between knowledge by acquaintance and knowledge by description—otherwise between immediate and mediate knowledge—when properly interpreted, is really between elements distinguishable in all apprehension, not between two separate kinds of apprehension.

Types are of two main forms, those which are simple and those which are complex. Let us, then, first consider what can be meant by a type, when the type is simple and is indistinguishable from its instances, as in the case of a precise shade of red. This shade can appear in separate particulars; and in these different embodiments, as regards the shade, i.e., type of colour, is indistinguishable from itself. In such a case, when the alleged particulars are thus admittedly exact replicas of the pattern, what precisely is involved in the contention that it is not an identical red which is appearing, but only instances of a type which can be distinguished from them? The reasons for desiring to make such a distinction, whether sufficient or insufficient as reasons, have already been stated. The question which I am now discussing is what, in the absence of observable differences, the distinction can mean, and how it can be possible.

Since there is danger of being carried too far from the question in hand, and also of my stating the issue in a manner so dependent upon what happen to be my own personal views as to be prejudging it, I shall safeguard myself by here making use of Cook Wilson's brief presentation of the question.[1] How, he asks, do we begin to notice things which we have not noticed before, and where therefore these beginnings are necessarily without language? In other words, what

[1] Cf. op. cit., pp. 340 ff.

must an act of apprehending anything involve, to be an act of apprehension at all?

> If we notice a particular A_1, we cannot apprehend it as a mere individual, but as having some distinctive quality A, this quality being individualised in A_1. . . . But, in thus noticing A in A_1 for the first time, we have *ex hypothesi* not more than one instance of A before us in apprehension. What we are apprehending as A is indeed a universal quality in a particular, and so far Aristotle is right (when he says 'perception is of the universal'), but it does not follow that we apprehend it as such, that we have, in his terminology, 'perception of the universal *qua* universal'.[1]

In the apprehension of the universal as a universal there is involved, Cook Wilson maintains, a *threefold* distinction, between the particulars, the 'something definite' identical in the particulars, and the universal. The two latter are, he holds, connected but yet distinct. The 'something definite' he also entitles the 'characteristic being of the universal', and distinguishes it from the universal as A from A-ness. Thus if we take, as an illustration, particular reds (A_1, A_2, A_3, etc.), by which as Cook Wilson is careful to point out, we should mean not red things but 'individual red colours', i.e., 'reds', then the quality red (A), usually represented by the adjective red, is the 'something definite', the 'characteristic being of the universal', and redness (A-ness), of which the particulars are the instances, is the universal. The fact that A is always a 'something definite' (e.g., the red in reds), and consequently is easily confused with particularity, explains, Cook Wilson suggests, why the nominalists have sought to reduce A to A_1 (e.g., red to this and that red). The directly opposite error, he seems to imply, has been committed by the adherents of the orthodox view. Regarding as unnecessary, and indeed as illegitimate, any distinction additional to that between things and universals, they reduce both A_1 and A to the only kind of A-ness which their position allows.

There are certain other points which Cook Wilson regards as essential for an understanding of these distinctions; first, that the 'characteristic being of the universal' is only to be understood by realizing what

[1] Loc. cit., pp. 340–1.

corresponds to the universal in the particular instances; it cannot be known apart from the particulars: and secondly, that the process of noticing, however elementary, necessitates distinction of what is noticed from something else, which is therefore also so far noticed. Thus if we notice an individual A_1, and notice its quality A as distinct, we need to be noticing at least one other individual, B_1. A third, and last point is that we cannot say that in apprehending A_1, in its distinction from B_1, as a particular and as having the 'characteristic being' A, we have therefore apprehended it as a particular of A-ness.

We are now, I think, in position to understand Cook Wilson's answer to our main question.[1] While the apprehension of the difference of A and B, when they thus appear as different qualities in A_1 and B_1, enables us to distinguish A_1 and B_1 as particular beings, and so to recognize, for instance, the particularity of A_1, *we have not so far made any distinction between A and the particularity of A_1*. For though we are apprehending A, 'the characteristic being' of the universal, in its difference from B, we are *not apprehending A as having an existence beyond A_1*, that is, *not as a universal in particulars*; and similarly, though we apprehend A_1 as a particular, in its distinction from B_1, we are *not apprehending A_1 as a particularization of A*. What is before us is, indeed, Cook Wilson maintains, 'a particularized universal of "characteristic being" A' but what we thus far actually apprehend *in* it is only this 'characteristic being'; and this 'characteristic being' in being thus apprehended is apprehended neither as universal nor as particular. Accordingly those who hold that perception is always of a universal and those who hold that it is always of the mere particular are, Cook Wilson argues, alike in error. For though everything which we apprehend in perception is a particular of a universal and never a mere particular, it need not be apprehended either *as* particular or *as* a universal.[2]

---

[1] For brevity's sake, I have omitted one factor in Cook Wilson's account, namely his insistence—it is another of the main tenets in the idealist theories of knowledge, and as such is no less insisted upon by Stout than by Bradley and Bosanquet—that particulars can be distinguished only within the sphere of some kind of being which is common to them all and so universal, i.e., that all advance in knowledge is specification of previously existing less specific knowledge. Cf. op. cit., pp. 337, 340–1.

[2] Op. cit., p. 344.

Cook Wilson, it will be noted, owing to his fundamental conviction, which he shares with the orthodox view, that the distinction between the particular and the universal is an ultimate fact and that neither is intelligible in the absence of the other, holds that every finite existence— and he counts characters as belonging to this class—is a particular of a universal, or to use his terminology, is a particularization of the 'characteristic being' of a universal. Consequently the 'characteristic being' having been identified in one particular can be identified in another particular. Such identification would be impossible if A, in the first instance, had been apprehended as confined to A_1, that is, if we had apprehended A_1 merely as a particular. (One particular, needless to say, can never be identified with another.) But having apprehended it, from the start, neither as particular nor as universal, and it (i.e., 'the characteristic being' A) being in itself identical in the various different particulars, there is no obstacle to our recognizing it as being thus identical. When we have done so, then for the first time we have recognized the universal *as* universal.

The only part of the above account which I find reason for questioning is Cook Wilson's distinction between A and A-ness, that is, between the 'characteristic being' of a universal and the universal itself. The sole reason which he here gives for drawing this distinction is the fact, which I see no ground for questioning, that on first apprehending the universal we need not explicitly apprehend it as being a universal, just as we also need not explicitly apprehend the particular as being particular. But this surely is no sufficient ground for denying that it *is* the universal which is being apprehended when we apprehend A. The universal (A-ness) cannot, of course, be identified with A, if A-ness has to be defined in concrete, extensional fashion, as being the totality of its instances. But this reason apart, I can find in Cook Wilson no justification for the drawing of the distinction between A and A-ness. He admits that the distinction between A_1 and A in such a case as red is a philosophical distinction, with which ordinary language is not concerned. Redness is, however, a term which we do employ in ordinary speech; and it seems a very forced interpretation to take it as a name not for 'the characteristic being' of the universal 'red', but as a name for the totality of all the actual and possible instances of red. Cook Wilson's and

Stout's interpretation of the universal, as a name for the totality of the actual and possible instances, seems still more unnatural when applied to relations. Surely in conceiving the universal 'to the right of', we do not require to be thinking of a class constituted of all those cases, actual and possible, in which the relation may exist.

My contention therefore is that in the case of absolutely specific types, which being simple do not allow of variation, the whole nature of the particular is determined by the type: each instance is apprehensible only as a 'such', and the 'such' is the type. The distinction can be quite adequately symbolized as being between A_1, A_2, A_3, etc., and A. The type or universal, A, as such, is a predicate, not a character; but A_1, A_2, A_3, etc., being what they are, it is truly predicable of them. Hence when we say, 'This flower is red', what we are asserting is 'This flower has a character which is of the type "being red" '.

A chief respect in which 'being a character' differs from 'being a type' is that the latter involves, as already noted, consideration of more than the character, or even than the thing or event which has the character. I may express this difference by saying that even when the character in question is a quite simple character, our apprehension of the corresponding type involves reference to a complex situation in which there is more than one instance, observed, or if not observed, thought of, of the character, and in which the instances are severally identified as of the same 'so and so'. Only one instance may be supplied to us in actual experience; the other may be directly inspected or observed, or may be obtained through ideal construction. But whatever the means, the complex situation must be mentally entertained, if the type, i.e., a universal as a universal, is to be apprehended. The difference between 'being a character' and 'being a type' may therefore be taken as the difference between a mode of existence and that mode of existence as reflected upon. *Universalia* belong to the reflective sphere, but are *bene fundata* in the nature of things.

These considerations suggest a method of answering our next question: namely as to the nature of the complex types, such as 'being a colour', 'being a shape', 'being a number', types of living organism, and the types, normative and other, dealt with by the humanistic disciplines. All the strictly logical issues come up in connexion with any one of these types, and further discussion of the type 'being a colour', with occasional references to other types, will, I think, indicate sufficiently clearly the nature of the proposed standpoint.

This is the most difficult part of my inquiry. For in connexion with it I have to meet the objection that there are certain non-specific, or as we usually say, *general* characters, which appear to be in no respect particular, such, for instance, as 'colour', 'shape', 'number'. Can type be understood in a connotative manner, save by adoption of the orthodox view that such characters as these are of necessity universal, and can never exist as particulars? I have already touched upon this point in other connexions. The interpretation which I have given to the proposition, 'Red is a colour', is that it asserts, 'Red has a character of the general type "being a colour"'. The question itself, however, has not yet been answered. What is meant by 'being of the type colour', or in other words, having a character of which this predicate can be truly asserted? Though 'red' is that to which this predicate is being applied, what is asserted is not simply that it is red, but that it has a character distinguishable from simply being red. For since the predicate 'being a colour' can also be asserted of what is *not* red, for instance, of green, quite clearly it is not being simply equated, in its existential being, with red. The answer is, I think, fairly obvious, when the complex spatial situation in which colours exhibit their properties is taken into account. We then find, in addition to the qualitative types constituted by the different colours, a certain other type *of a highly relational nature*, which is uniform for all the colours, namely that of defining outline through contrast of colouring. This is a type of property found in connexion with every colour, and found only in colours; and is, I have maintained, our reason for assigning to each and all of them the title 'colour'.

Now the situation which is experienced when we observe two different colours defining the limit between them is a particular situation—particular in the same sense in which a simple character is particular, namely, as being a particular instance of such and such a type. In one important respect it does, indeed, differ from a simple quality. Being complex, many of its simpler terms and relations can vary without destroying the uniformity of the type. This would seem to be what is meant by saying that a certain type is a general type. We may merely mean that it is a type which has many duplicate instances; and this is one meaning of the term 'general'. But we recognize different degrees of generality in types and universals; and what is then meant would seem to be that the more general types are not merely general in contrast to the particularity of their instances, but are general in contrast to their distinguishable sub-species. But does this mean more than that one and the same result can be obtained by different methods? Uniformities are of different orders; those which depend upon a variety of contributory conditions can, in certain cases, be achieved in more than one way. The variety of the sub-types, distinguishable according to the variety of means employed, is, however, so far as type is concerned, really irrelevant. Either the type is achieved or it is not; and if it is, the relation between it and its instances is interpretable in the same manner as the relation between a precise type of red and the particulars in which it is found.

What tends to conceal this from view is that the sub-types are always more than simply embodiments of the more general type, and therefore involve for their apprehension the recognition of further types. The sub-grouping does not, however, in the least diminish the uniformity of the more general type. Visual definition of outline can be achieved through the contrast of red and green or through the contrast of yellow and blue; and adequately to apprehend the two situations involves identification through each of the four qualitative types. But in the case of the predicate 'being a colour', which is equally applicable to any one of the four colours, there is identification only through one type, a type which is constant in both situations. In distinguishing, therefore, within the type 'being a colour' the subordinate species, 'red', 'green', etc., we are not required to hold that the property which leads us to identify both red and green as colours is a general property in any sense in which the sub-type 'red' is not itself a general property. What has been said in regard to simple types, that the whole nature of the particular character in question is determined by the type, will also apply to this complex type.

To take an instance from another field: if triangularity be defined as the type 'three-sided rectilineal figure', then through all variations of type the number, straightness and closedness of the sides remain unvaried. In these respects the type is absolutely uniform and identical in all triangles, however otherwise they may vary. Every existing triangle must, of course, be more than simply an embodiment of the type triangle; but to whichever of the sub-types, equilateral, isosceles or scalene, it may belong, the unvarying identity of the main type is not affected by the diverse ways in which it is thus achieved. Here as in all other such cases, identity is not in any degree diluted by the intervention of differences. In simple types the 'instances' are *characters*, and the only differences discoverable in them reduce to existential differences, and as such ultimately to differences of position within some system; in the more complex types, the 'instances', strictly interpreted, are again the *characters* of which the types are types. We can, of course, in the manner of the customary view of universals, regard the 'instances', as being the 'things' which, while having these characters, also have other characters; and only in such a way of speaking can the differences be said to enter into the constitution of the 'particulars', i.e., not of the characters but of the things.

Similarly, though 'being a living organism' is a highly general type, judged by the number of its distinguishable sub-types, this type must none the less be definable in absolutely precise terms. Its generality is in no sense equivalent to vagueness or indefiniteness of character; and this is as true of 'being a living organism' as of 'being a specific shade of red'; the type must remain throughout *the same identical type*, and in respect of the *type*, the instances must be indistinguishable from one another. And just as a certain amount of abstractive analysis is required to get at the type 'red'—every red that we experience being apprehended as a red patch or surface, with a multiplicity of features which are not relevant— so likewise in the case of the type 'being a living organism'. Indeed it is a task requiring the scientifically trained observer. In ordinary consciousness such terms are used vaguely and loosely; and as Socrates discovered in reference to moral concepts, the capacity to define them is often more than can be expected even of the professional thinker. But preciseness of nature, however difficult to discern or to formulate, is none the less always presupposed, and, so far as I can see, is in no way incompatible with particularity of existence. I am proceeding, of course, on the very large assumption that the corresponding argument has been made good in regard to simple characters. If, however, this can be granted, it would seem to follow that whatever meaning is to be ascribed to the phrase 'degrees of generality', this meaning cannot be such as will affect the issue. I do not mean to suggest that complex types are analysable without remainder into simple types. But complex types of whatever order of unity are, I should maintain, to be viewed as being, like simple types, identical in their instances, and therefore as being compatible with thoroughgoing particularity in all the characters and relations which we can observe in the instances, or which in view of the requirements of the type, we are constrained to ascribe to them.

I may here intercalate a reference to that part of Bosanquet's teaching which bears upon the question before us. If the above position be tenable, then even when the type is 'a scheme of modifiable relations',[1] the scheme is not *itself* modifiable: it stands for what is uniform in all the instances in which it is found. In apprehending triangularity or animality, we are, of course, alive to various alternative possibilities; but this only means that we are interested in other characters besides triangularity and animality; there are different sorts of triangles and animals, but not different sorts of triangularity and animality. If it be not so, what can be meant by saying that all the types of triangularity or of animality are *triangular* or *animal* types? Bosanquet asserts that in man animality is of a modified type: what he ought to have asserted is that man is a type of animal of a highly specific kind. Similarly, animals, not animality, are either vertebrate or invertebrate.

To allege that no conception of triangularity or animality is adequate unless it contains reference to the different species in which it can be embodied is virtually to allege that no conception is adequate unless it extends to the detail of all the varying particulars to which it applies. Short of this, there is no consistent stopping place. If, for instance, the conception of triangularity must in itself, in order to be adequate, involve explicit reference to its having three main species, must it not also take account of the fact that in every triangle the three angles are equal to two right-angles, and that when a triangle is right-angled the square on its hypotenuse equals the squares on its other two sides, etc.?

---

[1] Cf. above, p. 266 (in first article).

If humanity has to include 'Frenchmanity', must it not make reference to the differences of racial origin, of outlook and temperament, in the various Provinces of France, as also to all the innumerable differences in individual Frenchmen whether of the past, of the present, or of the possible future?

Bosanquet's contention[1] that though certain characters have always to be included in the universal concept, one or more of them may be at zero value, cannot, I should say, be granted. He would appear to be claiming the right to say 'yes' in a predicate and 'no' in the subject to which the predicate is applied. Take, for instance, the example to which in this connexion, Mr. Hoernlé has recently[2] drawn attention, viz., 'nationality'. Is it legitimate to maintain that an adequate concept of 'nationality' *must always* involve the characters of political subjection and political domination, and that the concept is yet applicable even when, as in the case of the Swiss, both these characters are non-existent? Is not this to confuse the question as to the range of historical contingencies contributory to the emergence of national unities with the very different question as to the characters which are required to justify the assertion, in any given case, that this type of unity has or has not been attained? Nationality has certainly been achieved under very varying conditions. Does it, therefore, follow that the understanding of what is meant by nationality is impossible if we be ignorant of these diverse historical influences, and that it cannot be conceived save by reference to them? Is it not the very negation of any effective precision in reasoned discourse, when we thus obscure (in the favoured Hegelian fashion) the distinction between the accepted or postulated meaning of terms and the never-ending task of obtaining detailed understanding of the diverse historical or natural entities to which each can be applied? I do not press the further point that since, on Bosanquet's view, 'Frenchmanity' (and not merely the negro)[3] falls short of much that is implied in humanity, the term 'human', so regarded, is not fully applicable to individual Frenchmen; and that we are therefore left with none but the vaguest of pronouncements as to the conditions under which, in this and other

[1] Cf. above, pp. 266 ff. (in first article).
[2] In the issue of *Mind* above referred to, vol. xxxvi, no. 142, pp. 190 ff.
[3] Cf. loc. cit., p. 152.

cases, a universal is or is not applicable, or as to what precisely it signifies when actually applied.

Some such 'elastic'[1] use of concepts, whatever be its disadvantages, is doubtless obligatory upon an absolutist philosophy. In giving up the doctrine of a distinguishable essence (or as I should prefer to describe it, of definitely distinguishable factors or contents), and so in disavowing, in fact, if not intention, any distinction between properties and accidents, Bradley and Bosanquet, while yet endeavouring to retain much of the older teaching, have set their feet upon the very different road that leads—in the expectation of transcending relations by exhausting them —to their relationless Absolute.

To return to my main argument: from the standpoint which I have adopted, universals are either simple or complex, that is, represent types of lower and of higher order. The main difference between these two classes of universals is that whereas simple types allow of possible (i.e., conceivably possible), as well as actual instances, they do not allow of possible sub-types. Complex types, on the other hand, owing to variability in their accompaniments, may allow of possible sub-types as well as of possible instances. If, however, we are classing, not universals but relations and characters, and thereby the entities (things and events) which are so related and characterized,[2] then the above types, through their recurrence, give rise in turn to a fourfold division—classes of relations, classes of characters, classes of things (i.e., continuants), and classes of events.

When universality is thus regarded, as consisting in recurrence of type, there is no longer any serious difficulty in explaining the chief characteristics through which universals are distinguished from particulars. We are in position, for instance, to explain why universals do not allow of quantitative predicates. Multiplication of instances does not increase the amount of a type *qua* type. There is as much of the type 'green colour' in a single blade of grass as in two blades, in a half-blade as in a whole blade.

Hence also the 'inoperativeness' of universals. This is only what we should expect if characters are not identical save simply in type. A type,

---

[1] Cf. Hoernlé, loc. cit., p. 192.
[2] Cf. above, p. 297.

as a type, is not directly operative. What can alone operate are the causal and other factors in the system within which it appears, the factors which have conditioned its emergence as a type, which favour or do not favour its continuance, and which consequently determine how many instances embody it in actual existence, and in what precise modes. In an indirect, and none the less effective, fashion, type does, of course, determine consequences. The causal factors which operate are themselves of certain sorts, and act differently according to the sorts of things they are.

And lastly, to the question how universals can appear in different times and places, and in connexion with numerically distinct things, the answer is simple and obvious. Universality consists not in identity of existence or of occurrence, but solely in the identity of a type that is recurrent in separate particulars.

There are certain further questions, bearing on the existential status of universals, which are much too complicated to be dealt with in a few pages, but which are so directly relevant that before concluding I must attempt to indicate my attitude towards them. In maintaining that no existent can be apprehended save as a 'so-and-so', as a 'such', I have intended to suggest, though on wider grounds than can here be discussed, that the mode in which particulars are thus known is also the form in which they exist. Accordingly I have agreed in one quite fundamental respect with the orthodox view, namely that universals are integral to reality, and are predicable of it in a direct and not in a merely extensional manner. In this sense, while distinguishing, as the orthodox view does not, between characters and predicates, I have maintained that every actual universal is truly predicable of one or more actual particulars, namely, as being their type, i.e., as being a pattern of which there are other instances, possible, if not actual. I have further suggested that every non-actual, but conceivable, universal is a differentiation of some other, complex, universal which is thus actual.[1]

In this last statement I indicate my answer to the question—so important in connexion with the controversy as to the possibility of

---

[1] I have discussed the matter somewhat more fully in an article on 'Whitehead's Philosophy of Nature', in *Issues and Tendencies in Contemporary Philosophy* (University of California Publications, 1923), pp. 218 ff. (reprinted above, pp. 226–50).

distinguishing between existence and subsistence—whether types are conceivable beyond any that have been actualized in the Universe as we find it to exist. If we can hold that every actual universal has possible (i.e., abstractly conceivable) as well as actual instances, and also that certain complex universals have possible as well as actual sub-species— their possibility being determined solely by reference to the universals, without consideration of the factors which would have to be reckoned with, if we were considering whether they could also be actual—we shall escape what I should describe as the two evil alternatives, either of having to agree with Bradley and Bosanquet that nothing is possible which is not also real, or of having to hold that supplementary to the real there is a second realm, that of the subsistent. The possible, in so far as it is relative to some *actual* universal will be genuinely, though only abstractly, possible.

When we further ask whether the abstractly possible—as a possible additional instance of an existing type or as a possible new sub-type of an existing type—can be or become itself actual, we are asking a legitimate and quite intelligible question, namely as to whether the supplementary conditions required for making it actual (in addition to those which have determined the actuality of the presupposed type) are themselves possible, e.g., as to whether, and if so by what means, air can be made to exist in solidified form, or as to whether, and if so by what means, poverty can be abolished by advances in chemistry, or war by changes in international organization and in human nature. Special, detailed knowledge is required to answer either the 'whether' or the 'what' of any such questions; and we cannot, ahead of experience or at least of adequate theory, dogmatize in regard to them. And for the same reasons, when similar questions of a more metaphysical character are propounded, we cannot hope to answer them simply in terms of any doctrine of universals, or indeed from any purely logical standpoint, but only in this or that differing manner, according as our general philosophy, based on wider grounds, is of this or that kind. No universals —at least, as it would seem, none of those humanly accessible to us—are ever self-justifying, not even when they are of the normative character dealt with in the humanistic disciplines. For even in those fields in which rights and values come up for consideration, type does not seem to be any more independent of the rest of reality than happens in the case of what we presume to call the merely *de facto*.

In other words, one main consequence of the view here taken of universals is that they will have to be regarded as being in all cases *conditioned* modes of existence—a conclusion which, if true, will result in a very different type of rationalism than is usually favoured by the idealist philosophies. This, indeed, is of the nature of a corollary to the conclusion arrived at in the previous article, that relatedness within a system, not identity in difference, is the more ultimate category. System conditions both characters and relations, and therewith the types in which they recur.

The Fruitfulness of the Abstract

THAT the abstract should so frequently be spoken of in depreciatory terms, as being the *merely* abstract, would seem to indicate a very general lack of understanding of its many services. Indeed it is because I have detected myself as yielding, without much reflection and almost by inattention, to this usual way of speaking, that this paper has come to be written. It is an attempt to remedy in my own thinking what I have found disturbing when its consequences appear, as they do, in the teaching of Bradley and Bosanquet.

I may also add, in explanation of my purpose, that I regard the abstract and the universal as standing in the closest possible connexion, the sole difference between them being a difference in the point of view from which their common function can be regarded. The abstract, I shall maintain, is the content of the universal viewed on its negative side, namely, as distinguished from what in the complexes in which it is found is other than itself, and that the universal is the abstract viewed as constituting a type.

Resort to the abstract is necessitated by the same general conditions that justify asceticism in ethics and the prescription of a traditional technique in the arts, namely, the requirement of restraint and of indirect methods of procedure in every field of human endeavour. In all enterprises in which ultimate issues are in any degree involved, the difficulties to be faced and the limitations under which the struggle to overcome them has to be conducted are usually such as to rule out as impracticable any method of direct attack. Indeed, it is only in and through the processes of circumventing these limitations that we can obtain the opportunities for arriving at an enlightened understanding of what it really is that we are desirous of doing. There is, however, a very natural reluctance to recognize, or at least to keep constantly before the mind, the fruitfulness of limitation, and it is not therefore surprising that our first reactions to the notion of the abstract should be somewhat lacking in warmth of appreciation. The abstract is represented by a term in which all the emphasis appears to fall upon the fact of omission. The abstract, it would seem to be implied, is arrived at simply by dropping out of mind the manifold factors which go along with it in actual experience. It has, indeed, a quite positive nature, being that which is left on our hands when the processes of omission have been completed. This, however, is always less than what we started with, and would therefore seem to involve the sacrifice of much that we should desire to retain. Thus regarded, abstraction is little more than an unfortunate necessity due to the limitations in our powers of attention; it is a methodological device whereby we study partial features, with the ultimate purpose of so mastering the material, part by part, that through gradual reversal of this abstractive procedure, we may finally be in position to grapple with the experienced in all its concreteness. From this point of view, it is analogous to increase of microscopic power, the narrowing of the field being compensated by a proportionate effectiveness in the apprehension of that which remains.

Were this an adequate account of the services rendered by the processes of abstraction, we should certainly not be justified in regarding them as an independent source of insight. In resorting to them, we should still be seeking precisely what is sought in the more synoptic vision of ordinary consciousness, knowledge of what is present to the mind as the object of its scrutiny. The only difference would be that the processes of ordinary apprehension, in being limited and therefore supposedly concentrated, have been rendered more than usually effective.

We need not, I think, question the assertion that the cognitive processes at work in abstraction are those of ordinary apprehension, especially when it is granted that they are a highly effective application of them. The problem to be solved is that of explaining in what this special effectiveness consists, and to what precisely it is due.

It is a commonplace of the psychologist that all consciousness is focalized. This, I take it, is a way of stating that the total object of cognitive apprehension is always a perspective, i.e., a field complete with foreground and background, and that this field is so completely unified that it changes as a whole with every alteration in the distribution of attention. To limit attention is not merely to omit part of what was previously attended to; it is by the shift of attention to adopt a new total field in place of the previous total field. The object of consciousness, even when we are endeavouring to carry out abstraction to its uttermost limits, is never simple. What is simple may be brought into the focus of consciousness, but even so it is never apprehended save in its relations to what is other than itself. Nor should we overlook the fact that in conceiving the distribution of attention on the analogy of focusing the eyes, we are representing it in a metaphorical manner. We can, of course, be inattentive to what we are looking at. There are purely mental factors which determine the mental, as distinguished from the merely visual, perspective; a visual landscape can at any moment become for the observer no more than merely the background to what is not in any manner sensibly present. It is under these complex conditions that a meaning has to be found for the processes of abstraction, and for their product, that which is thereby discerned. How does the mind, in pursuing a continuous train of thought, contrive to secure itself against what Whitehead has entitled the 'infinitude of irrelevance'? And can it be guarded against, save in so far as it is in some degree apprehended?

When we approach our problem with these considerations in view, it is at once obvious that abstraction is not merely omission. Indeed, it is questionable whether the term omission has any relevance. All that we are justified in asserting is that the mind abstracts from certain factors, not that it omits them. That, however, is a minor point. What calls for special insistence is that the process mainly at work is integrative, not separative in character. This is a statement which I shall later endeavour to justify. Meantime an illustration may perhaps suffice. Though the red of a red object is but one of its manifold characters, in saying 'This object is red', so far from merely narrowing our field of attention by abstracting from part of what is being at the moment experienced, we are, as a matter of fact, widening it. What we are saying is: 'This manifold object is, as regards its redness, of a type elsewhere and otherwise previously experienced'. We are integrating experience, synthesizing in the act of analysing, recognizing identities in experiences that otherwise would remain in isolation, and therefore lacking in the significance which they thus acquire. And, *ipso facto*, we are obtaining knowledge of more than the separate items that make up the real world; we have made a beginning in the task of deciphering what is equally important, its structural pattern. Natural existences are not types but individuals, and they are known to us only in and through events which as one-time occurrences have to be regarded as in their existence absolutely unique. None the less it is likewise true that there can be no apprehension of nature save in proportion as it is found to embody what as 'rhythmic' or non-unique allows of recurrence. Abstraction, as consisting in preoccupation with those features which in type are recurrent, is for this reason of supreme importance, and makes its own distinctive contribution in the acquisition of knowledge.

Before proceeding to my main argument, it is perhaps well that I should state, somewhat more fully, the view of abstraction which I have been criticizing. According to that view, we start with knowledge of the concrete, and therefore with knowledge of a multiplicity of factors, any of which, as being thus already known, can at will be selected for special attention. Abstraction, that is to say, is not to be looked to for disclosure of anything genuinely new. It is merely the more attentive apprehension of what has been antecedently known in some concrete setting; and it would thus seem to be simply the rendering of our initial awareness more definite and precise.

This is the view which underlies the doctrine of the general or universal concept, as usually formulated in the cruder textbooks of Formal Logic. There is, it is assumed, no problem as to how we apprehend concrete particularity, in ordinary experience. The only question raised is as to how, from concrete particulars antecedently known, we come into possession of universal concepts. These, it is maintained, are the outcome of abstraction. Observing particulars which, in resembling one another, also differ, we abstract out their common qualities, and so arrive at a knowledge of the class-concept under which they all fall.

Two very strange assumptions are here being made: first, that it is easy to apprehend the individual in the uniqueness 'of its individuality, and, secondly, that it is also easy—namely, by processes of mere omission—to arrive at knowledge of the universal. Both these assumptions are in flat contradiction with what we find to be the actual facts.

Nothing is more difficult than to carry discrimination to the point of apprehending the uniquely individual. Indeed, may we not say that this is an ideal goal towards which we can only approximate? The shepherd may indeed succeed in distinguishing each of his sheep: members of a family can distinguish the twins of their family; but even so, they do this by noting features, or rather by noting special combinations of features, any one of which is or may be found in other individuals. As the saying goes, 'every man has his double'. We start, in experience and knowledge, not with the individual, but with the vaguely generic, and advance in knowledge is to be measured quite as much by increased appreciation of differences as by capacity to generalize. The child can usually recognize trees before he can distinguish the different species of trees; and to the end all recognition, even of what is discriminated as being an individual distinct from all others, is by means not of absolutely unique features, but of types. The absolutely unique can be *postulated*, and we constantly do postulate it, on the ground of what we judge or naïvely assume to be adequate evidence; but such evidence can never be merely that of purely immediate experience. Were it otherwise, it would not be possible to err, as we so frequently err, in our identification of individuals. Such identification always implies inference, though it is, of course, only by exception, in cases of difficulty and consequent hesitation, that we formulate to ourselves the grounds of the inference. 'The individual in the distance has surely', we say, 'the figure and gait of so and so.' 'That airedale looks strangely like our own dog: can it be? Look at the patches of grey on its shoulders.'

In view of these obvious facts, it is indeed something of a problem to explain how the traditional doctrine should ever have come to be formulated, and Cook Wilson is doubtless correct in suggesting[1] that it has been occasioned by the Sophistic and Socratic preoccupation with moral concepts. For the situation in ethics has always been, as it still remains, one of fairly common agreement as to what is right and what is wrong, so far as regards *particular* actions, combined with lack of agreement as to what are the wider concepts—whether of practical utility, of pleasurable consequences, or of absolute standards—under

---

[1] *Statement and Inference*, pp. 28, 379.

which the agreed particulars have to be subsumed; and it was therefore very naturally supposed that it is by way of analysis of the agreed particulars that the universals are to be discovered.

Yet it is precisely in this field that the perversity of the procedure is most strikingly evident. If we are to arrive at an adequate concept of justice by comparing particular just acts, we must be able to guard against the possibility of our having included among our data any acts that are not just. This, however, is only possible if we are able infallibly to *recognize* which acts are just and which are unjust, and since justice is nothing in the nature of a sensible character or other directly experienced quality, it is evident that in this case at least we are presupposing possession of the very concept which we profess to be seeking. We must have knowledge of justice sufficiently infallible to be able to discriminate just from unjust acts, and it is from the acts thus classed as just that we profess to obtain the concept. The process is merely 'a manner of looking for our spectacles by aid of the spectacles themselves'. It also has the further defect that it would rule us out from ever being in position to criticize the data from which we start. Socrates, needless to say, was very well aware of these objections. It was, indeed, these very objections that led him to formulate his doctrine of reminiscence, a doctrine which is the beginning of the end of the view under criticism, and which in Plato's restatement of it amounts, in all essentials, to the doctrine to which I have already made reference, that all cognition is recognition. The problems which on the traditional view have been made to appear so simple and easy are, on the contrary, complex and difficult.

I may now return to my main argument. As already remarked, the unitary object of cognitive experience is a complex situation or domain, a perspective. Anything less complex is a product of mental selection. What, then, determines such selection? There can be no doubt as to the correct answer. The conditions are those which favour comparison, namely, conflict of presentations—the same and yet not the same, same shape but differing colour, same colour but differing shape, same for observation yet differing in practical consequences. These, however, are merely the conditions which favour abstraction; they do not in themselves amount to an actual abstraction. For completion of the act an additional, all-important factor is required—the apprehension of what is thus the same as being the same. The common element must be *identified* as a common element, and since such identification has to be compatible with the experienced separateness, it must take the form of recognition of a *type* or *kind*—that is to say, of a universal. The abstracted factor is, therefore, abstracted in this sense only, that it is at once distinguished from the conflicting features that accompany it in the various instances, and at the same time identified, not *qua* existent but in type or kind, as being the same in them all.

Thus the abstract and the universal come to consciousness in one and the same act—the highly complex act that constitutes cognitive apprehension in any and all of its possible modes. To cognize is to recognize, to recognize is to identify a recurrent type, and to identify a recurrent type is to have selected for special—i.e. abstractive—attention, in one or more instances of the type, the feature or features which go to make up the content of the type. As features of the particulars they share in the 'thisness' of the particulars: they are themselves particulars. On the other hand, as making up the content of the type, they are apprehended as 'suchnesses'; and thus, in their regard, as in regard to all else, we have to accept as ultimate the dual 'this-such' nature of everything experienced.

This is as true of relations as of qualities, but is only indirectly true of the individual. I say 'indirectly', for, as already remarked, it is only in respect of this or that character, or set of characters, that an individual can be regarded as being of a type. And for this reason it is improper to speak of an individual (or any part of an individual), considered in and by itself, as being an abstraction. The individual is, indeed, initially known only in its relations within some complex context, and this context may be temporarily left out of account. But this yields an *incomplete*, not an abstract view of the individual. What is peculiar to that which allows of abstraction is that its nature (though not, of course, the conditions of its existing or occurring) can be exhaustively known in being considered in and by itself. The enigmatic features exhibited by the individual, and by the accompanying efficacies peculiar to it (or at least never found save when individuals, that is, continuants, have to be postulated as being present), do not have to be reckoned with in the case of the abstract. Abstractive treatment is therefore entirely adequate in dealing with characters and relations, in a manner in which it can never be adequate in dealing with the individual.

This calls for fuller statement. Identity, and consequently recognition, is found in two forms. There is recognition as ordinarily understood, namely, recognition of an individual as having been previously experienced. Secondly, there is the recognition which logic has mainly in view, but which is not ordinarily so called,[1] namely, recognition of a particular as being in this or that regard of this and that kind. In other words, there is recognition of the individual, and there is recognition of type. The two forms of recognition are correlative to the two species of identity—the self-identity of a particular and the identity of a type in distinguishable particulars. It is important to discriminate the two species of identity as sharply as possible. The identity of a type or kind I take as being precisely what is meant by a universal. It is that which can be asserted to be identically the same in one and all of a number of instances; and as such it is invariable. While allowing of combination with this and that other universal, it does not in any such combination admit of modification by these others. It is an identity that is found amidst differences, but which is never in any degree or fashion altered in its identity by these differences. It is, indeed, a condition of the combination of universals that together they are found to constitute a new type—that is, to constitute what is more than a mere combination of the simpler types. Otherwise we should not be conceiving a new type, but only conceiving simultaneously the previously conceived types.[2] But into the conception of the new type the simpler universals enter without change of meaning. Thus the universal or type 'triangularity' enters into the more complex universals, 'equilateral' and 'scalene', and as a constituent of the two latter has a meaning that is uniform for both; though they are species of 'triangle', they are not species of 'triangularity'. Similarly, 'animality' has a uniform meaning as predicated of man and of the various species of brutes, and this is why they can all alike be said to be animal species. Universals, being thus fixed in meaning, can always be represented by symbols that are invariables.

[1] Usually we simply say that we *know* an object to be red or square, not that we *recognize* it as being such.

[2] This is an important topic, and raises issues which I cannot here discuss.

Individual things, on the other hand, are admittedly variable; each is an identity that is compatible with, and indeed can be conceived at all only in and through the diversity of its distinguishable qualities, and in and through the changes whereby it responds to changes in its environment. It is not merely, like type, an identity amidst differences, it is an identity in and through its differences. The differences enter into its innermost being; and yet do so in a manner which not only allows of, but requires, their own variation. Universals, it may be objected, are also inconceivable save as embodied in changing particulars. This, I should agree, is true; my point is simply that they find a quite constant, not a variable embodiment. What differentiates the individual from the universal, in this regard, is that the former, consistently with its self-identity, can itself vary.

Secondly, as a consequence of this difference, it follows that whereas the universal, as being a type, consists in a definitely enumerable set of constituents, each of which can be abstractly considered, and in this manner exhaustively known, the individual can never be equated with any finitely exhaustible number of known characters. This is true even when we leave out of account its capacity for variation in response to change of conditions. And obviously it is still more true when this latter possibility is counted into the reckoning. For these reasons, then, every individual, though apprehensible in terms of an indefinite variety of different types, according as it is regarded in this or that aspect, is never thereby exhausted. But though thus apprehensible, it is also at the same time abidingly enigmatic. Accordingly, the symbol by which we make reference to an individual has to be a variable—in this sense that, though fixed in meaning (a primary requisite of every logical symbol), it has as part of its intended meaning a recognized ignorance.

But though identity is of these two species, identity *in and through* difference, i.e., identity of a continuant, and identity *amidst* difference, i.e., identity of type, the mode of their recognition is found, on closer examination, to be one and the same in both cases. We cannot recognize what we do not apprehend. What then is it, in the individual, that is apprehended, and in being apprehended, recognized as identical? As we have already had occasion to observe, the answer would seem to be that what we recognize as evidencing the continuing identity of a being, elsewhere or otherwise experienced, is the special manner in which the types (all of which are also found in other individuals) are combined with one another. The special manner of their combination, that is, the special permutation of common factors, is our sole clue to the identity of the individual, as found at different times and in differing situations. In other words, identification of the individual is thus itself still a form of identification by type. It is capacity to recognize type, 'suchness', that makes possible the capacity to apprehend the individual. When, in any class of individuals, the types which they embody are few in number, or when the relations between the types are very definitely fixed, the instances of the type are not separately identifiable, save numerically through difference of position. This is the case in the physical field, as, for instance, with samples of water; and is also what may render the members of a biological species difficult of discrimination.

Such, then, is a chief mode in which the abstract exhibits its fruitfulness; it makes possible apprehension of its counterpart, the uniquely individual. And owing to the manner in which it does this, we likewise owe to it a further service. No inferences are possible either from or to the unique, considered as unique. They are possible only in virtue of some identity, as defined by means of type. Accordingly, in apprehending the individual in terms of type, we bring it, notwithstanding its uniqueness, within the range of all those inferences which are relevant to the type. In the case of the individual, which as such is liable to variation, the type may, indeed, be a type which the individual embodies only in one set of relations, and the inferences from or to the type have, therefore, to be correspondingly guarded. None the less, it remains true that apprehension of type is what can alone bring the individual within the province of reasoning. A universal is a prerequisite of all inference; and the fixity of the abstract type is what enables the concept of the type to supply this need.

This, it may be observed, is true even when the inference is an induction by so-called simple enumeration. Even in such inference the main question, from the logical point of view, is as to our justification for *isolating* the universal, i.e., for treating differences as irrelevant. Thus, when we say A1, A2, A3, . . . are M, therefore all observed A's are

M, what we are virtually saying is that A1, A2, A3, . . . notwithstanding their many differences, are one and all M. It is not A1 in the features by which it is distinguished from A2, A3 . . . that is recognized as being M, but A as a such, and therefore as in type identical with the others. *A fortiori*, therefore, this must hold of all other forms of inference.

I have left over for concluding consideration yet another function of the abstract universal, no less important than those thus far dealt with, but differing from them in the nature and magnitude of the benefits, both practical and theoretical, which it carries in its train, namely, the use to which the abstract is put in the entertaining of possibilities, and thereby in the apprehension of whatever, in the absence of direct experience, must be known indirectly, if it is to be known at all.

In the purely practical sphere this is in some degree achieved, though much less effectively and within narrow limits, by the higher animals as well as by man, through the employment of concrete images which are generic in character. So long, however, as the types selected keep close to the concrete, the possible new combinations must themselves be correspondingly concrete, and there can be little in them that is genuinely novel. The rearrangements are, of necessity, mainly spatial and temporal; for instance, the huntsman's dreams of the choicest kinds of game as falling plentifully to his spear and arrows, or the imagining of a pit to be dug for the capture of the larger animals. The attempt to obtain any higher degree of novelty by such means results, as a rule, in the fantastically impossible. Thus it is easy to picture the types, man and horse, in novel combination; but the resulting type, the centaur, is utterly impossible as a type of living animal. As pictured, it is allowed to have two sets of lungs and only one throat, presumably two kinds of stomach and yet only one mouth.

The situation undergoes an almost magical transformation when by means of a more thoroughgoing analysis we succeed in arriving at the simpler factors which go to constitute the types first selected, when, in other words, we come to rely, not on images, but on abstract concepts— a change which would seem to be due to a threefold feature in the situation which then discloses itself.

In the first place, the simpler factors are few in number compared with the composite derivate types, and in proportion to their paucity[1] are found to be widely pervasive of reality, entering into an indefinite variety of differing entities. Secondly, not only do they account for the experienced types, they also render possible of conception types that are novel with a quite new kind of novelty, widely diverging from any apprehended in actual experience. And, thirdly, these novel types, though often almost fantastically novel—planetary systems within the compass of the atom, curved space and the like—are just for this very reason such as are required to open our eyes to what is illusory in ordinary experience, and to supplement it where it can be shown to have fallen short.

I may add a few comments in fuller statement of these last three points. If we are to arrive at knowledge of what is not itself experienced, the means of conceiving it must none the less still be supplied in experience. For just as the mind can only isolate what is actually given, so it can only synthesize what has already been apprehended. An ideal combination can, therefore, be a *new* combination only in this sense, that the elements combined, though all of them given in experience, are not given in this special combination. This is the extent of the mind's creativeness. If when such novel combinations are made, reality further discloses itself to the mind, the disclosure is due to reality, that is, to the nature of the elements (be they types of term or types of relation) which are being made use of to obtain the new type of grouping, and to the manner in which they then generate types that *are* genuinely new.[2] The mind has at most supplied only the opportunity for the disclosure. Thought is here creative in precisely the same general manner as in the making of physical experiments—the mind waiting upon reality, alert to take notice of its reactions, in the novel situations which have been brought about by 'artificial' rearrangement of natural existences.

Further, if all ideal construction is synthetic rearrangement, and if the materials rearranged are the elements arrived at by abstractive

[1] Dr. Broad, in his Presidential Address on 7 November 1927 (*Proceedings*, p. 45), has directed attention, with special reference to the problems of inductive inference, to this 'Principle of Limited Variety'.

[2] This, as observed above, is a question which I am not in this paper attempting to discuss.

analysis, it follows, as above suggested, that what we rearrange are types or kinds, not particulars. We employ simpler types, all of which are actually given, to yield, through recombination, complex types which are not given. Thus, to take the usual trivial instance, which yet is fully representative, we combine 'gold' and 'mountain'—two types revealed in experience—in conceiving, through ideal construction, the new non-experienced type, 'gold mountain'. What is true of this standard illustration will be found to hold in all other cases, however recondite, namely, that the new type is new only to the extent of being a new variation of actually experienced types, a variation that arises upon prescription of a type of connexion, likewise experienced, different from any under which the types in question have hitherto been found to exist. Some combinations can be at once set aside as impossible, e.g., 'square circle'. The types 'square' and 'circle', as being alternative embodiments of the same more general type, spatial figure, refuse to qualify one another. In other cases, such as in the concept of 'curved space' or of 'four-dimensioned space', the question of their legitimacy is one upon which only the mathematician and physicist—the metaphysician giving such aid as he can—are in position to pass an informed judgement.

When, as in physical science, we have to deal with types that are seemingly arbitrary, as, for instance, the complex types of structure appropriate to the various species of molecule and atom, an examination of each of the conceivable combinations is impracticable; for though the abstract factors involved may be few in number, the modes of their possible combinations are almost inexhaustible, especially as regards their quantitative aspect. We have therefore to proceed by indirect methods, scrupulously reckoning with the relevant sensible appearances, and resorting to measurements of meticulous exactitude. When these precautions are duly observed, the new combinations, hypothetically arrived at, are found to have a fruitfulness, in the explanation of appearances, that justifies the assumption of their objective reality.

We are now in position to determine what in this connexion are the fruits of conceptual abstraction. In its absence we should be confined to such knowledge of reality as is supplied in the perspectives of ordinary sense-experience, that is, to those combinations of types which it yields to 'passive' observation. Thought would, at most, be merely analytic of the immediately given; it could never, save in very modest degree, arrive at knowledge of what is other than given. The long-past in time—such as the state of the earth when its crust was being formed or the historical processes which have given rise to our present civilization —all such happenings, in proportion as they differ from conditions now prevailing, could not have become known to us. Similarly, the molecular, atomic and sub-atomic constitution of bodies would have remained quite outside our mental horizon. In short, science, whether positive or historical, would not have been possible. The capacity for what may be entitled ideal or conceptual reconstruction has so freed the mind from the limitations imposed by the conditions of its creaturely existence, that it can range freely over all time and over all space, and that in regard to what is experienced here and now, it is enabled to penetrate beyond the seeming simplicities of the sensory appearances to the structural complexities which they mask from view.

On the one hand, we have human experience, very limited in extent and highly conditioned in character. On the other hand, we have the Universe articulated in minutest detail and yet at the same time infinitely vast. None the less a bridge is provided over which the mind is able to travel from the one to the other—a bridge that is made possible by the unity of the real, as exhibited at once in the paucity and in the universality of the factors that constitute it. The paucity of the ultimate elements is as distinctive a feature of reality as is the unexhausted variety to which they supply the key. Reality is as conservative in its means as it is prodigal in its effects. The endless variety of its particulars is achieved without departure from the broad simplicities of its structural types. The abstract factors, if considered each apart, do not, indeed, yield to contemplation anything more than can be gathered from their first apprehension. So regarded, they are barren, not fruitful. They are apprehended in their whole nature, even in those narrow and distorted perspectives of immediate experience in which alone they can present themselves to our human consciousness. But when discriminated and freely recombined, they are the effectual instruments of the wide-reaching, more impersonal insights of science and philosophy.

In resorting to abstract thinking we are indeed carried so very far away from the brightly-coloured world of ordinary consciousness that we experience considerable difficulty in retracing our steps. This, however, is not surprising. In selecting out certain factors, to the neglect of others, we have predetermined the highly partial character of any insights to which we may attain. If we can succeed in correlating certain features in the wider and different world, disclosed in abstract thinking, with what that world appears to us as being in direct experience, this is as much as can reasonably be demanded under the circumstances. In disclosing the disparity between independent reality and the modes in which it is immediately experienced, abstract thinking has indeed set to us a novel set of problems. But there is no reason to conclude that abstract thinking which has led to the discovery of these problems is not equally competent in any possible further treatment of them.

John Locke (1632–1704)

PLATO has suggested that action is so much more natural to us than contemplation, that only those who are handicapped by ill-health or in some other way are likely to adopt the philosophic life, contenting themselves with the less immediately vivid satisfactions of the looker-on. Is it fanciful to find in John Locke an example of the justice of this remark? After being privately tutored, Locke entered Westminster School at the age of fourteen; and taking one year longer than the usual curriculum of five years, did not proceed to Oxford until he was in his twenty-first year. There he continued his linguistic and other studies, following out what seems to have been his first intention, or at least his father's intention, of preparing himself for the Church. He early came to have doubts as to whether this was his proper calling, but it was not until 1666, when he was thirty-four years of age, that he finally abandoned all thoughts of it. Meantime, thanks to his intimacy with Boyle and his scientific circle, he had become interested in the physical sciences, and especially in their practical application in medicine; and as these new interests gained upon him, he resolved to become a physician.

Whereas up to this point we have no information as to Locke's general health, we may reasonably suppose that it had been somewhat delicate, handicapping him in many ways, accounting for his late entry to the University, and so abating his energies as to prevent his earlier adoption of a permanent profession. We hear nothing of any sudden failure of health, but from 1666 onwards there are constant references in his correspondence to his ailments; and notwithstanding the anxious care of devoted friends, these infirmities were his constant companions through all his later years. They constrained him again to change his programme of life. As Lady Masham—the source of our most intimate knowledge of Locke—tells us: 'Some time after that Mr. Locke had begun to study in earnest, he applied himself principally to physic—a science which he yet never afterwards made use of to his profit, as not being well able to bear the fatigue those must undergo who would bring themselves into any considerable practice.'

Happily, at this juncture, a new way of life, highly congenial to him, and consistent with his poor health, was suddenly opened out by a chance meeting with Lord Ashley, afterwards the first Earl of Shaftesbury. The meeting resulted in their becoming lifelong friends. Lord Ashley installed Locke in his London house, in the Strand, as his private physician, and as tutor to his son; and later when he became President of the Board of Trade and Lord Chancellor, from 1672 onwards, as a trusted secretary and adviser in his political concerns. Locke also received a Government appointment as Secretary of Presentations (to benefices), and later as Secretary to the Council of Trade and Foreign Plantations. Thus far, Locke's health, though troublesome, had sufficed for these varied calls upon his energies. It gradually worsened, however; and in 1675 he went into retirement in France, where he spent three years, partly in Paris, chiefly in Montpellier. Writing to a friend from Paris in 1677 he says: 'My health is the only mistress I have a long time courted, and is so coy a one that I think it will take up the remainder of my days to obtain her good graces and keep her in good humour.'[1]

On his return to England, Locke was again engaged with Shaftesbury in political activities of various kinds; but sharing in the consequences of his fall from power, he followed him into exile in Holland. And so at last, in the enforced inactivities of a life at once of ill-health and of exile, he became, what otherwise the preoccupations of active life would probably never have permitted, a professional thinker and writer on philosophical subjects, his first work appearing some seven years later, when he was fifty-eight years of age.

There was one later occasion on which the enticements of practical life again presented themselves. In returning to England in February 1689 in the train of King William, he was offered the Ambassadorship to the Court of Frederick the First, Elector of Brandenburg, one of the most important positions in the diplomatic service, Frederick being the ally on whom William had mainly to rely in his opposition to Louis XIV. But Locke's good genius, in the guise of ill-health, again, happily

---

[1] Fox Bourne, *Life of John Locke*, i, p. 370.

for Philosophy, entered an interdict. His letter of refusal, addressed to Lord Mordaunt, has survived, and contains these passages: 'I cannot but in the highest degree be sensible of the great honour his Majesty has done me in those gracious intentions towards me which I have understood from your Lordship; and it is the most touching displeasure I have ever received from that weak and broken constitution of my health which has so long threatened my life, that it now affords me not a body suitable to my mind in so desirable an occasion of serving his Majesty. . . . My Lord, the post that is mentioned to me is at this time, if I mistake not, one of the busiest and most important in all Europe. . . . But what shall a man do in the necessity of application and variety of attendance on business to be followed there, who sometimes after a little motion has not breath to speak, and cannot borrow an hour or two of watching from the night without repaying it with a great waste of time the next day?'[1]

Locke did, indeed, accept the modest office of Commissioner of Appeals, and later very reluctantly agreed to act for a time as one of the Commissioners of the Board of Trade. But save for his occasional visits to London, in discharge of the duties of these offices, the remaining fourteen years of his life were spent in the country, in almost complete retirement, under the devoted care of Lady Masham and her family. And there we can picture him, as he describes himself in a letter to his Quaker friend, Benjamin Furley, resident in Rotterdam: 'Do not think now I am grown either a stoic or a mystic. I can laugh as heartily as ever, and be in pain for the public as much as you. . . . You may easily conclude this written in a chimney corner, in some obscure hole out of the way of the lazy men of this world and I think not the worse for being so, and I pray heartily it may continue as long as I live. I live in fear of the bustlers, and would not have them come near me. Such quiet fellows as you are, that come without drum and trumpet, with whom we can talk upon equal terms and receive some benefit by their company, I should be glad to have in my neighbourhood, or to see sometimes though they come from the other side of the water.'[2]

In reviewing Locke's life, there are two points to which I may direct

[1] Lord King, *Life of John Locke* (1830 ed.), i, pp. 319–20.
[2] Fox Bourne, op. cit., ii, p. 506.

attention: first, the fact that he published nothing under his own name until he published his main work, the *Essay Concerning Human Understanding*, in his fifty-eighth year; and secondly, that almost immediately upon its appearance Locke became the dominant philosophical influence throughout Europe, displacing Descartes—most notably so in France. Why, having delayed so long, did Locke publish at all? And why was his message so immediately influential, once it had been delivered? The answer which we have to give to the first of these questions also affords in part the answer to the second.

Why was Locke so late in finding his vocation? It does not suffice to say that Locke was one of those whose powers mature slowly and late. The main reason seems to have been that, in the very modest estimate which he had formed of his abilities, he had never been tempted to picture himself as destined to be a leader in the world of thought. Time and again, in his correspondence and writings, we find him protesting with obvious sincerity, that any merit his writings might have was not due to unusual abilities. This unawareness of his powers may, in part, have been caused by the uncongeniality of the linguistic studies to which he had to devote so large a proportion of his time at school and in Oxford, and to the bewilderment of mind occasioned by the scholastic philosophy into which his not very competent teachers sought to initiate him. One of the consolations which he drew from his first eager reading of Descartes was that perhaps, after all, this had not proceeded from any defect in his understanding, since however often he might differ in opinion from Descartes, he never failed to find him intelligible.

Fortunately Locke early acquired the habit—so much more usual than in these modern days—of writing out his views on any topic that might interest him, and of communicating them in epistolary form to his friends. While at Oxford, he was not, Lady Masham tells us, 'any very hard student', but 'sought the company of pleasant and witty men, with whom he likewise took great delight in corresponding by letters, and in conversation and these correspondences he spent for some years much of his time'. Practically all his writings originated in this way. It was the appreciative response of his friends, and their urgent petitions that these papers be used for the instruction of the world at large, that alone ultimately induced Locke to venture upon publication. In this regard the origins of his *Essay Concerning Human Understanding* are typical. Five or six of his friends, he tells us, meeting at his chamber, and discoursing on a subject very remote from that of the *Essay*—as we know from one of these friends they were discussing the 'principles of morality and revealed religion'—found themselves quickly at a stand by the difficulties that rose on every side. 'After we had a while puzzled ourselves . . . it came into my thoughts, that we took a wrong course; and that before we set ourselves upon enquiries of that nature, it was necessary to examine our own abilities, and see what objects our understandings were or were not fitted to deal with. . . . Some hasty and undigested thoughts . . . which I set down against our next meeting, gave the first entrance into this discourse, which being thus begun by chance, *was continued by—treaty*; written by incoherent parcels; and after long intervals of neglect, resumed again, as my humour or occasions permitted; and at last, in a retirement, where an attendance upon my health gave me leisure, was brought into that order thou now seest it.'[1] And Locke, addressing his Reader, proceeds: 'It will possibly be censured as a great piece of vanity or insolence in me to pretend to instruct this our knowing age, it amounting to little less when I own that I publish this *Essay* with hopes it may be useful to others. If I have not the luck to please, yet nobody ought to be offended with me. I plainly tell all my readers, except half a dozen, this treatise was not at first intended for them; and therefore they need not be at the trouble to be of that number. . . . I shall always have the satisfaction to have aimed sincerely at truth and usefulness, though in one of the meanest ways. . . . Everyone must not hope to be a Boyle or a Sydenham; . . . it is ambition enough to be employed as an under-labourer in clearing the ground a little, and removing some of the rubbish that lies in the way to knowledge.'

Locke's own account of the origins of the *Essay* is, however, incomplete, and can now be supplemented. An early draft of the *Essay* was discovered a few years ago by Dr. Benjamin Rand in the Lovelace collection of the Locke manuscripts, and is now accessible in the edition which he published last year. The meeting of friends, as we previously knew, was in and about the year 1670. What is a matter of considerable

---

[1] *Essay: Epistle to the Reader.*

interest, and in view of Locke's own utterances, very unexpected, is that this early draft, which is in Locke's own handwriting and dated by him 1671, and which is about one-tenth the length of the *Essay*, treats in consecutive form, though in a somewhat different order, nearly all the problems later dealt with in the four books into which he divided the *Essay*, and that all his main doctrines are already at this early date more or less definitely formulated. It is therefore the more surprising that Locke should not have thought of publication until some nineteen years later. We hear of him rewriting and extending this material during his stay at Montpellier. He showed his manuscript to friends; and Lord Shaftesbury had read it prior to his death, which took place in 1683. But it was subsequently to that date, during his exile in Holland, that Locke made his final revisions and additions. In all probability, Lady Masham declares, the work never would have been finished had he continued in England.[1] It was, not unlikely, the importunity of his friend Leclerc, whom he first met during his exile in Holland, that finally overcame his disinclination to publish. Leclerc was the editor of a literary and scientific review, entitled the *Bibliothèque Universelle*. For this journal he succeeded in obtaining from Locke a few minor contributions,[2] and finally an outline of the *Essay*. This outline, in the French translation made by Leclerc himself, appeared in January 1687–8; and its reception so encouraged Locke that two years later, in 1690, he published the *Essay* in its complete form. As I have said, it was an immediate success, new editions being called for in rapid succession. It was at once adopted as a textbook at Trinity College, Dublin, where some years later it was studied by Berkeley. With Locke's approval an abridgement of it was prepared by John Wynne, afterwards Bishop of St. Asaph. The decision of the Heads of Colleges in Oxford in 1703 that tutors must not read it with their pupils is even better evidence of the interest which it had aroused. On hearing of the interdict, Locke wrote to his young friend, Anthony Collins: 'I take what has been done as a recommendation of that book to the world, as you do, and I conclude, when you and I next meet, we shall be merry upon the subject. For

---

[1] Fox Bourne, op. cit., ii, p. 16.
[2] Cf. Fox Bourne, op. cit., ii, pp. 44–45.

this is certain that, because some wink or turn their heads away, and will not see, others will not consent to have their eyes put out.'[1] A French translation of the *Essay*, by Pierre Coste, appeared in 1700; and the Latin translation begun in 1696, appeared in 1701. Meantime Locke had been publishing his other writings: his *Letters on Toleration*, his works on Government, on Education, and on Religion.

The welcome accorded to the *Essay* was sufficiently encouraging to dispel any doubts that Locke may still have entertained as to his vocation, but he would have been amazed, and probably more dismayed than gratified, had he lived to read the eulogies which were passed upon his writings on the Continent, and especially in France, in those formative decades in which Voltaire, Montesquieu, D'Alembert, Diderot, Condillac, and Rousseau were the outstanding figures. They one and all looked up to Locke as the philosopher in whose steps they were proud to follow. He is hailed as 'the wise Locke', the 'greatest of all philosophers since Plato'. Voltaire, in popularizing Newton's discoveries in optics and in astronomy, sought also to popularize the teaching of the *Essay*. 'Many', he says, and among them he included Descartes, 'have written the romance of the mind; a sage has come who has modestly written its history.' The Abbé de Condillac wrote his *Essay on the Origin of Human Knowledge* as a supplement to Locke's *Essay*. D'Alembert, in the *Discourse* with which he prefaces the first volume of the great *Encyclopédie*, claims for Locke that he had created metaphysics very much as Newton had created physics. In paying this tribute to Locke, D'Alembert is not, in any unpatriotic spirit, forgetting Descartes. Descartes he depicts as the great geometer, and as the protagonist of reason, liberating the European mind, as no other had done, from the yoke of tradition and authority, and yet all the while forging weapons that in the end had to be turned against himself—his positive teaching with its many reactionary doctrines have to yield place to the counter-teaching of Locke.

This strain of eulogy continued unabated, in France at least, throughout the century. As late as 1794, in Condorcet's posthumously published work, *An Historical View of the Progress of the Human Mind*, a work of which the National Assembly ordered three thousand copies to

[1] Fox Bourne, op. cit., ii, p. 523.

be printed at the public expense, we find Condorcet describing what he takes to be the new method first formulated by Locke, and which he roundly declares to have been the method to which all genuine philosophical thinking, alike in the physical and in the moral sciences has since conformed. While it was mainly Locke's *Essay*, it was not solely the *Essay* that earned for him this position of pre-eminence; his writings on toleration and government, on education, and on religion also played their part. Montesquieu in questions of government, and Rousseau in treating of education, bear witness to their indebtedness to him. Those who set themselves in opposition to the prevailing spirit of the times entertained of course no such reverence for Locke; but even they paid indirect homage to his influence by the violence of their denunciations. This is especially true of De Maistre; he depicts Locke as 'the evil genius' of the eighteenth century.

To proceed therefore to our second question: How came Locke—in such complete contrast to the neglect, and even obloquy, that awaited his predecessor Hobbes and his contemporary Spinoza—how came he to exert, in so short a space of time after the appearance of the *Essay*, a European influence of the first magnitude, and also to retain it over so long a period? Was this not a strange fate to befall so modest and so moderate a writer? Certainly it calls for explanation; and the explanation would seem to be mainly twofold: on the one hand the *representative* character of Locke's teaching, and on the other hand, the relations in which he stood to Descartes and to Newton.

Let us consider each of these two points in turn. In the course of his life Locke enjoyed an extraordinary range of varied experiences. 'I no sooner perceived myself in the world,' he wrote in 1660, 'but I found myself in a storm which has lasted hitherto.' When he was a boy of ten, the Civil War was raging around his home in Bristol; and political troubles again came very near him when King Charles was beheaded within a few hundred yards of the school in which he was a pupil. Prayers were said that morning in the school for the preservation of the life of the King. While at first Locke, like his Father, had Puritan sympathies, many of his friends were Royalists; and he was caught up into the vortex of their competing interests, learning by bitter experience that the Presbyterians and the Independents, in coming to power, could be just as intolerant as the most extreme of their opponents. Welcoming the Restoration, he found opportunity, in the service of the Earl of Shaftesbury, to acquire first-hand experience in the management of public affairs, and this from a point of vantage which enabled him to follow their course, with first-hand knowledge of the issues and personalities involved. Partly in the service of the State and partly, as we have seen, for reasons of health, he travelled and resided in France, in Germany, and as an exile in Holland, his keen mind eager and open to almost every human interest. Even when politically engaged, he maintained the scientific and other contacts which had been formed in Oxford and elsewhere, corresponding on all kinds of topics with a large circle of friends. In particular he very early came to stand in intimate personal relations with the chief scientific workers of his time. The scientific group which was concerned in the founding of the Royal Society, the group of which Boyle was the centre, occasionally met in Locke's rooms in Oxford. Locke was himself elected a Fellow of the Society in 1668; and presumably it was at its meetings that he first became acquainted with Newton. After Boyle's death Locke edited Boyle's *General History of the Air*, a work which Boyle had started at Locke's instigation, and for which Locke had himself made observations.

But it was not only Locke's general interest, however intelligent, in all these matters, that gave its characteristic cast to his thinking. We must also bear in mind that he had very thoroughly equipped himself to be a practising physician, and that throughout his life he practised the art from time to time, placing his knowledge and skill freely at the disposal of his friends. When Shaftesbury had to undergo a delicate and difficult operation, it was upon Locke's judgement and practical skill that he chose to rely. Was some acquaintance in despair over persistent ill-health or have a child that was sickly, it was to Locke, sooner or later, that an appeal for aid and advice came to be made. His knowledge of methods of treatment and of the effects of drugs, and still more of diet, he was constantly adding to, with the consequence that the bodily conditions of our human existence were never in danger of being lost sight of when as a philosopher he came to speculate on the nature and limits of the human understanding or to formulate views on education and on government.

Locke was thus quite peculiarly equipped to appreciate the specific needs and the major tendencies of his age, equipped as no other contemporary thinker could claim to be; and this is, therefore, one very obvious explanation of the welcome accorded to his writings. But these considerations, relevant and important as they are, by no means suffice to answer our question. Locke could never have gained so immediate and so universal a welcome in England and throughout Europe had it not been for the favouring relations in which, thanks to historical contingencies, he happened to stand to the two great figures of the philosophy and science of his time, namely to Descartes and to Newton. Like two great planets in conjunction, they created the tide that swept Locke's venturing argosies into so many foreign ports.

Though Locke gained his first relish for philosophical inquiry from Descartes, his interest in the empirical sciences, and especially his medical studies, enabled him to adopt, from the very start, a critical and detached attitude towards Descartes' teaching. In particular, they acted as a prophylactic, guarding Locke against any temptation to regard as satisfactory its dualistic foundations. He insisted that man is not to be understood apart from the body, that the problem of the interrelation of mind and body, in its metaphysical aspects, has for us no very special urgency; and in consequence he set aside, as of little value, almost the whole of Descartes' metaphysics. What, on the other hand, he gratefully adopted from Descartes, his doctrine of clear and distinct ideas, and his rationalist method of approach to all problems, are precisely those features in Descartes' philosophy that allowed of a general welcome, especially when, as in Locke, they were supplemented by due recognition, so completely absent in Descartes, of the part which experience must play in providing the materials with which reason has to cope. Since Locke could thus take over all those elements in Descartes' philosophy which were suited to the needs of his contemporaries, and also was able, in place of much that Descartes had retained from the older ways of thinking, to substitute doctrines more in keeping with the scientific and other tendencies of the times, it is not surprising that the Cartesian philosophy put up so poor a fight, and everywhere yielded place, not least quickly and completely in France itself, to Locke's type of teaching.

In yet another regard Locke is a carrier of Cartesian doctrine, namely, in his insistence upon the necessity of new beginnings, through an abrupt break with the past. Alike in Descartes and in Locke, this takes the form of a depreciatory estimate of the value both of history and of learning. Truth, they argue, is independent of time. To engage our energies in study of the ever-changing opinions and beliefs of men is therefore worse than useless; when truth is our goal, to carry a weight of learning is to be handicapped in the race with the simple and the merely ignorant. Fired by this conviction, Descartes and Locke lived provincially in the age to which they belonged; and in respect of the many prejudices and limitations to which their teaching became thereby subject, neither had the advantage over the other. In the century that followed—a century even less historically minded than the seventeenth—no small part of Locke's influence was due to his unquestioning adherence to this way of thinking.

The history of seventeenth-century science reads, as Whitehead has said, 'as though it were some vivid dream of Plato or Pythagoras'.[1] Starting with Descartes' creation of analytic geometry, the mathematical sciences, entering upon a period of fruitful development, had given rise to the most extravagant hopes that by analogous methods metaphysics might be enabled to make corresponding advances. Such, indeed, is the philosophical ideal for which Descartes stood, or rather, since this statement is not wholly just, it is the ideal to which Descartes' successors believed him to be committed. Descartes was conceived as the great geometer, and as teaching that philosophy must itself be geometrical in method, that it is in a position to start from principles which are guaranteed by reason, and which, when followed by reason into their necessary consequences, place in our hands the keys adequate to the solution of all the problems of science and philosophy. This interpretation of Descartes' purposes is, as we have seen, somewhat unfair to him; but it is by no means so unfair, if the spirit of his teaching be gathered from the programme which he set himself in physics and astronomy. And, as it happened, it was almost exclusively by his teaching in these fields that his philosophy as a whole came to be judged.

The subsequent course of events, which was highly dramatic, is

[1] *Science and the Modern World* (Cambridge, 1926), p. 46.

unintelligible save in the light of the dominant influence exercised by Newton, an influence which in philosophy no less than in science has all the importance of a watershed dividing two epochs from one another. Notwithstanding the character of the work done by Kepler, Galileo and Huyghens—all of whom were concerned with the problems of applied mathematics—prior to Newton, it was still possible to argue, in the Cartesian manner, that the mathematical ideal of a purely deductive science is the idea also for physical science, and that it is possible of early achievement. To this type of rationalism Newton, through his discoveries in optics and in astronomy, gave—at least so far as the next two centuries were concerned—what was virtually the death-blow, the issue being decided in the great controversy between the Newtonian and the Cartesian types of cosmology. Thanks to Voltaire,[1] it became a hotly debated subject among the intelligent public. Descartes professed to have demonstrated '*by means of reason*' that light must be so and so constituted and is instantaneous in its action; Newton '*by means of a prism*' proved that in actual fact it is otherwise constituted and takes (on his estimate) six and a half minutes in travelling to us from the sun. Descartes professed to show '*by the natural light of reason*' that there must be vortices of subtle matter, and that in these vortices is to be found the explanation of the movements of the planets; Newton '*by observations upon comets*' proved that there are in actual fact no such vortices. Newton thus made clear beyond all questioning, that however important be the part played by mathematics in physical inquiry, observation and experiment are no less indispensable as supplying the brute data, the 'irreducible and stubborn facts', which reason may not ignore and is required to interpret.

Whitehead has asserted[2] that in consequence of this revolution the men of science became anti-rationalist, being content with a simple faith in the order of nature, and that it was the clergy alone who continued to uphold the rights of reason. But this, surely, is a perverse reading of what actually happened. The typical thinkers of the eighteenth century are, indeed, in striking contrast to those of the seventeenth century, *anti-*

[1] Voltaire's *Lettres Philosophiques*, ed. F. A. Taylor (Blackwell, 1946), Letters xiv, xv and xvi.

[2] *Science and the Modern World*, p. 73.

metaphysical; but this did not in the least weaken their conviction that in all matters of controversy reason is the sole ultimate court of appeal. What they had come to recognize—and it is here that Locke, following Newton, seemed to them to have shown the way—was that while reason is the instrument, it is not in and by itself the source of insight; and that speculation is therefore idle save when we are constrained to it in our efforts to define what it is that is being vouched for by experience.

Newton's *Principia*, it is important to remember, appeared just four years prior to Locke's *Essay*. Being at one in the empirical character of their teaching as in the time of their publication, they came to be associated in men's minds, each work assisting in the spread of the other. And in this partnership it was, of course, Locke who stood to be the main beneficiary. The battle-cry which Voltaire adopted in his great crusade was: 'the Newtonian Philosophy and Locke as its Prophet'.

To return for a moment to the subject of my original question—Locke's vogue in France throughout the eighteenth century. When we bear in mind what Descartes has meant, and still means, to the French people, as giving classical expression to so much that is native to their genius, it seems strangely paradoxical that an Englishman, and so very English an Englishman as John Locke, should have been allowed, for the space of a century, to eclipse in their esteem their own native teacher—a teacher who, assuredly, is the greater figure of the two. But the paradox is more seeming than real. As I have already said, Locke took over from Descartes precisely those elements in his teaching which were suited to the needs of the times, his insistence on clear and distinct ideas, and his trust in reason as exercising supreme sovereignty in all matters of controversy. Locke restated these doctrines in the manner demanded by the results of the empirical sciences, and especially of Newton's great discoveries. Thereby Locke became the chief channel through which all that could be immediately fruitful in Descartes' teaching came to its own; and it was these parts of Locke's philosophy that gained support for it in France. The Locke they adopted was not the complete Locke, but Locke cut to a French pattern, as befitted the role assigned to him. It is accordingly no exaggeration to say that what France, in the eighteenth century, received from England at the hands of Locke is in large part what France, in the seventeenth century, had herself given to

England, in the person of Descartes. In substituting Locke the philosopher for Descartes the metaphysician, the French were not therefore proving false to their own traditions; they were conserving them, and this in a manner which allowed their realist aptitudes—surely no less typical of the French genius—to gain more adequate expression than was possible within the limits of the Cartesian system.

In the comedy of human life time plays strange tricks with men and affairs. Here we have Locke, the most modest of men, being set on a pedestal as a rival to Plato, or when attacked by his enemies treated as an influence so powerful as to have poisoned the mind of a whole century. That Locke should have lent himself to such apotheosis and attack, is easily understandable as regards his controversial writings—Locke the protagonist of toleration, Locke as standing for constitutional rights and for individual liberty, and for a simplified theology, Locke the educationalist, Locke the opponent of innate ideas in the first book of the *Essay*. It was natural that the importance of these writings should be overestimated. Just because of their immediate serviceableness, being written to meet contemporary needs, nothing in them was likely to fail of effect. But as regards the *Essay*, outside the first book, only a few of its main doctrines, not always those that we should now regard as the most important, received attention; and as a rule these were formulated in some doctrinaire manner, quite contrary to the temperate, tentative, qualified spirit in which they were put forward by Locke himself. Accordingly the passing away of the eighteenth-century overestimate of Locke has not, so far as the *Essay* is concerned, brought any excessive reaction in its train. On the contrary, when the clouds of incense ceased to rise, in place of the cosmopolitan figure, there emerged the plain honest features of the genuine Locke, less imposing but more individual, distinctively English, and with a great deal more in his teaching than the eighteenth century, notwithstanding its exaggerated worship of him, had ever been sufficiently interested to study and appreciate.

Let us then, in the time that remains, turn to the complete Locke, the English Locke, as he reveals himself to us in his writings, and especially in the *Essay*. No one can read these writings without being struck by the predominance of the moral note. Sober and discriminating in all his judgements, he tested everything by a twofold criterion, truth and usefulness, neither, as he seems to have believed, being possible in the absence of the other. On first hearing, this may seem to be a somewhat commonplace and prosaic creed; it is redeemed by the freshness and liberality, no less than by the religious intensity, with which Locke held it. 'It is a duty we owe to God, as the fountain and author of all truth, who is truth itself; and it is a duty also we owe our own selves, if we will deal candidly and sincerely with our own souls, to have our minds constantly disposed to entertain and receive truth wheresoever we meet with it, and under whatsoever appearance of plain or ordinary, strange, new, or perhaps displeasing, it may come in our way. Truth is the proper object, the proper riches and furniture of the mind, and according as his stock of this, so is the difference and value of one man above another. . . . Our first and great duty then is, to bring to our studies and to our enquiries after knowledge a mind covetous of truth; that seeks after nothing else, and after that impartially, and embraces it, how poor, how contemptible, how unfashionable soever it may seem.'[1] For Locke, truth is no mere abstract term; it came to him weighted with the benefits and powers that, as he believed, may confidently be counted to follow in its train.

No less characteristic of Locke's writings are certain features which I may perhaps not unfairly describe as distinctively English, moderation, preference for qualified over unqualified statement, for adequacy over consistency, distrust of logic so long as contrary facts are in evidence, and consequent comparative lack of interest in the more metaphysical aspects of philosophy. These characteristics have been very happily summed up by Professor S. Alexander. '[The] general tone [of Locke's writings] is that of equable common-sense, without emphasis, without enthusiasm, restrained in its judgement, careful of measure, never dull but reflecting evenly from a candid surface, modest when it is most original, because concerned with the faithful presentment of things, rather lambent than fiery, an inspired pedestrianism.'[2]

Yet another general characteristic of Locke's teaching—I have already referred to it as common to him and to Descartes—is his insistence that in matters of knowledge and belief each man must stand on his own

[1] Lord King, op. cit., i, pp. 187–8.
[2] *Locke* (Constable, 1908), p. 23.

feet. 'He that distrusts his own judgement in everything, and thinks his understanding not to be relied on in the search of truth, cuts off his own legs that he may be carried up and down by others, and makes himself a ridiculous dependent upon the knowledge of others, which can possibly be of no use to him; for I can no more know anything by another man's understanding than I can see by another man's eyes.'[1] Why, Locke asks, 'make it one's business to study what have been other men's sentiments in things where reason is only to be judge?'[2] The teaching which Locke thus inculcated he himself practised, and to it his philosophy owes many of its chief merits, and some of its defects. He lived almost entirely in his time, reading, for the most part, the works only of his contemporaries, and even these but sparingly. Every field in which he worked he prospected as if it were virgin country, never before explored. This, indeed, is the key-note of all Locke's writings, no matter on what topic he may be writing: not that he himself made extravagant claims to originality—that he left to his eighteenth-century eulogists. 'He who has raised himself above the alms-basket, and not content to live lazily on scraps of begged opinions, sets his own thoughts on work, to find and follow truth, will (whatever he lights on) not miss the hunter's satisfaction; every moment of his pursuit will reward his pains with some delight, and he will have reason to think his time not ill-spent, even when he cannot much boast of any great acquisition.'[3]

Take, for instance, Locke's *Thoughts Concerning Education*. Here indeed was a virgin territory, for Locke the physician, for Locke who looked back with such regrets upon the opportunities that his teachers had failed to open out to him, for Locke the lover, and himself the especial favourite, of children. Consider some of the many novel maxims that he propounds. That children should live much in the open air, and should go bareheaded; that it is custom alone that makes children more liable to catch cold through the feet than through the hands, and that their shoes should therefore be so constructed that they do *not* keep out the wet—in a word, the present-day sandals; that the ideal breakfast for children is plain brown bread, preferably without

---

[1] Lord King, op. cit., i, p. 196.

[2] Op. cit., i, p. 175.

[3] *Essay: Epistle to the Reader.*

butter, and small beer; that children be not too warmly clad, winter or summer; that their beds be hard and made in different fashions, the pillow now high and now low, that they may not in after-life be put out when something is amiss. 'The great cordial is sleep. He that misses that, will suffer by it; and he is very unfortunate who can take his cordial only in his mother's fine gilt cup, and not in a wooden dish.' Nor is Locke above dwelling upon the evils of costiveness, and the duty of paying 'court'—as he expresses it—'to Madame Cloacina'. 'It being an indisposition I had a particular reason to enquire into, and not finding the cure of it in books, I set my thoughts on work, believing that greater changes than that might be made in our bodies, if we took the right course, and proceeded by rational steps.'

In things of the mind, the formation of character, he holds, takes first place. Next in importance he reckons wisdom in the management of affairs; third he places good-breeding; and only thereafter book-learning. Dancing he regards as a main instrument of education; and would have children disciplined by its means from their earliest years. 'For, though this consist only in outward gracefulness of motion, yet, I know not how, it gives children manly thoughts and carriage, more than anything.' The ordinary school curriculum, as he had himself known it, he regarded with little favour. 'What ado', he says, 'is made about a little Latin and Greek, how many years spent in it, and what a noise and business it makes to no purpose.' But the defender of the classics will be apt to think that Locke, in his candour, weakens his case, in disclosing his mind somewhat further. 'If [a child] have a poetic vein, it is to me the strangest thing in the world, that the father should desire or suffer it to be cherished or improved. Methinks the parents should labour to have it stifled or suppressed as much as maybe; and I know not what reason a father can have to wish his son a poet, who does not desire to have him bid defiance to all other callings and business . . . for it is very seldom seen that any one discovers mines of gold or silver in Parnassus. It is a pleasant air, but a barren soil; and there are very few instances of those who have added to their patrimony by anything they have reaped from thence.' Poetry and the fine arts lay outside the range of Locke's otherwise very catholic interests.

In general, Locke is confident that the road to knowledge can, by new and proper methods, be made short and easy. French and Latin are to be learned by reading and talking. 'Latin is no more unknown to a child, when he comes into the world, than English; and yet he learns English without master, rule or grammar; and so might he Latin too as Tully did, if he had somebody always to talk to him in this language.' In the curriculum for school and college he would also include the study of the sciences, of law, and of philosophy, but not either rhetoric or logic; and he would give prime importance to the pupil's mother-tongue. Would it, he asks, 'be very unreasonable to require a learned schoolmaster (who has all the tropes and figures in Farnaby's rhetoric at his fingers' ends) to teach his scholar to express himself handsomely in English, when it appears to be so little his business or thought, that the boy's mother . . . outdoes him in it?' In addition Locke would have every child learn 'a manual trade; if practicable two or three, but one more particularly'.

But we should not pass from Locke's work on education without noting what is one of its great qualities, namely his sympathetic understanding of child-life, and his demand that the discipline and training which he recognized to be very necessary be by gentler methods than those which had hitherto prevailed. The article on Locke in Diderot's *Encyclopaédie* is unsigned; but internal evidence reveals the author. Who but Rousseau could have written the following passage, which gives a very French version of what is not untrue to the essential spirit of Locke's teaching? 'Accustom the mind to the spectacle of nature . . . it is always great and simple. . . . Unhappy the children who have never seen the tears of their parents flow at the sight of the misfortune of others. Fable relates that Deucalion and Pyrrha repeopled the earth by throwing stones behind them. There remains in the soul of the most sensible something of its stony origins; and we must labour to recognize and to soften it.'

Locke's independent approach to every subject that came to occupy his attention can similarly be illustrated in the case of his other writings. These, however, in even greater degree than his *Thoughts Concerning Education*, are now of almost purely historical interest. It is the *Essay Concerning Human Understanding* by which Locke's genius must mainly be judged. It has stood the test of time as no other of his writings has done. His influence throughout the eighteenth century, as I have sought to show, was favoured by circumstances which conferred upon his writings a timeliness and an importance thay could not otherwise have had; and there was consequently an element of happy accident in the recognition accorded to Locke. But this cannot be said as regards the present-day reputation of the *Essay*. It has attained the assured rank of a philosophical classic, thanks to the sane, solid, and at the same time original, qualities of Locke's native genius.

The four Books into which the *Essay* is divided are of very unequal value. Books I and III are much shorter than the others, forming between them only one-fourth of the *Essay*. As I have already suggested, Book I is little more than a controversial tract, with almost no present-day relevance. Book III, which treats of language, though expository in character, has also little present value. In it Locke shows no appreciation of the closeness and subtlety of the inter-relations between thought and language. He is merely repeating and applying the kind of views which were then current—that language, while socially indispensable, is from an intellectual point of view a necessary evil, and the prime cause of fallacy—views not unnatural when we bear in mind that the type of philosophy then still dominant in the universities was a weakened form of Scholasticism, which employed an archaic and highly technical phraseology, and which was so out of keeping with the times that even its most reputable teachers had no genuine and living appreciation of the truths for which it stood. The intellectual life, Locke seems to say—as did Berkeley after him—should largely be spent in dodging out of the way of words. I am apt, Locke says, to imagine that when we quit words, and think upon things, we all think the same; whereas when we have some strange, outlandish doctrine to propound, it is upon legions of obscure, doubtful and undefined words that reliance is placed, so that the positions defended are more like the dens of robbers or the holes of foxes than the fortress of truth. This view of language is still occasionally to be met with among workers in the sciences; students of the humanities have, happily, freed themselves from it.

It is, therefore, to the other two Books of the *Essay*, to Books II and IV, that we have to look for Locke's main contribution to philosophy. What is that contribution? Usually the opening sections of Book II have been given such prominence that Locke's purposes and teaching in the *Essay* have been set in a very misleading light, as if he were mainly intent upon showing that the materials of knowledge are all-important, and are all, without exception, empirically obtained. This is part of the teaching of the *Essay*, but in Locke's own view—and he was entirely justified in so believing—the less important and the less original part. The primary purpose of the *Essay* is to determine the nature, conditions and limits of knowledge, the term 'knowledge' being employed in an unusually strict and narrow sense. As Professor Gibson, in his masterly work on *Locke's Theory of Knowledge* has pointed out,[1] for Locke knowledge and certainty are equivalent terms. Knowledge, Locke holds, excludes the possibility not only of doubt but of error. It is a form of absolutely certain cognition; and to possess it is to recognize it as such. 'With me,' he says, 'to know and to be certain is the same thing: what I know, that I am certain of; and what I am certain of, that I know. What reaches to knowledge, I think may be called certainty; and what comes short of certainty, I think cannot be called knowledge.'[2]

How, Locke asks, is this knowledge possible; in what fields is it possible; and what are the substitutes for it, where it is not available? Locke believed himself to have quite definite answers to these questions. Knowledge proper, he declares, is scientific; and consists of truths which are abstract and universal. The most *obvious* examples of such knowledge are, he recognizes, to be found in the mathematical sciences. But since 'our business here is not to know all things, but those which concern our conduct,' it is in 'morality' and in 'divinity' that we must look for its most *important* instances. Outside these three fields, we have at best only an assurance resting on probabilities—an assurance which for practical purposes may amount to certainty but still never is certainty.

Such is the very strange answer that Locke gives to his fundamental question: what is the nature and what are the limits of knowledge? Knowledge, absolutely certain knowledge, is possible in mathematics, in ethics, and in natural theology; it is possible nowhere else. Both physics and metaphysics are excluded from the domain of knowledge; they are concerned with the dark, not with the possibly 'enlightened' parts of

[1] Op. cit., p. 2.
[2] Second Letter to Stillingfleet, *Works*, vol. iv, p. 145.

things; and accordingly they should be pursued no further than practical need compels.

Now had Locke been true to his own programme, had he in the *Essay* consistently held to these positions, and succeeded in formulating a body of teaching in harmony with them, the *Essay* would, by now, have been, like his other writings, of purely historical interest. What he actually achieved, as distinguished from what he believed himself to have achieved, was to show, with admirable force and suggestiveness, that such hard and fast distinctions, such attempts at clear-cut delimitation of the knowable from the unknowable, are far from tenable, and that the metaphysical issues, the discussion of which he has deprecated, are not to be evaded in any such off-hand fashion. This, indeed, is precisely what lends to the *Essay* its permanent value. Locke does more than merely abstain from concealing counter-considerations. He was much too deeply interested in the problems, as problems, to be under any temptation to do other than emphasize them; and for the same reason, the metaphysical issues, though ruled out on principle, received, in the course of the *Essay*, no small share of attention.

All this comes about in the following manner. There is a conflict between the account given in Book II of the origins and nature of our ideas, and the teaching of Book IV, which deals with the validity of the knowledge we have by means of them. In Book II Locke declares sensation and reflection to be the two possible sources of all our ideas, reflection being described as itself a kind of inner sense. To these two sources, he tells us, all our simple ideas are due; we can have no complex ideas that are not reducible, without remainder, to such simple ideas. Yet later in the *Essay*, when Locke passes from the consideration of sense-experience to the treatment of knowledge, when, that is to say, he passes from the consideration of how we acquire experience in time to the consideration of truth, which holds independently of time, we find that he traces such knowledge neither to sensation nor to reflection, but to a quite new source of experience, which he entitles 'intuition'. And patently there is such a third source of experience. The apprehension that two units added to two units make four units is not a set of simple ideas; it is a proposition, the truth of which is learned through direct inspection. In what relation, then, does such direct intuitive inspection stand to sense-experience? Locke's answer is virtually to accentuate the distinction until it becomes an opposition between what is given to the mind and what the mind does for itself, and so paradoxically enough to base truth not on experience but on constructions of which the mind is alleged to be the author. Sense-experience, like the world from which we receive it, is ever-changing and gives, he says, no assurance beyond the moment. Like time it is a perpetual perishing; once past it can never recur. Intuition, on the other hand, yields knowledge that is universal and holds independently of time: a proposition, if true at all, has always been true and must remain true. This difference between our changing sense-experiences and the propositions in which intuition expresses its insights points back, Locke argues, to an equally marked difference in the nature of their objects. Sense-experience is of the real, which as real is always changing and in each of its changing states is inexhaustibly complex. For both reasons, that the real changes and that it is inexhaustibly complex, it is not being known even when it is being experienced. Sense-experience does not carry us beyond the moment of its own occurrence, and even at the moment we apprehend only the simple ideas present to the mind, not the reality to which they are due. Intuitive knowledge, on the other hand, is not of the real but of the abstract, not of the changing but of the immutable, not of terms—that is, not of simple ideas—but of relations which presuppose at least two terms, two ideas. Indeed, it is the relations, and not the terms, the structural features of the compound, and not its separate constituents, of which alone we come to have understanding, when we formulate propositions and recognize them as true.

Thus the objects of intuition are not ideas at all, not at least of any kind allowed for by Locke in his account of the sources of experience. They are immutable essences, each with a complex nature that is no longer itself if any, even the least, alteration be made in it. Locke adds, indeed, that they are essences and not realities, nominal not real, abstract with none of the inexhaustibleness that is proper to the genuinely actual. But while thus seeming to withdraw with one hand what he puts forward with the other, he does not withdraw from either of the two opposed positions, that sense-experience is never knowledge, and that there is a knowledge which is otherwise obtained. The nearest that experience can come to having the certainty proper to knowledge is in experimental sampling and the generalizations based on such sampling; but this, Locke insists, is worlds apart from the certainty attained in mathematical and other intuited propositions.

From logic and the theory of knowledge Locke then leads us on, in his speculations regarding 'substance' and what he entitles '*real* essences', to the problems of metaphysics. Is existence, like time, a perpetual perishing; or have we the right to posit what direct experience, in Locke's view, never discloses, a something that survives the passing of time, a something that fulfils itself in and through change? Or to state the problem in a wider form, is the compound resolvable into the simple, is the enduring reducible to the successive; and if so, is the complex and enduring nothing in its own right, is it a mere aggregate or series, without any structure proper and peculiar to itself? To these questions Locke suggests the same antithetic answers as to those we have just been considering. His theory of the sources of experience leads him in one direction, the nature of the knowledge which we actually possess leads him in a quite opposite direction. Thus to read Locke is constantly to be made to question what the author is saying in any one passage in the light of what he has said elsewhere, with the result that the *Essay*, when we are studying it, is—is it not?—as often on the knee as in the hand. And is not this the best tribute that a reader can pay to a reflective work of this kind?

To employ a distinction drawn by Whitehead, what we have come to value in Locke's *Essay* is his adequacy, an adequacy constantly obtained in disregard of consistency. He opens out fundamental problems in a manner none the less admirable that quite patently he fails to afford an answer that is final or satisfactory. This, under the circumstances, is a positive merit. For the questions which he sets us asking are problems which, as we have to recognize, still retain their central position, and to which, after two centuries of philosophical speculation, there is still no agreed solution. In respect of this considered, balanced, weighty character of its teaching, the *Essay* stands apart from Locke's other writings. As we have seen, it was Locke's main interest for a period of thirty years, from the time when he first drafted it in 1671 to the year 1700, when he made his final revisions for its fourth edition. Compared with the *Essay*, his other writings—with the possible exception of his second *Treatise of Government*—might almost be said to be in the nature of *parerga*. They are propagandist in character, and are seldom elaborated beyond what the immediate needs of the contemporary audience for which they were written seemed to him to demand.

The account which I have given of Locke in this lecture is, I need hardly say, very far from complete, even as an outline. I have barely touched on his writings on religion and on government, and have entirely passed over his writings on finance and currency. I have said nothing about his influence on Berkeley, on Hume, on the Mills and Herbert Spencer, or of the manner in which his *Essay* has contributed to the establishment of psychology as a positive science. I have preferred to dwell on those features of his personality and of his time which enable us to understand how so immense a range of influence has fallen to the lot of a writer so moderate, so candid, so unpretentious; and why, in especial, his *Essay Concerning Human Understanding* has acquired the unquestioned status of a philosophical classic, each succeeding generation of readers, not least so in these present days, finding in its pages something suited to its needs.

Immortality

IN upholding, as I propose to do, the belief in immortality, I shall dwell upon what I take to be the two main points at issue: first, the nature and sufficiency of the grounds appealed to in support of the belief; and, secondly, the question whether the belief can be a genuinely disinterested belief, and such therefore as can be coveted by the disinterestedly minded. These two points are not really separate, and I shall discuss them conjointly.

But let me first say a word in regard to a very usual interpretation of the issues before us. Those who deny the possibility of an after-life frequently base their denial upon what they consider to be the established results of the natural sciences, and especially of physiology. This, I shall contend, is a mistaken estimate of what the positive sciences have so far succeeded in proving. I venture the statement—and it would have the support, I think, of almost all workers in the field of philosophy— that the positive sciences leave us free either to affirm or to deny survival after death. There is no evidence that the body has the power of generating thought and feeling; and there is no evidence, except strictly negative evidence, that the consciousness of the individual ceases for ever when the functioning of his brain is at an end.

Certainly, we have overwhelming evidence that in our present state of existence our conscious life is conditioned by the body. The relation of mind and body is, however, a two-sided relation. Each influences the other; and the influence can start from either end. The mind is at least sufficiently independent of the body to influence the body; and this being so, the possibility remains that it may be sufficiently independent to survive the body.

This, however, is a mere possibility; and is indeed, so far as the natural sciences are concerned, so empty and so idle a possibility, that were not evidence of a positive character forthcoming in other fields of human

363

experience, we should not be justified in allowing it to occupy our attention.

Returning to my two main questions, we may first note how very doubtful are the uses to which the belief in an after-life has often been put. There is, for instance, the hortatory use of it to enforce a low-grade morality of rewards and punishments—the threat of eternal punishment to terrify those who find no intrinsic attractions in the good life, and, for those who are but half-hearted in the pursuit of the good life, the bribe of eternal bliss. Such teaching is now happily more rarely heard; but it is not so long since it has been so; and the belief in a future life still tends to be associated in the popular mind with a crude and anti-quated morality of punishment and reward.

But the belief in an after-life has been compromised and handicapped in yet other, more subtle ways. Here, for instance, is a passage from a sermon on immortality, delivered by John Henry Newman, early in his Oxford period. It depicts an attitude not unusual in past centuries, but which is now widely, and I should say very rightly, repudiated. The passage is as follows:

'The unprofitableness and feebleness of the things of this world are forced upon our minds; they promise but cannot perform; they disap-point us. Or, if they do perform what they promise, still (so it is) they do not satisfy us. . . . And should it so happen that misfortunes come upon us (as they often do), then still more are we led to understand the nothingness of this world; then still more are we led to distrust it, and are weaned from the love of it, till at length it floats before our eyes merely as some idle veil, which, notwithstanding its many tints, cannot hide the view of what is beyond it; and we begin, by degrees, to perceive that there are but two beings in the whole universe, our own soul, and the God who made it.'

And Newman then proceeds: 'As to those others nearer to us, who are not to be classed with the vain world, I mean our friends and rela-tions, whom we are right in loving, these, too, after all, are nothing to us here. They cannot really help or profit us; we see them, and they act upon us only (as it were) at a distance, through the medium of sense; they cannot get at our souls; they cannot enter into our thoughts, or really be companions to us. In the next world it will, through God's mercy, be otherwise; but here we enjoy not their presence, but the anticipation of what one day shall be.'

Now, while recognizing that Newman, with his flame-like spirituality, may well be allowed to use expressions that in another might be criticized as over-strained and excessive, none the less is there not here shown a quite undue preoccupation with the self and its future destiny? And when Newman speaks of the unsatisfying character of our relations with our fellow-men, are not his sentiments, in this regard, bound up with the defects of his own great qualities—due, that is to say, to his exacting, over-sensitive, difficult temperament that came between him and his fellows, throwing him back, as it constantly did, defeated upon himself? Certainly these views, when expressed by others less exceptionally gifted, have a repellent quality. They are felt to encourage an evasion of our natural duties, a disloyalty to our immediate goods, and so for this reason also have tended to alienate all those to whom the natural pieties disinterestedly appeal. They are out of keeping with much that is best in our present-day civilization—delight in the study of nature, delight in contact with nature, the love of animals, co-operation with our fellows in the tasks of life, and all the manifold goods that follow therefrom. A vividly held belief in an after-life may—it is often contended—be an assurance, and a consolation, to those who have suffered disablement in the battle of life, through bereavement or otherwise. But can it be other than a distraction to those whose tasks call for an undivided allegiance? Hence the mood, so prevalent in these days, that the possibility of an after-life had best be counted as one of the many questions that should wisely be left unanswered, as making no important difference in the true conduct of life.

Allow me now to formulate my argument, on behalf of immortality, by reference to a personality more modern in type than Newman— David Hume. Hume is the opposite of Newman in almost every main regard—as is shown in his whole manner of life, and in his refusal to consider as even desirable the belief in a life after death. It has been said of Hume that 'he was probably the worst-hated author and the best-liked and most likeable man of his day'. As he himself has playfully declared in one of his letters, he was loved by all men, except by all the Tories, all the Whigs, and all the Christians. This Hume could justly claim. For whatever men's prejudices against him, whether religious or political, in his immediate presence these prejudices vanished away. By general testimony no one could come near him without liking him. Especially notable in him were his equanimity of temper, his simplicity and good sense, his unfailing gaiety of spirit, his zestful interest in things human—not to speak of the vigour of intellect in respect of which alone he and Newman bear comparison with one another.

What was Hume's attitude to the question of the immortality of the soul? He expressed his disbelief in the most unequivocal terms. Our powers are, he held, no more superior to our present terrestrial wants than those of foxes and hares are, 'compared to *their* wants and to *their* period of existence'. The whole scope and intention of man's creation are, he declared, limited to the present life. So far are our powers from exceeding our present needs, that, on his view, they are frequently, nay, almost always, 'too slender for the business assigned to them'.

Now, to what is this fundamental difference of conviction concerning immortality, in Newman and Hume, due? How are we to account for it?

Much can be said in answer to this question. We may note, on the one hand, the absence in Hume of those excessive tensions of spirit, the costing character of which is exhibited in the unhappiness and depression from which Newman so greatly suffered through all the middle period of his life; and, on the other hand, Hume's zestful and effective adjustment to the demands and duties of his day by day living. On both accounts, Hume, handicapped by a life which was placid and uniformly happy, and which save for some minor disappointments was so well within his powers, had little reason to regard life as unsatisfying, and as requiring him to look further for its meaning and justification. But this hardly suffices as an answer to our question. For, it was not merely that Hume did not allow his mind to be preoccupied with the possibility of an after-life; he definitely rejected it. If, however, we still press the question, we find an answer which is obvious and, I hold, sufficient— namely, that whereas for Newman religion and its preoccupations meant everything in life, for Hume religion meant practically nothing. Hume had, indeed, a due sense of the mysteriousness of life, and of our incapacity to plumb the depths that lie beneath its surface. There was nothing, therefore, in his sceptical philosophy to prevent him accepting the belief in immortality, had he found in himself the inclination to do so. But it was to him uncongenial; and, as it seemed to him, unsupported by evidence, either scientific or moral. I have referred to what I have presumed to describe as Newman's temperamental limitations. Hume also had the defects of his great qualities; and they are, it seems to me, very evident when he is speaking of the inner life, in the moral, aesthetic, or religious fields. When he deals with these matters his writing has little of the subtlety of thought that has given him so high a place in the history of philosophy. He formulates the issues in the external, simplified form in which they were discussed in the 'enlightenment' circles of his day. And being, as he was, secular-minded—with, if anything, a positive distaste for religion and what it seemed to him to stand for in the world of his time—his negative attitude to the belief in immortality, as I shall now proceed to argue, inevitably followed.

For the thesis which I propose to maintain is this: the belief in immortality cannot stand alone; it draws its strength from another belief more fundamental than itself. It follows upon belief in Divine Existence, and save as a corollary or consequence of such belief we can have no right to it. Only if the Universe is divinely ordered are the conditions provided under which an after-life is credible, and under which reasons can be found sufficient to justify the conviction that personality survives the disintegration of the body. Only so can the belief spring from roots that will maintain it in health and vigour. I am not intending to suggest that belief in the existence of God is an easy belief. On the contrary, it is, as Newman has declared, the most difficult of all beliefs; and this for the very sufficient reason that in committing ourselves to it we are at the same time committing ourselves to so much else.

Let us now consider some of the objections to which these assertions may appear to lie open. Even granting, it may be said, that immortality is a belief which rests upon the prior acceptance of Divine Existence, even so, does it at all follow that we, the creatures of time, will share in the eternity of Divine Existence?

What, from the religious standpoint, is the answer to this question? The answer, be it right or be it wrong, is not in doubt. The answer made by all the greatest religious teachers is that we are *already* sharing in

Divine Existence; that our life is already in eternity and not solely in time; and that it is precisely for this reason that the assurance of immortality is possible to us. Our present life is the eternal life already begun, and contains, therefore, the guarantee of its continuance in its actually experienced nature. The guarantee—if this line of argument be valid—is twofold: first, the nature of that Divine Existence which is apprehended as conditioning our creaturely existence; and, secondly, the nature of our creaturely existence as thus divinely upheld.

This, too, is the answer to the objection that we have no power of conceiving how an eternal life could be even tolerable for creaturely beings such as ourselves. The objection is certainly a forcible objection. Even our highest satisfactions are bound up with the animal and physical conditions that are integral to our present life. Are not the fine arts inseparable from pigments and other materials? Does not all music depend upon the time-span of our human consciousness and upon our sensations? Must not Dante's poetry perish if Italian be not spoken in heaven? All attempts that have been made to render specific and definite the nature and conditions of an after-life, whether in the *Book of Revelation* or in Dante's *Paradiso*, or in any other way, are patently inadequate, being merely diminished and circumscribed versions of our present existence. Other, more modern, versions repel by the familiarity with which they treat of these mysteries, duplicating our present existence by another all too like it. So poverty-stricken are we in the materials for even the symbolizing of an after-life that we have to employ fire to symbolize alike the sufferings of souls in torment and the ardours of the saints in bliss. Light and darkness symbolize for us the good and the evil; yet in bodying forth the mysteries of Divine Existence we speak of God as dark by excess of light.

But does the belief in immortality demand any precise picture, geographical or other? Or to put my question more forcibly: is the belief, when held on genuinely religious grounds, one which must necessarily preoccupy the mind with the future? What the belief, thus held, stands for is that a life partaking in the quality of the Divine Life is already begun and will continue. The belief, that is to say, is not so much belief in *future* life as confidence in the quality of the life now being lived and its abiding conditions—a confidence which, so far from distracting the individual from present living, enables him the more serenely to concentrate upon it. To quote a passage already cited in one of the talks earlier in this series: 'The goldsmith takes a piece of carving, and from it chisels out a fairer form. So will it be with the man that does good. Hereafter he will be better. As the caterpillar, having eaten one leaf, begins at the tip of the next, so man, having ended one existence, will begin anew, beginning always where he left off.'

This is one reason why bereavement is not only so frequent an occasion for reflection upon the problem of immortality, but also is one of the legitimate and healthful approaches to it. For what in bereavement leads the individual to desire to hold the belief is not preoccupation with another life, different from that which he is already living, but the desire for the continuance of a relation which death has interrupted, and which he has, just thereby, been brought to value the more. A conviction of the continuing *presence* of the dead is consequently of the essence of the belief, when it is vividly held. Here again, therefore, the belief, if healthy and not morbid, need not carry the individual away from actual living; it may stabilize it.

Or consider this same objection in another form. In H. G. Wells's *Invisible King* there is the following frequently quoted passage: 'Whether we live for ever or die tomorrow does not affect righteousness. Many people seem to find the prospect of a final personal death unendurable. This impresses me as egotism. I have no such appetite for a separate immortality; what, of me, is identified with God, is God; what is not is of no more permanent value than the snows of yester-year.'

What reply is there to this? We shall probably all of us agree that this is a frequent mood, and may be a very wholesome mood, for the individual towards himself. But can such a position be taken, ought it to be taken, in regard to others? For is there anything known to us of higher intrinsic value than personality? Certainly there are many sorts of being much more finished and complete than human personalities are ever found to be. Indeed, no other type of creaturely existence falls so far short of perfection in its kind. Hume, in the words which I have quoted, declares that the powers of men are no more superior to their present terrestrial wants than those of foxes and hares are, 'compared to *their* wants and to *their* period of existence'. That may be so, but is not this because among our terrestrial needs are some that can never be fully satisfied in our present life, and that require even for their partial satisfaction the sciences, the arts and religion? It is only among the animals that we find fixity of need and completeness of satisfaction. Man has an abiding sense of imperfection which does not diminish, but increases, as advance is made.

Indeed, it is in the sphere of human life that the problem of evil rises before us in its most baffling forms. Evil is so widespread, it is so closely woven into the very texture of our existence, that it is difficult, and in certain of our moods well-nigh impossible, to deny that frustration, and the loose ends that go therewith, are among the ultimate facts of life. There is, however, another side to the picture. For is there not another problem more fundamental and even more challenging than that of evil—the problem of good? Why do we take good for granted and question only evil? Is it not because, widespread as evil is, the good is incomparably more so? The good is the very substance of life; evil is only what checks and thwarts it. There being so much good in life, how are we to account for the good being there in this degree, or even for its being there at all, unless we are prepared to recognize that there must be even more good than first appearances seem to show?

Agreed, some of you will say. Our present life, properly lived, would be sufficiently satisfying. As we have seen, it was found so by David Hume. Ought we not to cultivate those zestful qualities of which Hume is so admirable a representative? And will not life, lived in this spirit, justify itself by further fruits, and by increased control over the evils that may still remain?

Before attempting to answer this objection, let me restate it in yet another form that reinforces it. For I have left till the last certain considerations which probably, more than any other, have weighed in deciding so many against the belief in immortality. The very essence of morality, the secret of happiness in life, it is urged, is devotion to causes greater than the self and outlasting it. Only by this path can the frustrations, so inevitable in all self-seeking, fade into insignificance in comparison with the satisfactions that attend upon the pursuit of disinterested ends. The individual, it is claimed, *does* then have an immortality—the only immortality for which he ought to have any care, namely, that of the interests and causes with which he has identified himself, and to which he has given of his best. He himself is shortly to be scrapped; and the qualities *proper* to his personality do not, therefore, in comparison, supremely matter.

Now all that is positive in this argument may at once be accepted. This capacity for disinterestedness man can truly claim; and it marks him off, as nothing else does, from the rest of the animal world. Nature has indeed seen to it that each generation of animals spends itself in the maintenance of the species. In the mating season birds pair, build their nests, and rear their young—no labour being too great for them, that Nature's purposes in them be effected. In man also, Nature, in similar fashion, has made secure the maintenance of the species. But in man this end is complicated in manifold ways, which find no proper analogy in the strictly animal realm. Man is governed by reason as well as by instinct; as a reflective being, demanding the why and the wherefore of what he does, and as a moral being, stirred by aspirations for a life better and more satisfying than any ever yet attained, he is summoned to live not only for the continuance of the species, but also for other, more comprehensive ends. The crucial question for us, in our inquiry, is as to how these further ends are to be conceived.

Men, it may be agreed, should be impersonal, demanding but little for themselves and everything for the ends after which they strive. But what are these ends? Are they, too, describable as impersonal in character?

The term 'impersonal' has two distinct meanings. It may be distinguished either from the merely personal, meaning the selfishly and illegitimately self-interested; or it may be distinguished from the personal as such, and so be taken as signifying the non-personal. Now is it the case that the meaning and value of life consists in the furtherance of non-personal ends—ends which are self-justifying quite apart from any bearing thay may have on the felicity of personal beings? Surely not. Truth is an end in itself, partly because the pursuit of it is an intrinsically self-satisfying activity for a conscious being, and partly because of the fruits which, in the furtherance of life, physical and spiritual, it brings in its train. Beauty and goodness are ends in themselves, for similar reasons. If we eliminate all personality, Divine and creaturely, these goods are no longer even barely conceivable. Dispute can arise only as to whether the personalities, so enriched, are or are not mortal beings.

The argument that is here being directed against the belief in immortality is, I should contend, a two-edged argument. For are not those who thus argue both running with the hare and hunting with the hounds? They are finding the meaning of life in the pursuit of ends which depend for their value on personality, and yet at the same time are assigning to personality a secondary role, as merely instrumental, in the furtherance of ends which they conceive as existing in and by themselves. And it is from this standpoint that they declare immortality to be not even desirable.

To state my point as concretely as possible: here, say, is a person devoting his main energies to a political party or to the achievement of certain social reforms. This gives him a governing purpose in his life. The political party may prove successful and effective, or, for reasons for which the individual may not be at all responsible, may make shipwreck. The social reforms may be achieved or they too may prove abortive. On this interpretation of life the pattern which gives meaning to the individual's life is a *single* pattern; the individual's eggs, so to speak, are in the one basket; and if it be upset, as in this difficult world it so frequently is, then for the individual the frustration is, so far, complete.

On the other interpretation, that which assumes survival, all life has a complex, simultaneous, *double* pattern. In every activity two ends are simultaneously being pursued. While we are furthering some scheme of social and political reform we know that we are at the same time, through communion with and in co-operation with what is other than the self, building up in ourselves and others the personal powers upon which this and all other possible enterprises supremely depend. And in view of this latter end, the failure of the political party or the defeat of the reforms may be no ultimate defeat, but may have afforded precisely the opportunity required in preparation for larger tasks. Life is being lived simultaneously on two levels, and not wholly on one; and each level, in its own appropriate fashion, contributes to the enrichment of the other. The true believers in immortality are the twice-born.

Also, is not the believer in immortality the more likely to be the effective worker, even for terrestrial ends? Is not a certain degree of detachment the supreme condition of effective action; or at least is not the alternation between whole-hearted absorption in social activity and such retirement into the self as secures it against all fanatical insistence upon the programme in hand, the only healthful attitude? Other things being equal, is not this necessary degree of detachment more likely to be achieved in and through belief in immortality than in its absence? If there be an eternal life now lived, that, secure in a divine basis, assures us of its continuance, can there be any better balance-wheel in our living here and now? Will it not supply both serenity in the times of stress or disaster, and an added zest, with overtones of heightened meaning, in the occupations that satisfy and succeed?

As we have noted, the symbols at our disposal are few in number, and each can be put to contrary uses. The secularist outlook can be symbolized by the brightly coloured flower that to yield the seeds of a continuing species must itself fade and perish. The religious outlook finds its symbol in the dark seed that in disrupting itself breaks through its envelope and with its fresh shoots responds to the potencies through which it is drawn to the sources of light. But there is, as we must recognize, this difference between the two uses of the symbol. The one can be understood in terms of experienced happenings. Through the other we are only, in a manner, saying: 'As the sky extends beyond the valley, so I know that there are ideas beyond the valley of my thought.'

As I have said, my argument has not been in the nature of an attempted *proof* of immortality. My argument, so far as I have outlined it, is simply this. If we are unable to believe that our present lives are divinely conditioned, we can have no sufficient grounds for believing in survival after death. If, on the other hand, we are able to achieve this most difficult of all beliefs—as I have already noted, that is how Newman has himself described belief in Divine Existence—if we are able to take this first most difficult step, the belief in immortality then follows in natural sequence. And so obtained, the belief is not a way of escape from the difficulties of actual living, but the clue to its present and proper meaning.

Such a belief is not, of course, to be acquired merely by listening to argument on the question. Argument may play its part. But the argument, in such matters, is argument from evidence; and the evidence is accessible to us only in the actual processes of actual living, practical, aesthetic, and contemplative. Only belief thus achieved can be counted upon to withstand the stresses and strains to which, as creaturely beings, we remain irretrievably subject.

Is Divine Existence Credible?

IN residing, some years ago, at an American State University, one of the things that most impressed me was the prevalence, alike among the students and among members of the Staff, of the view that belief in God is no longer possible for any really enlightened mind. This point of view was naïvely militant in the student-body; among members of the Staff, with comparatively rare exceptions, it seemed to be assumed as a matter of course. That such a way of thinking should be thus widespread in America is not, indeed, surprising. It owes much of its strength to the yet wider currency of the Fundamentalist counter-position; each creates a field highly favourable to the other. This sceptical way of thinking finds, however, notable representatives in every university and in every age; and in our European universities—at least until the past decade—there has probably been more of it than there has ever been at any time in the past. You may recall the passage in the Encyclical Letter of the Archbishops and Bishops in session at the Lambeth Conference: 'We are aware of the extent to which the very thought of God seems to be passing away from the minds and hearts of many even in nominally Christian nations.'

What—I propose to ask—are the positive grounds that lend to this negative attitude its assured confidence? Why is it that what was, at the least, an open question for David Hume, is for so many no longer worthy even of debate?

We have, of course, to distinguish between crude-minded types of disbelief and the more refined questionings of those who, though well aware of the many-sided character of the issues involved, yet arrive with conviction at a negative answer. It is with the latter that I am mainly concerned; but the two are interconnected, and I shall begin by considering certain misunderstandings, which by intervening tend to

375

prejudice the issues, and indeed so to conceal them, that they are never properly even raised.

The first and main type of misunderstanding I should trace to the fact that those who are of this way of thinking, however they may have thrown over the religious beliefs of the communities in which they have been nurtured, still continue to be influenced by the phraseology of religious devotion—a phraseology which, in its endeavour to be concrete and universally intelligible, is at little pains to guard against the misunderstandings to which it may so easily give rise. As they insist upon, and even exaggerate, the merely literal meaning of this phraseology, the God in whom they have ceased to believe is a Being whom they picture in an utterly anthropomorphic fashion—a kind of Being whom it is not wholly absurd to picture as seated on a throne—a kind of Being who even if he were able to say to himself, 'All things are due to me', would still of necessity be pursued by the question, 'But whence then am I?' Such a Being could not be otherwise than abashed before the immensities of space and time for which, as Divine, he has to be conceived as responsible. For whatever be the honorific attributes assigned to him, he is in essentials finite; and as Hume has so convincingly argued in his *Dialogues*—in Philo's reply to Cleanthes—a limited and finite God can meet the needs neither of religion nor of theology.

Connected with this first cause of misunderstanding is the assertion, so frequently made in religious circles, that belief in God is easy, and indeed almost self-evident. Belief in the existence of God is indeed easy for those who already so believe. But this is true of any and every belief. All belief, once acquired, is thereafter easy. But this proves nothing as regards the ease or difficulty of first acquiring it. And as a matter of fact, is it not the case that there is no belief *more* difficult to acquire than belief in the existence of God? If we avoid non-committal terms, such as 'the Absolute', and if we profess to believe in a Being who has the attributes customarily assigned to the Divine, and who is at the same time a Being with whom we may have personal relations, can there be any belief more difficult to acquire, for those who do not find themselves already possessed by it? To believe in such a Being is not a minimum belief, to be counted upon whatever else the believer may or may not accept; it is a maximum belief, and commits us to all the many other beliefs congruent with, and consequent upon, itself. To represent such a belief as easy of acquisition is to set it in a misleading light, and is to discourage precisely those who are most sincere in their approaches to it.

One main reason why the situation has been thus falsely represented is, I think, the continuing influence of the eighteenth-century view that the existence of God can be demonstrated from the facts of Nature and history—the actual situation being—is it not?—that the existence of God cannot be demonstrated in any such manner. If we come to Nature and to history with an *antecedent* belief in the existence of God, they may be shown to be, conceivably, not incompatible with such belief; but they never suffice to demonstrate it.

I can best lead up to the points upon which I wish to dwell by an examination of this usual assumption that God, if God exists, must be demonstrable from the facts of Nature and history. But before I do so, allow me to interpose a further word of general explanation. Dr. F. R. Tennant, in the second and concluding volume of his *Philosophical Theology*, contends that belief in the existence of God cannot be justified either from *a priori* premisses or from purely ethical data. So far I find myself in agreement with him. Now there are, he says, only two other methods of justifying belief in the existence of God. We may attempt to do so either by way of direct experience of the Divine or else by some form of the argument to design. Again I should agree; but I am unable to follow him in the alternative which he proceeds to adopt. Dr. Tennant holds that we have no direct acquaintance with the Divine, and that the argument to design is by itself valid and sufficient. The position from which my paper is written is that the argument to design can play no such part as he assigns to it, and that if certain important qualifications and reservations be made, we are justified in maintaining that belief in God does ultimately rest upon immediate experience.

Hume and Kant deal with the argument to design in a strangely hesitant manner. Thus Kant begins by eulogizing it as 'the oldest, the clearest, the best suited to ordinary human reason', and then straightway proceeds to show that as argument it is the least satisfactory of the traditional proofs, involving not only those fallacies which, as he teaches, render the more speculative types of argument impossible of acceptance, but in addition a number of fallacies peculiar to itself.

This is also the manner in which Hume has argued in his *Dialogues concerning Natural Religion*, only in his case the inconsistency, if inconsistency it be, is rendered the more flagrant in that he reverses the sequence. Instead of beginning with praise and ending with criticism, he first gives a quite devastating criticism of the argument and evidence for design—criticism placed in the mouth of Philo—and then in the concluding section of the *Dialogues*, and again through the mouth of Philo, in violent contradiction with the results previously arrived at, he proceeds to allege that 'a purpose, an intention, a design strikes everywhere [in Nature] the most careless, the most stupid thinker; and [that] no man can be so hardened in absurd systems, as at all times to reject it'.[1]

Recently Sir Arthur Keith has made a somewhat similar pronouncement. After stating the influences which have led to the destruction of his belief in a personal God—'a super-being endowed with human attributes'—stating more particularly the irresistible body of evidence which shows that creation does 'not work from without but from within', and that 'the human soul is but the manifestation of the living brain, as light and heat are the manifestations of a glowing bar of steel', he none the less arrives at the following conclusion:

> The human brain is a poor instrument to solve such ultimate problems. We have to recognize its limitations. Yet it perceives how well-ordered all things are and how wonderful are the inventions of nature. *Design is manifest everywhere*. Whether we are laymen or scientists, we must postulate a Lord of the Universe— give Him what shape we will. But it is certain that the anthropomorphic God of the Hebrews cannot meet our modern needs.[2]

Now why is it that Hume, Kant, Sir Arthur Keith, and so many others, proceed in this manner? Why do they thus, while rejecting the *argument* to design, none the less still accept the *fact* of design? Is their formal inconsistency a real inconsistency? Are they in their own persons nullifying their own conclusions? Or are they no more than recognizing the conflicting requirements of the complex situation with which they are attempting to deal? As I shall try to show, their procedure cannot

---

[1] Op. cit., pt. xii, at the beginning.
[2] *The Forum* (April 1930), p. 225. Italics not in text.

be defended against the charge of inconsistency. As I shall also try to show, the inconsistency is for them unavoidable. For however they may agree that it is not possible to prove God's existence from the facts of Nature and of history, they still have not been able to clarify their minds in regard to certain immediate experiences, which, as they believe, are undeniably aroused in them by the contemplation of Nature.

I shall dwell briefly on each of these two points. What are those defects in the argument to design which constrain us to reject it? In the first place, it ignores the radical character of the distinction between the natural and the artificial. The existence of an artificial product is only possible in and through the existence of an external artificer: the natural, on the other hand, is, *qua* natural, self-evolving and self-maintaining; that is to say, its form is as native and natural to it as the matter of which it is composed. Indeed the argument is at its weakest precisely in those fields in which it professes to find its chief evidence—the evidence upon which Paley, for instance, mainly relied—the amazingly complex and effective adjustments exhibited in vegetable and animal organisms. The hinge of a door affords conclusive proof of the existence of an artificer: the hinge of the bivalve shell, though incomparably superior as a hinge, affords no such proof;[1] it is as natural in its origin as anything in physical Nature can be known to be.

This brings us to a second, even more fundamental, objection, namely, that to conceive God as a Designer is to conceive God in terms of attributes proper only to a creaturely being. The concept of 'purpose' is so bound up with the distinction between present and future, and with the distinction between means and end, that when we combine it with the further concepts involved in the notion of 'design', we are really endeavouring to conceive God in terms of that part of our human experience which is least appropriate thereto. Design implies foresight. But when do we possess foresight? In our repetitive activities. When our activities are describable as being creative, then precisely in the degree in which they are so, they tend to be tentative, purposive indeed, but proceeding by trial and failure. Such activities are not conceivable save in reference to a being who is faced by an external environment

[1] Cf. *The Life and Letters of Charles Darwin* (Murray, 1887), ed. Francis Darwin, i, p. 309.

which determines the possibilities among which he may choose, and supplies the materials through which they can be realized.

To state the point in the manner of Hume. Design involves a plan, and only if the plan be granted as pre-existing, can the designing activities act with foresight, namely, in accordance with the plan. But how does the plan itself originate? If we say that the plan must itself be planned, we are landed in an infinite self-defeating series. We must perforce admit a first stage, in which there is action that is not dependent upon a previously planned plan. To do so, however, is to conceive God not as a Designer but as a Creator. For we are then conceiving him, not as planning his plans, but as creating them; and if so, if we thus admit that design is not necessary to the creation of a plan (and the plan to be effective must be complete, down to the minutest details), we are no longer justified in requiring design as a stage preliminary to the creation of Nature. Either, therefore, we have no right to the assumption of a Creative Being, even in respect of a plan; or if we have, it is as a Creator, not as a Designer, that he must be conceived.

In what respects, then, does the concept of creation differ from that of design? As already stated, only our repetitive activities can be designed, that is, performed with foresight. They are conditioned, therefore, by some prior activity that is not repetitive; and this prior activity, in being creative, is by no means out of line with other everyday happenings. As Whitehead teaches: Nature is constantly advancing into novelty. *Nature is made up*—with supplementary factors no less enigmatic—*of events which, as one-time occurrences, are unique.* Thus should I move my hand, the movement has never occurred before and will never occur again; events are not repeatable in being but only in type. I can say that I repeat the *same* motion of my hand; but it is not the same motion; it is a quite new motion; it is the *same* only in type or kind, not in being. It is in and through creativity, in and through one-time occurrences, that any continuing modes of being which we may have to recognize are maintained in existence.

It is commonly supposed that we can avoid this conclusion by resorting to the concept of substance, as that in and through which change is alone possible—this substance being conceived either as matter, or as energy, or as spirit. But even so, we do not really escape the acceptance of creativity. Substance, as thus postulated, is in all three forms an enigmatic type of existence; and in conditioning change it still exhibits that very creativity with which we are professing, by its means, to dispense. Substance is doubtless one of the factors conditioning creativity; it cannot be a substitute for it. For consider, again, the motions of my hand: at least, it may be said, the hand that makes the motions is the same throughout them all. But what is the hand? Like a vortex in water, it is the fixed form taken by certain changing constituents; and even as such a form, it is only relatively fixed. It too is always in process of passing; it too is a one-time occurrence, and so far unique. The change from caterpillar to butterfly is indeed 'a gesture in creation', but is not on that account a departure from Nature's ordinary course.

Now we do not possess even the beginnings of an understanding of creative activity: whenever and wherever it occurs—and it is occurring at every moment in all places—we are presented with something to which we can find no analogy in anything other than itself. Though it is thus omnipresent, exemplified in all that occurs, it is abidingly mysterious. It is one of the many opaque elements with which reason has to reckon when it endeavours to define the situations in which we find ourselves to be placed. If, with Samuel Alexander, we define the *a priori* as being not what is due to mind but as what is pervasive of all reality, creativity may be so described; and like all other ultimates, it has to be used in explanation, while remaining itself unexplained.

The typical attitude of the eighteenth-century thinkers in regard to the argument to design may perhaps be stated thus. The self was taken to be a self-subsistent being, naturally immortal, and capable of exercising purposive activities. In regard to it, no further questions of a metaphysical character were asked. Creation might be spoken of in the Creeds: it was tacitly ignored, as hardly respectable in philosophy. God was accordingly conceived as a magnified self, related to the natural world in what was supposed to be the easily understandable relation in which man stands to the works of his hands. God is the Divine Artificer, doing on the cosmic scale precisely what man is capable of doing in his own smaller world. On this view neither the self nor God is mysterious; they differ only in degree, and both are adequately known for what they are. The shift which has taken place in Hume and in Kant is precisely that further questions have been asked in regard to the self, both in regard to the nature of its purposive activities, and in regard to its supposedly self-conditioned existence, and mysteries are discerned where none had been suspected. The self is in fact not self-maintaining; it is upheld by the body, and the body is integral to its natural setting. The self is indeed, like all other existences, capable of creativity; but it is a conditioned and delegated creativity; and if we are to believe in a Divine Being on analogy of the self, we must carry over into the conception of it all that is thus mysterious in the self, at the same time recognizing its possession of a creativity which is not thus conditioned and creaturely, and which is therefore proportionately the more mysterious. Certainly in this and that attribute the Divine must allow of being known to us—otherwise we should have no right to entitle it the Divine —but precisely in being thus known it will still be known as abidingly mysterious. For the concepts which we employ are problematic concepts; their function is to enable us to locate and to specify the mysteries of Divine Existence, not to resolve them.

This may be illustrated by reference to the attributes of 'omnipotence', 'omniscience', 'eternity' and 'omnipresence'—leaving aside for later consideration the question as to the general nature of the evidence upon which they may be predicable of the Divine. There is nothing in our human experience adequate to the concept of omnipotence. We do, of course, experience power in ourselves; but when we pass from the concept of power to that of omnipotence, the concept of power is modified in ways which presuppose for their possibility the existence of a Being quite other than the creaturely. All our powers are upheld and made possible by conditions which they do not themselves provide; they are conferred or delegated powers. Our power of knowing, for example, is conditioned by the brain, and the brain in turn by the whole natural order. Accordingly omnipotence remains a problematic concept. It is theomorphic, not anthropomorphic. It *presupposes* the possibility of the Divine; it can be allowed as possible only to the extent to which the Divine can be alleged to be itself possible.

So also with the attribute, omniscience. In two respects it presupposes what no human experience ever manifests. In us conscious experience is conditioned by the possession and use of sense-organs; God, if God there be, must be able to apprehend physical and other existences in some immediate non-sensible manner. Secondly, we have no power of looking into the minds of others, and so of knowing their thoughts and feelings by direct inspection. In this regard also, omniscience is no mere enlargement of our human powers of knowledge. It too is theomorphic; it is conceivable only in a Being who in these fundamental respects is quite other than ourselves; and it therefore presupposes the independently established existence of that Being.

So also with eternity; as predicated of the Divine, it cannot mean merely endurance throughout all time. God, so conceived, would apprehend creaturely existence mainly through memory and foresight. In memory he would reach back into the 'immemorial' past, and through foresight would anticipate the interminable ages still to come. A Being, thus conceived, would be in creaturely subjection to the conditions of time. Should a Being thus situated claim to be Divine, he would be an upstart, posing in a role for which he is unfitted. Either Divine Existence is an utterly incredible mode of Being, or we must be prepared to allow that God transcends the present in some other manner than merely in this human fashion by memory and anticipation. This, I take it, is one main reason why my colleague, Professor Taylor, has recently been maintaining,[1] in agreement with Whitehead, that the problem of time is a central problem in present-day philosophy, and especially in theology. As a clue in terms of which we may endeavour to conceive such transcendence of time, we have the apprehension of the specious present, as in reading a poem or listening to a piece of music—a present which is 'a slab of duration' made up of the just-past and of the not-yet, as well as of the 'actually' present. But the step from durational time to eternity is precisely the step which has to be justified, and for the possibility of which such apprehension, in and by itself, affords no sufficient evidence.

Similarly with the attribute of omnipresence. Admittedly, we can find nothing analogous in the physical realm. Thus should we, speaking in the manner of the older physics, say that ether is present throughout all space, we mean only that its parts are external to one another and that there is enough of it to supply a distinguishable part corresponding

[1] A. E. Taylor, *The Faith of a Moralist* (Macmillan, 1930), i, p. 66; ii, p. 320.

to each distinguishable space. Obviously this is not omnipresence in the theological sense. But neither do we find any sufficient analogy in the dynamical efficacies whereby bodies exert influence on other bodies, or even in the cognitive processes whereby we apprehend what is distant in space and past in time. These are modes not of omnipresence but at most only of compresence; and even so, they rest on a number of highly specific limiting conditions. The step from compresence to omnipresence is again precisely the step that has to be accounted for, and for which our experiences of the creaturely can yet afford no sufficient support.

Thus in respect of each and all the ontological attributes the Divine is not known through analogy with the self, or with any other creaturely mode of existence. These divine attributes *presuppose* God's existence, and save in this reference even their bare possibility cannot be established. If, without any antecedent or independent apprehension of the Divine, we have to start from the creaturely, as exhibited in Nature and in man, and by way of inference and of analogy—on the pattern of what is found in the creaturely—through enlargement or other processes of ideal completion, to construct for ourselves concepts of the Divine, then the sceptics have been in the right; the attempt is an impossible one, condemned to failure from the start. We cannot reach the Divine merely by way of inference, not even if the inference be analogical in character. By no idealization of the creaturely can we transcend the creaturely. To this extent, therefore, Hume's and Kant's negative criticisms of the argument to design must, I am contending, be accepted as unanswerable.

We may now turn to the second main point, the attitude of Hume and Kant to certain immediate experiences which, as they assert, induce belief which is independent of evidence, and which indeed transform the traditional argument from being an argument *to* design into being an argument *from* design. Hume and Kant are here, I shall further contend, guilty of a flagrant inconsistency—an inconsistency due to their failure to clarify their minds in regard to the modes in which the direct contemplation of Nature does and does not reinforce belief in Divine Existence. Faced by Nature and the overwhelming impression which in certain situations it generates in us, they see no option save to cast doubt upon their own conclusions. In Hume this is the less surprising; in his eyes it is merely one more instance of the non-rational character of our natural beliefs, which arise independently of evidence and persist in despite of logical refutation. In Kant, however, it is, I should say, a sheer inconsistency.

To quote from Hume's *Dialogues* the words of Philo—they express, we may believe, the personal attitude of Hume himself:

> You, in particular, Cleanthes, with whom I live in unreserved intimacy; you are sensible that notwithstanding the freedom of my conversation, and my love of singular arguments, no one has a deeper sense of religion impressed on his mind, or pays more profound adoration to the Divine Being, as he discovers himself to reason, in the inexplicable contrivance and artifice of Nature. A purpose, an intention, a design strikes everywhere the most careless, the most stupid thinker; and no man can be so hardened in absurd systems as at all times to reject it.[1]

Kant's statements, while less definite, are in similar terms: '[The argument from design] is the oldest, the clearest, and the best suited to ordinary human reason. It enlivens the study of nature, just as it itself derives its existence and gains ever new vigour from that source.'[2]

The question to be answered is therefore this: how far is it true to say that 'a purpose, an intention, a design [in Nature], strikes everywhere the most careless'? Certainly we receive an overwhelming impression of inexhaustible fertility in the generation of elaborate types of existence, mutually adjusted the one to the other, but of 'a purpose, an intention, a design', surely we have no discernment!

Consider the following comment upon Wordsworth's attitude to Nature:

> The Wordsworthian adoration of Nature has two principal defects. The first . . . is that it is only possible in a country where Nature has been nearly or quite enslaved to man. The second is that it is only possible for those who are prepared to falsify their immediate intuitions of Nature. For Nature, even

---

[1] Op. cit., pt. xii.
[2] *Critique of Pure Reason*, A 623.

in the temperate zone, is always alien and unknown, and occasionally diabolic. . . . [Wordsworth] will not admit that a yellow primrose is simply a yellow primrose—beautiful, but essentially strange, having its own alien life apart. He wants it to possess some sort of soul, to exist humanly, not simply flowerily. . . . Our direct intuitions of Nature tell us that the world is bottomlessly strange; alien, even when it is kind and beautiful; having innumerable modes of being that are not our modes; always mysteriously not personal, not conscious, not moral; often hostile and sinister; sometimes even unimaginably, because inhumanly, evil. . . . A voyage through the tropics would have cured [Wordsworth] of his too easy and comfortable pantheism. A few months in the jungle would have convinced him that the diversity and utter strangeness of Nature are at least as real and significant as its intellectually discovered unity. Nor would he have felt as certain, in the damp and stifling darkness, among the leeches and the malevolently tangled rattans, of the divinely anglican character of that fundamental unity. He would have learned once more to treat Nature naturally, as he treated it in his youth; to react to it spontaneously, loving where love was the appropriate emotion, fearing, hating, fighting whenever Nature presented itself to his intuition as being, not merely strange, but hostile, inhumanly evil. . . . Europe is so well gardened that it resembles a work of art. . . . Man has re-created Europe in his own image. Its tamed and temperate Nature confirmed Wordsworth in his philosophizings.[1]

Hume (again in the person of Philo) can be cited against himself:

Look around this Universe. What an immense profusion of beings, animated and organized, sensible and active! You admire this prodigious variety and fecundity. But inspect a little more narrowly these living existences, the only beings worth regarding. How hostile and destructive to each other! How insufficient all of them for their own happiness! . . . The whole presents nothing but the idea of a blind Nature, impregnated by a great vivifying principle, and pouring forth from her lap, without discernment or parental care, her maimed and abortive children![2]

[1] Aldous Huxley, *Do What You Will* (Chatto & Windus, 1929), p. 116.
[2] Op. cit., pt. xi.

This may be over-statement, but whatever qualifications may have to be made, do we not find ourselves in some degree approving the terms employed? Man himself, like all other animal existences, is a parasite. He lives parasitically upon vegetables and upon other animals; and in their absence could not survive. Bread, which we entitle the staff of life, itself consists of thwarted seed. The practice of the old-time gardener was to plant five seeds in each hole:

> One for the raven, one for the crow,
> Two to die, and one to grow.

There is a passage in Leopardi's *Dialogues*,[1] in which an Icelander who has wandered over the Earth in search of an answer to these and similar questions, propounds them to a Sphinx in the heart of Africa. The answer came in the form of two lions that crept up out of the desert. The beasts were so enfeebled and emaciated with long fasting that they had scarce strength left to devour the Icelander. And even so, he was sustenance to them for only one more day.

As Cardinal Newman has declared in the same general connexion, though more specifically in regard to the world of men: 'All this is a vision to dizzy and appal; and inflicts upon the mind the sense of a profound mystery, which is absolutely beyond human solution.'[2]

Undoubtedly, Hume and Kant are correct in maintaining that when the mind, freed for a time from its practical preoccupations, allows Nature to be the object of its contemplation, then no matter whether it be the complexities of animal existence or of our own bodies, or the immensities of the heavens that occupy our attention, Nature produces an overwhelming impression upon us. As John Stuart Mill has said: 'To a mind thus occupied it seems unutterable presumption in so puny a creature as man to look critically on things so far above him.'[3] Does this amount, however, to the apprehension of 'a purpose, an intention, a design'? That it did so in the minds of Hume and of Kant, their sceptical questionings notwithstanding, there is no reason to doubt. The best possible testimony to the sincerity of their statements is that

---

[1] *Operette Morali* (1928), ed. A. Donati, pp. 81–82.

[2] *Apologia pro Vita Sua* (Longmans, 1864), p. 378.

[3] *Three Essays on Religion* (Longmans, 1874), p. 26.

they were surprised to discover these feelings, and were puzzled as to how they could persist so obstinately when the evidence, impartially considered, points so very definitely in the opposite direction.

But something is evidently wrong in their statement of the situation. How can data which, when impartially considered, are found to be worthless as *evidence* of design, suffice for producing an overwhelming *impression* of design? The answer would seem to be that while undoubtedly Nature produces an impression which is overwhelming, the impression is being misinterpreted when described as being the impression of design. Minds which have been moulded upon the anthropomorphic Deistic ways of thinking so prevalent in the eighteenth century, and which in popular religious circles are still so usual, will indeed be apt to interpret the impression in this fashion. That Hume and Kant should have done so shows the extent to which they were still under their influence. Immediately the tension of their thought was relaxed, the accustomed ways of thinking resumed their sway.

When we turn to the spontaneous utterances of the religious mind, we find quite a different response to the impression made by Nature. We may take as typical the Old Testament writers. As A. B. Davidson has made so convincingly clear in his *Theology of the Old Testament*, 'it never occurred to any prophet or writer of the Old Testament to prove the existence of God.'[1] For them that was quite needless. They moved among ideas that presuppose God's existence—a Being with whom they stood in relations of religious fellowship. This conception of God already possessed is used by them to explain the world. In Davidson's own words:

> The Hebrew thinker came down from his thought of God upon the world; he did not rise from the world up to his thought of God. . . . There seems no passage in the Old Testament which represents men as reaching the knowledge of the existence of God through nature or the events of providence, although there are some passages which imply that false ideas of what God is may be corrected by the observation of nature and life.[2]

[1] Op. cit. (T. & T. Clark, 1904), p. 30.
[2] Op. cit., pp. 32–33.

If we are in danger of likening God to any of his creatures, or of measuring his powers by the powers of man, then the knowledge which we otherwise have 'may be refreshed, and if needful corrected by the contemplation of Nature'.[1] In the words of Isaiah:[2] 'To whom then will ye liken me? . . . Lift up your eyes on high, and see who hath created these, that bringeth out their host by number.' Or as in the 8th Psalm:

> When I consider thy heavens, the work of thy fingers, the moon and the stars, which thou hast ordained; what is man, that thou art mindful of him? and the son of man, that thou visitest him?[3]

But just because their belief in God was not based on evidence obtained by study of Nature and human life, they used it the more freely, and with greater assurance, to interpret both Nature and history. As God is for them the Being upon whom all things are dependent, nothing in Nature or history *can*, on their view, be contrary to his Will. And the facts which they choose to enforce this teaching are often precisely those that are a stumbling-block in the way of any argument to design. In the words of the Psalmist, God creates the darkness 'wherein all the beasts of the forest do creep forth. The young lions roar after their prey, and seek'—precisely Leopardi's counter-instance—'their meat from God'.[4]

As A. B. Davidson has also pointed out,[5] the nearest approach to an argument to design is in a passage in one of the Psalms:[6]

> They break in pieces thy people, O Lord, and afflict thine heritage. They slay the widow and the stranger, and murder the fatherless. And they say, The Lord shall not see, neither shall the God of Jacob consider. Consider, ye brutish among the people: and ye fools, when will ye be wise? He that planted the ear, shall he not hear? He that formed the eye, shall he not see? He that chastiseth the nations, shall he not correct, even he that teacheth man knowledge?

[1] Op. cit., p. 78.
[2] Isa. xl. 25–26. Revised Version.
[3] Ps. viii. 3.
[4] Ps. civ. 20.
[5] Op. cit., pp. 79–80.
[6] Ps. xciv. 5–11. Revised Version.

This is by no means an argument to design. The argument here is that the Being who *has been* able to plant the ear and to form the eye, who *is able* to instruct the nations and to teach men knowledge—all of which is taken as being beyond question—that such a Being must surely be omniscient, with powers which utterly transcend those of any of his creatures.

Hence, too, the kind of facts cited as witness of God's *providential* care. They were so assured of the existence of God, and *therefore* of his providential rule, that in all times of trial and disaster, to however contrary a conclusion the events, taken by themselves, might seem to point, the assurance remained unshaken. Not being obtained by reflection upon the course of events, it could not be overthrown by them.

The position, then, as regards the convictions of religious writers, whether in the Old Testament or elsewhere, is this. In and through their religious experience of fellowship with God, they have belief in God, and coming to Nature and history with this belief in their minds, they interpret Nature and history freely in accordance therewith. They do not observe order and design, and *therefore* infer a Designer: they argue that order and design must be present even where they are not apparent, because all existences other than God have their source in him. They start, that is to say, from an *immediate* experience of the Divine; and only so are their methods of argument and modes of expression possible at all.

Now Hume and Kant entirely overlooked this fundamental difference in standpoint. They took it as a matter of common agreement that there is no immediate experience of the Divine, and that the existence of God must be established, if it is to be established at all, in and through inference, that is, in and through study of what is other than God. And accordingly when they found religious writers interpreting Nature as divinely conditioned, they were confirmed in the view that Nature, in and by itself, yields the impression of intention and design, and in this fashion generates belief. Had they been as thorough in their scepticism as they professed to be, the experiences which they continued to have would have ceased to find lodgment in their minds.

But if the Divine cannot be reached by way of inference, if it cannot be gathered from any antecedent knowledge of the phenomena of

Nature and of the events of history, and if also it cannot be arrived at through analogical reasoning, by magnification of attributes and processes which we experience in the self—if, in other words, it cannot be gathered from any knowledge antecedent to itself—then either we have no right to claim belief in the existence of God, or the one remaining alternative must be accepted, that we experience the Divine in a direct and immediate manner. It is to this alternative that I shall devote my remaining remarks.

'Immediate experience' is a phrase which calls for a good deal of explanation. As a mode of experience, it involves all the conditions that are required for the possibility of experience; and had I in this lecture been engaged in an epistemological discussion much would have to be said in regard to the *a priori* factors which, as I believe, enter into all experience, conferring upon our human consciousness its persistently questioning and characteristically metaphysical outlook. I cannot here do more than indicate, in passing, certain *negative* features of immediate experience.

Immediate experience is not equivalent to exhaustive knowledge. We have, it will probably be granted, immediate experience of the self; and the self, as I have already suggested, is an abidingly mysterious mode of existence.

Nor does it follow that what we immediately experience, we experience in isolation from what is other than itself. We may, or may not, do so. Each of us, for instance, experiences his own body in distinction from the bodies of his fellows. But in regard to the self, it is quite otherwise. If we attempt to isolate the self from all that is other than the self, then, as Kant long ago pointed out, nothing whatsoever is left. Though we experience the self directly, we never experience it sheerly in and by itself. At most we experience situations, past and present, and the self as integral to them; the attempt to locate the self at points within such situations—at points in which nothing but the self is present—is doomed to failure. This, it would seem, is likewise true of our experience of the Divine. We never experience the Divine sheerly in and by itself: we experience the Divine solely through and in connexion with what is other than the Divine.

There is no such temptation in regard to *other* selves, as there is in regard to the self, to hold that we can experience them in isolation. Indeed in the past the tendency has been all the other way. The prevailing view has been that our knowledge of other selves is indirect and inferential, consisting in the interpretation of signs and indications— consisting, indeed, in some mode of reasoning by analogy from the self. Observing the *bodies* of others, and noting that in their actions, as disclosed to us through the senses of sight and hearing, they behave as do we ourselves, we infer—so it is alleged—that accompanying their bodies there are inner conscious experiences analogous to our own. This is the point of view which the argument to design carries over into the theological domain, contending that it is by similar processes of analogical reasoning that we infer the existence of a Divine Being. Now it may be agreed that we do not experience other selves—any more then we experience the self—in isolation from all else, and certainly not independently of their bodily actions; but while doing so, we may still maintain that through, and in connexion with, these bodily activities other selves are experienced with the same immediacy with which we experience the self, our conviction as to their existence being based on directly experienced fellowship, and not upon inference. There is, indeed, growing agreement among philosophical thinkers on this point.

In consequence of this altered theory of knowledge, there is readiness to recognize, as is done by such different thinkers as Cook Wilson, Samuel Alexander, and C. C. J. Webb, that this is likewise true of our experience of the Divine. Should this position be accepted, our grounds for believing in the self, in other selves, and in the Divine will so far be identical in type. In all three cases, the question under discussion will be a *question strictly of fact*—namely, as to whether there is or is not any such type of immediate experience, *not a question as to the adequacy of argument from facts otherwise unquestioned.*

But in restating the issue in this manner, we must at the same time allow that the problems which emerge in connexion with our experience of the Divine are much more difficult than any which arise in connexion with our experience of the self and of other selves. I have already emphasized that what we immediately experience need not be, and indeed, when properly envisaged never is, other than mysterious. If we try to define the nature of the self, or even of natural events, we are at

once in the midst of controversy; immediate experience, while it justifies belief, yields belief only in what, in proportion as we become
enlightened and self-critical in our beliefs, are admittedly highly problematic types of existence. But while this problematic, that is to say,
mysterious character is, so far as regards the self and natural events, a
late discovery, due to philosophical reflection and critical analysis, and
save for occasional experiences in this and that individual, is almost
entirely absent from the minds of the unsophisticated, in the case of
the Divine, from the very start, mystery is a chief and prominent
characteristic.

You are acquainted with the distinction between feeling and emotion.
Feeling, such as pleasure or pain, is in itself a purely subjective experience; emotion implies an objective situation within which there is
something which arouses the emotion, and towards which the emotion
is directed. The Divine is, it would seem, first experienced in such a
situation; and is initially apprehended solely and exclusively as that
which arouses certain types of emotion. If the emotion be awe, then the
Divine is so far apprehended as the awesome, what Otto has so helpfully
entitled the numinous.

Even apart from the *a priori* factors—to which I have already referred,
and which equip the mind for apprehending what is thus experienced—
the considerations involved are extremely complicated. I may draw
attention to four that are of chief importance. First, we have to recognize one main difference between the experience of other selves and the
experience of the Divine. Owing to the fact that we experience other
selves only through, and in connexion with, their bodies, other selves
are experienced by us only in the situations in which these bodies are
found; and whenever these bodies, or the indirect manifestations of
such bodies, are apprehended, we have the immediate experience that
other selves are there. In the case of the Divine, on the other hand, there
are no such *isolable and constant* accompaniments. Potentially any situation may yield an immediate awareness of the Divine; actually there is
no situation whatsoever which invariably yields it.

Secondly, consciousness of the Divine seems to have been first
aroused through, and in connexion with, Nature and its occurrences,
not in connexion with our specifically human modes of life. If we take

Nature not only in its larger physical aspects, but also as exhibited in birth and death, and particularly in the dead body of the once-living man—the object of such awesome dread among primitive peoples—we would seem to be justified in saying that in the beginnings of civilization the natural world alone has the strangeness and mystery, the unfamiliar otherness, in the degree necessary to arouse the religious sentiment. It is only later, through the institution of impressive rites and ceremonies, and through the choice or provision of an artificial environment, such as the cave of Altamira or the temples of Carnac and Stonehenge, that the sentiment is brought under social control, being canalized in the direction of, and aroused in connexion with, the specifically human activities of the group life.

Thirdly, when religion is considered historically, in reference to its origins, we are faced by the strangely ambiguous character of its infant stages. Religion begins as a not very promising, and indeed highly questionable, set of rites and practices. The underlying conception of the Divine is quite indefinite. To quote a description which, according to Marett, is typical and applies almost universally: speaking of the Masai, a people very low in the scale of culture, an authority has said: 'Their conception of the deity seems marvellously vague. I was *Ngai*. My camp was *Ngai*. *Ngai* was in the steaming holds. His house was in the eternal snows of Kilimanjaro. In fact, whatever struck them as strange or incomprehensible, that they at once assumed had some connexion with *Ngai*.'[1] And the initial experience of the Divine is not only thus vague in conception; it is also highly ambiguous in its *practical* bearings. Since it is predominantly emotional, and so is more instinctive than reflective, it easily degenerates into the orgiastic, and tends to excesses and violences of every kind. When other sides of our nature, such as the sexual, join forces with it, it becomes an energy of extraordinarily high potential, and proportionately incalculable in its methods of release. Accordingly it stands in more imperative need of moralization than any other aspect of human life. And just as it starts by being other than morals, so it continues to the end to be more than morals. It has its own independent roots; and it is out of them, not out of morals, though with the favouring aid of morals, that it has to grow.

[1] Quoted by R. R. Marett, *The Threshold of Religion* (Methuen, 1909), p. 12.

Fourthly, religion in any high form comes only late, when through mutual action and reaction religious experiences and social exigencies have, by mutual adaptation each to the other, brought into existence modes of group activity in which a way of life is prescribed to the members of the group—a way of life through which, in virtue of the discipline which it affords, they are given access to certain types of experience not otherwise possible to them—types of experience in which the Divine is apprehended no less directly than in regard to Nature and its occurrences, but which differ in that they reveal the Divine as not merely other than man but also as akin to man. The Mosaic Law of the Hebrews, for instance, with its prescribed ways of life and modes of worship supplied a discipline that made possible a society within which the Prophets could appear—what is specific in their teaching could not have appeared among the Polynesians or even among the Greeks—and could have those experiences in and through which the character of the Divine is further disclosed. The concepts of omnipotence, omniscience, eternity, and omnipresence are not, of course, part of any such experiences, taken in their first immediacy; they are the problematic concepts whereby we endeavour—it may be rightly or it may be wrongly—to define what the immediate experiences are to be taken as revealing. It is precisely in the control of these hazardous processes of interpretation, eventuating in this and that type of theology, that the great religious traditions exercise their distinctive functions; and they do so not merely by the guidance which they afford in matters of theory, but also, in a more radical fashion, by the supplementary, more specific data which they make accessible to us, and in the absence of which our reasoning faculties can have no sufficient material upon which to work.

These statements are too summary to be really definite; but they may suffice to indicate the thesis which is an essential part of my argument—that only by thus assigning a central role to the immediately experienced can we hope satisfactorily to account for the presence of religion already at the very beginnings of human civilization, for the ambiguous character of the first manifestations of religion, and for the part played by institutions and by tradition in determining its higher forms.

I come now to my last point, which is also my main point; it can be quite briefly stated. Though religion of any high type thus comes late, and is made possible only through and in connexion with our specifically human modes of activity, none the less the initial experiences in which religion takes its rise continue to be the source from which we can still best learn, and from which indeed we can alone learn, one all-important side of Divine Existence. It is, we may still maintain, through and in connexion with the *cosmic* setting of our human life, that we can alone experience that aspect of the Divine which is so essential to its credibility, because so essential to its possibility, and which is also required in order to give proper perspective to all our other assertions in regard to the Divine—the otherness, the non-creatureliness, of the Divine, as a Being whose throne is the heavens and whose footstool is the earth. Unless we are to resort to the concept of a finite God—and that by very general agreement is insufficient to meet the needs either of religion or of theology—then by the Divine we must, at the least, mean that upon which all things rest. This is a prime condition required of any Being to which we can legitimately assign the title 'God'; and it is a condition which can be fulfilled only by a Being endowed with attributes other than any to which the creaturely can lay claim. The conception of the Divine as merely other than the creaturely, even if we add that the Divine also conditions all that is creaturely, is in itself, indeed, a jejune and savourless conception. Yet when retained and carried over, in the manner of the higher religions, into further assertions, it is precisely what gives to these further assertions their supreme importance. Admittedly, power is not the highest of the Divine attributes. None the less it is fundamental since only on the basis of such power can the other attributes have a sufficing efficacy—an efficacy which will justify us in looking for them alike in the works of Nature and in those of Grace. They are deeply hidden, and there may not be in us the virtue to discern them; none the less, relying on such powers, we may still be justified in proceeding on the assumption of their universal presence. Certainly the Divine, to justify the title, must possess such further attributes— attributes in which the Divine exhibits kinship with man—but even these are *divine* attributes only as being the attributes of a *Divine Being*; and so again we are brought back to the non-creatureliness, that is, to the otherness of God, as that in reference to which alone any such assertions are legitimate and have meaning. And there is, I have argued, no other path to the apprehension of *this* aspect of Divine Existence save that by which it first breaks in upon the consciousness of man, namely, in connexion with the inexhaustibly varied, infinitely vast, and profoundly mysterious natural order, of which we are integral constituents and whereby we are upheld. To quote a favourite saying of Baron von Hügel: 'God is the God of Nature as of Grace. He provides the meal as well as the yeast.'

The answer to my question is therefore this: Divine Existence is more than merely credible: it is immediately experienced; and is experienced in increasing degree in proportion as the individual, under the discipline and through the way of life prescribed by religion in this or that of its great traditional forms, is enabled to supplement his initial experiences by others of a more definite character. And in Divine Existence, as thus revealed, the non-creatureliness, that is, the otherness of God, is fundamental, as that under assumption of which alone any further, more specific assertions can be made.

Henri Bergson, Mem.F.A., Hon.F.R.S.E.

HENRI BERGSON died in Paris on 5 January 1941, in his eighty-second year. He had a twofold association with Edinburgh: in 1913 he gave the series of Gifford Lectures, and in 1923 he was elected Honorary Fellow.

Bergson's parents were of British nationality. His father was a Jew, a musician by profession, and his mother English. It has been stated—with what truth I have not been able to verify—that there was a Polish strain in his father's ancestry and both an Irish and a Jewish strain in his mother's ancestry. Born, however, in Paris (18 October 1859), he was educated, with only brief residence in London, at the Lycée Condorcet, where he distinguished himself in classics and in mathematics. His first published work was the solution of a mathematical problem, printed in the *Annales mathématiques* in 1878. After hesitating between the faculties of Letters and Science, Bergson entered the École Normale on the classical side, obtaining special distinction as a Hellenist; and it was to the teaching of philosophy in Lycées, first in the provinces and later in Paris, that he devoted the next sixteen years of his life. In 1897 he was appointed to a Chair at the École Normale, and in 1900 transferred to a Chair in the Collège de France. Almost every possible academic honour came to him in due course, including election to the French Academy in 1914, and the award of the Nobel Prize for Literature in 1927.

Bergson established his philosophical reputation by what still remains the most original and important of all his writings, the work which he submitted as a doctorate thesis in 1887: *Essai sur les données immédiates de la conscience*. The philosophy of Herbert Spencer was then still in the heyday of its popular influence; and it was by questioning one of

398

Spencer's fundamental presuppositions that Bergson made entry into his own philosophy. On Spencer's view, time is an independent variable; physical and biological evolution might, conceivably, in all its sequential detail and without essential distortion, have taken place, not in the millennial periods which it has in fact occupied, but in the infinitely divisible periods yielded by even the 'shortest' time. In direct opposition Bergson formulated a doctrine of *durée réelle*.

Some one philosophical problem is made central, to the deliberate exclusion of others, in each of Bergson's chief writings; and in his second main work—*Matière et Mémoire* (1896)—he concentrated on the problems of mind–body relation, treating them in a Cartesian dualistic manner which seemed to rule out as erroneous any conception of 'the living' as in any manner or degree mediating between the physical and the psychical. His disciples were accordingly faced with many surprises when, eleven years later (1907), he published *L'Évolution Créatrice*, the more so that the highly coloured metaphorical modes of expression in which he there so freely indulges, while certainly one of the reasons why this work has proved the most popular of all his writings, are more disconcerting than helpful to the more careful of his readers. Contrary to popular belief, his teaching has no true affinity with the anti-rationalist schools of philosophy, such as that of Georges Sorel, which have claimed him as their Master. It is the indiscretions—as in his equating of 'intuition' with 'instinct'—not the insights in Bergson's teaching, which they have underlined and developed.

Unhappily, a chronic condition of semi-invalidism prevented Bergson from expounding his philosophy in more systematic form. It was only through a triumph of mind over body that twenty-five years later (1932) he contrived to complete his fourth main work, *Les Deux Sources de la Morale et de la Religion*; and, as he frankly recognized, the teaching which it contains calls for a reconsideration of many of his earlier utterances. All that he could himself do, in aid of this revision, was to edit, under the title *La Pensée et le Mouvant* (1935), a series of essays and addresses in which he has drawn attention to what he regarded as fundamental in his teaching, and in which he has also been concerned to give a carefully balanced restatement of his views on the capacities and limits of discursive reason. It is probably true to say that Bergson, so 'perilously popular' in the years immediately subsequent to the publication of his *L'Évolution Créatrice*, has not even yet rightly come into his own, and that he will not do so until he has been read backwards, in the light of his own later comments on his earlier writings.

When the Vichy authorities in 1940 introduced racial discrimination, on the Nazi model, Bergson was exempted, in recognition of his services to French and European culture. He refused, however, to be thus dissociated from his Jewish compatriots. One of his last acts was to report himself with them, invalid as he was, in his dressing-gown, at the police station.

Bergson's Manner of Approach to Moral and Social Questions

HOW great is the contrast between the immense prestige of Bergson in the years 1910–1925 and the present somewhat tepid interest in his writings! There are two quite good reasons why this change has come about. The interest of the general reader was awakened by, and for the most part based on, the least original of his works, his *L'Évolution Créatrice*, published in 1907. The most important of his earlier writings, *Les Données Immédiates de la Conscience*, was known only through the popularized versions which professed to expound it. Contrary to popular belief, his teaching had no true affinity with the anti-rationalist schools of philosophy, such as that of Georges Sorel, which claimed Bergson as their master. It is Bergson's indiscretions—as in his equating of intuitive awareness with instinct—not the insights in Bergson's teaching, that have been underlined and developed.

Secondly, a chronic condition of semi-invalidism prevented Bergson from expounding his philosophy in more systematic form. It was only through a triumph of mind over body that, twenty-five years later in 1932, he published his next main work, *Les Deux Sources de la Morale et de la Religion*; and as he frankly recognized, the teaching which it contains calls for a reconsideration of several of his earlier utterances. All that he could himself do, in aid of revision, during the years that remained to him, was to edit under the title *La Pensée et le mouvant*, a series of essays and addresses in which he has drawn attention to what he regarded as fundamental in his teaching, and in which he has also been concerned to give a carefully balanced restatement of his views on the capacities and limits of discursive reason. It is probably true to say that Bergson, so 'perilously popular' in the years immediately subsequent to the publication of his *L'Évolution Créatrice*, has not even yet rightly come into his own, and that he will not do so until he has been read backwards, in the light of his own final comments on his earlier writings.

One further remark of a general kind. The markedly dualistic character of Bergson's ethical teaching, as expounded in his last main work, enables us to apprehend more clearly what his previous writings had already seemed to indicate, namely, that his metaphysic, so far as he claims to have a metaphysic, is neo-Platonic in character. In solving his problems he resorts to a supra-naturalism of an extreme type—a supra-naturalism so extreme that for him, as for the neo-Platonists, the difficulty is to secure for the natural a character sufficiently positive to permit of its being receptive of the supra-natural and not merely resistent of it.

What I now propose doing in this address is to limit myself to a discussion of the central thesis of Bergson's ethical teaching. Whether or not we can agree with his teaching—and I find myself unable to do so—we can all of us, I think, recognize that it is quite peculiarly relevant to the issues that face us in these present difficult days. There are, Bergson contends, two types of moral obligation—natural obligation and spiritual obligation. Natural obligation he traces to the non-moral pressure of natural necessities, spiritual obligation to our intuitive apprehension of spiritual goods, i.e., of the value-factors in experience, aesthetic, moral and religious. Natural obligation, when acting by itself, gives rise, he says, to a static morality; spiritual obligation makes possible a creative morality.

To illustrate. Nature prescribed that each human being must be either male or female, that he must spend a certain proportion of his day in sleep, that he must secure a sufficiency of food for the maintenance of his body in health and vigour, that he must agree with his fellows in a code of behaviour, a code which may take various forms, but which in whatever form it is developed must, as a minimum requirement, be for each group relatively fixed and generally conformed to.

These do not, however, exhaust the natural necessities. Nature, in creating man as a social species, has created him in groups which act as groups, in competition with other similar groups, and under conditions which have made war, with all its allied forms of rivalry and strife, inevitable. The lower animals are created under conditions which constrain them to have as their food other living species. It is the very nature of animal life to destroy life; life, as we find it in the world around us, is only possible in and through such self-conflict. Similarly man comes into being in circumstances which leave him no alternative save to attack, and to defend himself against, other beings, human like himself. It is this basis of natural necessity which has made so imperative those social duties which find their field of exercise in the carrying out of the blood-feud code, in inter-tribal warfare, and the like.

Common to all the specifically human forms of natural necessity is the manner in which nature, while prescribing certain general requirements, leaves the individual, or at least the group, free to operate them in very various ways. In this regard the customs of a society and its moral code are comparable to its language. Language is a product of usage; nothing in its vocabulary or syntax comes from nature; it is a body of agreed conventions, any one of which is more or less arbitrary, and could well be otherwise. What is inexorably exacted is that in each group there should be that amount of common usage and agreed practice which is necessary, if there is to be a language serving the purposes of intercommunication. In its absence the group would perish.

Similarly as regards the *modes* of warfare, the *times* and *occasions* for warfare. These vary from one tribe to another, from one continent to another; man in his changing moods and changing conditions may act now in this way and now in that; but in all past stages of civilization each group has had to accept the duties and obligations of warlike defence and attack. Where they have been shirked or ineffectively discharged, the group has perished, either completely, or by incorporation in a larger group, in which the natural duties have been more wholeheartedly observed.

These requirements of natural necessity may be fulfilled either instinctively or intelligently; and as civilization advances, the part played by critical intelligence becomes more and more important. Since natural obligation acts by way of conscious awareness, the alternatives left open by nature are weighed against one another; and under favouring conditions established customs, in proportion as they can be recognized as ineffective or self-defeating, come to be modified. Such criticism, however, is strictly limited in its scope. Nature has fixed the ends; intelligence can judge only of the suitability and effectiveness of the means employed; there is improvement in the adjustment of means to ends, that is, in the technique of life; there is no fundamental alteration in the quality of the life itself.

This, then, is one type of obligation. Such obligation, Bergson argues, is the form which natural necessity takes when it operates in and through choice. Consequently, it is the form which natural necessity takes in the case of man. Nature, while leaving man the choice between alternatives, predetermines the range of the alternatives.

The human situation involves, however, as Bergson proceeds to point out, further factors, which cause stresses and strains of a very different type, alike within the limits of the natural situations, and in respect of these limits. Alongside the natural ends appear those aspirations which are awakened by the discernment of spiritual values; and with these also reason has to reckon.

For man, as a child of nature, war is a necessity. He may regard it as a good or as an evil—according to circumstance he regards it as partly the one and partly the other—but has to accept it as an integral factor in the kind of life which he has no option save to lead. On the other hand, for man, as a creature stirred by aspiration, war can come to be regarded as morally evil, and from which he is therefore bound in duty to abstain. The two types of obligation then clash; and man as a reasoning animal, discerning the conflict, finds that his freedom is not merely that of intelligent choice as regards the means to be employed in forwarding natural ends, but a freedom to criticize nature, and so far as may be practicable to circumvent it, achieving purposes of an order other than, and it may be, in conflict with, nature's own.

As we have seen, among the natural necessities is the requirement that man be social in his habits and customs. To what type of society are we here referring? Is it closed or open? Is it a group in rivalry with other groups, or is it a society co-extensive with mankind? To put the question more definitely, when we accept as a fundamental requirement of social life the duty of respecting the life and property of others, of what society are we speaking? Before attempting to reply Bergson would have us consider what happens in time of war. Slaughter and pillage, as also perfidy, fraud and lying, not only become permissible, they are meritorious. For the belligerents, as for the witches in *Macbeth*, 'fair is foul, and foul is fair'. Would this be possible, would the transformation operate so easily and so generally, if the duties which society has been recommending were duties of man to man? It may, of course, be argued that *in principle* they are duties towards society at large, and that only the exceptional character of circumstance from time to time suspends their operation. But if so, how are we to explain that peace has always hitherto been a preparation for war?

Moralists, Bergson argues, have been misled, on the one hand by their failure to distinguish between natural and spiritual obligation; and on the other hand by a misunderstanding of the empirical fact, to which history bears witness, that, as civilization develops, larger and larger societies come to be formed, and that in conformity therewith the range of our sympathies is progressively widened.

To take the second set of considerations first: moralists have argued that just as apprenticeship for the civic virtues is secured in the family, so in love of the fatherland there is being prepared love towards mankind. The argument is, Bergson points out, *a priori* and intellectualist in character. It is noted that the three groups, the family, the nation, mankind, include an increasing number of individuals, and from this the conclusion is drawn that corresponding to the successive enlargement of the object cherished, there corresponds a progressive widening of sentiment. The first part of the reasoning is in agreement with fact; and civic virtues *are* closely bound up with the domestic virtues; and this for the very good reason that the family and society, indistinguishable in their origins, have remained in close connexion. But between the society in which we live and humanity in general, there is the distance that separates the finite from the indefinite, the closed from the open, and the difference between the two, Bergson argues, is a difference of nature, and not simply of degree. This, he claims, is confirmed, when we examine the states of mind corresponding to the two sentiments, attachment to fatherland and love of humanity. The one is rooted in the natural conditions of our life. It enlists the combative and acquisitive instincts in its support; and save as thus strengthened would fail to fulfil its natural ends. As a rule, it is most strongly felt when its interests are threatened by other units of the same type. By contrast, the love of humanity is indirect and acquired.

This brings us to the second cause of misunderstanding—failure to distinguish between natural and spiritual obligation. The patriotic sentiments, as has just been pointed out, are articulated and intensified by the combative and acquisitive instincts which are fed and favoured by the closed type of society. Love of humanity on the other hand, is arrived at by an indirect path—primarily, in the history of mankind, through religion, that is, by recognition that all men stand in the same relation to God, and that in this relation each has a worth which does not rest on natural conditions, and is unaffected by social or other natural differences. Reason, if it bases its argument upon recognition of spiritual values, may confirm these conclusions, setting aside all differences of sex, colour, race, and natural capacities, as being of quite secondary importance compared to the dignity native to man as man, and so claiming for all men the respect due to such dignity. But whichever language be used, whether that of religion or that of philosophy, we do not, Bergson contends, arrive at humanity by stages, passing to it by way of the family and the State; we pass to it at a leap, and in being carried to it we are also carried beyond it to the Divine, or failing that, to values which are self-justifying. Humanity is not simply the city or State enlarged. The obligation appealed to is other than that which has its roots in the natural necessities of family and group life.

The conception of justice, which incorporates in itself so many of our other moral concepts, and which consequently expresses itself in a great variety of ways, is, Bergson contends, peculiarly instructive in regard to the interrelations of the two forms of obligation. Justice is symbolized by a balance, evoking ideas of regularity, proportion, compensation. One of its earliest expressions is 'an eye for an eye, a tooth for a tooth'. In primitive societies, however, this recognition of equality is limited in two ways. In the first place, it is applicable only within some group, and not to individuals outside the group; it is considered just to discriminate between fellow-tribesmen and strangers. And in the second place, within the group there are differences of status and class; and justice is conceived as proportioning itself to these differences—the law of justice being formulated as that of equals to equals, and of unequals to unequals—what is just conduct to a slave or to a social inferior being different from what is due to an equal.

In all such cases the mode of formulation is determined by the prevailing natural necessities. In a society in which slavery is a recognized institution, justice must be so defined as to authorize, and indeed to impose, on the free men the duties involved in upholding it, as, for instance, the duty of returning runaway slaves. Similarly in a society in which war is a recognized institution, justice must be so defined as not merely to allow of war, but as imposing on the individual the duties required, alike in the preparation for war, and in the carrying on of war. Thus conceived, justice is one obligation among others; and like the others its limits are predetermined by natural necessities. It is the pressure of natural necessities which makes it obligatory in these forms.

Bergson asks us to contrast with these definitions of justice the concept of justice which emerges when natural necessities of every kind are ruled out, and spiritual values are alone appealed to, men being conceived as having rights which no natural necessity can ever justify us in violating. This, as Bergson points out, is the old-time question: what would we do if we learned that for the safety of the State, or even for the very existence of humanity, an innocent man—he may, if we please so to suppose, be of another race, and of a lower civilization—has been condemned to suffer eternal torments? Could we consent to this? Would we not have to say: let the State, or even humanity, perish, rather than that the innocent man be condemned?

What, then, has happened? How has justice, which previously was one obligation on a level with others, interior, as it were, to society, and limited by its necessities—how has justice come to have this categorical and transcendent authority, hovering above society, independent of, and superior to, social exigencies of every kind? How came this attitude to be adopted, as historically it seems first to have been adopted, in the religious sphere by the Hebrew prophets, and in the philosophical field by Socrates and Plato?

And is it not the gate, upon the opening of which the road has led to the abolition of slavery, and at the present time to the endeavour to abolish poverty and the allied forms of economic servitude, and through

limitation of national sovereignties to end war and its concomitant evils?
Are we here inaugurating a new dispensation? Is closed morality yielding place to morality of a creative type? Is spiritual obligation, in
attaining its majority, becoming the sole sovereignty, to the complete
displacement of social necessities of every kind? Is obligation now on the
way to be single, and purely spiritual, and not as previously a hybrid
amalgam of natural necessity and moral choice?

Bergson, in distinguishing between the obligations due to natural
necessities and the obligations due to spiritual values, has, it may be
observed, described both as being *moral* obligations, and having done so,
proceeds to set them in opposition to one another, and to trace to this
opposition his further distinction between static and creative morality.
Morality, it is thus implied, exists in two opposite modes; and so far as
they can be defined in distinction from one another, they are opposed as
the purely natural and the sheerly spiritual—the static and the creative.
Static morality, in Bergson's view, consists in taking moral advantage of
the possibilities left open by the natural necessities. Creative morality,
on the other hand, signifies for Bergson moral action which is so
directed as to make new alternatives possible for the first time.

There are many indications in the course of Bergson's book, that he
is conscious of the doubtfully legitimate character of this distinction,
and of the many difficulties which lie in its way. But in the moral, as
in the natural sphere, a dualism he must have at whatever cost. Otherwise his neo-Platonic supra-naturalism will fail to work. Accordingly,
in the moral sphere, he ascribes to the non-moral factors in moral situations precisely those functions which he has ascribed to matter in the
biological sphere. Just as he has maintained that the materiality of an
organism does not represent a sum of means employed but a sum of
obstacles avoided, so he here maintains that spirit can discover itself only
in and through *antagonism* to the natural conditions under which it is
coming to its own. And here also, in his attempt to justify this thesis,
he has to allow to the negating factors a much more positive nature than
his ultimate convictions would seem to justify him in doing.

But I do not wish to enter further into Bergson's metaphysics. That
would carry us too far afield, and also would involve a discussion of his
view of religion. Keeping to my main problem, that part played by the

non-moral factors in moral situations, Bergson's thesis—if I may re-capitulate—is twofold: first, that moral obligation is dual, not single in type, that non-moral, natural necessities, give rise to a type of obligation upon which a static morality is based, and that the spiritual values give rise to a very different type of obligation, upon which a creative morality is based. And then, secondly, as implied in this thesis, the further thesis that there are values which can be determined in complete abstraction from natural necessities of every kind.

Neither thesis seems to me to be tenable. Natural necessities, it is agreed, enter into *certain* moral situations. Must we not recognize that they enter into every situation that is in any degree moral? If so, a morality based exclusively on natural necessities, and a morality con-ceived as emancipated from all such necessities, are alike fictitious, and are out of keeping with the actual facts of the moral life. Man is an amphibious being, and his nature is no less violated in the futile endea-vour to be sheerly spiritual, than in any undue preoccupation with the merely animal. Morality precisely consists in the tensions due to the constant presence of the twofold factors.

Some of you may recall the following passage in Aldous Huxley's Preface to his edition of the *Letters of D. H. Lawrence*: 'Pascal was horrified that human beings could so far forget the infinite and eternal as to "dance and play the lute and sing and make verses". Lawrence was no less appalled that they could so far forget the delights and difficulties of immediate living as to remember eternity and infinity.' Lawrence, I take it, was not asserting that true delight comes only when the infinite is shut out and forgotten. The eternal and infinite are, he holds, to be found, not by turning our backs upon the immediate, but only in and through the immediate, which is always freighted with what is more than simply itself. Unless we 'dance and play the lute and sing and make verses', or indulge in some other appropriate activity, how is the eternal to find opportunity of revealing itself to us?

To put my point in yet another way. What I wish to argue, as against Bergson, is that *all* moral choices, not merely certain of them, are in some measure *forced* choices; and that all choices, *however forced*, are at the same time based on appreciation of values.

Consider the evidence of history. St. Paul found no alternative save to accept the institution of slavery as an integral part of the established order of society, just as he had to accept so much else in it. Was this, in his view, a mere acceptance of natural necessity? And did it consequently commit him to a morality static in type? The answer, surely, is in the negative. Had St. Paul propounded a revolutionary programme, calling for the rule of the Saints, and the immediate establishment of an equalitarian communistic order of society, would not Christianity have proved false to its own lights? Would it then have been other than a form of fanaticism—a grasping at more than it could have had the moral resources to achieve, or rather a grasping at the lesser ends under the illusion that they were the greater? St. Paul, and the groups which he established, believed themselves to be *justified* in accepting the institution of slavery. The established order of society was, in their view, the arena within which, in the wisdom of Providence, the moral and religious life could alone be lived. The willing acceptance of the relation of master and slave, and the working of it in a humane and worthy manner were, in their view, moral duties.

So long as the groups of Christians scattered throughout the cities of the Roman Empire held themselves apart from the general life, and from the responsibilities of government, this attitude was admirably suited to their needs. In recognizing the established institutions, they could still urge that they must be humanized in accordance with Christian standards. In their own ranks, as fellow-Christians, bond and free were equal in standing; the relation of master and slave, like that of father and son, was a relation between moral beings: and for it there was, therefore, by admission, in all cases a morally right and a morally wrong way of treating it. This is the standpoint of Christian patriarchalism—a type of social ethics which attained its full development only under feudal conditions in the Middle Ages.

It was not until the Christian groups combined to form a Church, and the Church to ally itself with the State, that the consequences which follow from this attitude were explicitly recognized. Since the Church then became responsible for the spiritual guidance of the State, it had to justify the State institutions by sanctions compatible with its own teaching. The rationalization adopted was, of course, a rationalization by means of the doctrine of original sin. Owing to the consequences of the Fall, we have to live—so it was argued—under conditions which are undeniably evil—the signs, indeed, of moral evil. From the point of view of the Sermon on the Mount, the enslaving of a fellow-man stands condemned; yet none the less the institution of slavery, a consequence of our continuing sinful estate, is, it was held, a social necessity, and as such must be recognized and worked.

This, clearly, is an insufficient rationalization. Accepting the doctrine of original sin, and combining it with a belief in Divine Providence, the Church became quietist and ultra-conservative in its social teaching, endeavouring indeed, to humanize slavery and to humanize war, but denouncing as immoral any attempt on the part of the slave to vindicate his freedom, or of the free man to withhold his services in preparing for, or carrying on, war.

This, however, it will be observed, involved no acceptance of the institutions as merely and solely due to natural necessity; the grounds of acceptance—whether sufficient or insufficient I am not at present discussing—were as genuinely moral as the grounds upon which the further, consequent choices had to be made. But the acceptance was a *forced* acceptance. For the alternative, it was believed, is not a situation without slavery and without war, but a situation in which existing society, if not accepted and loyally worked by us, would come to exhibit even worse evils, and even perhaps dissolve in complete anarchy.

This conservative position, was, in some degree, qualified by the various opportunities which the Church provided for those who found the prescribed social duties uncongenial or intolerable, and who in revulsion against the evils of the general life felt called upon to conform their lives more closely to the ideal morality of the Sermon on the Mount. This seems to have been a main reason for the rise of monasticism. It is not sufficient to trace the spread of monastic institutions to a supposed wave of asceticism. This asceticism was itself due to the demand for a way of life more consistent with itself than any possible in the social conditions then prevailing.

But this too was a quietist method of meeting the difficulties. The world with its institutions and practices was allowed to be beyond remedy; its compromises, it was believed, could not be challenged within their own sphere. Two moralities were recognized as legitimate and right—one for those who live in the world, another for those who seek to anticipate the future life, by living apart, as witnesses of the higher life rendered impracticable by the Fall. Accordingly, in the Medieval Church not even the Saints challenged the established institutions, though in their ideals, as in their own persons, they sought to prefigure a higher order than these institutions allowed.

Thus, so long as natural factors were regarded as prescribed and un-changeable, there was a moral responsibility, not only to endure them, but also to make them inwardly fruitful: the acceptance, that is to say, could be a moral acceptance, and be accompanied by every effort to extract advantage, not in spite of, but precisely by means of, what was thus viewed as outside human control.

If, however, the non-moral factors can be regarded as modifiable, we are morally responsible for attempting or not attempting to alter their character. Their capacity for modification is as natural to them as any present modes in which they exist. And hence arose a second type of attitude—the sectarian, revolutionary type of attitude. Instead of shouldering the responsibilities involved in the existing social situation, the individual set up standards which condemned certain of the duties which society exacted, and retreating into a group, either held himself apart, or actively attacked the society for acquiescing in the supposed necessities and the duties following thereupon.

The objection to this attitude is that so long as the wider society persists, the sect or group is living parasitically, benefiting by the protec-tion of the society which it is refusing to uphold. This, however, in the view of the smaller group, is no sufficient objection; for it believes that it is conferring greater benefits than it is receiving, namely, in offering society the opportunity of so remodelling itself that its ends can be achieved without the evils against which the sect is protesting.

But this revolutionary attitude, no less than the conservative, is the outcome of *forced* choice. The individual is faced by the alternatives, either acceptance of what in his view moral standards condemn, or dissociation from the general life around him, and the impoverishment of life which this involves. For not only does he lose by segregation among the like-minded, with diminished contacts with types other than his own, he also incurs new dangers to himself and to society. To himself, in that he has to dispense with the discipline proper to ordinary life, namely that gained through working unsatisfactory conditions while still holding to the ideals with which they conflict. If the quietist, conservative attitude tends to blunt conscience, the absence of those duties, often disconcerting and humiliating, may tend to self-righteousness and to sentimentalism. Also the sectarian must often have it brought home to him—as in the case, say, of Gandhi—that in proportion as he fails to influence society at large, the general effect of his criticisms, especially when they are quite radical criticisms, is to weaken the social sanctions generally, and so, in proportion as they fail, to lead towards anarchy.

To come now to Bergson's second thesis; that there are values purely and sheerly spiritual. It is closely bound up with his conviction that all our human activities, when at their highest, that is to say, in proportion as they are truly creative, are then, however purposive, without foresight. The insights which guide them are due, he declares, to supranatural influences breaking in upon the normal course of our usual activities. As Bergson emphasizes, this first befalls some one individual, the prophet or leader. From him the influence spreads to a group, and through the group to some larger society, to a sect, a church, or a nation—even, it may be, beyond all societies to humanity at large.

In this teaching, Bergson seems to me to be unduly influenced by the conclusions which he has previously arrived at in other fields, and to be supporting them in this new field by arguments which he could hardly have regarded as sufficient, had he been approaching the questions without previous commitments. In his earlier teaching Bergson has declared that foresight is possible only when the ends pursued are predetermined: free creative activity must, he holds, be lacking in foresight. But he is not on this account tempted to deny that reality can and does constantly emerge into novelty; on the contrary, he maintains that the gates of the future are so wide open that we can have no ground for asserting anything to be either possible or impossible until it has occurred. It is, Bergson tells us, an illusion that there is, in addition to the actual, any such thing as the possible. Prior to actualization, it is, so to speak, only possibly possible. When the future has through creative activities been rendered actual, it casts back into the past the mirage of its own possibility; and so leads us, if we be not careful in observation, to believe that, had our previous experience been more extensive, we could have anticipated the future prior to its arrival. In Bergson's view, there must always therefore—to make an activity creative—be something which cannot be anticipated through any possible insight into the antecedently known conditions.

Then further—and this is the part of Bergson's teaching which I am most concerned to question—what is new is traceable, he declares, not to anything positive in the natural constituents of the situation, but solely and exclusively to an incursion, from above, of some factor or factors sheerly spiritual in character. Must we not maintain, in opposition to such contentions, that in mastery of natural necessities, the inspiration comes quite as much through new possibilities detected in these necessities as through the spiritual values to which we are endeavouring to give embodiment by their means?

Bergson, I should contend, fails to distinguish between ideals and utopias, or in other words, between ends which are schematic and formal, and those which are concrete and specific. An ideal, strictly and properly regarded, is not a programme that specifies and predetermines the goal to be reached, in the manner in which a utopia specifies what is sought ahead of its actualization. An ideal, that is to say, is not analogous to the plans supplied by an architect to a contractor. The ideal is that which, while the mind of the architect is occupied with the concrete conditions to be met and satisfied—the ideal is that which, *while he is so occupied*, keeps him persistently in search of a solution which in satisfying all of these prescribed conditions will also satisfy his more general demands for effectiveness and beauty. In discovering a satisfying solution, the contingencies and natural necessities play—do they not?—a no less essential part than do the ideal factors strictly so called.

I am the more interested to press these criticisms, because otherwise I find myself in sympathy with Bergson's plea that we recognize, as fundamental in all situations, the presence of the supra-natural, or at least of the supra-physical. I cannot myself even begin to understand, philosophically, any naturalistic doctrine of emergent evolution, any doctrine which regards the spiritual as having first come into being out of conditions not themselves spiritual in character. But equally I am unable to understand or find grounds for any type of teaching which seeks to define itself in a dualistic manner, in isolation from, or in sheer antagonism to, the natural conditions of our human life. Is not the presence of the supra-natural or spiritual vouched for by what is characteristic of the moral life on all its levels—namely, by the feature of *obligation*? If obligation is not of two types but is uniform with itself throughout; if in all its modes it has an obligatoriness, an absoluteness other than that of any natural necessity; and if, further, obligation is a feature of total situations, and not determinable by reference to any single factors within the situations, then we shall have to recognize that the supra-natural acts through the pressure of natural necessities, as well as through spiritual values, and that in the presence of natural necessities we are therefore already in contact with what is likewise drawing us to itself from in front. Either this, or what he is entitling the supra-natural is non-existent.

Bergson argues that in recognizing duties to man as man, we are making an absolute break with natural conditions. My contention has been that, in so arguing, Bergson is viewing the positive *modification* of natural necessities as if it were an *elimination* of them. Should, for instance, war be eliminated as between States, this would be analogous to many similar changes which have been successfully brought about in the past. We should still have to reckon with force and with strife. Within the State they exhibit their continuing presence in the functions of Courts of Justice and of the police; between nations they would still have to be reckoned with in some similar fashion. Strife and rivalry may in themselves be genuine goods. Even forceful compulsion, provided it be moralized, is not an evil; it is only a lesser good.

The relation of the artist to his materials is a fitting analogy. His materials are recalcitrant, and their resistance is what necessitates the labours which are only now and then successful. But none the less the contribution made by the materials is positive in character—as positive as are the ideal factors which keep the artist persistently active in face of defeat. So, to repeat my conclusion: when we seek to determine the nature of obligation, we find that while obligation is in itself single and uniform, being a feature of total situations, and not adequately determinable by reference to any single factors within the situations, it acts always through a twofold simultaneous influence, natural and spiritual. It is only in the stress of natural necessities that we can ever succeed in obtaining effective contact with that which is likewise drawing us to itself from in front, i.e., through the values to which we have access in conscious awareness.

Our moral obligation is, in all cases, that of moralizing existing situations, whatever these situations may be; and the specific nature of the duties to which we are obliged is therefore determined, and rightly determined, by the non-moral factors as well as by the spiritual values which claim to control them.

Fear: its Nature and Diverse Uses

> 'Fear has an ambivalent character, it may be beneficent or malignant, it may be Jekyll or Hyde.' D. K. HENDERSON, *Psychopathic States* (1939, p. 115).

THE 'Hyde' character of fear has been so widely, and generally so exclusively, dwelt upon, that a review of what can be truthfully said in praise of its 'Jekyll' character is, I trust, not untimely. I shall proceed on the assumption that all the natural passions, without exception, are essential, ineradicable factors in our human make-up, each allowing of both use and abuse. This, as I shall endeavour to show, is no less true of fear than of what we quite justly call the higher emotions.

Fear and unsatisfied desire are, it has been said, the twin sources of all unhappiness; and there are those who would represent fear as being the more formidable of the two evils, both as leading us astray in our pursuit of happiness, and as incapacitating us from enjoying it when brought within our grasp.

There are two periods in the world's history when this question has bulked very largely, alike in popular thought and in philosophical controversy—the Hellenistic period in the ancient world and the Enlightenment period in the modern world. In the Hellenistic period there is practical unanimity—not surprising in view of the political and religious conditions of the centuries before and after the birth of Christ —that fear is a main source of evil. The Stoics, it is true, gave it second place: it is easier, they seem to have believed, to subjugate fear than to satisfy desire. The Epicureans, on the other hand, as naturally followed from their hedonistic standpoint, had no manner of doubt to which of the two sources of evil to assign the primacy, as is indicated by the refrain that recurs throughout Lucretius' poem, and which we meet again, in heightened form, in Montaigne's declaration—surprising, surely, as coming from Montaigne—'the thing in the world I am most afraid of is fear'.

A very similar attitude was adopted in the seventeenth and eighteenth centuries by those English and French thinkers who represented the newer tendencies of the times. While agreeing with traditional teaching so far as to hold that human nature in its existing forms is perverted and distraught, they singled out as the instrument of such perversion not pride, or love of power, or love of pleasure, but the obsessive and debasing influence of fear. Fear, in its present intensity, they maintained, is an extraneous influence generated in us by the agency of political institutions and of educational methods devised in the interest of kings and statesmen, and has been further unnaturally stimulated by the superstitious inventions of their allies, the priests.

Some of the responsibility for this teaching must be recognized as having lain with the representatives of the traditional views. And in especial we have to take into account the maleficent influence exercised by Hobbes. For it was Hobbes who, in upholding the old-time views, rested them upon a psychology in which fear, in its lower and least worthy forms, plays the leading part.

> Hobbes got over the psychological facts which told against him either by treating them as exceptional, or by classifying every disposition which can restrain men from unsocial conduct as a form of fear. 'Pity ariseth from the imagination that the like calamity may befall himself', the 'fear of things invisible is the natural seed of that which every man in himself calleth religion, and in them that worship or fear that power otherwise than they do, superstition.'[1]

But to keep meantime to the Enlightenment thinkers. With few exceptions—Hume being one of the exceptions—they had but little understanding of the part played in the mental life by instinct and emotion. Emphasizing, as they did, the influence of social environment, and especially of education, they welcomed Locke's view of the mind as being at birth like a sheet of white paper, void of all characters. The only original tendencies which, as a rule, they admitted were the

[1] Graham Wallas, *The Great Society* (Macmillan, 1914), p. 92.

impulse towards pleasure and the aversion from pain. Society, they believed, acting through education, public opinion and government, can fashion the child as it pleases, generating this and that emotion, in this and that intensity, as prescribed by the needs of the social system. Fear, they contended, is the agency which has been chiefly favoured by the societies of the past; hence its present enslaving power. Men are born free; everywhere they are in chains, forged by their servile acquired fears.

Though nineteenth-century writers on educational and social topics have a more adequate conception of man's emotional equipment, the great majority have continued to represent fear in a very unfavourable light. Thus Mosso, the Italian physiologist—the inventor of the plethysmograph and other psychological instruments—in his book, entitled *Fear*, does not hesitate to describe fear as a disease. Appearing in the animals as one of nature's many and strange devices for furtherance of its own supreme end, the preservation of the species, it has, Mosso contends, been so exacerbated, especially, as he claims, during the Stone Age, that it has since remained one of the main causes of the evils of human existence, generating insanities, phobias, and the various obsessions which account in particular for the unhappy history of religious belief and practice. 'Let us remember,' he remarks, 'that fear is a disease to be cured; the brave man may fail sometimes, but the coward fails always.'[1]

These writers, it may be noted, interpret fear as directed chiefly to what threatens life and limb, or more broadly, to whatever is painful. In their educational theories it is conceived mainly as fear of punishment, not as fear of proving unworthy and so of losing self-respect and the esteem of others. Being conceived in such narrow fashion, it compares unfavourably with the higher motives which they delight to set in contrast to it—love of the end sought and of the esteem of our fellows. Similarly in religion, it is represented as fear of punishment in an after-life, or at best as failure to face the cold hard truths of a scientific-ally enlightened philosophy, not as fear of the essentially evil or of

---

[1] Op. cit., in the English translation by E. Lough and F. Kiesow of its 5th Italian edition (Longmans, 1896), p. 278.

failure in achieving the qualities of character in terms of which the religious spirit conceives of happiness.

Secondly, in their desire to emphasize the continuity of man with his animal ancestors, they give what is surely a very distorted account of our human make-up. Thus Graham Wallas would trace the origin of our fears back to the period when our fish-like ancestors disported themselves in the sea. In his *Human Nature in Politics* we find the following passage:

> A man, whose life's dream it has been to get sight and speech of the King, is accidentally brought face to face with him. He is 'rooted to the spot', becomes pale, and is unable to speak, because a movement might have betrayed his ancestors to a lion or a bear, or, earlier still, to a hungry cuttlefish.[1]

But surely, what such an incident illustrates is not the grip which our marine ancestors still exercise over the nervous system, but the tricks which the imagination can play with us. The courtier who thus obtains sight of his king does not see before him in the king a fellow-mortal. His imagination is so filled with the splendours of the nation's history that the king before him becomes their embodied symbol. He is dazzled not by what he sees, but by what imaginatively possesses him. His emotions are stirred as are those of a communist by the red flag. Is a communist thus stirred because red is the colour of blood, and therefore bound up with all the most exciting experiences of our animal and human ancestors? That may be a part of it, but if so only a quite minor part. The power lies in what is symbolized, not in the symbol denuded of its meaning. The red flag to its worshippers stands for the Utopia of their dreams.

Part of the case urged against fear consists in the contention that the child inherits quite definite fears of specific objects that have no real relevance to human or at least to modern life. Thus Stanley Hall in his *Study of Fears*, based on a questionnaire replied to by 1,701 persons, claims that there are 298 different things towards which man inherits atavistic fears; and he would have us agree that 'reason always fears emotion, and is shocked by its outbreaks, and well it may be, for they

---

[1] (Constable, 1908), p. 34.

mark the incursions of the race into the narrow life of the individual'.[1]

The evidence, impartially weighed, seems very decidedly to point to the counter-conclusion that, in man at least, there are no *specific* atavistic fears. Unfamiliar or strikingly novel objects, sudden or sharp or very loud sounds, unexpected movements of anything in our environment, these appear to be the only sensuous stimuli capable of causing fear. All other causes of fear appear to be due to factors determined by the individual's own earlier personal experiences. The human race is not hagridden by the long-past experience of its animal and human ancestors. The mind of man is not a palimpsest all underwritten with savage tattoos. We have indeed come heir to a rich animal inheritance, but not in that crude fashion. The emotion of fear is automatically aroused only through the stimuli—the stimuli that must always have acted in order that the emotion may be of service in rendering adaptation to threatening dangers rapid and effective.

This appears to be true even of the animals. Unhatched chicks pecking at their shells will at once become quiescent if the mother-bird utters the danger-note; but they also do so upon any strange sound or shock. The cry of a hawk frightens birds, but so does any harsh, shrill or grating cry. If it be true, as has been asserted, that a horse becomes restive at the smell of a lion in a passing menagerie, this need not be because its ancestors, thousands of years before, while roaming wild, had it stamped in upon their nervous systems that this particular odour is a sign of the presence of an enemy; it is presumably only because this particular horse has never before smelt this particular odour, and therefore is startled by its unfamiliarity, just as any of us may be by a sudden movement. Blind kittens show fear at the smell of a dog; but they also do so, as experiment shows, at any strong odour, such as ammonia.

There is, however, one type of fear which is at once highly specific, and yet apparently not explicable in terms of the individual's past experience. I mean those fears which are popularly entitled fears of the supernatural—fears to which, probably, most, if not all of us, are in some degree subject, the feeling of the eerie and uncanny, the sense of oppression, easily yielding to panic, which is especially liable to be aroused in the dark and when the individual is alone.

[1] 'A Synthetic Genetic Study of Fear', *American Journal of Psychology* (1914), p. 183.

By general admission, it is impossible to explain these fears by reference to our animal ancestors; and this is why the Stone Age has been assigned so important a role in the naturalistic treatment of the emotional life. And it may at once be allowed that in the period when man was in process of becoming man, profound changes must have taken place in his mental endowments, and that he lay open to new and unfamiliar dangers, which to his dawning intelligence and widening imagination *may* (we have no precise information on the point) have given to the emotion of fear an exaggerated and unwholesome intensity.

But it is further contended that the fears, thus unwholesomely intensified, generated religion, and that religion, once invented, reacted upon the fears, extending their range still further and multiplying their forms, until we are presented with the spectacle of a race of beings not satisfied with the very real dangers that encompass them on every hand, but duplicating them by imaginary terrors of a fanciful character, complicating their existence to a degree that finds no parallel in any other living species—a complication which still constitutes, it is maintained, the chief barrier to a healthy-minded amelioration of life.

In this naturalistic explanation several points call for notice. First, the vagueness of the explanation. Located in the Stone Age, regarding which, on the side of *mental* history, we know so little, it is, by the nature of the case, unsupported by independent evidence. The one point that alone stands out clearly is the tacit admission that at this stage in human development there occurred a transition from animal existence to that which is specifically human, and that with this transition is also bound up the first beginnings of the religious view of life, the history of religion and the history of man being coextensive.

Secondly, 'exacerbation of our *animal* fears' is a very inadequate description of what by admission has actually taken place. A quite new set of fears, directed to a new set of objects, now makes its appearance. On the naturalistic view these fears are altogether unreal and imaginary; and yet once conceived acquire even greater influence than fears of actual dangers. This recognition of the part which imagination plays in human life we may welcome; but its sudden introduction, to carry the naturalistic theory over a difficult bit of the road, is somewhat surprising.

Thirdly, we may question the legitimacy of singling out one specific factor, such as fear, and of laying upon it the burden of accounting for the transition to a religious and therefore metaphysical interpretation of life. Such procedure is in keeping with the naturalistic philosophies whose usual tendency is to analyse the complex into its elements, and to treat the elements as more operative than the compound they constitute. That emotion plays a more important part than intellect or even imagination, in the beginnings of religion, can hardly be doubted, but the emotion at work, while involving fear, is much more complex. It is the emotion of awe, an emotion into which there would appear to be almost no human factor that does not enter. That to which it is directed both attracts and alarms; it is an object of worship as well as of self-abasement. Peculiar to this type of experience is a sense of being drawn—*in spite of fear*—to the object which is arousing it, leaving us with the desire for further experience of it. The experience is inexplicable in the absence of fear, and yet involves, in some measure, a transcendence of fear. The emotion is, indeed, so distinctively and exclusively human, that to understand it we must have understanding of the self as a whole. And if this be so, the naturalistic explanation of the origin of religion through fear breaks down. To explain the possibility of religion we need to postulate something else than *animal* fears; and yet when we have such *non*-animal fears as we find in the emotion of awe, the religious attitude has already been adopted.[1]

Setting aside, therefore, all specific fears, as arising only through the individual's own experience, let us consider fear in general. Can it be regarded as an emotion which was necessary so long as men were placed in an environment threatening to life and limb, but really an anachronism under present civilized conditions, or at least of an intensity out of all proportion to practical needs?

There is universal agreement that fear in its milder forms, when it is little more than surprise or expectation, gives just sufficient shock to the nervous system to arouse its energies, and to render it sensitive to all

[1] In Hebrew the same word is used to cover both fear and reverence. Moffatt has therefore felt justified in substituting for the traditional translation of Ps. cxi. 10— 'Fear of the Lord is the beginning of wisdom'—'The first thing in knowledge is reverence for the Eternal.'

signs of possible danger. On the bodily side it achieves these ends by a reflex contraction of the blood-vessels and a quickening of the heart-beat. Thereby the blood is withdrawn to the nerve-centres and driven more quickly through them. The nerve-centres are thus stimulated, and reserve energies set in readiness for immediate use.

Those psychologists, however, who assert that the emotion of fear is largely irrelevant to civilization claim that fear tends to be of such intensity as to thwart its own ends. The body gets out of hand; the heart beats more wildly and rapidly than is necessary for stimulation of the nerve-centres, and in consequence of excessive contraction of the blood-vessels disturbances are caused in the glands and viscera in all parts of the body, the skin perspiring a cold sweat, the mouth becoming dry and the voice hoarse; and as these disturbances spread, the body loses its alert posture, the muscles and even the skin tremble, and the eye and ear lose the power of distinct perception.

Thus fear, in proportion as it is intense, would seem to interfere with delicacy and precision of movement, and with clearness of perception. The greater the danger, the more ill-adapted and hurtful it would appear to become in its manifestations. Such manifestations, it is argued, are symptoms of disease. And when to the reckoning we add the wider range and greater intensity which fear acquires in a man through the free workings of imagination and thought, we would seem constrained to recognize that in fear Nature has overreached herself, and has given birth to a vampire which feeds on our vitals, just as it has done in devising, with elaborate ingenuity and disastrous effectiveness, the life-cycle of the malarial mosquito.[1] Fear, that is to say, is conceived as a sort of mental disease with which human nature has, by some perverse accident or evil fate, become inoculated, and which we are summoned to eradicate, by guarding children from fear as from infection, by re-editing our literature, especially that of the young, and by substituting persuasion for authority in School and State. Some such view of fear, however qualified and restated, is indeed now, as in the eighteenth century, an almost invariable concomitant of humanitarian teaching in its secularist forms; and the fallacy which lies at its root is, I shall argue, that most

---

[1] Cf. Sherrington, *Man on his Nature* (Cambridge, 1940), pp. 367 ff.

frequent of all the sources of false reasoning, an arbitrary and unduly narrow selection of the data to be considered. Fear does indeed rule over the night-side of life, being the source of many psychopathic ailments, major and minor, as well as of the fret and worry to which even the most healthy-minded must occasionally succumb. But have those who thus disapprove of fear ever asked themselves what the starving of its legitimate forms would involve, and whether its elimination from our human make-up would not carry with it such emotions as shame, respect, reverence and awe?

In raising, therefore, the direct question—what is the nature and what are the proper functions of fear?—I would first draw attention to the complexity of our motives of action. The influences, reasoned and unreasoned, conscious and subconscious, which determine our conduct at any one moment can seldom, if ever, be completely analysed, at least not in such manner as to enable us to say with certainty that such and such motives alone decide it. There is a corresponding complexity in the emotional life. No single emotion, it would seem, is ever experienced by itself, unmodified by other emotions congruent or incongruent with it. Hatred, for instance, may be qualified by respect, intensified by jealousy, or coloured by contempt. To take fear itself: consider through what a remarkable range of variations it may pass while still maintaining its generic character. Fear of physical pain, fear of social disapproval, fear of losing the esteem of those we most respect, the mother's disinterested fears for the physical and spiritual welfare of her child, the politician's fears for the success of his party, the patriot's fears for his country's future. The list, to be complete, and to be adequate, would have to divide each of these fears into groups according to the complexity of the concurrent emotions which contribute to intensify, to modify, and to articulate them.

I may here make use of A. F. Shand's theory of the emotions, as expounded in his book entitled *The Foundations of Character*.[1] He has there discussed the nature of the emotions with full recognition of their complexity and variability, and of the manner in which each of them functions only in subordination to the conditions supplied by the

[1] Though published in 1914 (Macmillan), with a second edition in 1920, it has, it would seem, never yet received the attention it deserves.

organized self, on the various levels of the mental life. Shand develops his theory of the emotions in opposition to what was then the current view, as represented by William James, McDougall, Westermarck and others, that is, in opposition to the view that each fundamental instinct is rigidly attached to a primary emotion, and each primary emotion to a particular instinct. On Shand's view the mental correlate of instinct is not emotion but impulse. Emotion is more complex than impulse; and its function is to co-ordinate all the various instincts and impulses which can in any particular case be of service in adjusting the self to what arouses the emotion. Thus fear may organize in its service the instinctive reactions either of flight, or of hiding and keeping silent, or of desperate resistance. And though in the last-named form, fear frequently acts by first awakening anger, the anger is then a supplementary emotion arising alongside the fear and acting in its service. And fear itself in turn enters as an element into those more complex emotions which may be entitled sentiments, such as shame, respect, reverence and awe.

To understand the emotion of fear, we have therefore to determine its relation to our instincts on the one hand and to our sentiments on the other. Its relation to instinct is twofold. In fear impulsive tendencies are at once excited and obstructed. That which arouses fear must call for action, but the occasion of the fear must also at the same time, in all save the simplest and most usual dangers, come before consciousness as something which cannot be evaded with ease and certainty. That is to say, while fear calls for action, it also calls for caution and circumspection; and these two features are at variance with one another. In the one aspect the emotion presses towards action; in the other it checks action, and throws the individual back upon himself, imposing the delay required for reviewing the situation. In other words, the same emotion at once stimulates and checks; and this is the explanation of its seemingly ambiguous character as protecting against danger and yet as tending to destroy presence of mind. It seems to check the very activity it excites. Consequently its nature can only be defined through opposites. Fear is at once prompt and very wary, at once impulsive and deliberate. Its impulsive aspect reduces to the various instincts which fall within it; as emotion it at once arouses these diverse instincts and holds them in leash. So long as fear lasts, it marks a state of tension[1] or conflict: the release of the tension is always in favour of certain instincts which until the moment of release are balanced by others. Thus fear, to this extent, frees us from the tyranny of any one instinct. As Plato has said, courage calls for right knowledge of the things to be feared. That is to say, courage is not the absence of inner tension and strain, but the resolving of it in the manner which the self, when unstrained, would choose deliberately and upon full reflection.

But I must carry the analysis of fear a step further. I have described its ambiguous dual nature, but I have not yet stated its divers uses.

It is a general psychological law that, accompanying circumstances permitting, we spontaneously attend to what is pleasant, and withdraw attention from what is painful. Were everything detached from everything else, this law might be accepted as the rule of life. But since we prefer certain ends to others, in adopting these ends—if we are to succeed in our pursuit of them—we have likewise to accept all the necessary labour, frequently disagreeable, thereby demanded. Consequently, in order that life may be consistent and progressive, we have to work counter to the general law, attending to the painful so far as our wider ends demand. How is this psychologically possible? If all pleasure tends to further attention, and all pain tends to suppress or thwart it, how is attention to the disagreeable ever secured?

The means are supplied by the emotions and sentiments, acting under the general control of the will. Were pleasure and pain the only lieutenants to which an agent could look for aid, even animal life, in its higher forms, would not have been possible. 'The spirit whether of brute or man is impotent of accomplishment unless it have emotion. Without emotion could a bird build its nest?'[2]

In this connexion, it is all-important to take account of a distinction of which professional psychologists make little use, but which is well known to writers on religion—it is emphasized by Cardinal Newman—between the softer and the more astringent emotions. The softer, or as they may also be named, the positive emotions, love in all its forms, as

---

[1] Cf. Dean Acheson, *An American Vista* (Hamish Hamilton, 1956): 'Tension is bad for people with weak nerves, but very little is ever accomplished without it.'

[2] Sherrington, op. cit., p. 401.

liking, affection, parental love, are invariably themselves pleasant in character. The astringent emotions, on the other hand, such as fear and hatred, are in themselves painful. Now 'the will', which, properly understood signifies not a separate faculty of the self, but the self as agent, i.e., the total self *qua* active, is enabled, thanks to the assistance afforded by the astringent emotions, to meet the calls made upon it by the positive emotions. I have already made reference to the complexity of the emotional life, and the relation in which the astringent stands to the positive emotions is a particularly interesting illustration of this. The astringent emotions never, it would seem, act independently of the positive emotions and sentiments. We feel fear only of that which endangers what we cherish, just as we hate only what threatens or thwarts us in the ends we are pursuing. Fear holds the painful before consciousness, and keeps it there until the difficulties or dangers which arouse the fear have been removed or avoided. The positive emotions are thus reinforced by such other emotions as are relevant and helpful to them; and in all great and critical enterprises it is in fear that they find their first, or at least their readiest, lieutenant. It then awakens alert, imperative and circumspect, to stir the flagging energies at every turn, adding its own primitive intensity and momentum to the positive emotions in whose service it has been enlisted. Mosso, and his like, are in the right when they contend that fear is the most soul-shaking of all the emotions; and this is what enables it to be an invaluable ingredient in many emotions and sentiments to which it does not give its name.

Thus I have already in large part answered my second question: how fear stands related to the sentiments. In proportion as civilization develops, fear as a reaction to purely sensuous stimuli, i.e., as warning us against physical dangers, though still indispensable, becomes of relatively subordinate importance. Nature, however, delights to adapt existing organs to novel uses, rather than to multiply new ones; and fear is a supreme example of the spiritual employment of what in its first appearance is a strictly natural device. In the sentiments it acts in the service of the positive emotions, reinforcing them with its own primitive intensity, and adding to their softness and sweetness the astringency necessary for their own proper fulfilment.

In support of this view of the function of fear, we have Wordsworth's account, in the *Prelude*, of the influences which presided over the development of his mind. As Wordsworth's testimony is, I think, quite remarkably illuminating, I shall dwell upon it at some length.

> Fair seed-time had my soul, and I grew up
> Fostered alike by beauty and by fear.

Looking back he recognized that natural beauty had produced in him as a child peace and delight. 'Even then I felt gleams like the flashing of a shield.' But, as he found, even then it was fear which had exercised the deeper awakening power.

To appreciate the extent of Wordsworth's surprise at this discovery we must bear in mind the attitude which he had for a time been led to adopt in his earlier Godwinian period. According to William Godwin, his philosophical mentor at that time, emotion, no matter in what form it presents itself, is a dangerous and perverting influence. Take the examples which Godwin cites. Gratitude leads us to discriminate unjustly. It leads children to prefer their parents to other worthier people. With it also many of the evils of misgovernment are inseparably bound up. Is not gratitude for past or prospective services the politician's excuse for his worst jobberies? Similarly pity can distort our judgement and remorse weaken it. And as regards fear, is it not the instrument by which the despot and the priest hold their victims in helpless vassalage? Reason is the sole reliable, and by itself a sufficient incentive to action. As moral agents our duty, according to Godwin, is in face of each specific situation, without preconception or prejudice, and in a quite impersonal manner, by pure reason, to judge what is best in the given circumstances. If we allow our actions to be influenced in any degree by feeling and emotion, we hand ourselves over to influences which are all too likely to pervert and mislead.

When Wordsworth, bemused by this philosophy, began to come to himself and to realize the part which feeling and emotion actually play, and rightly play, in human life, he was filled with amazement. Human nature, as he found, is so much more complex, and in its workings so much more mysterious than Godwin had led him to believe. Many of Wordsworth's poems are, of course, directly attributable to this discovery. Gratitude he found in Simon Lee in an utterly disinterested and indeed pathetic form, and hence his poem of that name. The affections attaching to private property, the cause as Godwin had taught, of so many vices and of so much misery, Wordsworth discovers to be closely interwoven with the noblest feelings of the heart; and hence his poem 'The Last of the Flock'.

But what amazed Wordsworth most of all—he is constantly remarking upon it—was that fear, which for Godwin is the most debasing and enslaving of the emotions, should on occasion not only have a useful function, but should, in certain of its uses, turn out to be one of the supremely beneficent forces in human life. The strangeness of this leads Wordsworth again and again to exclaim upon the mysterious character of our human powers.

> Oh! Mystery of man, from what a depth
>   Proceed thy honours!
> . . . there is a dark
> Inscrutable workmanship that reconciles
> Discordant elements. . . .

Fear, he has discovered, is one of the 'hiding-places of man's power', releasing us from the trivial but absorbing preoccupations of ordinary life, and thereby awakening us to consciousness of our deeper needs.

Wordsworth cites four special occasions on which fear was aroused in him as a child; and records them as critical turning-points, whose influence persisted his life long. The first, in the order in which he relates them in the *Prelude*, occurred when, one summer evening, having stolen a boat, he rowed out upon Esthwaite. He guided his course by the crest of a ridge; and as he rowed away

> . . . from behind that craggy steep till then
> The horizon's bound, a huge peak, black and huge,
> As if with voluntary power instinct,
> Upreared its head.

Panic fear then suddenly descended upon Wordsworth's childish spirit. With trembling oars, he turned and moored his bark.

> And through the meadows homeward went, in grave
> And serious mood; but after I had seen

That spectacle, for many days, my brain
Worked with a dim and undetermined sense
Of unknown modes of being; o'er my thoughts
There hung a darkness, call it solitude
Or blank desertion. No familiar shapes
Remained, no pleasant images of trees,
Of sea or sky, no colours of green fields;
But huge and mighty forms, that do not live
Like living men, moved slowly through the mind
By day, and were a trouble to my dreams.

In this, as in other cases, it was not, Wordsworth is careful to indicate, in the first panic-producing onset of the emotion, but in its after-effects, in the ground-swell, so to speak, that followed upon it, that the mind profited by the experience. As already noted, fear is the most soul-shaking of all the emotions; and as Wordsworth here relates, the ground-swell which it had generated lasted for several days, and revealed its continuing presence even in his dreams. As thus persisting, it gave to all the experiences which it accompanied an unwonted intensity and vividness which made them stand out in the memory with a freshness and a power not otherwise obtainable.

His meaning is made clearer by his description of another kind of experience—the fear awakened while climbing on high places during his boyish bird-nesting expeditions. The fear, though in this case of mild intensity, acted, he tells us, as a pleasurable stimulant to all his mental powers, so that the sky and landscape no longer seemed to be the world of everyday experience, but to be magically transformed with a strangeness and beauty beyond the ordinary. And these experiences, also, were thus, through their strangeness and vivacity, under the stimulating excitability of the fear, indelibly stamped upon the memory, and so handed on as a permanent source of inspiration, as recollected in tranquillity, for later years.

The third instance, related in Book V, is made the more significant by being set by Wordsworth in immediate sequence to the passage in which he criticizes the educationalists who, finding their inspiration in Rousseau, would so supervise and guard the child, playing, as they believe, the part of a higher Providence, that, in Wordsworth's words,

> . . . natural or supernatural fear,
> Unless it leap upon him in a dream,
> Touches him not.
>
> When [he asks] will their presumption learn,
> That in the unreasoning progress of the world
> A wiser spirit is at work for us,
> A better eye than theirs, most prodigal
> Of blessings, and most studious of our good,
> Even in what seem our most unfruitful hours?

The incident, it may be recalled, was as follows. Wordsworth observed one evening, on the opposite shore of Esthwaite, a heap of garments, as if left by some bather. Long he watched as the darkness increased, but no one claimed them. The succeeding day a crowd had collected, and the bather was sought with grappling irons and long poles.

> At last, the dead man, 'mid that beauteous scene
> Of trees and hills and water, bolt upright
> Rose, with his ghastly face, a spectre shape
> Of terror; yet no soul-debasing fear,
> Young as I was, a child not nine years old,
> Possessed me, for my inner eye had seen
> Such sights before, among the shining streams
> Of faëry land, the forest of romance.
> Their spirit hallowed the sad spectacle
> With decoration of ideal grace;
> A dignity, a smoothness, like the works
> Of Grecian art, and purest poesy.

The fourth incident is told in Book XII, where Wordsworth is again speaking of those childhood's

> Spots of time
> That with distinct pre-eminence retain
> A renovating virtue whence . . .
> . . . our minds
> Are nourished and invisibly repaired.

Riding over a moor, while still so young that he could scarcely hold a bridle, he had lost touch with the servant who was accompanying him.

In fear, dismounting, he led his horse down the rough and stony moor
till he came to a bottom where in former times a murderer had been
hung in chains. On the turf the murderer's name was still inscribed in
monumental letters. His preceding fears were immediately intensified.
'Faltering and faint,' he fled, and

> . . . reascending the bare common, saw . . .
> A naked pool that lay beneath the hills,
> The beacon on the summit, and, more near,
> A girl, who bore a pitcher on her head,
> And seemed with difficult steps to force her way
> Against the blowing wind. It was, in truth,
> An ordinary sight; but I should need
> Colours and words that are unknown to man,
> To paint the visionary dreariness
> Which, while I looked round for my lost guide,
> Invested moorland waste, and naked pool,
> The beacon crowning the lone eminence,
> The female and her garments vexed and tossed
> By the strong wind.

The complete passage would take too long to quote: in it Wordsworth
dwells further upon this incident and upon its influence through his
later years. It stood out in his memory and had, as he says, a renovating
virtue by which in later years he frequently nourished and repaired his
spirit.

At the conclusion of the *Prelude*, Wordsworth, speaking of the
beneficent influence of his sister Dorothy, exclaims:

> I too exclusively esteemed *that* love
> And sought *that* beauty, which, as Milton sings,
> Hath terror in it.

And in another passage, in which he is again referring to Dorothy, he
says she taught him 'delicate fears'. And speaking of how, throughout
life, his spiritual freedom had been preserved and enlarged, he exclaims:

> To fear and love,
> To love as prime and chief, for there fear ends

[i.e., Wordsworth clearly recognized the subordination of the astringent to the positive emotions.]

> Be this ascribed; to early intercourse
> In presence of sublime or beautiful forms,
> With the adverse principles of pain and joy—
> Evil as one is rashly named by men
> Who know not what they speak.

And so I am brought back to my main thesis, that fear, properly used, works in the service and under the control of the positive emotions.

It is true, of course, that the misuse of fear has done incalculable mischief, and has played havoc with a multitude of lives. But this perverting power it shares with much that is best in human nature. All that is darkest or most tragic in human history is bound up with those emotions which, when rightly directed, are also the highest. There are none of the higher emotions but have their dark side; and the extent of the evil which fear, when misdirected, admittedly can cause, instead of leading us to regard it as a disease ought, by all the analogies, rather to be taken as proving its fundamental and all-pervasive character, and to prepare us for finding that it is one of the elemental forces, for good as well as for evil—both for the greatest goods and for the greatest evils—with which human nature is endowed. Were it merely a diseased excrescence, to be lopped off, its influence would be more purely local, and more easily dealt with. Let there, therefore, be a dragon in every child's book of fairy tales; and let us abstain from eliminating the exciting incidents from such thrilling stories as that of 'The Unhappy Man who could not Shiver and Shake'.

It is understandable that those who take a purely naturalistic view of the self should tend to regard with disfavour any emotion or sentiment in which fear is an ingredient. If the purpose of life is to bring the self and the given environment mutually into adjustment, modifying the environment, so as to satisfy the self in a maximum degree, and limiting our desires to what nature, when thus controlled, can be made to supply, fear, in its present continuing intensity, may have to be viewed as an unhappy survival from the days when, in the infancy of physical and medical science, our capacity to guard against threatening evils was so much less equal to its tasks. But if, on the other hand, it be the very nature of man to seek for more than his natural conditions themselves supply, and if these conditions through friction generate capacities which have no animal analogue, if every advance in human life reveals new tasks and dangers not previously discerned, and if these demand not merely further labours, but the sacrifice and undoing of much that was previously cherished, then fear may well be expected to widen its range in due proportion. The higher excellence, if higher in kind and not merely in degree, on first discernment alarms, and may even repel, quite as much as it attracts. If it sufficiently transcends our acquired standards of excellence, its approach will be heralded by fear no less surely than if it were an evil. It threatens the actual self, undermining the achievements upon which the self has hitherto prided itself—disclosing new and unanticipated labours, from the hardness of which the natural man inevitably shrinks.

To quote a typical expression of the older view at its best—the view which regards 'fear' as the beginning of wisdom—from the magnificent opening chapter of Calvin's *Institutes*:

> It is plain that no man can arrive at the true knowledge of himself, without having first contemplated the divine character, and then descended to the consideration of his own. . . . The eye, accustomed to see nothing but black, judges that to be very white, which is but whitish, or perhaps brown. . . . Hence that horror and amazement with which the Scripture always represents the saints to have been impressed and disturbed, on every discovery of the presence of God. . . . Of this consternation we have frequent examples in the Judges and Prophets; so that it was a common expression among the Lord's people—'We shall die, because we have seen God'. . . . And what can man do . . . when fear constrains the cherubim themselves to veil their faces? This is what the prophet Isaiah speaks of—'the moon shall be confounded, and the sun ashamed, when the Lord of hosts shall reign'; that is, when he shall make a fuller and nearer exhibition of his splendour, it shall eclipse the splendour of the brightest object besides. (Allen's translation.)

Contrast with this the following passage, from Sir Oliver Lodge:

The range of art and of enjoyment must increase infinitely with perfect knowledge. This is the atmosphere of God. Where dwells enjoyment, there is He. . . . This is the way with the greatest things. The sun is the centre of the solar system, a glorious object full of mystery and unknown forces, but the sunshine is a friendly and homely thing, which shines in at a cottage window, and touches common objects with radiance, and brings warmth and comfort even to the cat.

The attitudes alike of Calvin and of Sir Oliver are indeed not a little over-strained; but surely that of Calvin is nearer to the truth. Sir Oliver's domestic interior, with his window looking out on a landscape bathed in the very temperate sunshine of our English climate, is a decidedly foreshortened substitute for the glories, hazards and sub-limities of our terrestrial and cosmic setting.

Ought not those who regard fear as essentially evil to bethink themselves what it is they are maintaining? They are declaring that the most soul-shaking of all the instinctive emotions is by its very nature so intrinsically evil that the energies which it releases can never be bene-ficially employed. If that be so, are we not committed to the conclusion that in the emotional life we must be prepared to reckon with a permanent and irremediable twofold loss. First, of the emotional driving-force which fear represents: it will be no more legitimate to tap this source of energy than to employ an opiate in the doing of the day's work. And secondly, part of the emotional energies supplied by the other emotions will have to be set aside for the suppressing of this most ancient, and on their own showing deeply ingrained, excitability of fear. On this pessimistic view, we are summoned to curse Nature that ever it was so ill-advised as to create and employ this dangerous, and insidiously obsessive, type of emotional incentive.

Do not these considerations suffice to show that fear, whatever be its past record, cannot be so irremediably evil as its critics, whether senti-mental or naturalistic, have sought to make out? Is it not that they are so afraid of fear that they have never domesticated it, and therefore, unlike Wordsworth, have never got to terms sufficiently friendly to allow of acquaintance with its many redeeming qualities? Fear may be a very rough diamond; but it has the qualities of its defects, and how very sterling these are. Fear is, so to speak, very humble-minded, very teachable; so much so that it is ever on the look-out for a master wiser than itself; and when it finds such it is the most trusty of lieutenants. It is indeed precisely by its fearless use of fear that Nature has succeeded in evolving the most favoured of its creatures. For, as we find, it has not been by way of the nobler animals, so much less open to fear, but by way of the timorous inhabitants of the tree-tops that it has secured for itself the means required in the creation of man. Nimble-witted and highly excitable, they are also alertly distrustful. And it is on these foundations that Nature has built.

And now to draw my summary conclusions.[1] Fear, as I have tried to show, is the inevitable companion of all great and difficult enterprises. They require both tenacity and caution; and these fear is supremely fitted to supply. Its tenacity comes to it from the positive emotion in whose service it is acting. At the same time it is circumspect and open-minded. It is its nature to be ever on the watch. It is the very opposite of that complacent reliance on acquired powers, on past prestige, on previous success, which is so detrimental to further advance and to open-minded recognition of new issues as they arise.

But, it will be urged, the cultivation of this emotion must destroy legitimate self-confidence, engendering an anxious-minded preoccupation, not with the good but rather with the manifold evils by which it is threatened on every hand. This objection overlooks the fundamental fact, upon which I have been dwelling, that fear is aroused only in subordination to emotions and sentiments of an *opposite* character. That to which our affections are pledged is the determining ground of corresponding fears; and the intensity of these fears is proportioned to our positive attachment to the ends which are endangered. That is to say, fear in all its higher forms—fear properly directed and morally controlled, *disinterested* fear—operates within the complex emotional systems to which it is subordinated and in which its powers are usefully

---

[1] As helping to make good some of the many lacunae and other short-comings in this brief review, I can refer the reader to Lord Moran's *The Anatomy of Courage* (Constable, 1945), and to Paul Tillich's *The Courage to Be* (Yale, 1952). As the latter indicates, there is no English word precisely corresponding to the German word *Angst*—a distinctive, highly complex, species of anxiety.

and effectively utilized. Love generates fear of whatever threatens the beloved; and these fears, rightly directed—no easy task, yet within our powers—do not weaken the love but intensify it; while it in turn, if appropriately guided under the control of the will, regulates them in such manner as to render them contributory to the ends in view. Fear, which engulfs the coward, is a source of valour in the brave.

And lastly, the emotions when thus controlled, diminish in crude intensity, while increasing in power. As organized in the more complex sentiments, they stabilize the mind, freeing it from the feverish and diffusive restlessness characteristic of the immature. They contribute to the fervour, while lessening the turmoil of the soul. The objective sources of our positive affections lie beyond the individual self, and yet none the less constitute the centre of gravity of the self, lending the mind serenity, and enabling it to gain control over those fears which all supreme ends must inevitably generate, and generate in greater degree and in higher intensity, in proportion as they are found to be bound up with and to concern the more immediate purposes of our practical and social life.

Index

Aberdeen, University of, 9, 21
Absolute idealism, criticism of, 273–90
Abstract universal, *see* Universals
Abstraction, 68–75. *See also* Universals, esp. 324–38
Act–Character (in Avenarius), 61, 82–84, 147–8, 155–6
Adamson, Robert, 7–10, 86, 87 n. 1, 105 n. 1
Albee, E., 125 n. 3
Alberta, University of, viii
Alexander, Ian, 89 n. 2
Alexander, Samuel, 12, 20, 88 n. 1, 353, 381, 392
Allen (translator of Calvin's *Institutes*), 199 n. 1, 435
Alquié, F., 90
American Philosophical Association, 14, 184
Analysis, rational, 68
Anderson, John, 24
Anglo-Hegelians, 77–80
Animism, 154, 164–72
a priori, *v.* empirical, 62; of Alexander, 381
Armstrong, D. M., 88 n. 1
Arnauld, A., 174
Arnold, Matthew, 29
Ashley, Lord, *see* Shaftesbury
Asquith, H. H. (Earl), 20
Atomism, of G. E. Moore, 47, 76
Avenarius, Richard, 12–13, 80–84, 139–73 *passim*, 175, 180

Awareness of awareness, denial of, 85
Ayer, A. J., 89

Bacon, Francis (Lord), 193, 199 n. 2, 203–4, 211
Baillie, Sir James, 21–22
Baldwin, J. M., 162
Balfour, A. J. (Earl), 23
Balliol College, Oxford, 6, 8, 21
Barbour, G. F., 6 n. 1
Barker, Henry, 23
Barnes, H. E., 74 n. 1
Barth, Karl, 59
Bayle, Pierre, 98
Beibegriffe (in Avenarius), 154, 170
Belfast, Queen's University, 21
Belief, Hume's theory of, 97–122, esp. 106, 112–18, 118 n. 3
Bergson, Henri, 22, 27, 48, 54, 64–69, 74, 77–78, 81–82, 84, 87–90, 175, 180–3, 212, 245–7, 398–416 *passim*
Berkeley, Bishop George, 12, 34, 95–98, 101–2, 108 n. 2, 116, 118 n. 3, 174, 242, 344, 362
Berkeley, University of California, 12, 24, 36
Berlin, University of, 5, 9
Bifurcation of Nature (in Whitehead), 233–8
Binet, Alfred, 178
Birmingham, University of, 22, 24
Boole, George, 186

439